SHAKESPEARE AND LOST PLAYS

Shakespeare and Lost Plays returns Shakespeare's dramatic work to its most immediate and (arguably) pivotal context; by situating it alongside the hundreds of plays known to Shakespeare's original audiences, but lost to us. David McInnis reassesses the value of lost plays in relation to both the companies that originally performed them, and to contemporary scholars of early modern drama. This innovative study revisits key moments in Shakespeare's career and the development of his company and, by prioritising the immense volume of information we now possess about lost plays, provides a richer, more accurate picture of dramatic activity than has hitherto been possible. By considering a variety of ways to grapple with the problem of lost, imperceptible or ignored texts, this volume presents a methodology for working with lacunae in archival evidence and the distorting effect of Shakespeare-centric narratives, thus reinterpreting our perception of the field of early modern drama.

DAVID MCINNIS is Associate Professor of Shakespeare and Early Modern Drama at the University of Melbourne. With Roslyn L. Knutson and Matthew Steggle, he founded and co-edits the *Lost Plays Database*. He is also co-editor of *Lost Plays in Shakespeare's England* (2014) and a sequel volume, *Loss and the Literary Culture of Shakespeare's Time* (2020). His other books include *Mind-Travelling and Voyage Drama in Early Modern England* (2013), *Travel and Drama in Early Modern England: The Journeying Play* (Cambridge University Press, 2018; with Claire Jowitt), *Tamburlaine: A Critical Reader* (2020) and the Revels Plays edition of Dekker's *Old Fortunatus* (2020).

SHAKESPEARE AND LOST PLAYS

Reimagining Drama in Early Modern England

DAVID MCINNIS

University of Melbourne

CAMBRIDGE
UNIVERSITY PRESS

CAMBRIDGE
UNIVERSITY PRESS

University Printing House, Cambridge CB2 8BS, United Kingdom

One Liberty Plaza, 20th Floor, New York, NY 10006, USA

477 Williamstown Road, Port Melbourne, VIC 3207, Australia

314–321, 3rd Floor, Plot 3, Splendor Forum, Jasola District Centre, New Delhi – 110025, India

79 Anson Road, #06–04/06, Singapore 079906

Cambridge University Press is part of the University of Cambridge.

It furthers the University's mission by disseminating knowledge in the pursuit of education, learning, and research at the highest international levels of excellence.

www.cambridge.org
Information on this title: www.cambridge.org/9781108843263
DOI: 10.1017/9781108915250

First published 2021

Printed in the United Kingdom by TJ Books Limited, Padstow Cornwall

A catalogue record for this publication is available from the British Library.

Library of Congress Cataloging-in-Publication Data
Names: McInnis, David, author.
TITLE: Shakespeare and lost plays : reimagining drama in early modern England / David McInnis.
DESCRIPTION: Cambridge, United Kingdom ; New York, NY, USA : Cambridge University Press, 2021. | Includes bibliographical references and index. | Summary: "Shakespeare and Lost Plays returns Shakespeare's dramatic work to its most immediate and (arguably) pivotal context; by situating it alongside the hundreds of plays known to Shakespeare's original audiences, but lost to us. David McInnis reassesses the value of lost plays in relation to both the companies that originally performed them, and to contemporary scholars of early modern drama. This innovative study revisits key moments in Shakespeare's career and the development of his company and, by prioritising the immense volume of information we now possess about lost plays, provides a richer, more accurate picture of dramatic activity than has hitherto been possible. By considering a variety of ways to grapple with the problem of lost, imperceptible, or ignored texts, this volume presents a methodology for working with lacunae in archival evidence and the distorting effect of Shakespeare-centric narratives, thus reinterpreting our perception of the field of early modern drama"– Provided by publisher.
IDENTIFIERS: LCCN 2020036494 (print) | LCCN 2020036495 (ebook) | ISBN 9781108843263 (hardback) | ISBN 9781108824156 (paperback) | ISBN 9781108915250 (epub)
SUBJECTS: LCSH: English drama–Early modern and Elizabethan, 1500-1600–History and criticism. | English drama–17th century–History and criticism. | Shakespeare, William, 1564-1616–Contemporaries. | Lost literature–England.
CLASSIFICATION: LCC PR658.L6 M35 2021 (print) | LCC PR658.L6 (ebook) | DDC 822/.309–DC23
LC record available at https://lccn.loc.gov/2020036494
LC ebook record available at https://lccn.loc.gov/2020036495

ISBN 978-1-108-84326-3 Hardback

For Roslyn Knutson, of course

Contents

List of Figures and Tables	*page*	ix
Acknowledgements		x
A Note on Conventions for the Titles of Lost Plays		xiii
Introduction		1
Why Do Plays Become Lost?		2
A Case Study: 'Love's Labour's Won'		11
Where to from Here?		14
Lost Plays and Rubin's Vase		20
1 Charting the Landscape of Loss		27
Lost Plays and Shakespeare's Company		29
The Value of Lost Plays		36
The Composition of a Company's Repertory: The Admiral's Men		41
2 Early Shakespeare: 1594–1598		58
'Beginning at Newington': 1594		59
Moving to the Curtain: 1597–1598		70
3 Shakespeare at the Turn of the Century: 1599–1603		89
Love and War: 'Owen Tudor' and *Henry V*		91
Denmark without Shakespeare		95
Hamlet and 'felmelanco'		104
4 Courting Controversy – Shakespeare and the King's Men:		
1604–1608		118
'[T]he tragedie of Gowrie'		120
'A Tragidye of The Spanishe Maz:'		129
The Blackfriars: 1608		137
5 Late Shakespeare: 1609–1613		150
Recycling Romance		153
Shakespeare and the King's Men at Court: 1612–1613		160
What Was 'Cardenio'?		166
'Cardenio' at Court: 1612–1613		175

6   Loose Canons: The Lost Shakespeare Apocrypha   185
    'Henry I' and 'Henry II'   187
    'Duke Humphrey', with a Note on 'King Stephen' and 'Iphis and Ianthe'   191
    'Eurialus and Lucretia'   197

Conclusion   205

Index   208

Figures and Tables

Figures

I.1 Rubin's Vase   *page* 21
4.1 Illustration 5 from Rubin's work   148

Tables

1.1 Extant plays associated with the Chamberlain's Men's repertory:
1594–1603   30
1.2 Critical estimates of the size and loss rate of the
Admiral's repertory   46
1.3 Critical estimates of the size and loss rate of the
Admiral's repertory   55

Acknowledgements

Roslyn Knutson and I first began discussing lost plays in the summer of 2008, at the British Library. During that first conversation it became apparent very quickly that we each possessed snippets of knowledge that the other lacked. We realised that the same must be true of other scholars working on the history of early modern English drama, and we set about creating the *Lost Plays Database* (*LPD*) as a formal mechanism for facilitating the exchange of such knowledge. Neither of us quite anticipated how much that project would grow, or how much we would learn – to say nothing of how much fun we would have along the way. I could not have hoped for a better mentor, colleague and friend than Ros, who twice travelled from Little Rock, Arkansas to Melbourne, Australia, and who carefully read and meticulously critiqued drafts of this book in manuscript form. The advice and expertise that she is uniquely poised to provide have always improved my work. I cannot conceive of a more generous collaborator.

As the *LPD* continued to grow, the numerous contributors who added to entries according to their own interests all greatly expanded my knowledge. Two in particular, Matthew Steggle and Misha Teramura, have been models of intellectual generosity, excitedly sharing discoveries, pushing the project in new directions, and offering support and feedback on virtually everything any of us associated with the project has ever written for publication or conferences. This includes reading a draft of the full manuscript of this book and providing constructive suggestions. Thanks, Matt and Misha.

My work on lost plays has been supported over the years by an Australian Research Council (ARC) Discovery Project grant (DP140102297), 2014–17, which included work undertaken towards this monograph; a Dyason Fellowship at the University of Melbourne, which brought Roslyn Knutson to Australia; and a Folger Shakespeare Library Short-Term Fellowship (2011) and a SAA research grant (in the brief period they were offered), which facilitated archival research at a very early stage (2012). The Folger subsequently offered to host the *Lost Plays Database* and has been tremendously supportive in numerous ways (including image reproduction, in-kind support, financial support and the promotion of our resource). In particular, I would like to thank Meg Brown and Eric Johnson at the Folger for being so generous with their time and resources in ensuring a smooth migration of the *LPD* to Capitol Hill in 2018. The Folger Institute also provided the invaluable opportunity to participate in the 'Shakespeare's Theatrical Documents' symposium convened by Tiffany Stern in 2016. Tiffany's support of this work on lost plays and her generosity in offering advice on work in progress has been hugely appreciated.

A number of libraries and librarians around the world have been remarkably kind in supplying digitizations of archival material pertaining to lost plays, for reproduction in the *LPD*, which has been extraordinarily enabling for the kinds of research contained in this book: The Beinecke Library, Yale University; The Bodleian Libraries, the University of Oxford; The British Library; Cardiff Libraries; Christ Church Library, the University of Oxford; Dulwich College; The Folger Shakespeare Library; Fondation Martin Bodmer (Cologny, Geneve); Hatfield House; Houghton Library, Harvard University; The Huntington Library; The National Archives; The Schøyen Collection, Oslo and London; Society of Antiquaries of London Library; Thomas Plume's Library; Rare Book & Manuscript Library, University of Illinois at Urbana-Champaign; and the Warwickshire County Records Office (WCRO).

Besides the staff at the libraries listed above in connection with the *LPD*, I would like to thank the University of Melbourne's Baillieu Library staff – without subscriptions to EEBO-TCP and other invaluable resources, this project would scarcely have been possible; I hope I've been able to 'pay forward' some of this kindness by ensuring that the *LPD* is, and always will be, open-access.

I have learned much and benefited from the insights of my fellow panellists for the 2016 plenary presentation on 'Theater History Mash-ups' at SAA (New Orleans, 2016), and the participants at the two SAA seminars I co-led on lost plays: 'Lost Plays in Early Modern England' (Toronto, 2013, co-led with Matt Steggle) and 'Lost Plays and their Contexts' (Atlanta, 2017, co-led with Knutson and Steggle). Adam Hooks and Kirk Melnikoff kindly invited me to share my work in their SAA workshop in St Louis, 2014, as did Jeremy Lopez for his seminar in Vancouver, 2015. Other conferences where I've benefited from feedback from auditors include the World Shakespeare Congress (Prague, 2011);

the Australian and New Zealand Shakespeare Association's conference (University of Waikato, 2016); the Marlowe Society of America's international conference (Wittenberg, 2018); the MLA convention (Seattle, 2012); as well as at Sheffield Hallam University, Massey University, the University of Sydney, the Australian National University, the University of Queensland and the University of Southern Queensland.

The contributors to the two edited collections on lost plays for Palgrave and the numerous editors who have overseen the publication of my research have helped shape and refine my ideas about lost plays: these include John Astington, Dennis Austin Britton, Christie Carson, Susan Cerasano, Ian Donaldson, Richard Dutton, James Evans, Ian Gadd, David Irving, Claire Jowitt, Pete Kirwan, Tara L. Lyons, Larry Manley, Chris Matusiak, John Milton, Lucy Munro, Helen Ostovich, Michael Stapleton, Tiffany Stern and Melissa Walter. Thanks, too, to the following friends and colleagues who have helped along the way: Régis Augustus Bars Closel, Heidi Craig, Hugh Craig, Carla Della Gatta, Brett Greatley-Hirsch, Mike Hirrel, Lisa Hopkins, Laurie Johnson, John Jowett, Andy Kesson, Pete Kirwan, Heather Knight, Zachary Lesser, Domenico Lovascio, José A. Pérez Díez, Tom Rutter, Alexander Samson, Geoff Saw, June Schlueter, Lyn Tribble, Jesús Trónch, William Proctor Williams and especially (as ever) Martin Wiggins, who generously and frequently shared his work on the *Catalogue* ahead of publication.

Closer to home, I am grateful to have such wonderful colleagues in the English and Theatre Studies program, who have always supported the seemingly peculiar work I do on lost plays. I owe a debt to André Bastian, Elena Benthaus, David Rowland, Miriam Webster and especially Alex Thom for their research and translation assistance throughout the duration of this project. Thanks, too, to my Honours students in particular, for bearing with me during our Renaissance drama seminars whilst I prattled on about plays that don't even exist.

My greatest thanks, as always, is to my family: Emma, Imogen and Kit.

A Note on Conventions for the Titles
of Lost Plays

Since the earliest stages of our collaborative work, Roslyn Knutson and I have opted to reserve the use of italics for the titles of extant plays and to use quotation marks to denote lost play titles, and I follow this practice throughout this book. I modernize titles when there's no question of identity but where the play titles are ambiguous or there is a need for scholarly interpretation, I quote the spelling of documentary records instead.

Introduction

Shakespeare scholars face a significant challenge: our understanding of Shakespeare benefits from appreciation of the plays that he was responding to and influencing in the repertories of the London-based companies, but most of the play-texts from those repertories have been lost. Recent estimates suggest that for the period of c.1567–1642, whilst only 543 plays from the London commercial theatres have survived, as many as 744 plays are identifiably lost, with hundreds more completely untraceable.[1] At the same time, recent scholarship suggests that the data available about lost plays from Shakespeare's lifetime has never been greater, better assembled or more accessible. The advent of the *Lost Plays Database* (2009) and the publication of instalments of Martin Wiggins' multivolume *Catalogue* of British drama (since 2012) have been instrumental in making this information available.[2] What can be done with all this new knowledge? Scholars have long been fascinated by the influence of the lost 'Ur-Hamlet' on Shakespeare's *Hamlet* and by the fact that two plays actually written by Shakespeare ('Love's Labour's Won' and 'Cardenio') have been lost, but those three lost plays are only a small part of a much bigger picture. In this book I am interested in how we cope with such loss. I return Shakespeare's dramatic work to its most immediate and (arguably) important context by situating it alongside the hundreds of plays known to Shakespeare's

---

[1] D. McInnis and M. Steggle, 'Introduction: *Nothing* Will Come of Nothing? Or, What Can We Learn from Plays that Don't Exist?' in D. McInnis and M. Steggle (eds.), *Lost Plays in Shakespeare's England* (Basingstoke: Palgrave Macmillan, 2014), 1, drawing on figures generously provided by Martin Wiggins. London playhouses were not the only venues where the plays of Shakespeare and his contemporaries were performed, but for the purposes of this book and the repertory studies approach that I use throughout, I tend to restrict my focus to the wealth of data about theatrical production in London where analysis of direct engagement between companies is clearer.

[2] R. L. Knutson, D. McInnis and M. Steggle (eds.), *Lost Plays Database* (hereafter 'LPD') (Washington, DC: Folger Shakespeare Library, 2009–), https://lostplays.folger.edu; M. Wiggins in association with C. Richardson, *British Drama, 1533–1642: A Catalogue*, 11 vols (Oxford: Oxford University Press, 2012–).

original audiences, but lost to us. I reassess the value of lost plays both to the companies that originally performed them and to scholars who write about early modern drama now. I revisit key moments in Shakespeare's career and the development of the Chamberlain's (later King's) Men and, by prioritising the immense volume of information we now possess about lost plays, provide a richer, more accurate picture of dramatic activity than has hitherto been possible.

Why Do Plays Become Lost?

Beyond the impetus provided by the availability of copious new information, this study is timely and necessary because – despite their best intentions – those early scholars such as Frederick Gard Fleay who did glance in the direction of lost plays were as likely to distort the evidence as to handle it responsibly. More recent theatre historians have subsequently perpetuated those errors. One of my intentions in this book is to model a method of scholarship for working with lost plays; a method that is responsible, sceptical and which sees the value in complicating our understanding of the period rather than necessarily offering neat solutions. The early critics' neglect of lost plays is compounded by the baseless value judgments advanced by some scholars. Bernard Beckerman, a pioneer in privileging the commercial reality of what he called the 'repertory system' over 'an idolatrous love of Shakespeare', nevertheless dismissed lost plays as repertorial 'filler' of dubious aesthetic worth: 'As lovers of literature', he wrote, 'we need be grieved little by the disappearance of 75 per cent of the plays'.[3] In a similar fashion, Andrew Gurr has more recently offered his readers consolation by adopting what he calls 'the self-comforting assumption' that 'only those plays that were most famous and successful in their own day' were likely to survive.[4] There is no basis for these disparaging remarks, but the consequences are significant.

---

[3] B. Beckerman, *Shakespeare at the Globe: 1599–1606* (New York: Macmillan, 1962), 2, 14 and 16.

[4] A. Gurr, 'What Is Lost of Shakespearean Plays, Besides a Few Titles?' in D. McInnis and M. Steggle (eds.), *Lost Plays in Shakespeare's England* (Basingstoke: Palgrave Macmillan, 2014), 56. Gurr is here reiterating sentiments he expressed earlier in *The Shakespearian Playing Companies* (Oxford: Oxford University Press, 1998), where he supposed that '[t]he survivors are very likely to be the best or at least the most popular of the many original scripts' written for the London stages (26), and in his *The Shakespearean Stage, 1574–1642*, 3rd ed (Cambridge: Cambridge University Press, 1994), 18, where he characterised the majority of playwriting from the period as 'hack-work … to supply an entertainment industry' and alleged that '[w]hat has survived into this century is probably not a large proportion of the total output, though it is likely to include most of the cream'.

Plays become lost for a variety of reasons and appeals to 'quality' as the basis of non-preservation are not genuine explanations: without comparative data, 'quality' is unmeasurable. Yet even those recent critics who have been willing to acknowledge that 'plays were printed (or not) and survived (or not) for multiple reasons' paradoxically insist that 'there is no reason to suggest that the plays that survive are either unrepresentative or over-representative of the general performance trends'.[5] Unfortunately for us, the great variety of causes of loss means that the surviving drama is, statistically speaking, atypical precisely because of its survival; these plays constitute the distinct minority of the total dramatic output for the period. Unpredictable and arbitrary causes including fire and vandalism, for example, are responsible for the loss of a large number of play-texts. John Warburton (1682–1759) notoriously claimed that his invaluable collection of unpublished play manuscripts was lost through the callousness of his cook Betsy, under whose care 'they was unluckily burnd or put under Pye bottoms'.[6] (In the final chapter of this book I explore in greater detail the veracity of Warburton's scapegoating of Betsy and the implication that he owned the titles from his list.) The tragedies that befell the playing companies who occupied the Cockpit and the Fortune playhouses are less contentious, in that they demonstrably did occur. On Shrove Tuesday, 1617, the Queen's Men became the victims of the riots accompanying what was the traditional holiday for apprentices. Thousands of rioters took to the streets, some of them breaking into the Cockpit theatre in Drury Lane and (as one contemporary letter-writer reports) 'cutting the players apparell all in pieces, and all other theyre furniture and burnt theyre play books and did what other mischief they could'.[7] The immolation of the Fortune playhouse in December 1621, in which all the 'apparell and play-bookes' were lost, likewise struck a significant blow to the survival rate of plays in the repertory of the Palsgrave's Men.[8]

Censorship has also played a hand in the loss of drama. Most famously, performances of Ben Jonson and Thomas Nashe's seditious 'Isle of Dogs' play (1597) almost brought about the tearing down of playhouses and the suppression of playing across London and further afield. Quite how the play caused offense is a matter of conjecture and dispute. E. K. Chambers

---

[5] S. Dustagheer, *Shakespeare's Two Playhouses: Repertory and Theatre Space at the Globe and the Blackfriars, 1599–1613* (Cambridge: Cambridge University Press, 2017), 6.

[6] British Library, Lansdowne MS 807, fo. 1ʳ; digitised in the *LPD* entry for 'Warburton's List'.

[7] John Chamberlain to Sir Dudley Carleton, 8 March 1617, quoted in G. E. Bentley, *The Jacobean and Caroline Stage* (Oxford: Clarendon Press, 1968), 6.55.

[8] John Chamberlain, quoted in Bentley, *The Jacobean and Caroline Stage*, 6.153.

suggested that the offence centred on the King of Poland, whose ambassador had been in London very recently to visit Elizabeth.[9] Glynne Wickham thought the play must have been critical of the government.[10] More recently, Ian Donaldson has provocatively suggested that the topicality of the rivalry between the Cecils and Robert Devereux, 2nd Earl of Essex, may be relevant: around the time of the play, Essex had voyaged to the Canary Islands, whose Latin name (*canaria insula*) translates as 'Isle of Dogs'.[11] Whatever the supposed offence, the Privy Council instructed the governmental inquisitor Richard Topcliffe to ascertain 'what copies' of the play had been circulated and to 'peruse soch papers as were fownde in Nash his lodgings'.[12] Ultimately, these attempts to locate and destroy copies of the play-text may have had less to do with the play's actual contents than the exaggerations of the governmental informer, William Udall, in his testimony to Topcliffe about the play.[13]

Legal notoriety, if not explicit censorship *per se*, also took its toll on a play by George Chapman. In 1603, a bookbinder named John Flasket allegedly approached Chapman and supplied him with the plot of a play that Flasket wanted written. The play, 'The Old Joiner of Aldgate', was performed several times by the Children of Paul's; it was purportedly intended to humiliate Flasket's lover, Agnes How, who had recently married one John Milward despite being affianced to Flasket. Though the accused parties strenuously denied the charges, the Attorney-General's Bill alleges that Flasket devised the play in order to intimidate How into marrying him 'rather then to suffer her name to be so traduced in euery play house as it was lyke to be'.[14] In his deposition, Thomas Woodford, who bought the play from Chapman, claimed that 'he hath the booke itself without alteringe of it'.[15] Presumably such a play, though the 'booke' was still extant in 1603, was not going to find a willing publisher, given the Star Chamber proceedings. Chapman's play was at least performed: a play about the Dutch massacre of English merchants in

---

[9] E. K. Chambers, *The Elizabethan Stage*, 4 vols. (Oxford: Clarendon Press, 1923), 3.455.

[10] G. Wickham, *Early English Stages, 1300 to 1660*, 3 vols. (London: Routledge and Kegan Paul, 1963), 2.12.

[11] I. Donaldson, *Ben Jonson: A Life* (Oxford: Oxford University Press, 2011), 118.

[12] J. R. Dasent et al. (eds.), *Acts of the Privy Council of England, New Series: 1542–1631*, 46 vols. (London: HMSO, 1890–1964), 27.338 (via British History Online).

[13] See M. Teramura, 'Richard Topcliffe's Informant: New Light on *The Isle of Dogs*', *Review of English Studies*, 68 (2017), 44–59.

[14] Attorney-General's Bill, quoted in C. J. Sisson, *Lost Plays of Shakespeare's Age* (Cambridge: Cambridge University Press, 1936), 58.

[15] Thomas Woodford's deposition, quoted in Sisson, *Lost Plays of Shakespeare's Age*, 70–71.

Amboyna, Indonesia was suppressed by the Privy Council in 1625 following appeals by Dutch ministers in London, who feared that the scheduled Shrove Tuesday performance at an unknown playhouse would incite riots.[16]

Wilful destruction of play-texts also accounts for the loss of some plays. Sir Fulke Greville, first Baron Brooke of Beauchamps Court, is best known as the author of short poems and Senecan closet dramas including *Mustapha* (c.1596) and *Alahum* (c.1600). He also wrote a play about Antony and Cleopatra, but it perished in an act of self-censorship. In the wake of the failed coup and subsequent execution of the Earl of Essex in 1600, Greville realised that the play he had recently written might be misconstrued as dangerous political commentary. Fearing the repercussions of such an identification, Greville decided to burn his manuscript himself, even though he maintained that no such allegory was intended. (He likened himself to the Greek philosopher Thales, who was so preoccupied with gazing at the stars that he fell down a well).[17]

The logistics involved in bringing a play from the stage to the page were also undoubtedly a contributing factor to the loss of so many play-texts. As Donaldson observes, 'for a variety of aesthetic, social, religious, and political reasons', when Ben Jonson published his First Folio in 1616, he did not attempt to print everything he had written.[18] Jonson told William Drummond of Hawthornden in 1619 that 'half of his comedies were not in print', despite his First Folio having been published just three years previously. Although some of these comedies eventually found a home in the two-volume folio published in 1640 (e.g. *Bartholomew Fair* and *The Devil is an Ass*), Jonson was also presumably alluding to comedies now lost altogether, such as 'Hot Anger Soon Cold', which he wrote with Henry Porter and Henry Chettle in 1598, and which he must have knowingly excluded or been unable to include in the 1616 folio.[19] He notably omitted co-authored plays such as 'Page of Plymouth' (1599), early works he likely judged to be 'artistically inferior' (*The Case is Altered*) and

---

[16] See Chamberlain's letter to Carleton dated 26 February 1625 in N. E. McClure (ed.), *The Letters of John Chamberlain* (Philadelphia: The American Philosophical Society, 1939), 2.602 and the *LPD* entry for 'Amboyna'.

[17] F. Greville, 'Dedication to Sir Philip Sidney' in J. Gouws (ed.), *The Prose Works of Fulke Greville, Lord Brooke* (Oxford: Clarendon Press, 1986), 93.

[18] I. Donaldson, 'Collecting Ben Jonson' in A. Nash (ed.), *The Culture of Collected Editions* (Basingstoke: Palgrave Macmillan, 2003), 27 (and see 25–27 in general on the rationale of Folio inclusions/exclusions).

[19] See I. Donaldson (ed.), 'Informations to William Drummond of Hawthornden', line 306 in *The Cambridge Edition of the Works of Ben Jonson* (Cambridge: Cambridge University Press), 5.378.

controversial plays such as 'The Isle of Dogs', as well as other poetry and writings.[20]

Claims that half of Shakespeare's plays would have been lost had they not appeared in his First Folio of 1623 are somewhat overstated (presumably attempts would have been made to publish at least some of them in cheaper formats), but it is certainly the case that eighteen plays by Shakespeare appeared in print for the very first time in *Mr. William Shakespeare's Comedies, Histories, & Tragedies*. Drawing a comparison with palaeontology and the singular events that produce exceptional preservation conditions, Matthew Steggle describes the publication of the First Folio as 'one of the biggest and most significant mudslides of early modern drama'.[21] Unlike Jonson, Shakespeare could not assist with the publication of his collected works, having died in 1616. Play selection seems to have been determined by availability (what the stationers involved in the project already had rights to or could acquire) and perhaps some other principle of aesthetic resembling Jonson's criteria for folio inclusion. *All is True* (*Henry VIII*), co-authored with Fletcher, was included, but *The Two Noble Kinsmen* and 'Cardenio' (also Fletcher collaborations) were not, and neither was *Pericles*, co-authored with George Wilkins. 'Love's Labour's Won', which was apparently in print by 1603, was also omitted.[22] (More on this play below.) The plays that were included stem from a variety of copytexts of varying quality: it was not simply the case that the 'best' were published. The *New Oxford Shakespeare* editors conclude that scribal copy underlies seven of the previously unpublished plays, though the nature of those transcribed manuscripts remains uncertain, with *Two Gentlemen of Verona* probably a playhouse manuscript, *Measure for Measure* probably a late playhouse manuscript (including additions made after Shakespeare's death), and *The Tempest* probably not originating in

---

[20] Donaldson, 'Collecting Ben Jonson', 26; see also Donaldson, *Ben Jonson: A Life*, 332. Loss could actually be beneficial on occasion. Jonson seems to have preferred to let some plays disappear, and at least one critic of Dekker has unkindly suggested that judicious jettisoning of that playwright's works may have increased his reputation: 'Oddly enough, it seems likely that Dekker's reputation would be greater if all but *Shoemakers' Holiday*, *Old Fortunatus*, both parts of *Honest Whore*, and the delightful *Gull's Hornbook* had been lost'. See J. H. Conover, *Thomas Dekker: An Analysis of Dramatic Structure* (The Hague: Mouton, 1969), 213.

[21] M. Steggle, 'They are all Fossils: A Paleontology of Early Modern Drama', in R. L. Knutson, D. McInnis and M. Steggle (eds.), *Loss and the Literary Culture of Shakespeare's Time* (Cham: Springer/ Palgrave Macmillan, 2020), 186.

[22] The inclusion of 'Love's Labour's Won' on the inventory list of Exeter-based bookseller Christopher Hunt (1603) strongly implies that this lost Shakespeare play had been printed; see T. W. Baldwin, *Shakspere's Love's Labor's Won* (Carbondale, IL: Southern Illinois University Press, 1957).

the playhouse at all, given its permissive stage directions.[23] A further three plays evidently seem to have been printed from theatrical manuscripts (*All's Well*, *Julius Caesar* and *Macbeth*); three appear to be authorial papers annotated for performance (*Coriolanus*, *King John* and *1 Henry VI*); and one (*All is True*) seems authorial but lacks theatrical annotations. The nature of the copytext for the remaining four plays that appeared in print for the first time in the Folio (*As You Like It*, *Comedy of Errors*, *The Taming of the Shrew* and *Timon*) remains unclear.[24]

The 'mudslide' of the Folio offers a just cause for celebration, but the process of its creation also helpfully illuminates the various contingencies associated with attempting to preserve plays in print. The variety of copytexts used, from disparate moments along the continuum from authorial papers to scribal copies and performance texts, suggests that manuscripts were not superseded by newer transcriptions, and that the latest iteration of a play-text did not offer cause to discard earlier iterations. As Paul Werstine has recently shown, although older generations of critics (influenced by W. W. Greg) postulated 'that for every play some company once possessed just a single document', it must actually have been the case that multiple playhouse manuscripts of individual plays co-existed simultaneously.[25] The versions of extant plays that survive are not necessarily the most recent, authoritative or any other ostensible index of quality – they might be old or inferior copies that happened to still be available when the Folio editors began their project of assembling Shakespeare's works. The above editorial inferences can be supplemented with historical evidence from 1623, the year that the First Folio was printed, when the Master of the Revels had to re-license for the King's Men '[a]n olde playe called Winter's Tale' since 'the allowed booke was missinge': the licensed text was not available, but clearly the company had recourse to an alternative manuscript, and the play was printed that year.[26]

Certainly some early modern readers accorded little value to playbooks. Sir Thomas Bodley famously classed 'Englishe plaies' alongside almanacs and pamphlets as 'riffe raffes' and 'baggage books' that his first Keeper, Thomas James, should take care not to admit into the Bodleian library ('hardly one in fortie' of them being 'worthy the keeping'). Nicholas Ferrar expressed a

---

[23] The other scribal plays are *Antony and Cleopatra*, *Cymbeline*, *Twelfth Night* and *The Winter's Tale*.

[24] See discussions under each title in *The New Oxford Shakespeare: Critical Reference Edition* (Oxford: Oxford University Press, 2017).

[25] Werstine, 'Lost Playhouse Manuscripts' in Knutson, McInnis and Steggle (eds.), *Loss and the Literary Culture of Shakespeare's Time*, 41.

[26] N. W. Bawcutt (ed.), *The Control and Censorship of Caroline Drama: The Records of Sir Henry Herbert, Master of the Revels, 1623–73* (Oxford: Clarendon Press, 1996), 142 (item 43).

similar attitude to vernacular literature with his dying wish: he ordered his brother John to 'take out of my Study those three great Hampers full of Bookes' (being his collection of 'Comedies, Tragedies, Love-Hymns, Heroicall Poems, & such like') and have them carried 'to the place of my grave, & upon it, see you burn them all'.[27] Critics no longer uniformly accept such disdain for playbooks as representative of early modern attitudes to English plays, and the reputation of playbooks has been recuperated by book historians.[28] However, it would be a mistake to assume that the incidence of play loss decreased in the early seventeenth century, when the market for playbooks became more established.[29] In an examination of playbook publication patterns in the period spanning 1576–1660, Alan B. Farmer and Zachary Lesser describe 1576–1597 as 'an initial period of low production' and the subsequent period covering 1598–1613 as a 'boom followed by sustained high production'.[30] Moreover, Farmer and Lesser's work demonstrates that stationers appear to have embraced the opportunity to print playbooks (which is not to say that it was a lucrative business so much as a valued one: lower in risk and not as low in profit as previously assumed).[31] In the course of comparing the 'popularity' of playbooks to other print publications of the period (in particular sermons and treatises), they note that market share was determined not only by demand (the public's willingness to purchase certain kinds of books), but also by supply (i.e. the availability of manuscripts to print).[32] Acknowledging that play-texts occupied a smaller

---

[27] See Letter 220 (1 January 1612) and Letter 221 (15 January 1612) in G. W. Wheeler (ed.), *Letters of Sir Thomas Bodley to Thomas James, First Keeper of the Bodleian Library* (Oxford: Clarendon Press, 1926), 219–222; and B. Blackstone (ed.), *The Ferrar Papers* (Cambridge: Cambridge University Press, 1938), 60–61.

[28] See, e.g. Aaron T. Pratt's recent recuperation of the status of playbooks as they appeared in stab-stitched quarto format, the pamphlet form of which 'did as much to align playbooks with respectable forms and genres as it did to set them apart': A. T. Pratt, 'Stab-Stitching and the Status of Early English Playbooks as Literature', *The Library*, 16(3) (2015), 304–328, esp. 308–309 and 327–328). See also L. Erne, *Shakespeare as Literary Dramatist* (Cambridge: Cambridge University Press, 2003).

[29] On the status of playbooks and Bodley's sentiments, see L. Erne, *Shakespeare and the Book Trade* (Cambridge: Cambridge University Press, 2013), 194ff.

[30] A. B. Farmer and Z. Lesser, 'The Popularity of Playbooks Revisited', *Shakespeare Quarterly*, 56 (2005), 7. This 'boom' was in turn followed by a 'gradual contraction' (1614–1628) with only thirty-one first editions. Successive periods within their date range alternate between booms and contraction, but are beyond the scope of this book's own date range.

[31] Farmer and Lesser, 'The Popularity of Playbooks Revisited', 25. Their article was written in response to the very different conclusion offered in Peter W. M. Blayney's still influential 'The Publication of Playbooks' in J. D. Cox and D. S. Kastan (eds.), *A New History of Early English Drama* (New York: Columbia University Press, 1997), 383–422.

[32] A. B. Farmer and Z. Lesser, 'Structures of Popularity in the Early Modern Book Trade', *Shakespeare Quarterly*, 56 (2005), 212.

portion of the marketplace than sermons, Farmer and Lesser nevertheless imply that if publishers had been furnished with more playscripts, the market would have happily absorbed them:

> We simply do not know how many more playbooks stationers would have published if theaters had produced plays in the same quantities that preachers produced sermons or divines produced treatises (although the high reprint rate for playbooks seems a good clue).[33]

The implication is that once the market for playbooks began to enjoy its first 'boom' in 1598 or so, the rate of loss was curtailed.

Writing in 2005, Farmer and Lesser were distinctly ahead of the curve in acknowledging the peculiar problem that lost plays pose to such calculations. Their method of calculating the popularity of playbooks takes loss rates into account in two distinct ways. First, they note that approximately thirty-six titles entered in the Stationers' Register in anticipation of publication pertain to manuscripts that may have been professional plays, but for which there are no extant specimens. ('Cloth Breeches and Velvet Hose', a 'morall ... As yt is Acted by my lord Chamberlens servantes', entered for James Roberts in the Stationers' Register on 27 May 1600, is a good example.)[34] Although their study sometimes covers a chronological range of 1576–1660, this particular statistic is derived from W. W. Greg's bibliography of printed drama, and pertains to the more limited period of c.1591–1646 (being the titles of ostensibly professional drama appearing on pages 965–977 of the 'lost plays' section of Greg's work).[35] It therefore omits reference (for example) to the approximately fifty-eight old plays registered for publication by Humphrey Moseley on 9 September 1653, forty-seven of which appear to be lost.[36] To what extent did the actions of stationers such as Moseley result in the non-survival of plays that could have been saved by printing? Second, Farmer and Lesser offer the salient reminder that not everything that was printed was necessarily registered beforehand at Stationers' Hall; in fact, by their calculations, only four-fifths of the first-edition playbooks printed between 1576–1640 were registered. If the thirty-six entries (by their count) for lost plays represent four-fifths of the plays that stationers intended to publish (but which are

---

[33] Farmer and Lesser, 'Structures of Popularity', 212.

[34] E. Arber (ed.), *A Transcript of the Registers of the Company of Stationers of London, 1554–1640 AD* (London, 1875–1894), 3.161 (accessed via Columbia University Libraries' digitisation).

[35] Farmer and Lesser, 'The Popularity of Playbooks Revisited', 29, citing W. W. Greg, *A Bibliography of the English Printed Drama to the Restoration* (London: Bibliographical Society, 1939–1959), 2.965–977 (hereafter '*BEPD*').

[36] See Greg, *BEPD*, 2.979 (header note for entries 'θ 58 to 102').

not known to exist), Farmer and Lesser project an upper limit total of
forty-six lost first editions of play-texts – or 'less than one playbook per
year' of their studied range. They subsequently qualify their assumptions
to arrive at an even leaner range of between one and twenty lost first
editions.[37]

Farmer and Lesser's conception of lostness pertains exclusively to those
presumed play-texts which had made their way into the hands of willing
stationers, but which were either not printed or, if they were, did not
survive. Similarly, Alexandra Hill (in her more recent analysis), claims that
of the 411 plays registered for publication at Stationers' Hall between
1557 and 1640, 319 saw their way into a printed edition that still survives
today. This implies a survival rate of something like eighty percent.[38] Such
reassuring statistics need to be understood within context, however.
Several plays – e.g. *The Second Maiden's Tragedy*, *The Welsh Ambassador*
or *Sir Thomas More* – survive in manuscript but not in print sources.
Survival is not to be equated with whether stationers printed something
and whether that printed edition survives.[39]

What of the many hundreds, if not thousands, of plays that never even
made it as far as the stationers? In his preface to *The English Traveller*
(1633), Thomas Heywood offers an unusually explicit commentary on the
process of loss and survival in the period:

> True it is, that my Playes are not exposed unto the world in Volumes, to beare
> the title of Workes, (as others) one reason is, That many of them by shifting and
> change of Companies, haue beene negligently lost, Others of them are still
> retained in the hands of some Actors, who thinke it against their peculiar profit
> to haue them come in Print, and a third, That it never was any great ambition
> in me, to bee in this kind Voluminously read.[40]

Heywood's claim of having had '*either an entire hand, or at the least a maine
finger*' in the composition of some 220 plays remains unverified, but if his
explanation for their non-appearance in print is to be trusted, Heywood's
lost plays were unlikely to have ever been offered to stationers, and thus

---

[37] Farmer and Lesser, 'The Popularity of Playbooks Revisited', 29.
[38] A. Hill, *Lost Books and Printing in London, 1557–1640: An Analysis of the Stationers' Company
Register* (Leiden: Brill, 2018), 135.
[39] The question of why certain manuscripts survive and not others warrants more space than I can
devote to it here; that a mere eighteen theatrically annotated play manuscripts survive from the
period implies a kind of randomness yet the provenance of these manuscripts offers insights into the
complex reasons for survival.
[40] T. Heywood, 'To the Reader' in *The English Traveller* (London, 1633), sig.A3ʳ.

would not factor into Farmer and Lesser's calculations.[41] (This is utterly appropriate, given the print focus of Farmer and Lesser's study.) Moreover, of the reasons Heywood offers – negligent loss arising from the plays' shifting and changing between companies; the alleged greed of profiteering actors who retained play-texts to their own advantage; and the playwright's lack of ambition to see his works monumentalised in a Jonsonian or Shakespearean folio – none offers support for Beckerman and Gurr's suggestion that quality is a factor in deciding which plays survived and which were lost.

A Case Study: 'Love's Labour's Won'

The example of Shakespeare's 'Love's Labour's Won' helps illustrate my point about the paradoxes and idiosyncrasies of loss. This play does not appear in the Stationers' Register or in any playhouse-related documents. The earliest reference to the play was made by Elizabethan schoolmaster Francis Meres in his *Palladis Tamia* (1598), where he ranked Shakespeare as the English equivalent of Plautus for comedy, citing Shakespeare's '*Gentlemen of Verona*, his *Errors*, his *Loue labors lost*, his *Loue labours wonne*, his *Midsummers night dreame*, and his *Merchant of Venice*' as examples.[42] Of these, only *Love's Labour's Lost* had been printed at the time Meres was writing; his ability to commend them indicates a familiarity either with performances or manuscripts, rather than print. He may therefore have seen 'Love's Labour's Won' at the Theatre or the Curtain if he saw it in London, as these were the venues used by the Chamberlain's Men around this time. Martin Wiggins cautiously observes that when Robert Allot compiled *England's Parnassus* (a collection of *sententiae* organised by thematic headings) in 1600, he quoted extracts from every Shakespeare play published up until 1599 with the playwright's name on the title page; Wiggins therefore concludes that 'Love's Labour's Won' was 'probably not printed until 1600 at the earliest', else we might expect to have found it cited by Allot.[43] When Meres' reference was the only known mention of 'Love's Labour's Won', even such scholars as E. K. Chambers thought it was 'most natural to take this as an alternative title for some

---

[41] Heywood, 'To the Reader', *The English Traveller*, sig.A3[r].

[42] F. Meres, *Palladis tamia. Wits treasury being the second part of Wits common wealth* (London: Peter Short for Cuthbert Burby, 1598), sig.Oo2[r].

[43] Wiggins #1109; he further notes that there are 'no untraceable quotations assigned to Shakespeare' either.

extant play'.[44] But a bookseller's list datable to 1603 was brought to the world's attention by T. W. Baldwin in 1953, offering independent confirmation that a play called 'Love's Labour's Won' was known to Shakespeare's contemporaries by that title.[45] Under the heading '[inte]-rludes & tragedyes' appears a list of sixteen English plays including both 'loves labor lost' and 'loves labor won'.[46] The list is associated with Christopher Hunt, a bookseller who began his career in London but had apparently set up shop in Exeter (or Salisbury) by 1603.[47] Although only two of the extant plays in Hunt's list were printed without first being entered in the Stationers' Register, *Love's Labour's Lost* happens to be one of them, hence the absence of a registration for 'Love's Labour's Won' is no obstacle to our believing that it had been printed, as indeed it appears to have been, at some point between 1600 and 1603.

Unfortunately, little more of value can be gleaned from Hunt's list. As might be expected, he possessed multiple copies of some of the most recent titles in his stock: two each of *Thomas Lord Cromwell* (1602), *1+2 Edward IV* (1600; if this is what is meant by 'Jane Shore' in Hunt's list) and *1 Sir John Oldcastle* (1600); but surprisingly he had three copies of Robert Greene's *Friar Bacon* (1594), two copies of Richard Bower's *Appius and Virginia* (1575), and most bafflingly, *four* copies of William Wager's *Enough is as Good as a Feast* (c.1568). Wager's play was printed by John Allde, however, who had also printed *Nice Wanton* (1565), *Jack Juggler* (1570) and *Like Will to Like* (1587) from Hunt's inventory; possibly Hunt had acquired or inherited a batch of Allde plays as part of his stock (their failure to sell explaining both why Hunt was able to acquire them and why he too was apparently not selling them). Baldwin's conclusion is precisely that Hunt

---

[44] E. K. Chambers, *William Shakespeare: A Study of Facts and Problems* (Oxford: Clarendon Press, 1930), 1.272.

[45] T. W. Baldwin, *Shakspere's Love's Labor's Won* (Carbondale, IL: Southern Illinois University Press, 1957). Baldwin himself, despite this evidence, rejected the independent existence of 'Love's Labour's Won' and lumped the title together with the extant *All's Well That Ends Well* (15). Contrary to popular interpretations, the list does not categorically rule out the possibility that the title was an alternative for *The Taming of The Shrew*: it includes the anonymous *A Shrew*, not Shakespeare's *The Shrew* (though Shakespeare's *Shrew* had not yet been published, so its absence from a list of printed/saleable plays makes sense).

[46] The relevant portion of the list is reproduced and transcribed in Baldwin, *Shakspere's Love's Labor's Won*, 30–31.

[47] In his review of Baldwin's book, G. K. Hunter casts doubt on Baldwin's interpretation of the manuscript fragment's list of place names as being suggestive of an Exeter location for Hunt's shop, suggesting instead that Salisbury would be 'a more natural centre' for the places named; see G. K. Hunter, 'Shakespeare's Love's Labor's Won' (review), *Review of English Studies* 10(40) (1959), 412.

had 'recently bought out someone's accumulated stock of plays in London',[48] though he doesn't hazard a guess as to whose stock this might be. In a review of Baldwin's book, G. K. Hunter cast doubt on the conclusion that the list is an inventory of Hunt's stock, suggesting instead that it may have been a list of titles to be ordered.[49] However, he does not attempt to justify why, in 1603, a stationer or his customers might want four copies of Wager's thirty-five year-old interlude. Even if we assume, though, that Hunt's list was an inventory of stock rather than *desiderata*, we immediately run into trouble if we attempt to think of the bookseller's list as an alternative 'repertory' to consider for 'Love's Labour's Won', because it seems to be at least partially comprised of bulk acquisition obtained (presumably) at an attractive price rather than strategically selected.[50]

Unless new archival discoveries are made, very little further can be said about this title. A potentially rewarding avenue of exploration is the search for physical traces of the printed play: as Jeffrey Todd Knight and others have observed, plays once bound together in *sammelbande* can sometimes leave ghostly imprints on neighbouring titles in the collection, an 'almost imperceptible darkening of the paper that comes from the oil in ink or its acidity relative to a facing leaf'.[51] Knight has relied on this phenomenon to identify the one-time pairing of quartos of Heywood's *A Woman Killed With Kindness* and Shakespeare's *Henry V* printed for Thomas Pavier in 1619. The most logical place to look for such ghosting (or 'offsetting') of the 'Love's Labour's Won' title page would be the final leaf of *Love's Labour's Lost* (what better play to pair it with in a nonce collection?), but of the fourteen extant copies of the 1598 quarto, no ghosting is to be found.[52] Of

---

[48] Baldwin, *Shakspere's Love's Labor's Won*, 13.

[49] Hunter, 'Shakespeare's Love's Labor's Won' (review), 413.

[50] The situation does not improve if we ignore the old stock and focus on the more recent titles, which Hunt may have had a more active hand in selecting. Cuthbert Burby (who had published Meres' *Palladis Tamia*) is somewhat prominent in the list; he published nine extant plays (some of them twice), and Hunt had four of them, including *Love's Labor's Lost*. An intuitive conclusion would be that 'Love's Labour's Won' might also have been printed as 'a pleasant conceited comedy' for Burby, but against this logic, Hunt seems to have acquired *A Knack to Know and Honest Man* (printed by Thomas Scarlet for Cuthbert Burby in 1596) seemingly as a companion piece to the similarly named but unrelated *A Knack to Know a Knave* (1594), even though that play was printed by Alice Charlewood or James Roberts for Richard Jones (rather than Burby). The Chamberlain's Men are best represented in Hunt's list, but only by a very slender (and statistically insignificant) margin: three plays, as opposed to two from the Admiral's repertory and only a single play from other companies (Queen's, Strange's, Pembroke's, etc.); the auspices of several are unknown.

[51] J. T. Knight, *Bound to Read: Compilations, Collections, and the Making of Renaissance Literature* (Philadelphia: University of Pennsylvania Press, 2013), 151.

[52] I.e. the Bodleian Library, Dartmouth College, Edinburgh University Library, Folger Shakespeare Library (three), Harvard University Houghton Library, Newberry Library, Princeton University Firestone Library, the Fondation Martin Bodmer, the British Library, the Huntington Library

course, an early owner of a 'Love's Labour's Won' quarto may have had it bound with another play or text altogether.[53] The idiosyncratic logic of individual collectors' organisation of their *sammelbande* means that aside from some basic categorical principles ('comedy'?), such ghosting – if it exists – could theoretically turn up anywhere.[54]

From the available evidence, then, the most we can say is that for Meres to have recalled it, the play had probably been performed by 1598 (placing it at the Curtain, though perhaps not exclusively); that it had been printed during or after 1600 (its absence from *England's Parnassus* in 1600 suggests its unavailability in print at the time); and that it was still available to purchase in 1603. A striking feature of this lost play's history is that, contrary to every generalisation about why plays become lost, 'Love's Labour's Won' was sole-authored (the prejudice of the Jonson folio, for example, against collaboratively authored plays does not apply), its playwright was still with the same company (i.e. there were no issues around ownership of the play), it had been printed (so ought to have been available in quarto even if its manuscript versions had perished), and it had been singled out for its quality (by Meres; so it wasn't consigned to oblivion by virtue of being inferior).

Where to from Here?

A revaluation of the role played by lost drama in the repertories of early modern playing companies is urgently needed. C. J. Sisson was amongst the distinct minority of scholars when he wrote, in 1936, 'I am not ready to accept with confidence the belief that all the best of this abundant drama survived, and that the worst only is buried in the oblivion that fell

---

(two) and the Trinity College, Cambridge copies. I am grateful to the librarians who kindly assisted with my inquiries and to the libraries who have generously digitised their copies and made them readily available online.

[53] Sir John Harrington apparently had a *Love's Labour's Lost* Q1 bound between Nashe's *Summer's Last Will and Testament* and *Il Pastor Fido*, and vol. 10 of the Petworth House play collection has a copy of *Love's Labour's Lost* Q3 bound between Dekker's *The Wonder of a Kingdom* and Shakespeare's *King John*. The Petworth House *sammelbande* were probably compiled in 1638 by Sir John Borough for the 10th Earl of Northumberland, Algernon Percy. See Maria Kirk, 'Performing Consumption and Consuming Performance: A 17th Century Play Collection', unpublished PhD thesis, University of Sussex (2016) (see online at http://sro.sussex.ac.uk/61894/).

[54] Jeffrey Masten's discussion of a previously unreported copy of Q1 of Marlowe's *Edward II* (1594) in a seventeenth-century *sammelband* housed by the Universitäts-bibliothek Erlangen-Nürnberg is instructive in this regard; the English history play is bound with a lengthy theological tract and a history of the Turks. See J. Masten, 'Bound for Germany: Heresy, Sodomy, and a New Copy of Marlowe's Edward II', *Times Literary Supplement*, (21 December 2012), 17–19.

upon almost all plays neglected by the printer'.[55] His own response to the challenge focused on individual titles: he turned to legal records of the Court of Star Chamber to reconstruct in vivid detail the contents of two controversial London plays (George Chapman's 'The Old Joiner of Aldgate', 1603, and Thomas Dekker, William Rowley, John Ford and John Webster's 'Keep the Widow Waking', 1624), as well as jigs and May Games. The documentary evidence Sisson assembled is both rich and regrettably atypical: noting that the playbook of 'The Old Joiner of Aldgate' was used as evidence in court, Sisson tantalisingly suggests that at one point, 'the file of the case might well have contained Chapman's autograph play in full, licensed and prepared for the stage'.[56] He mourns the loss of the 'great prize' (meaning the absent manuscript) but consoles himself with the 'lesser' prize of the 'abundant evidence' about the play that *is* preserved in the records.[57] Sisson's terminology is unfortunate, as the spate of recent scholarship on lost plays has demonstrated how incredibly useful such 'lesser prizes' can be for theatre historians.

To study lost plays is to return to early modern drama with a Coleridgean 'freshness of sensation' in the representation of familiar things.[58] The object of inquiry is not a polished final product, but the skeleton or embryonic form of drama, which offers a productive reminder of drama's construction. (Of course, the same might be said of plays that scholars have regarded as being 'complete', but it is in the attention to lost plays that such a view becomes most obvious.) For example, there survive six backstage plots – single sheets of paper once hung backstage to help organise the actors and other participants in a play by providing an overview of the scenes – that correspond to such lost plays as 'Frederick and Basilea', '2 Fortune's Tennis' and 'The Dead Man's Fortune'. These backstage plots are devoid of actual lines from the play-texts, but they preserve the dramaturgy of lost plays in the sense that they record entrances, casting information and sometimes props or special effects.[59] The dramaturgy, but not the English language, is preserved too in a number of plays that found their way to the Continent and were adapted

---

[55] Sisson, *Lost Plays of Shakespeare's Age*, 1.   [56] Sisson, *Lost Plays of Shakespeare's Age*, 72.

[57] Sisson, *Lost Plays of Shakespeare's Age*, 8–9.

[58] S. Taylor Coleridge, 'Chapter IV' in *Biographia Literaria* (London, 1817), 1.85.

[59] The surviving plots are held by the Dulwich College ('2 Seven Deadly Sins') and the British Library ('The Dead Man's Fortune', '2 Fortune's Tennis', 'Frederick and Basilea' and 'Troilus and Cressida'; Add. MS.10449); the plot of 'The First Parte of Tamar Cam' was transcribed by George Steevens and printed by Isaac Reed in the 'Variorum' *Shakespeare* of 1803 (foldout after leaf 2D8^v/p. 414); the original has since disappeared.

into German by travelling players: *Comoedia von der Königin Esther und hoffertigen Haman*, a 'Hester' play published in German in Leipzig in 1620, for example, may well constitute direct evidence of the 'Hester and Ahasuerus' play performed at the Rose in 1594, and is almost certainly a partial source for *The Taming of the Shrew* (I discuss this play in Chapter 2). Performance scholars could extrapolate a great deal from a full play-text like this, despite the fact that not a word of the original English survives.[60] Emma Whipday, Lucy Munro and others have recently experimented with a form of performance-based research centring on lost plays (which they call 'early modern verbatim theatre'). They used legal records pertaining to the lost Dekker, Ford, Rowley and Webster play, 'Keep the Widow Waking' (1624) as the basis for exploring archival traces through performance.[61]

Occasionally a playwright's plot-scenario (their summary of a projected play's action, composed before the play itself is written) is accompanied by a fragmentary draft of the play, as with James Cobbes' tragedy called 'Romanus', possibly written for the King's Men in the early 1620s.[62] Textual analysis is clearly possible in such instances, as it is too in the case of the actor's 'part' for the role of 'God' in the Welbeck Abbey MS, 'Old verses frō Limebrook' (c.1575) or the role of 'Poore' in Houghton MS Thr 10.1 (c.1616); in these plays, the lines of only these single characters survive.[63] In his recent monograph on digital humanities and lost plays, Matthew Steggle helpfully suggests that a lost play's title itself might be regarded as a very short document of performance; we should thus add the records of play-titles – as recorded in the diary of Rose playhouse manager Philip Henslowe; in court records; and Masters of the Revels

---

[60] For a detailed analysis of another such play, lost in English but extant in a German adaptation, see my chapter, 'Magic Mirrors, Moors, and Marriage: A Lost English Play Surviving in German' (which focuses on 'The King of England's Son and the King of Scotland's Daughter', c.1597–1598) in Knutson, McInnis and Steggle (eds.), *Loss and the Literary Culture of Shakespeare's Time*, 215–231.

[61] The experiment was conceived for 'A Symposium on Early Modern Verbatim Theatre', The Anatomy Museum, King's College London (Strand Campus), 6 May 2016; see also the chapter by Munro and Whipday, 'Making Early Modern "Verbatim Theater" or "Keep the Widow Waking"' in Knutson, McInnis and Steggle (eds.), *Loss and the Literary Culture of Shakespeare's Time*, 233–249.

[62] British Library Harley MS 4268, fo.272ʳ–282ᵛ; see the *LPD* entry for a digitisation of the MS. On this critically neglected play, see R. M. Schuler, 'James Cobbes: Jacobean Dramatist and Translator', *The Papers of the Bibliographical Society of America*, 72(1) (1978), 68–74.

[63] See the *LPD* entry for 'Processus Satanae' and 'Play of Poore' for full digitisations of the 'parts' and, in the case of 'Poore', an accompanying transcription by David Carnegie, reproduced courtesy of the Malone Society.

accounts – to the examples above.[64] If we as Shakespeare scholars take these various forms of documentary records into consideration, we have ample data on which to base arguments about sources, genre, themes and authorship. This wealth of documentary evidence affords a more nuanced appreciation than previously possible of the repertory system in which Shakespeare – playwright, player and shareholder in the Chamberlain's/ King's Men – operated.

In this book I approach the question of coping with loss by thinking in pragmatic terms about how scholars can and should incorporate discussion of lost plays into their work on substantially extant texts. At its heart is my desire to better understand Shakespeare's plays by restoring them to their most immediate and pressing context: the lost drama of the day, which also constitutes the majority of drama of the day – and thus the most severely neglected yet relevant of all contexts. Although the book is informed by the logic and insights of repertory studies (concisely defined by Tom Rutter as 'an approach to the study of drama that takes the acting company – rather than, say, the individual dramatist or play – as the subject of its enquiry'), and a concern with how the commercial playing companies of Shakespeare's London competed with each other for play-goer patronage, I am not bound to a season-by-season analysis of the Chamberlain's-King's repertory in conjunction with that of their competitors per se.[65] Rather, I am interested in how the comparison of Shakespeare's works with lost plays might enrich our understanding of Shakespeare's plays, his company and the theatrical marketplace for which he wrote.

When Roslyn Knutson published her pioneering study of the repertory of Shakespeare's company in 1991, lost plays formed a component of her analysis and she was amongst the earliest of critics to refute old assumptions about the value of non-extant drama, suggesting that Beckerman's so-called 'fillers' (the lost and extant drama by playwrights other than Shakespeare) were 'valuable items in the company repertory – if only because of their number, conventionality, and appeal to a spectrum of tastes'.[66] When Scott McMillin and Sally-Beth MacLean published their seminal study of the Queen's Men in 1998, they acknowledged six plays once in that company's repertory but which have not survived, yet they

---

[64] M. Steggle, *Digital Humanities and the Lost Drama of Early Modern England* (Farnham: Ashgate, 2015).

[65] T. Rutter, 'Repertory Studies: A Survey', *Shakespeare* 4(3) (2008), 352.

[66] R. L. Knutson, *The Repertory of Shakespeare's Company, 1594–1613* (Fayetteville: University of Arkansas Press, 1991), 13.

consciously adopted what they called a 'conservative approach' to repertory, studying only the nine extant plays confidently attributable to the
Queen's Men, because their intention was to 'read closely' for 'evidence of
an acting company's artistic identity'.[67] By the time Lawrence Manley and
Sally-Beth MacLean produced their study of the Lord Strange's Men in
2014, theatre historians had come to prefer a 'maximal rather than minimal discussion of what might reasonably be suspected to have been in the
repertory'. Manley and MacLean devote two chapters to a census of
'candidate plays', thereby giving prominence to the numerous lost plays
associated with that company.[68]

　　With the central tenets of repertory studies well and truly established,
and a gradual elevation in the status accorded to lost plays by critics, it is
now possible for me to do what was unthinkable thirty years ago and focus
primarily on lost plays as the context for understanding Shakespeare's work
and the commercial marketplace of the London theatres during his lifetime.[69] Moreover, recent years have seen the advent of game-changing
digital tools (including Early English Books Online's Text Creation
Partnership wing, EEBO-TCP; the Internet Archive; and Google Books)
that facilitate rigorous searching of large data sets, significantly improving
the likelihood of illuminating the subject matter of opaquely titled lost
plays. Matthew Steggle, for example, has used such search tools to great
success in his monograph, *Digital Humanities and the Lost Drama of Early
Modern England* (2015), in which he recovers the subjects of 'Albere
Galles' (actually 'Alba Regalis', 1602), 'Richard the Confessor' (a medieval
saint, not a mistake for a pre-Norman king, 1593) and others. His strategy
involves 'intensive study of single plays whose titles have been entirely
uninterpreted, or else misinterpreted', with a view to 'establish the title's
meaning and to enable the play to be placed in terms of genre and other
features'.[70] In what follows, I too take advantage of the available digital
tools in order to propose several new identifications of my own, but more
importantly I begin the more macroscopic work of integrating discussion

---

[67] S. McMillin and S.-B. MacLean, *The Queen's Men and Their Plays* (Cambridge: Cambridge
University Press, 1998), 86. The six plays are listed on pp. 92–93; another play, which I have
described as 'A Lord and his Three Sons', featured Tarlton, dates to the mid-1580s, and is therefore
likely to also be a lost Queen's Men play: see D. McInnis, 'Evidence of a Lost Tarlton Play, c.1585,
Probably for The Queen's Men', *Notes & Queries*, 59(1) (2012), 43–45.
[68] L. Manley and S.-B. MacLean, *Lord Strange's Men and Their Plays* (New Haven: Yale University
Press, 2014), 9.
[69] On the evolution of repertory studies, see T. Rutter, 'Repertory Studies: A Survey', *Shakespeare*, 4
(2008), 336–350.
[70] Steggle, *Digital Humanities*, 8.

of lost plays with discussion of extant plays as a mutually illuminating enterprise.

With the notable exceptions of destroyed plays (Greville's 'Antony and Cleopatra') or famously unfinished works (Jonson's 'Mortimer, His Fall'), what I refer to in this book as 'lost plays' were not, of course, lost in their own day. Rather, they were part of the rich fabric of the early modern stage, influencing and influenced by the drama that *has* survived to this day. All early modern drama must be understood in this context; as part of an elaborate playing system characterised by the interactivity of the plays offered by various companies, with no sense that certain plays might somehow be doomed to loss in centuries to come or be less worthy of attention in their own day or ours. Examination of lost plays should not be restricted to passing footnotes – acknowledged, but segregated from main discussions. For an analysis of early modern theatre to be meaningful, lost plays must be fully integrated in the discussion. At the same time, it is imperative that we acknowledge that lost plays *are* lost to us; that we do not assert, over-confidently, what they were about or how they handled their subject matter. In his introduction to the most recent scholarly translation of Sappho, a writer whose canon is characterised by loss, André Lardinois cautions against the critical desire to elide the notorious gaps in the archive and reconstruct more of Sappho's life and work than the limited evidence permits. He even cautions against relying on the ostensible authority of ancient writers who, we might think, were better placed to know the details of Sappho's achievements:

> [L]ike modern scholars, [ancient scholars] hated not to be able to give an answer and therefore deduced unknown details from better known ones. One should therefore always assess how likely it is that the ancient scholars could have known certain facts.[71]

One should similarly always assess how likely it is that any given scholar could know certain facts; a seductive narrative, confidently offered, is not a substitute for archival evidence. Whilst a certain amount of storytelling enhances readability, theatre historians do not need to force square pegs into round holes. A key contribution I hope to make with this book is the exploration of the unknown from a position of relative scepticism, and the recognition of the virtues of 'productive failure'. Our colleagues in the sciences are at least implicitly familiar with this concept: not all funded

---

[71] A. Lardinois, 'Introduction' in D. J. Rayor and A. Lardinois (eds.), *Sappho: A New Translation of the Complete Works* (Cambridge: Cambridge University Press, 2014), 2.

science projects find a cure for cancer, but there is value in positively ruling out certain approaches or potential cures, and subsequent studies build on the findings of previous studies. So too there is methodological value in rigorously exploring the evidence and potential clues to lost plays – especially those with opaque titles like 'the taner of denmarke' or 'felmelanco' – even if they stubbornly refuse to yield satisfying answers.

As long as the misconceptions popularised by Fleay and others continue to shape the current critical conversations, real progress is unlikely to be made. In the following chapters, I attempt to break down received narratives, clear the debris and create space for fresh perspectives. Rather than deducing unknown details from better known ones and over-confidently providing an answer where none is warranted, I aim to always provide transparency and accountability when working with evidence pertaining to lost plays. For this reason, the book is best read in conjunction with the relevant *Lost Plays Database* ('*LPD*') entries, which provide access to digitisations or transcriptions of the primary evidence in question, quite separate from summaries of critical commentary. Since 2009, the *LPD* has attempted to raise lost plays from obscurity by bringing together documentary evidence, critical commentary and new information or conjecture in the belief that the sum is greater than the parts and that such elusive subject matter is best served by collaboration among theatre historians, each of whom will have their own minor but important contributions to make to our overall understanding of any particular lost play under investigation. The impact that this website has had on early modern scholarship is testament to the benefits of having a curated data set, especially when it is open-access. That project, which isolates and documents lost plays, is well advanced. It is now vital to restore lost plays to their natural environment. In this book, I return the newly visible lost plays to their commercial context alongside the surviving drama from the London companies' repertories, offering a timely critical reassessment of early modern drama.

Lost Plays and Rubin's Vase

In the chapters that follow, I want to draw attention to how absence contributes to presence, or rather, to how that presence is perceived. On one level, every student of early modern drama knows this: during the hand-press period, compositors setting the type of an English playbook (for example) would justify their lines of type – or create a deliberate space in a line, perhaps at the end – not by passively neglecting to fill out the line, but by actively putting in a 'thick' or 'thin' space (or combination thereof) from a box of mixed spaces in his or her case of type.[72] What the reader perceives as a gap or a blank is in fact structured by the presence of a piece of physical type, a little under the height of the rest of the type, which ensured the line would lock up tightly in the forme. Likewise, the pictures that appeared in printed books of the period were typically produced from relief woodcuts: blocks of wood whose surfaces were cut to produce a design, whereby those elements of the image that were to remain white on the page were cut away and those elements that were to be inked remained uncut.[73]

However, there is a much more specific and useful metaphor that I wish to use. It derives from the work of the Danish psychologist Edgar Rubin, whose doctoral thesis on visually experienced figures included the now iconic two-dimensional image of a vase (see Figure I.1), the contours of which (one slowly notices) are shared with a contiguous image of two faces looking at one another:

Fig. I.1   Rubin's Vase.[74]

[72] See, e.g. P. Gaskell, *A New Introduction to Bibliography* (Oxford: Clarendon Press, 1979), 45.
[73] See, e.g. Gaskell, *A New Introduction*, 155.
[74] Illustration 3 from the German edition of Rubin's work, *Visuell Wahrgenommene Figuren* (Copenhagen: Gyldendalske Boghandel, 1921) (out of copyright) (available online at https://archive.org/details/visuellwahrgenomo1rubiuoft).

Commonly known as 'Rubin's Vase', this image demonstrates how when 'two fields have a common border', there exists the potential for the 'figure' and the 'ground' in an image to interrelate in unstable ways, such that '[a] field which had previously been experienced as ground can function in a surprising way when experienced as figure'.[75] Art historians sometimes refer to this interplay of the figure and ground in terms of 'negative space'; the space around a focal object in an artwork that itself 'constitutes a particularly powerful or significant part of the whole composition'.[76] Rubin's work helps explain why scholars are naturally drawn to extant plays as the 'figure' in our overall picture of early modern drama: it is a fundamental principle of Rubin's studies that 'an enclosed area, which is smaller than an enclosing area, is more likely than the surrounding area to be perceived as figure', and the corpus of extant plays is significantly smaller and more manageable – more knowable and familiar – and is metaphorically 'enclosed' by the amorphous mass of lost drama.[77] An equally significant contributing factor, of course, is the fact that the text-focused practices of literary critics (such as twentieth-century close-reading and formalist analysis) are quite distinct from the aims of literary and theatre historians. Close-reading is predicated on access to texts, and thus distorts our sense of what constitutes the field of literature or theatre. As long as Shakespeare scholars fixate on play-texts and ignore lost plays, we will only ever continue to gaze at the figure of the vase, and remain ignorant of the two faces (the ground) that give the vase its shape and which constitute a significant image in their own right. We are only seeing less than half the picture of early modern drama.

Beyond the absence of text, though, I would argue that lost plays suffer from the fact that the very shapelessness of the 'ground' works against attempts to understand it. But an important finding of Rubin's work is that often 'an area previously seen as a figure suddenly changes to ground, and vice versa'; in other words, a defamiliarising effect is possible – hence what was once a picture of a vase is now a picture of two faces.[78] What happens when a field dominated by the uber-canonical (Shakespeare) is reconceived in relation to the ultimate of peripherals (lost plays)? I am not

---

[75] E. Rubin, 'Figure and Ground' in S. Yantis (ed.), *Visual Perception* (Philadelphia: Psychology Press, 2001), 225.

[76] OED, 'negative space'.

[77] J. L. Pind, *Edgar Rubin and Psychology in Denmark: Figure and Ground* (Cham: Springer, 2014), 101.

[78] Pind, *Edgar Rubin*, 94.

so interested in how such visually experienced figures work as I am in asking why we have perceived the field of early modern drama the way we have and how it could it be perceived differently. Just as Rubin instructed the participants in his experiments to view 'either the positive or the negative areas [in the stimuli] as figure', in order to determine whether such instructions would affect perception, so too Beckerman and Gurr – through their disregard of the value of lost plays – have implicitly instructed Shakespeare scholars on how to perceive the canon of early modern drama. They have, effectively, nominated what is the figure and what is the ground, and in so doing have shaped our perception through their instruction.[79] What do the attitudes that govern our perceptions reveal about our biases and values?

The literal intersection of the figure and ground – the point at which they meet, and from which they derive their independent forms – is the 'contour' or 'common boundary' that ostensibly separates them.[80] This mutually defining relationship between the figure and the ground is key to Rubin's experiments in visually perceived figures, and the 'shaping effect emanating from the contour' is vital.[81] Rubin acknowledges the possibility of the contour having 'no shaping effect on either area in which case no figure is perceived', as well as the possibility in which the contour 'shapes both areas equally and two figures are experienced', but suggests that '[t]he figure is most directly affected by this shaping effect of the contour'.[82] This is important for my purposes, because it suggests that our perception of the surviving drama has been affected by the shaping power of a contour generated by the interplay of lost and extant plays. The contour is somewhat fuzzy though: some play-texts are substantially preserved but exhibit signs of having been cut down, or have missing scenes or plotlines; many plays that must have been written in order to furnish the London companies with sufficient material to perform in a competitive market-place have simply disappeared without leaving any trace by which to identify their one-time existence. Part of the work this book performs, then, is to trace the contour and help gauge the shape of both the figure and the ground, the corpora of extant and lost plays respectively. When all that was known of the lost play identified as 'Henry the Una...' was its fragmentary title, scholars might have assumed that it concerned a

---

[79] Pind, *Edgar Rubin*, 92.   [80] Pind, *Edgar Rubin*, 97.
[81] Pind, *Edgar Rubin*, 97, summarising Rubin's findings in *Synsoplevede Figurer* (University of Copenhagen, 1915), 36.
[82] Pind, *Edgar Rubin*, 97, summarising *Synsoplevede Figurer*, 35.

monarch named Henry who was perhaps the first of that name; the play might thus sit alongside numerous other history plays, including the lost 'Historye of Henry the First' play attributed to Davenport in 1624 (see Chapter 6). The contour needed significant reshaping once Matthew Steggle discovered that the play was actually about the impotent Castilian king, 'Henry the Unable', and thus more of a piece with Rowley's *All's Lost by Lust* and *The Changeling* than with history plays.[83] Through this metaphor of Rubin's Vase, I suggest that rather than thinking of lost plays as gaps in the overall corpus of early modern drama that resist scrutiny, we should revalue them more productively in terms of how they have contributed to the structure of the extant corpus.

My suggestion is that lost plays, as a kind of ground or negative space, bring our picture of early modern drama into sharper relief. By recovering the likely subject matter of plays known to have been in repertorial competition with surviving early modern plays, we recover an important and largely neglected context for understanding how and why the commercial playing companies acquired the plays they did, when they did. Moreover, the pursuit of a fuller, richer view of dramatic activity from this period offers an opportunity to reconsider what we take for granted about the surviving plays, and the chance to notice not just the figure but the ground; the element whose purported absence is actually structuring or giving shape to the element perceived as present. We have been conditioned to see one image – the image of the early modern dramatic corpus that has been shaped exclusively by surviving play-texts – but once the duality of the image is perceived, it is impossible to see it the same way again.[84] Unlike other optical illusions such as American psychologist Joseph Jastrow's famous 'duck-rabbit' (an ambiguous image perceived variously as either a duck or a rabbit) – or even Shakespeare's Antony, 'painted one way a Gorgon' and the other way 'a Mars' in the manner of 'anamorphic' or 'perspective' paintings (10.117–118) – this is not a matter of seeing the same thing in two different ways.[85] Rather, the key feature of

---

[83] See Steggle, *Digital Humanities*, 119–132.

[84] Of course, even for so-called extant plays, a staggering amount of information has been lost: as Knutson and I note in 'Lost Documents, Absent Documents, Forged Documents', although there are surviving texts, Stationers' Register entries, records of performance, an illustration, and a ballad related to *Titus Andronicus*, there is no manuscript, backstage plot, actors' parts, playbills, title or scene boards, or even confirmation of co-authorship between Shakespeare and Peele; see T. Stern (ed.), *Rethinking Theatrical Documents in Shakespeare's England* (London: Arden Shakespeare, 2020), 242.

[85] For a discussion of Jastrow's images, see L. Wittgenstein, *Philosophical Investigations*, 3rd ed, trans. G. E. M. Anscombe (Oxford: Basil Blackwell, 1986), 193–197.

Rubin's Vase is that it contains two elements that each gives form to the other by virtue of their interconnected presence and shared contour. It is the structural interplay between lost and extant plays in shaping the canon of early modern drama that interests me most.

I am not the first to use visually experienced figures as the impetus for inquiry in a seemingly unrelated discipline. In *The Selfish Gene*, the evolutionary biologist Richard Dawkins used a comparable optical illusion – the Necker cube – to explain that there can be 'two views of the same truth', and that in the case of natural selection, the 'gene's angle and that of the individual' each provides important insights. Dawkins subsequently explained that '[r]ather than propose a new theory or unearth a new fact, often the most important contribution a scientist can make is to discover a new way of seeing old theories or facts'.[86] I argue that the same holds true for Shakespeare scholars. I have not unearthed a single new play-text in the writing of this book, but what I have aimed to do, through Rubin's Vase (rather than the Necker cube), is to reassess and reconfigure the relationship between the lost and extant plays of Shakespeare's time, and to provide a new way of seeing the corpus of early modern drama.

After an initial chapter devoted to recuperating the reputation and value of lost plays, I follow a stable trajectory that maps roughly onto Shakespeare's career. The four central chapters each cover five-year periods in Shakespeare's professional life. These five-year periods are purely nominal increments, but they afford me the pleasing symmetry of four equally weighted chapters comparing Shakespearean plays from 1594–1598 (Chapter 2), 1599–1603 (Chapter 3), 1604–1608 (Chapter 4) and 1609–1613 (Chapter 5) with lost plays relevant to the Shakespearean examples. The precise dates of composition and early stage runs of Shakespeare's plays are often contested of course, but rarely (if ever) are plays from the very earliest periods reassigned to the later period of Shakespeare's working life (or vice versa) – hence even if there is some movement within a given five-year block, the impact on my overall argument should be minimal. Dating or re-dating the plays is not part of my agenda here; for the purposes of this study, I choose to rely on Martin Wiggins' extraordinarily useful and comprehensive *British Drama, 1533–1642: A Catalogue*. A notable virtue of Wiggins' *Catalogue* (unlike Alfred Harbage and S. Schoenbaum's *Annals of English Drama, 975–1700*)

---

[86] R. Dawkins, *The Selfish Gene: 40th Anniversary Edition* (Oxford: Oxford University Press, 2016), xx; the earlier work that Dawkins refers to is *The Extended Phenotype* (Oxford: Oxford University Press, 1982).

is the transparent handling of evidence: readers interested in dates and dating can easily find Wiggins' reasons for assigning plays to the dates that he has chosen by consulting the relevant entries of the *Catalogue*.

In the final, coda-like chapter on the lost Shakespeare Apocrypha, I turn to authorship attribution but harness the insights from repertory studies (rather than stylometric analysis, which cannot be applied in the absence of play-texts), in a bid to understand why it once seemed reasonable (to some at least) that half a dozen plays written after Shakespeare's death were attributed to him, and what these plays can teach us about Shakespeare's posthumous reputation.

In this study I am concerned with developing an appropriate methodology for working with lost plays; one that is sensitive to the lacunae in the archival evidence, the distorting effect produced by privileging Shakespeare-centric narratives, and the limitations of what we can assert with confidence. Although generations of scholars have been reluctant to acknowledge it (building narratives about Shakespeare's theatre with a compelling but unwarranted confidence), our field is actually characterised by extensive documentary loss.[87] Accordingly, this book is deliberately filled with scepticism, caveats and cautiously drawn inferences as I engage with some of the more obscure or seemingly impenetrable case studies: what interests me is a change in perspective. I believe that by considering a variety of ways to grapple with the problem of lost, imperceptible or ignored texts, Shakespeare scholars will find inspiration for productive approaches to working with the elusive drama that is not always perceptible at first glance.

---

[87] On turning 'hypotheses into fact', see S. McMillin, 'Building Stories: Greg, Fleay, and the Plot of *2 Seven Deadly Sins*', *Medieval and Renaissance Drama in England*, 4 (1989), 53–62. On the prevalence of documentary loss, see Knutson and McInnis, 'Lost Documents, Absent Documents, Forged Documents', 241–259.

CHAPTER I

Charting the Landscape of Loss

Why does a company's repertorial context matter? Because Shakespeare's plays were performed alongside the plays (lost and extant) in the commercial companies' repertories and because Shakespeare was writing his own plays to fit within that repertory context. Some of these must also have been the plays in which Shakespeare, as an actor, was performing. The diary of Philip Henslowe, theatrical impresario and manager of the Rose and Fortune playhouses, is indispensable as a source of relevant historical information on the repertories in London. Henslowe's theatrical accounts pertain to performances by multiple companies between 1592–1597,[1] and his expenditure on behalf of the Admiral's and the Earl of Worcester's Men between 1597–1603. The data about performances, takings, inventory lists and expenditure on costumes and playbooks is the most detailed account of company commerce from the period. In this chapter, I consider the finances of the Admiral's, Strange's and Sussex's Men as preserved in Henslowe's diary, with a view to comparing lost and extant plays in terms of the highest number of performances, the highest average takings and the single most profitable performances. If there is any truth to the suggestion made by older generations of scholars that lost plays were mere filler and that their failure to appear in print is an index of their perceived quality, I would expect to see such valuations reflected in the three financial measures I explore, but the results do not support such a conclusion. Instead, one of the key claims I make is that lost plays performed significantly better (financially) and were of greater value to a commercial company than scholars have traditionally acknowledged.

Unfortunately, Henslowe only documents the plays of Shakespeare's company, the Lord Chamberlain's Men, for a brief period of eleven days in June 1594 (see Chapter 2). To appreciate the nature and extent of loss in

---

[1] I.e. the Queen's Men, the Lord Strange's Men, the Earl of Sussex's Men, the Lord Admiral's Men, the Earl of Pembroke's Men and even the Lord Chamberlain's Men for a brief period in 1594.

the Chamberlain's repertory, I must approach the task obliquely by establishing what we can reliably claim about the better-documented repertory of the Admiral's Men. Using the metaphor of Rubin's Vase, I attempt what should be the straightforward task of distinguishing figure (extant plays) from ground (lost plays). Rubin's Vase contains two elements that give form to each other by virtue of their interconnected presence and shared contour, but it is not always so easy to distinguish the elements. The repertory of the Admiral's Men is an instructive example in this regard, for although we have copious documentary evidence in the form of Henslowe's diary entries, those entries can be opaque, and require careful interpretation. When confronted by a complicated or ambiguous image, the challenge for the viewer is to give identity to its interconnected but discrete features; to shape the ground and outline the figure. Rubin's biographer, Jörgen L. Pind, suggests that a 'noticeable difference between figure and ground' is the 'ease with which observers can describe the figure compared to the difficulty they often experience in giving a clear description of the ground with the exception of general remarks as to size or color'.[2] In the case of the Admiral's Men, this is particularly pronounced: scholars have wanted to see the extant plays as forming a coherent shape of some kind (featuring disguises and humoral comedy; being conducive to touring) and have had notable difficulty describing the ground, to the extent that no two scholars even agree on the number of lost plays associated with the company.

Likewise, in the case of the Chamberlain's Men, Shakespeare's plays (with their high survival rate) have become synonymous with the company's repertory to the extent that scholars have argued that it was basically a 'Shakespeare company': the ground has been underappreciated, if perceived at all. I therefore construct a census of the Admiral's known repertory, with the initial aim of identifying a ratio of lost-to-extant plays that may be indicative of the loss rates for other, less well-documented adult, commercial companies. The process of conducting this census also affords me the opportunity to explore in more nuanced detail the critical assumptions that distort the perception of lost plays. The answer to the simple question, 'How many plays did the Admiral's Men have?', turns out to be frustratingly elusive, but the process of answering it helps elucidate the sometimes opaque guiding principles of scholars' methodologies. This in turn has implications for our perception of the Chamberlain's Men's repertory and the likely extent of its losses in relation to the surviving

---

[2] Pind, *Edgar Rubin*, 97, summarising Rubin's findings in *Synsoplevede Figurer* (University of Copenhagen, 1915), 41.

'figure', which is dominated by a disproportionate number of plays by Shakespeare.

Lost Plays and Shakespeare's Company

The lack of records for the Chamberlain's Men during the years Henslowe was actively keeping records for other companies is a particularly important archival lacuna. The absence of a Chamberlain's Men equivalent of Henslowe's papers to illustrate the true depth and breadth of that company's repertory is a key factor in older critical assumptions that Shakespeare's company had a smaller repertory of higher quality plays that were more likely to have survived in print than those of the rival playing companies in London.[3] In fact, as Bernard Beckerman (despite his disparagement of lost plays) suggested long ago – and the data below reinforces – it is more likely the case that to remain competitive, the Chamberlain's Men had a repertory comparable in size to the Admiral's and other London companies.[4]

By my count, approximately thirty-five extant plays can be associated with the Chamberlain's Men's repertory between 1594–1603 (the years mapping onto Henslowe's records of the Newington Butts run of Admiral's–Chamberlain's performances and ending with the company's change of patron on 19 May 1603). In drafting my census, I have drawn on Wiggins' catalogue for plays written for performance by the Chamberlain's in the specified date range, but have also made allowance for old plays that may have carried over into performances during those years or that may have been revived by the company (sometimes at a remove of many years, as was the case during the court performances in the winter of 1604/5, when the King's Men performed such old plays as *The Comedy of Errors, The Merchant of Venice* and *Love's Labour's Lost*).[5] Because no such list of the Chamberlain's repertory is conveniently available, I provide it here (see Table 1.1).

---

[3] G. B. Harrison, for example, guessed that '[i]t is probable that at least 80 per cent of the plays acted by Shakespeare's company have perished, including not a few of his own. But these facts cannot be known until – if ever – Burbage's *Diary* comes to light!': see G. B. Harrison, *Elizabethan Plays and Players* (Ann Arbor, MI: University of Michigan Press, 1961), 139. Sally-Beth MacLean has lamented the absence of documents comparable to the Henslowe and Alleyn papers for the 1580s, too: 'There is no Burbage's diary or collection of Tarlton letters to tell us about playhouse management or touring and domestic arrangements made by actors while they were on the road in the 1580s': see S.-B. MacLean, 'Adult Playing Companies, 1583–1593' in R. Dutton (ed.), *The Oxford Handbook of Early Modern Theatre* (Oxford: Oxford University Press, 2009), 44.

[4] Beckerman, *Shakespeare at the Globe*, 14–15.

[5] W. R. Streitberger (ed.), *Malone Society Collections XIII: Jacobean and Caroline Revels Accounts, 1603–1642* (Oxford: David Stanford at the University Printing House, 1986), 7–9.

Table 1.1 *Extant plays associated with the Chamberlain's Men's repertory:*
1594–1603

#	Title	Wiggins Catalogue #	Wiggins Date
1	*The Spanish Tragedy* (1602 quarto version)[6]	#783	1587
2	*Mucedorus*[7]	#884	1591
3	*The First Part of the Contention betwixt the Two Famous Houses of York and Lancaster*	#888	1591
4	*The True Tragedy of Richard, Duke of York, and the Death of Good King Henry VI*	#902	1591
5	*The Taming of the Shrew*	#916	1592
6	'harey the vj' (*1 Henry VI*)[8]	#919	1592
7	*Titus Andronicus*	#928	1592
8	'a Comedy of Errors' (*The Comedy of Errors*)[9]	#944	1593
9	*Richard III*	#950	1593
10	*The Taming of a Shrew*[10]	#955	1594
11	*The Two Gentlemen of Verona*[11]	#970	1594
12	*Romeo and Juliet*	#987	1595
13	*Richard II*	#1002	1595
14	*A Midsummer Night's Dream*	#1012	1595
15	*Love's Labour's Lost*	#1031	1596
16	*King John*	#1043	1596

[6] See discussion of *The Spanish Tragedy* and the Admiral's 'Joronymo' play as its clone below. See also chs 13, 14, 15 and 16 in G. Taylor and G. Egan (eds.), *The New Oxford Shakespeare: Authorship Companion* (Oxford: Oxford University Press, 2017). Wiggins acknowledges that 'Jonson himself implies that there was more than one version' but nevertheless associates Kyd's play with the Admiral's 'Joronymo' of 1597 and does not discuss the possibility that it belonged to the Chamberlain's Men.

[7] The first and last scenes imply performance at court; Wiggins considers Queen's, Sussex's, and Pembroke's the 'likeliest candidates' but if the play were not new when performed at court, the Chamberlain's 'might enter the running'. The 1610 quarto's title page ascribes the play to the King's Men by Shrove Sunday of that year.

[8] Henslowe records a play by this title in the repertory of Strange's Men; see Wiggins #919 for the reasons for thinking this is (or is a version of) the play subsequently published as *1 Henry VI*.

[9] Described as such when performed at Gray's Inn in 1594 by an unspecified company (Pembroke's?); the King's Men subsequently performed 'The plaie of: Errors' by 'Shaxberd' in 1604 at Whitehall Palace: *Gesta Grayorum* (London, 1888), 22; Streitberger (ed.), *Malone Society Collections XIII*, 9. A reasonable assumption, then, is that these references both refer to *The Comedy of Errors*, and that whether or not the Chamberlain's were the company that performed it in 1594, they presumably acquired it at some point prior to the performance at court in 1604 (by which time they had changed patron). There is, however, no direct evidence as such for the Chamberlain's ownership of the play.

[10] '[P]ossibly performed at Newington Butts by the Admiral's and Lord Chamberlain's Men on Thursday 13 June ... recorded as Tuesday 11 June' (Wiggins #955; cf. #916).

[11] NB. not printed until 1623, with act divisions that suggest a post-1608 copytext; the only external evidence for stage history is a report in 1669 of the play having been in the King's Men's repertory prior to the closure of the theatres. Wiggins, however, notes that '[t]he strongest pull of the evidence is towards a date after 1592 and not long before 1595, placing *Two Gentlemen* early in Shakespeare's time with the Lord Chamberlain's Men.'

Table 1.1 (*cont.*)

#	Title	Wiggins Catalogue #	Wiggins Date
17	*The Merchant of Venice*	#1047	1596
18	*1 Henry IV*	#1059	1597
19	*The Merry Wives of Windsor*	#1079	1597
20	*A Warning for Fair Women*	#1080	1597
21	*2 Henry IV*	#1083	1597
22	*Every Man in His Humour*	#1143	1598
23	*Much Ado About Nothing*	#1148	1598
24	*Henry V*	#1183	1599
25	*A Larum for London*	#1191	1599
26	*Julius Caesar*	#1198	1599
27	*Every Man Out of His Humour*	#1216	1599
28	*As You Like It*	#1237	1600
29	*Hamlet*	#1259	1600
30	*Sir Thomas More*[12]	#1277	1601
31	*Thomas, Lord Cromwell*	#1290	1601
32	*Twelfth Night*	#1297	1601
33	*Satiromastix, or The Untrussing of the Humorous Poet*	#1304	1601
34	*Troilus and Cressida*	#1325	1602
35	*The Merry Devil of Edmonton*	#1392	1603

This total of thirty-five plays with a reasonably well-evidenced provenance might be supplemented by at least four jigs thought to be associated with performances by the Chamberlain's Men and by a number of extant plays whose stage history remains tantalisingly ambiguous.[13] Shakespeare's hand has been detected in *Arden of Faversham* and *Edward III*, but the theatrical auspices of each remains unknown. The play known as *The First Part of Ieronimo* (1600) would make a logical repertorial partner for *The Spanish Tragedy*, and although once ascribed to the Children of the Chapel Royal, its company affiliation is now

---

[12] Wiggins: 'The company ascription rests squarely on the putative involvement of Shakespeare: it is plausible that Heywood and Dekker (with or without Chettle) might have been hired to do the job for the Lord Chamberlain's/King's Men, but quite implausible that Shakespeare, an actor-sharer in that company, might have 'moonlighted' for a rival troupe.' (He notes Jowett's alternative hypothesis, that the play was originally composed for Derby's and the revision was for Worcester's/Queen Anne's after their association with Henslowe concluded.)

[13] The known jigs are: 'The Broom-Man' (1594; Wiggins #968); 'The Kitchen-Stuff Woman' (1595; Wiggins #996); 'The Slippers' (1595; Wiggins #997); and *Singing Simpkin* (1595; Wiggins #1006).

completely open-ended.[14] Manley and MacLean argue that it is 'in many of its parts a legible palimpsest of Lord Strange's Men's forepiece to *The Spanish Tragedy*', and Syme has hinted that it may have migrated to the Chamberlain's Men's repertory along with Kyd's play.[15] Jonson's *Sejanus His Fall* possibly warrants inclusion in the Chamberlain's list, inasmuch as Jonson had been working on the play since 1601 (when the company was still the Chamberlain's), but he claimed its premiere was under the auspices of the King's Men.[16] The dating of *All's Well That Ends Well* poses a comparable challenge. Knutson proposed a repertory date of 1602–1603, which would make it a Chamberlain's play; Wiggins notes a possible range of 1601–1608 for the play's composition but settles on 1605 (and thus the King's Men at the Globe) because dating it thus 'comfortably fills what would otherwise be an exceptionally long gap in Shakespeare's output' between *Othello* and *Lear*.[17]

Leaving aside the more ambiguous cases, the Chamberlain's total of thirty-five extant plays compares favourably with the twenty-four extant Admiral's plays for the same period (see below).[18] However, the survival rate of Chamberlain's Men's plays only looks proportionally higher because we remain ignorant of the true extent of loss. If this list were truly indicative of the Chamberlain's repertory, it would imply that for the greater part of the 1590s, the company seemingly relied on only one dramatist (Shakespeare). Knutson offers the sobering reminder that:

> [W]e have only partial playlists for the Chamberlain's and King's men from 1594–95 to 1612–13. There is not even a year in which we can name half of the plays in production unless it is 1612–13, when a clerk in the Office of the Chamber copied down on a draft of the accounts the titles of eighteen plays given by the King's men at Court.[19]

---

[14] Noting the play's references to Hieronimo's short stature, Wiggins observes that 'there is no way of knowing whether the role was written for a boy or for a short adult actor', and thus no way to confirm even which type of playing company it was written for (#1270).

[15] Manley and MacLean, *Lord Strange's Men*, 84; Syme, 'Shakespeare and *The Spanish Tragedy*: A Challenge for Theatre History'.

[16] Wiggins notes Jonson's statement in his First Folio (1616) that the play was 'first acted in the year 1603 by the King's Majesty's Servants' but notes that the closure of the London theatres between 19 March 1603 and 6 April 1604 (apart from a 'short period in May before the King's Men were patented on 19 May') makes Jonson's statement problematic. He suggests the play premiered at court that Christmas, by the King's Men (Wiggins #1412).

[17] Knutson, *The Repertory*, 179; Wiggins #1461.

[18] The Chamberlain's figure benefits from the Shakespeare First Folio's existence, of course; what if there had been a Heywood or Dekker folio?

[19] Knutson, *The Repertory*, 13.

Yet even by the most generous estimate, only thirteen lost plays from the Henslowe years (1594–1603)[20] have been associated with the Chamberlain's:

(i)   'Hester and Ahasuerus' (Wiggins #801), performed at Newington Butts in June 1594 during the joint run of the Admiral's and Chamberlain's Men, but not recorded thereafter in the Admiral's repertory;

(ii) 'Hamlet' (Wiggins #814), also performed at Newington Butts in June 1594. Possibly the subject of Thomas Lodge's reference to 'ye ghost which cried so miserally at ye Theator like an oister wife, *Hamlet, reuenge*' in 1596;[21]

(iii) The untitled play or plays (Wiggins #1040) that Thomas Nashe told William Cotton he hoped to write for the Chamberlain's during the vacation preceding Michaelmas Term, 1596;

(iv) '1 Seven Deadly Sins' (Wiggins #1061), not known directly through any documentary evidence, but inferable (and logically required) by the existence of the plot for '2 Seven Deadly Sins'. Scott McMillin and Sally-Beth MacLean argue that Richard Tarlton's 'The Seven Deadly Sins' (c.1585) is quite distinct from these later 'sins' plays;[22]

(v)   '2 Seven Deadly Sins' (Wiggins #1065), known from the existing backstage plot (Dulwich College MS xix). Formerly ascribed to the Lord Strange's Men c.1592 until David Kathman offered an alternative possibility for the provenance of the plot and a compelling attribution to the Chamberlain's Men, c.1597;[23]

(vi) 'Love's Labour's Won' (Wiggins #1109), known through Francis Meres' reference to Shakespeare's comedies (1598) and from Exeter bookseller Christopher Hunt's inventory list (1603);

(vii) (possibly) an anti-Scots play (Wiggins #1111). Wiggins deduces the existence of an otherwise unknown lost play from a 15 April 1598 letter to Lord Burghley written by George Nicolson, who notes the resentment felt in Scotland that 'the Comediens of

---

[20] Henslowe's systematic records cease in March 1603, even though his final reckoning is dated 14 March 1604.

[21] T. Lodge, *Wits miserie, and the worlds madnesse discouering the deuils incarnat of this age* (London, 1596), 56.

[22] S. McMillin and S.-B. MacLean, *The Queen's Men and Their Plays* (Cambridge: Cambridge University Press, 1998), 93.

[23] D. Kathman, 'Reconsidering *The Seven Deadly Sins*', *Early Theatre*, 7(1) (2004), 13–44.

London shoulde in their play, scorne the *king* and people of this lande'.[24] Wiggins acknowledges the possibility that the play causing offence might be 'The King of England's Son and the King of Scotland's Daughter' (#1112, which survives only in the German adaptation published in Liepzig in 1620), but finds insufficient evidence to lump the two together. Proceeding on the assumption that the anti-Scots play is distinct from the other, Wiggins tentatively attributes it to the Chamberlain's repertory on the basis that we know more about the Admiral's repertory at this point in time and 'none of its new plays in the spring of 1598 are promising candidates'. There were, of course, more than two companies operating in London at this time (possibly at the Swan, the Curtain, and the Boar's Head), so Wiggins' ascription to the Chamberlain's is necessarily conjectural;[25]

(viii)   (possibly) 'The Fair Maid of London' (Wiggins #1154), a play licensed for performance by Edmund Tilney on 24 May 1598 (the licence, however, is known only through a record by Henry Herbert in 1662).[26] Wiggins thinks the play's non-appearance in Henslowe's records 'allows the tentative hypothesis' that it was not an Admiral's play, and suggests that '[s]ince it was a play of local London interest, and since there was no other company performing in London in 1598, it follows that it most probably belonged to the Lord Chamberlain's Men'. As noted above, the Admiral's and the Chamberlain's were not the only companies in London, however. It is curious, too, that the licensing record allows three plays, the other two of which *did* belong to the Admiral's: 'Sir William Longsword' and 'Richard Cordelyon' (i.e. 'The Funeral of Richard Coeur de Lion');

(ix)   'The Tartarian Cripple, Emperor of Constantinople' (Wiggins #1181), known only from an ambiguous reference in the Stationers' Register. It might not be a play, but if it is, its registration with other Chamberlain's plays suggests that it too belonged to that company;

---

[24] National Archives, SP 52/62, fol. 19ᵛ (George Nicolson, letter to William Cecil, Lord Burghley, 15 April 1598); see the *LPD* entry for 'Anti-Scots Play'.

[25] On the Boar's Head, Herbert C. Berry observes that '[p]layers ... probably did not use the Boar's Head in any regular way before 1598', which implies that by 1598 there were at least sporadic performances at that playhouse: H. C. Berry, *The Boar's Head Playhouse* (Washington: Folger Shakespeare Library, 1986), 29.

[26] See Revels Documents (1660–1673) R29 and R33 in Bawcutt, *The Control and Censorship of Caroline Drama.*

(x) 'Cloth Breeches and Velvet Hose' (Wiggins #1193), entered in the Stationers' Register for James Roberts in May 1600;

(xi) 'Sir John Oldcastle'. The evidence for the possibility that the Chamberlain's Men had what Knutson describes as 'a more robust commercial and political answer to the Admiral's Men's two-part *Oldcastle* than killing off Falstaff in *Henry V*' is the letter from Rowland Whyte to Sir Robert Sidney (8 March 1600) in which he describes the Chamberlain's recent performance of a play he calls '*Sir John Old Castle*' before Ludovic Verreyken, the Archduke's Ambassador, at Carey Court, Blackfriars.[27] Wiggins does not list this as a discrete play on Oldcastle, including the Carey Court performance as part of the early stage history of Shakespeare's *1 Henry IV* instead (Wiggins #1059). There is some evidence that Falstaff had originally been called Oldcastle, until the Cobham family (Oldcastle's descendants) objected sometime in 1596–1597. The identity of this play turns on the question of how likely it is that the company, in 1600, would revert to the name that had previously caused offence; or if it was not the company but Whyte (in his letter) who adopted the 'Oldcastle' nomenclature for the play, how likely it is that he knew about the original controversy and was still inclined to refer to *1 Henry IV* by a character's superseded name;

(xii) 'The Freeman's Honour' (Wiggins #1361). W. Smith prefaced his play *The Hector of Germany* (1615) with a letter to Sir John Swinnerton, in which Smith reveals that he wrote '*a former Play, called the* Freemans Honour, *acted by the Now-seruants of the Kings Maiestie, to degnifie the worthy Compane of the Marchataylors*';[28] and

(xiii) 'A play of Robin Goodfellow' (Wiggins #1399), performed at court on New Year's Day in 1604 (according to Dudley Carleton), but necessarily written earlier (c.1603), and possibly before the Chamberlain's became the King's Men (the royal patent is dated 19 May 1603).[29]

---

[27] M. G. Brennan, N. J. Kinnamon and M. P. Hannay (eds.), *The Letters (1595–1608) of Rowland Whyte* (Philadelphia: American Philosophical Society, 2013), 439; see also Knutson's *LPD* entry for 'Oldcastle, Sir John (Chamberlain's)'.

[28] W. Smith, *The Hector of Germany, or the Palsgraue, Prime Elector* (London, 1615), sig.A2ʳ. See D. Kathman, 'William Smith, "The Freeman's Honour," and the Lord Chamberlain's Men' in Knutson, McInnis and Steggle (eds.), *Loss and the Literary Culture of Shakespeare's Time*, 161–171.

[29] Letter from Dudley Carleton to John Chamberlain (15 January 1604) in M. Lee, Jr (ed.), *Dudley Carleton to John Chamberlain, 1603–1624* (New Brunswick, NJ: Rutgers University Press, 1972), 53. Chambers lumped 'Robin Goodfellow' with Shakespeare's *Midsummer Night's Dream* but the identification has not been universally endorsed (see, e.g. Knutson, *Repertory*, 113–114).

As this brief and contentious list illustrates, what little is known to have been lost from the Chamberlain's repertory has been pieced together from Stationers' Register entries and historical references in letters, diaries and printed publications. Without Smith's reference to his earlier play, for example, its place in the Chamberlain's repertory (and its one-time existence at all) would not have been known to scholars. This is hardly a solid foundation from which to construct argument about the extent and quality of the company's offerings.

The Value of Lost Plays

The extent of loss from the Chamberlain's repertory matters: the plays lost to us once formed a vital and vibrant part of the commercial playing companies' repertories and possessed obvious financial value in their own time. The financial value of lost plays can be quantified by turning to Henslowe's diary and consulting the periods of relatively complete records for various professional companies in London.[30] The diary provides valuable data about the frequency of performances, the average takings and the highest takings for individual performances, enabling us to compare lost plays and extant plays using these metrics. For example, in the period spanning 12 April 1596 to 22 January 1597, the Admiral's Men performed at least thirty-three identifiable plays.[31] Scholars agree that five of these survive: *A Knack to Know an Honest Man*, *Doctor Faustus*, *The Blind Beggar of Alexandria*, *The Jew of Malta* and *Stukeley*.

The title of a sixth play recorded by Henslowe requires more careful interpretation: if the play Henslowe enters as 'Joronymo' is Thomas Kyd's *The Spanish Tragedy*, then a sixth extant play is in this repertory, but there are compelling grounds for rejecting this identification. Holger Syme has expressed repeated and justifiable scepticism over the identification of the Admiral's 'Joronymo' with Kyd's *Spanish Tragedy*.[32] In light of Douglas

---

[30] Henslowe's diary does contain significant omissions and gaps. Noting a lack of repayment records, inexplicable calculations of total outstanding debt, sudden absolution of debt etc., Neil Carson recognises that Henslowe's diary alone could not constitute the entirety of his record-keeping for financial purposes, but must have 'formed only part of Henslowe's accounting records, which included also formal bonds and very likely one or more ledgers' which probably 'became separated from the diary at the time of Henslowe's death': N. Carson, *A Companion to Henslowe's Diary* (Cambridge: Cambridge University Press, 1988), 13.

[31] P. Henslowe, *Henslowe's Diary*, 2nd ed, R. A. Foakes (ed.) (Cambridge: Cambridge University Press, 2002), 36–37, 47–48 and 54–56.

[32] See H. S. Syme, 'The Meaning of Success: Stories of 1594 and Its Aftermath', *Shakespeare Quarterly*, 61(4) (2010), 504 n 38.

Bruster's use of orthographic evidence to offer apparent confirmation that Shakespeare contributed to the version of *The Spanish Tragedy* published in 1602, Syme put the following dissonant 'facts' into dialogue with each other:[33]

(i) Strange's Men had plays called 'spanes comodye donne oracioe' (or variants thereof) *and* 'Jeronymo' in repertory together in 1592;[34]

(ii) Shakespeare apparently contributed lines to *The Spanish Tragedy* (1602 quarto) around 1596–1597 (Bruster prefers 1598–1599);[35]

(iii) the Admiral's Men also had a 'Jeronymo' play in their repertory in 1597 (but unlike the Strange's Men's play, it was not staged with a comic partner);

(iv) Henslowe paid Jonson (not Shakespeare) for additions to the play in 1601 and 1602 (but there is no Jonsonian influence detectable in the 1602 quarto);[36]

(v) sources from 1601 and 1619 strongly associate the role of Hieronimo with the Chamberlain's leading actor, Richard Burbage, rather than any of the Admiral's players;

(vi) by 1604 the Chamberlain's Men objected to the Children of the Revels apparently performing the Chamberlain's 'Jeronimo' play.

Syme offers various interpretations of these inconvenient pieces of information, but the narrative that best fits with the circumstantial evidence is as follows:

> The Strange's Men's 'Jeronymo' is *The Spanish Tragedy*. When they left the Rose, they took both it and the comedic counterpart with them, and both became part of the Chamberlain's Men's repertory. In 1597, the Admiral's Men acquired their own Hieronimo play (their first performance of 'Joronymo' is marked 'ne' in the diary, very unusually for a play previously listed), and revised that text extensively in 1601 and 1602; the revised version may well have remained in their repertory thereafter.[37]

If Syme is right, the Chamberlain's Men acquired Kyd's *Spanish Tragedy* from players migrating from Strange's Men and Shakespeare subsequently

[33] D. Bruster, 'Shakespearean Spellings and Handwriting in the Additional Passages Printed in the 1602 *Spanish Tragedy*', *Notes and Queries*, 60(3) (2013), 420–424.

[34] Foakes (ed.), *Henslowe's Diary*, 16–19.

[35] See Bruster, 'Shakespeare's hand in the additional passages to Kyd's *Spanish Tragedy*', OUP blog, 26 August 2013 (available online at https://blog.oup.com/2013/08/shakespeares-additional-passage-kyd-spanish-tragedy/).

[36] Foakes (ed.), *Henslowe's Diary*, 182, 203.

[37] Syme, 'Shakespeare and *The Spanish Tragedy*: A Challenge for Theatre History', dispositio blog, 31 August 2013 (available online at www.dispositio.net/archives/1667).

added to it; meanwhile, Henslowe paid Jonson for additions to what is more likely to be a lost clone of Kyd's play, for the Admiral's company. I am persuaded by Syme's provocations and assign the Admiral's 'Joronymo' to the 'lost' category.

Returning to the analysis of the Admiral's 12 April 1596 to 22 January 1597 run at the Rose, an extant play, *The Blind Beggar of Alexandria*, received the highest number of performances: fourteen. The next most frequently performed plays, though, were '1 Tamar Cham' and 'Vortigern', each of which was performed nine times. The highest average takings were recorded by lost plays, however: 'The Tinker of Totnes', 'Alexander and Lodowick' and 'Paradox' recorded 60s, 55s and 45s respectively on the single performance recorded for each that season. (Why these successful plays were not performed again that season remains a mystery.) The only extant play to average over 30s per performance was *Stukeley*, which averaged 36.6s over five performances. By contrast, eleven lost plays (including 'Joronymo') achieved an average of 30s or more during this period. In terms of highest takings for an individual performance, new plays (e.g. 'Troy', 22 June 1596) and plays that were performed close to holidays did well: 'Pythagoras' took £3 on Whit Monday (31 May 1596) and 'Nebuchadnezzar' took £3 8s on 'crismas day' (recorded as 27 December) 1596.[38] Even so, of the eight plays that made 60 shillings or more in a single performance, seven are lost: namely 'Troy', 'Nebuchadnezzar', 'The Tinker of Totnes', 'Joronymo', '2 Tamar Cham', 'Pythagoras' and 'Longshanks'. The only extant play to achieve this sum is *Stukeley*.

Examination of performance runs by the Strange's Men and by Sussex's Men yield comparable results and lend further support to the recuperation of the financial value of lost plays within a company's repertory. From 19 February to 22 June 1592, the Lord Strange's Men performed at least twenty-three identifiable plays.[39] Of these twenty-three, only seven are extant: *A Knack to Know an Honest Man*, *A Looking-Glass for London and England*, 'harey the vj' (if this is the basis of the play published as *1 Henry*

---

[38] As Foakes notes, when Henslowe enters his enigmatic 'ne' marker next to the record of a play's performance – seemingly indicating that the play was new in some way (new to the repertory, newly licensed; not necessarily newly written), the associated monetary sum is typically higher than usual: 'Clearly either a higher charge was made to spectators at these plays or they attracted much larger audiences': see Foakes (ed.), *Henslowe's Diary*, xxxiv.

[39] Lawrence Manley counts between twenty-four to twenty-six different plays in the company's repertory for this period in 1592, noting that the number 'depends on how the titles of plays listed by Henslowe are interpreted': L. Manley, 'Lost Plays and the Repertory of Lord Strange's Men' in D. McInnis and M. Steggle (eds.), *Lost Plays in Shakespeare's England*, 163.

VI in Shakespeare's First Folio),[40] *Orlando Furioso*, *The Jew of Malta*, 'Jeronymo' (which, unlike the Admiral's clone play discussed above, has a more compelling claim to being Kyd's *The Spanish Tragedy*)[41] and the 'fryer bacon' manuscript play (Alnwick Castle MS 507) referred to as *John of Bordeaux* by the Malone Society editor.[42] If 'harey the vj' is a version of *1 Henry VI*, an extant play was again the most performed play, with fifteen recorded performances. It is followed by a healthy mix of lost and extant plays: 'Jeronymo' (*The Spanish Tragedy*) (thirteen performances), 'Muly Molocco' (eleven), *The Jew of Malta* (ten), the 'spanes comodye donne oracioe' (perhaps partially preserved in *The First Part of Ieronimo*, 1605) (seven performances) and 'Titus and Vespasian' (seven performances). The 'harey the vj' play also received the highest takings from an individual performance with £3 16s 8d recorded next to its apparent premiere (the date marked 'ne') on 3 March 1592. However, a lost play, the ambiguously titled 'the taner of denmarke', was only three shillings behind with £3 13s 6d recorded against its single known performance on 23 May 1592.[43] Of the seven plays that made 60 shillings or more in a single performance, four are lost: 'the taner of denmarke', '2 Tamar Cham', 'Titus and Vespasian', and 'Muly Molocco'. The three extant plays to achieve this also are 'harey the vj' (*1 Henry VI*), *A Knack to Know a Knave* and 'Jeronymo' (*The Spanish Tragedy*). In terms of averages, even if we exclude 'the taner of denmarke' as an aberration (because it does not reappear in this dataset), the lost plays 'Titus and Vespasian', '2 Tamar Cham', 'Muly Molocco', 'Jerusalem' and 'Four Plays in One' all set the bar high by averaging 30+ shillings per performance across multiple performances. The extant plays to achieve this also are *A Knack to Know a Knave*, *The Jew of Malta*, 'harey the vj' (*1 Henry VI*) and 'Jeronymo' (*The Spanish Tragedy*).

If I take into account the subsequent string of performances by the Strange's Men, between 29 December 1592 and 1 February 1593, the

---

[40] Wiggins (#919) and Manley and Maclean (97–99) concur that Henslowe's 'harey the vj' (Foakes (ed.), *Henslowe's Diary*, 16) is indeed the play now known as *1 Henry VI*.

[41] Foakes (ed.), *Henslowe's Diary*, 17. It is here being performed in repertory with 'spanes comodye donne oracioe' (Foakes (ed.), *Henslowe's Diary*, 16) which seems to be partially preserved in *The First Part of Ieronimo* (1605). For a discussion of these two Spanish plays' identities, see Manley and MacLean, *Lord Strange's Men*, 81–85, where they draw on Lukas Erne's work in *Beyond* The Spanish Tragedy: *A Study of the Works of Thomas Kyd* (Manchester: Manchester University Press, 2001).

[42] Foakes (ed.), *Henslowe's Diary*, 17; W. L. Renwick (ed.), *John of Bordeaux: Or The Second Part of Friar Bacon* (Oxford: Malone Society, 1936).

[43] Foakes (ed.), *Henslowe's Diary*, 18; the title has conventionally been modernised as 'The Tanner of Denmark', but Lawrence Manley has proposed 'The Tamer of Denmark' as an alternative: Manley and MacLean, *Lord Strange's Men*, 151. I will return to this play and its significance in Chapter 3.

picture changes only a little. 'The Comedy of Cosmo', 'The Jealous Comedy' and *The Massacre at Paris* were performed in this run in addition to the plays recorded in 1592, but because this is such a short run, only *Knack to Know a Knave* was performed four times – the others, lost and extant, received between one and three performances each. Unsurprisingly, the 'ne' performance of *The Massacre at Paris* yielded the highest takings (74s) but 'Muly Molocco' was close behind with 70s and (unlike *Massacre*) it was far from being new by this date. If I combine the data from the two performance runs of the Lord Strange's Men (February to June 1592 and December 1592 to February 1593) to get an overall picture of that company's business at the Rose, the ranks of performance and total takings remain broadly the same. In terms of averages, one interesting comparison emerges, in which the two top plays (excluding 'the taner of denmarke' and *The Massacre at Paris*, both of which are one-off successes within the context of these data sets) are *The Jew of Malta* and the lost 'Titus and Vespasian'. Their average takings are both 45s 2d, across long runs of thirteen and ten performances respectively. A comparison of the lowest averages might also be instructive, with the extant *John of Bordeaux* ('fryer bacon') and *Orlando* performing as poorly as 'Pope Joan', 'Cloris and Ergasto', and 'Constantine', each of which averaged less than 20s. No further lost plays break into the 60s for a single-performance cohort when I include this additional data, but *The Massacre at Paris* and *The Jew of Malta* do. As usual, caution must be exercised when attempting to infer conclusions from such data: Henslowe's records do not always show the entire repertorial life of a given play. Here, the plays successful in the previous year might be reaching the end of their stage runs.[44]

Finally, Henslowe also records a short run with consequently limited data for the Earl of Sussex's Men between 27 December 1593 and 6 February 1594. During this run, the company performed at least twelve discrete plays, of which only three seem to be extant: *George-a-Greene*, *The Jew of Malta* and 'titus & ondronicus' (historically identified as Shakespeare's *Titus Andronicus*).[45] Given the limited nature of the data, I cannot draw meaningful conclusions about how often a play was performed. The three extant plays are distributed evenly within the performance frequency rankings: *George-a-Greene* receives the most performances (five), 'titus' receives three (the same number as 'Huon', 'Friar Francis' and 'Abraham and Lot', and

---

[44] See the discussion under 'Date' in Wiggins #878 ('Cloris and Ergasto').
[45] Foakes (ed.), *Henslowe's Diary*, 21.

one less than 'Buckingham'), and *The Jew of Malta* receives one performance (the same as 'King Lud' and 'William the Conqueror', and one less than 'God Speed the Plough', 'Richard the Confessor' and 'The Fair Maid of Italy'). In a single recorded performance in this run, *The Jew of Malta* returned healthy takings at 50s, and 'titus & ondronicus' averaged just over 49s for each of its three performances (one of them marked 'ne'). Six other plays – mostly lost ones – averaged around 30s or higher across multiple performances: 'Friar Francis' (42s 4d), 'Buckingham' (37s 4d), 'God Speed the Plough' (36s), 'Abraham and Lot' (31s 4d), *George-a-Greene* (31s 2d), and 'Huon of Bordeaux' (29s 8s). By highest takings, the extant *George-a-Greene* and the lost 'Huon of Bordeaux' are joint winners with 70s-performances each. Three other plays broke the 60s benchmark, including 'titus & ondronicus' (68s), 'Friar Francis' (61s) and 'God Speed the Plough' (61s), at least the last two of which are lost.

In the absence of play-texts, theatre historians cannot evaluate the literary or aesthetic quality of these lost plays. But it is equally true that examination of the copious data from Henslowe's accounts points to an incontrovertible conclusion: the evidence does not support the fanciful notion that lost plays were lost because they were somehow judged inferior to those plays that did survive in print or manuscript.

The Composition of a Company's Repertory: The Admiral's Men

Since lost plays provided demonstrable financial value to their playing companies and since the known number of lost Chamberlain's Men's plays seems suspiciously low at thirteen (cobbled together, as that figure is, from diverse sources and an incomplete archive), I see value in attempting to undertake a census of lost and extant plays in the more robust archive of the Admiral's Men. Doing so provides a better sense of what we don't know about the Chamberlain's Men's repertory *and* about the complex difficulty of even assessing that loss.

How many plays did the Admiral's Men have? Our perception of loss in the 1590s relative to later decades is largely a factor of the felicitous survival of Henslowe's extensive records. By my calculations, based on Henslowe's evidence, but also taking into account related documents of performance and logical inferences supported by those records, the Admiral's Men had approximately 235 plays in repertory between 1594 and 1603 (the Henslowe years), of which a mere twenty-four have survived. These statistics are necessarily contentious and differ from the statistics offered by other critics; I explore the reasoning and assumptions behind my counting in what follows, since the process of establishing something so seemingly simple as a census of plays calls attention to the precariousness of and biases involved in working with lost plays. The contour separating the figure from the ground is fuzzy, and each of those related elements is therefore subject to differing perceptions. Under these circumstances it is challenging to paint a picture of the repertory with great confidence, as we are basing our inter- pretation on the slightest of glances. The broader point, regardless of which scholar's statistics are used, is that only a distinct minority of plays in the Admiral's repertory has survived: somewhere in the vicinity of only 10.2 per cent (based on my numbers). Examination of Henslowe's financial accounts strongly suggests that lost plays account for the vast majority of a company's holdings and, as the calculations of receipts analysed above demonstrate, lost plays were at least as profitable as those plays that survived in print.

The availability of Henslowe's detailed financial accounts is not without complication, however, and the issues pertaining to their interpretation offer an instructive case study for the critical study of lost plays. Martin Wiggins is the most recent scholar to draw attention to the perils of assuming that Henslowe offers a complete overview of theatrical activity at his playhouse. Noting that the incomplete payments for 'Pierce of Exton' (1598) cannot be taken as evidence that the play was not completed – given that other plays with similarly incomplete payment records (Dekker's *The Shoemaker's Holiday*; Dekker and Chettle's 'Troilus and Cressida') demonstrably *were* completed and performed – Wiggins observes that:

> It follows that not all company expenditure went through Henslowe, and therefore that the expenditure noted during the period 1597–1603 will not necessarily contain a complete record of the companies' repertory during those years: there may have been plays which make no appearance in the account-book at all.[46]

Amongst the 'plays which make no appearance', *The Battle of Alcazar* and *Look About You* are only the most famous examples: their printed title page attributions associate them with the Admiral's company at this time, but they do not appear under these titles in Henslowe's paperwork.

Given these complications, it is not surprising that individual scholars' estimates of the size of the Admiral's repertory have ranged from as low as c.181 plays (E. K. Chambers) to 235 plays (my estimate), with no two scholars agreeing on including precisely the same plays in their own lists of

---

[46] Wiggins, 'Introduction' in *British Drama*, 1.xix. See also Carson, *A Companion*, 13, as cited above.

the Admiral's repertory.[47] To understand the discrepancies, we need to examine the individual rationales of the various scholars who have analysed the information in Henslowe's diary.

In the commentary volume accompanying his edition of Henslowe's diary, W. W. Greg includes a list of all the plays mentioned by Henslowe without regard to company affiliation, preserving the plays 'in the order of the Diary itself'.[48] Accordingly, it is outside his remit to list those plays known only from inventory lists ('Sturgflatery', 'Black Joan') or backstage plots ('2 Fortune's Tennis'), and those which are not recorded by Henslowe but which appeared in print with a relevant title page attribution (*The Battle of Alcazar*, *Look About You* and *1 The Two Angry Women of Abingdon*). Amongst the more controversial examples of plays he apparently considers extant (at least in adaptation) are:

- '2 Godfrey of Bulloigne' (tentatively associated with Heywood's *Four Prentices of London*);
- 'The Mack' ('possibly' *Wonder of a Kingdom*);
- '1 & 2 Hercules' (Heywood's *Silver* and *Brazen Age* plays);[49]
- 'Harry the Fifth' ('[p]robably ... the Admiral's men appropriated and revised the [Queen's men] play and stayed the publication till 1598');
- 'Troy' (Greg considers it 'an earlier and shorter version later expanded into the two-part play' known as *The Iron Age*, by Heywood');[50]
- 'Five Plays in One' (Greg hedges his bets about whether this corresponds to a combination of short pieces by Heywood published in 1637 as *Dialogues and Dramas*);

---

[47] Chambers counted fifty-five new plays and nineteen revived plays belonging to the initial period of Henslowe's records of activity for the company (1594–1597) (*Elizabethan Stage*, 2.143–146). To this figure of seventy-four discrete plays, Chambers added a further fifty-six new plays 'duly completed and paid for in full' and perhaps twenty 'possibly unfinished plays' for the 1597–1600 period (2.164). Complications arise immediately, for when he lists these plays by name and year (2.165–171), the new plays amount to fifty-*eight*, and when he begins to compare the periods he mysteriously attributes sixty-two new plays to a newly defined 1599–1600 period. For the final period of 1600–1603, Chambers traces thirty-one new plays (2.177–181). Chambers resists offering a definitive total, and supplements each of these periods' individual reckonings with qualifications about possible duplications, possibly unfinished or unperformed titles, and so on. Restricting the tally only to his explicit declarations leads to a total of approximately 181 plays in the Admiral's repertory.

[48] W. W. Greg (ed.), *Henslowe's Diary, Part II: Commentary* (London: A. H. Bullen, 1908), 148.

[49] Douglas Arrell has attempted to bolster the identification of these plays more recently: D. Arrell, 'Heywood, Henslowe and Hercules: Tracking 1 and 2 Hercules in Heywood's Silver and Brazen Ages', *Early Modern Literary Studies*, 17(1) (2014), 1–21.

[50] Arrell has supported and elaborated on this proposition more recently: D. Arrell, 'Heywood, Shakespeare, and the Mystery of *Troye*', *Early Modern Literary Studies*, 19(1) (2016), 1–22.

- 'Love Prevented' (Greg follows Fleay in thinking this is Porter's *1 Two Angry Women of Abingdon*);
- 'Truth's Supplication to Candlelight' (Greg thinks identification with Dekker's *Whore of Babylon* is 'practically certain');[51] and
- 'The Spanish Fig' (identification of which with Dekker's *Noble Spanish Soldier* 'seems plausible').

In total, Greg lists 227 Admiral's plays, thirty-six of which he thinks survive in some form.

In a much more recent study of the Admiral's Men, Andrew Gurr explicitly notes that '[o]f the 229 plays known by their titles to have been written for and most likely performed by the company, texts for no more than thirty-seven have survived, thirty-five in print and two in manuscript'.[52] Gurr's figure of 229 sounds comparable to Greg's 227, but it should be noted that Gurr significantly underestimates the number of Admiral's plays, for his 229 takes into consideration that company's extended history as patronised by Prince Henry and the Lord Palsgrave (subsequently Frederick V the Elector Palatine). Of the plays Gurr lists in his appended census, only 205 pertain to the Henslowe years, twenty-eight of them being extant in Gurr's reckoning and 177 lost.[53] Six of the plays Gurr lists as surviving only fall into that ontological category because he has conflated titles from Henslowe with different titles from printed texts or manuscripts that he proposes refer to the same play.[54] As John Astington has observed, a fundamental interpretative choice affecting the study of lost plays turns on the decision either to 'lump' two or more play titles together and assume they are variants applying to the one dramatic artefact, or to

---

[51] Matthew Steggle has convincingly demonstrated that 'Truth's Supplication' was a nocturnal play unrelated to *The Whore of Babylon*: see M. Steggle, *Digital Humanities and the Lost Drama of Early Modern England* (Farnham: Ashgate, 2015), 89–100.

[52] A. Gurr, *Shakespeare's Opposites: The Admiral's Company, 1594–1625* (Cambridge: Cambridge University Press, 2009), 109. In a subsequent publication, Gurr provides slightly altered figures: 'We know, for example, the titles of approximately 229 plays associated with the Admiral's men are known, with only 38 having survived': see A. Gurr, 'What Is Lost of Shakespearean Plays, Besides a Few Titles?' in D. McInnis and M. Steggle (eds.), *Lost Plays in Shakespeare's England* (Basingstoke: Palgrave Macmillan, 2014), 59.

[53] See Gurr's 'Appendix 1: The Plays' in *Shakespeare's Opposites*, 201–273. Gurr lists 'Medicine for a Curst Wife' but acknowledges that although the play seems initially to have been commissioned by the Admiral's, Dekker ultimately offered the play to Worcester's; I have excluded it from Gurr's total.

[54] Gurr problematically lists as extant: 'The Wise Man of West Chester' (Gurr #23), 'Longshanks' (Gurr #36), 'The Disguises' (Gurr #39), 'Thomas Merry (Beech's Tragedy)' (Gurr #139), 'Jugurth' (Gurr #145), and '2 The Blind Beggar of Bethnal Green, or Tom Strowd' (Gurr #163).

maintain a 'split' between the identity of the plays to which the various titles apply.[55] For scholars who resist Gurr's lumping of titles, the total would be twenty-two surviving plays.

Wiggins adopts significantly more rigorous and generous principles for inclusion/exclusion of plays than any of his predecessors, and arrives at a different figure again. He strives for completeness in his chronological catalogue; this means not only recording entries for plays known by titles and for untitled plays that are demonstrably distinct from them, but also entries for 'cases where an author is recorded as having written plays, but where no specific plays are ascribed to him'.[56] Accordingly, plays inferred from contemporary references feature uniquely in Wiggins' reckoning: for example, he includes an untitled comedy by Thomas Heywood (Wiggins #1044) and one by Richard Hathway (Wiggins #1068) on account of Francis Meres' celebration of each of these authors' comedies. I assume these are both Admiral's plays because Meres' reference occurs at a time (before 7 September 1598) when it is plausible that such a comedy or comedies by Heywood and Hathway would have been offered to the Admiral's.[57]

Wiggins also consciously 'seeks to apply a higher standard of analysis in the interpretation of documentary evidence' than some previous critics have done,[58] leading him to distinguish (for example) 'The Tragedy on Jonson's Plot' (Wiggins #1159) from 'Chapman's three acts' (Wiggins #1168) on the basis of the substantial gap between the October 1598 payment for the two acts on Jonson's plot and the January 1599 payments for Chapman's other three acts.[59] Greg thought the two groups of payments referred to a single play (Greg #157a); Neil Carson acknowledged but didn't count the two acts on Jonson's plot;[60] and Gurr ignored both. Another unique feature of Wiggins' pursuit of comprehensiveness is his inclusion of logical inferences:

---

[55] See J. H. Astington, 'Lumpers and Splitters' in McInnis and Steggle (eds.), *Lost Plays in Shakespeare's England*, 84–102; see also R. L. Knutson and D. McInnis, 'The *Lost Plays Database*: A Wiki for Lost Plays', *Medieval and Renaissance Drama in England*, 24 (2011), 48–49.

[56] Wiggins, 'Introduction', *British Drama*, 1.xvii.

[57] I base this plausibility on these dramatists' known company commerce. Heywood first appears in Henslowe's records in late October 1596 when Henslowe lent 30s to Alleyn and others 'for hawodes bocke', and Heywood subsequently agreed to act exclusively for Henslowe for a two year period commencing 25 March 1598 (Foakes (ed.), *Henslowe's Diary*, 50, 241). Hathway was associated with that company between 1598–1603, though Greg suggested that Hathway could have been working for other companies during that time (*Henslowe's Diary*, 2.270–271); a sentiment supported by Hathway's apparent request to withdraw his play of 'The Conquest of Spain by John a Gaunt' from Henslowe (see MS I, article 33 in Foakes (ed.), *Henslowe's Diary*, 294–295).

[58] Wiggins, 'Introduction', *British Drama*, xvii.

[59] For Chapman's untitled plays, see Foakes (ed.), *Henslowe's Diary*, 100, 102, and 103.

[60] Carson, *A Companion*, 55.

Table 1.2 *Critical estimates of the size and loss rate of the Admiral's repertory*

	Greg	Gurr	Wiggins
Extant plays	36	28	25
Lost plays	191 (84.14%)	177 (86.34%)	208 (89.27%)
Total	227	205	233

noting the record of a '2 Henry Richmond' play but not a first part, Wiggins explains that the existence of a part one is nevertheless presupposed (but that 'the principle is not reversible: a known first part does not necessarily imply a lost second part, because the second part may never have been written; the existence of *The First Part of the Tragical Reign of Selimus* is not evidence of the existence of a 2 *Selimus*').[61] By my calculation, Wiggins explicitly associates 233 plays with the Admiral's Men; of these, only twenty-five survive.[62]

The foregoing discussion is summarised in Table 1.2.

By now it should be apparent that to ask the seemingly simple question, 'How many plays did the Admiral's Men have?' is in fact to ask a much more complicated question about scholarly practices of interpreting historical documents. The key areas in which the seminal scholars have differed are the following: (1) the handling of evidence pertaining to untitled or incomplete plays; (2) the identification of plays with play-titles; and (3) the inferential licence afforded by the documentary evidence (that is, the tension between restricting oneself to literally what is recorded in the archive versus a more all-inclusive approach that reads between the lines).

Greg is relatively thorough in documenting the names of plays that appear in Henslowe's records; Carson's much more recent *Companion to Henslowe's Diary* arrives at a near-identical census, the two differing only on slight matters (for example, Carson's inclusion of 'Black Joan'[63] as #121 conveniently replaces Greg's #121 for 'two jigs', without interrupting the otherwise perfect correspondence in numbers each assigns to the plays).[64] However, Greg is slightly inconsistent in his handling of

---

[61] Wiggins, 'Introduction', *British Drama*, xix.

[62] I've qualified my statement in terms of 'my calculations' because Wiggins exercises admirable restraint when it comes to formally assigning plays to companies, authors and dates; in some cases (such as Hathway's comedy) I find the evidence sufficiently compelling to count a play as part of the Admiral's repertory even if Wiggins himself stops short of a formal declaration.

[63] See Foakes (ed.), *Henslowe's Diary*, 321 and 323.

[64] Carson, *A Companion*, 82–84. Carson's study counts 224 plays in the Admiral's repertory (cf. Greg's 227).

payments for unnamed plays. On the one hand, he lists the play in Chettle's pawn on 7 March 1603 (which Gurr does not), and the 'Play for court' known only through Henslowe's payment to Chettle on 29 December 1602 for a prologue and epilogue (which Wiggins, whose principles for inclusion require that the ostensible play is 'demonstrably not coextensive with any other', excludes).[65] On the other hand, he does not record Henslowe's payment of 10s to Chettle and John Day (19 June 1600) in earnest of an unnamed play, despite the fact that it has not been possible to associate this payment with any other Chettle-Day project.[66]

Gurr occasionally lists untitled plays known only from payment records, such as Chapman's pastoral tragedy of July 1599,[67] yet ignores others, such as the book by 'young' Haughton (1597),[68] the plot Jonson showed the company and promised to turn into a play in December 1597,[69] Munday's court comedy (1598),[70] the playbook by 'm^r Maxton [Marston?]' (1599),[71] Chapman's playbook,[72] Chapman's tragedy on Jonson's plot[73] and Chapman's three acts towards another play (1598–1599).[74] Other notable omissions by Gurr that are harder to explain (because clearly named in Henslowe) include Robert Wilson, Dekker, Michael Drayton and Chettle's 'Pierce of Exton' (1598);[75] Chettle's 'A Woman's Tragedy' (1598);[76] Porter's 'The Two Merry Women of Abingdon' (1599);[77] Dekker's 'The First Introduction of the Civil Wars of France' (1599);[78] William Haughton's 'playe called

---

[65] Greg #258, #252; Wiggins, *Catalogue*, vol.1, 'Introduction', xvi.
[66] Foakes (ed.), *Henslowe's Diary*, 135; the only critic to count this play is Wiggins (#1255).
[67] Gurr #127 and see Foakes (ed.), *Henslowe's Diary*, 122 and 266; cf. Wiggins #1197.
[68] Foakes (ed.), *Henslowe's Diary*, 72; Wiggins #1088.
[69] Foakes (ed.), *Henslowe's Diary*, 73; Wiggins #1099.
[70] Foakes (ed.), *Henslowe's Diary*, 96; Wiggins #1140.
[71] Foakes (ed.), *Henslowe's Diary*, 124; Wiggins #1209.
[72] Foakes (ed.), *Henslowe's Diary*, 100; Wiggins #1158.
[73] Foakes (ed.), *Henslowe's Diary*, 100; Wiggins #1159. Greg lists this and Chapman's three acts together as #157a; Gurr does not list it. Carson acknowledges this play on p. 55 but does not list it in his census.
[74] Foakes (ed.), *Henslowe's Diary*, 103; Wiggins #1168.
[75] Foakes (ed.), *Henslowe's Diary*, 88; Wiggins #1118.
[76] Foakes (ed.), *Henslowe's Diary*, 93; Wiggins #1138.
[77] Foakes (ed.), *Henslowe's Diary*, 105; Wiggins #1179. Gurr acknowledges that '[a]s may as three plays might be noted in the entries for Henry Porter' but does not elaborate further (*Shakespeare's Opposites*, 241 n 92).
[78] Foakes (ed.), *Henslowe's Diary*, 103; Wiggins #1175. Gurr lumps this title with '1 Civil Wars' and does not list separately, but Henslowe clearly lists this playtitle *after* '3 Civil Wars', making identification with '1 Civil Wars' extremely improbable.

of w[illia]^m cartwryght' (1602);[79] and the unattributed 'Mortimer' (1602)[80] and 'The Earl of Hertford' (1602).[81]

Differences between Greg's interpretation of Henslowe's titles and the interpretation of other scholars can be partially explained due to errors, both avoidable and otherwise. In the former category, Greg's howler of attributing Jonson and Nashe's 'The Isle of Dogs'[82] to the Admiral's company (instead of Pembroke's at the Swan) probably stems from confusion over the Pembroke's player William Bird (or Borne) and others approaching Edward Alleyn on 10 August 1597 with a view to joining the Admiral's Men after the Privy Council imposed a restraint against playing precisely because of 'the Ieylle of dooges'.[83] (Carson does not follow Greg with regards to the Jonson-Nashe play). Greg alone lists Henslowe's cancelled title, 'Better Late Than Never' separately to the title Henslowe entered in its stead (and consistently thereafter), 'Bear a Brain'.[84] (The case for lumping here is that 'Better Late' is patently an error, which Henslowe corrected immediately).

The lumping together of titles by scholars partially explains the variation in estimates of the overall number of Admiral's plays and the number of extant plays. In the majority of instances, the rationale for these lumpings is extra-documentary in nature, and depends on scholarly whim. Fleay abhorred the idea of positing the one-time existence of a play now lost, merely to make sense of an ambiguous reference; he referred to it as 'the imbecile resource of supposing a lost play'.[85] But in his haste to avoid such practices, he ventured numerous disingenuous guesses as to how lost plays might relate to surviving plays. His convoluted reasoning led him (on occasion) to have 'entirely misrepresented the nature of the printed piece in seeking to make his identification plausible' (which Greg rightly regarded as 'something very much worse' than supposing a lost play).[86] Gurr, however, embraces a number of the identifications made by Fleay and his method of lumping more generally. Gurr believes that the play Henslowe consistently calls 'The Wise Man [singular] of Westchester' can

---

[79] See Foakes (ed.), Henslowe's Diary, 204 for payment to Haughton for a 'playe called of w[illia]^m cartwryght'; Wiggins #1348 is struck by the ambiguity of the word 'of', which could mean 'about' or 'by' (the cancellation of 'called' suggests that 'William Cartwright' was not the name of the play, at any rate).

[80] Foakes (ed.), Henslowe's Diary, 205; Wiggins #1345.

[81] Foakes (ed.), Henslowe's Diary, 205; Wiggins #1347.   [82] Greg #112.

[83] Foakes (ed.), Henslowe's Diary, 240.   [84] Greg #178a and 179.   [85] Fleay, BCED, 2.31.

[86] Greg #161; the particularly convoluted reasoning by Fleay in this case of 'War without Blows' led Greg to glibly conclude that '[t]his is one of the cases that convince one that there may be something very much worse than the "imbecile resource of supposing a lost play"'.

be identified as the manuscript play *John a Kent and John a Cumber*, which is about two wise men and has a setting 'near Chester'; it is therefore listed as extant by Gurr.[87] Henslowe's 'Longshanks' is likewise lumped with Peele's extant *Edward I*; 'The Disguises' with *Look About You*; and 'Jugurth' with William Boyle's MS play, *Jugurtha* (which Gurr dates to 1600 despite the presence of anachronistic features including act division and scene locations).[88] Oddly, Gurr suggests that '2 The Blind Beggar of Bethnal Green, or Tom Strowd' might survive in quarto but doesn't offer any explanation.[89] Perhaps he has in mind the theory Wiggins alludes to in entry #1250, that the quarto of *1 Blind Beggar* actually represents a redaction of all three parts (Wiggins isn't at all persuaded).

In a more complex example, Gurr counts as extant the Day and Haughton collaboration, 'The Tragedy of Thomas Merry (Beech's Tragedy)' (1599) because he lumps it with Robert Yarington's *Two Lamentable Tragedies* (1601): presumably Yarington's absence from Henslowe's records and his not otherwise being known as a dramatist encouraged Gurr to assume that Yarrington had not independently written a play on the same subject matter as Day and Haughton. Yet Gurr resists the temptation to follow Fleay and also lump 'The Orphans Tragedy' with Yarington's printed playbook.[90] Rather, Gurr suggests an alternative interpretation of Henslowe's entry as 'The Tragedy of Orphenes' rather than 'orphans', and points to classical precedents including 'the story of Orphe, to whom Apollo gave the gift of prophecy but who Bachus changed to stone'.[91] Likewise, in the case of 'The Spanish Moor's Tragedy', a play widely accepted by scholars as having been printed in 1657 as *Lust's Dominion*, Gurr doesn't buy the lumping of these titles, citing Chambers on the absence of full payment information in Henslowe 'to mark its completion'.[92] For Gurr, 'The Spanish Moor's Tragedy' still counts as lost.

Gurr's lumpings have not gained widespread critical acceptance, but there is greater consensus on the identification of Henslowe's 'The Guise' with Marlowe's *Massacre at Paris* and 'The Comedy of Humours' with Chapman's *Humorous Day's Mirth*.[93] In the case of the former, the identification rests primarily on the distinctiveness of the named

---

87 Gurr, *Shakespeare's Opposites*, 58.
88 See Wiggins #1234; for an attempt to support Gurr's identification, see F. Kiefer, 'Lost and Found: William Boyle's *Jugurth*', *Medieval and Renaissance Drama in England* 28 (2015), 17–29.
89 Gurr #163; see Item 163 on p. 254 of *Shakespeare's Opposites*.
90 Gurr #139 and 140; see Fleay, *BCED*, 2.285–286.   91 Gurr, *Shakespeare's Opposites*, 249 n 105.
92 Gurr, *Shakespeare's Opposites*, 250 n 110; see also Gurr #146.
93 Wiggins #1073; Greg and Carson #106; Gurr #69.

protagonist, a phenomenon not unique to Henslowe. A comparable example of plays being referred to by their primary characters comes from the
accounts of the Treasurer of the Chamber, which record a play 'called
Benidicte and Bettris' and another called 'The Hotspurr' (probably *1
Henry IV*) amongst the twenty having been performed at court in May
1613 by the King's Men.[94] It should be noted, however, that character
names can feature in multiple plays and thus cannot alone guarantee the
identification of two titles with a single play. Greg was an unlucky casualty
of history when, in his edition of Henslowe published in 1908, he assumed
that Henslowe's reference to 'the playe of bacon' referred unambiguously
to Greene's *Friar Bacon and Friar Bungay*; Greg's edition of Henslowe was
published in 1908, and the Alnwick Castle manuscript of *John of Bordeaux,
or The Second Part of Friar Bacon* (MS 507) was not published until
1936.[95]

The cases of lumping two titles when both are recorded by Henslowe
are slightly different. Greg lists 'Vortigern' separately to 'Hengist' – a title
recorded only once by Henslowe, on 22 June 1597 – but admits that it is
'[v]ery probably the same as Valtegar'.[96] Gurr, Wiggins and the *LPD*
provide only a single entry for these titles. Wiggins offers cogent reasons
for lumping based on the inability of the subject matter to furnish two
separate plays in the order named by Henslowe, in the same company's
repertory. He notes that the *second* half of the material centres on
Vortigern's construction of the tower (so would not lead to a second,
Hengist-centred play on the need to construct the tower), and that 'there is
not enough usable material on the subsequent career of Hengist to sustain
a second play about his further adventures'.[97] Greg and Carson list
'Orestes' Furies' and 'Agamemnon' as separate plays; Gurr lumps them
without explanation; Wiggins notes that if they were two plays, 'Orestes'
would be the sequel to 'Agamemnon', yet it was commissioned first (which
makes the two-play theory unlikely).[98] He argues in favour of the company
asking the playwrights to 'cover the whole story in a single play, whose
balance and emphasis changed from avenging son to murdered father in

[94] D. Cook and F. P. Wilson (eds.), 'Dramatic Records in the Declared Accounts of the Treasurer of the
Chamber 1558–1642' in *Malone Society Collections VI* (Oxford: Oxford University Press, 1961
[1962]), 55–56.

[95] Foakes (ed.), *Henslowe's Diary*, 207; W. L. Renwick (ed.), *John of Bordeaux, or The Second Part of
Friar Bacon* (Oxford: Malone Society, 1936). Critics now tend to agree that the play mentioned by
Henslowe is not Greene's; see Wiggins #908 and L. Manley and S.-B. MacLean, *Lord Strange's Men
and Their Plays* (New Haven: Yale University Press, 2014), 93–96.

[96] Greg #95 and #109.   [97] Wiggins #1048.

[98] Greg and Carson #173 and 174; Gurr #125; Wiggins #1186.

the course of writing', as reflected in Henslowe's changing titles for the single play. A similar phenomenon might lie behind Henslowe's payments of £6 in total for a play called 'Judas' in December 1601 and subsequent payment of 10s to Dekker in January 1602 for a prologue and epilogue for the seemingly unrelated 'Pontius Pilate'.[99] These titles have always been treated as though referring to separate plays. Wiggins briefly entertains the concept of the two plays being one (#1318) but is unable to find a source text that unites them substantially enough to justify his hunch. But Paul Whitfield White has made a convincing case for lumping them based on Judas Iscariot and Pontius Pilate as 'two gospel villains whose accounts, in the Book of Mathew, immediately follow one another' and whose stories are intimately entwined in the ballad, *The Dream of Judas' Mother Fulfilled*.[100] Following White, I list these two titles together as a single play in my census of the Admiral's plays.

Subject matter can provide justification for splitting, as in the case of Henslowe's references to 'the conqueste of brute wth the firste fyndinge of the bathe' and to 'brute grensh*i*llde'.[101] As Misha Teramura has shown, both Brutes were useful inclusions in the Admiral's late sixteenth-century repertory, but they are obviously distinct personages.[102] (Gurr does not list 'Brute Greenshield'). Scholars since Greg have tended to lump together two disparate titles, 'Caesar's Fall' and 'Two Shapes', for no better reason than their chronological proximity in Henslowe's records (they occur a week apart in May 1602) and the significant overlap in writing teams involved.[103] The amount paid to the playwrights (£8) exceeds the usual rate for a new play, and as Wiggins observes, 'Two Shapes' (the later title) 'does not relate to anything in the likely narrative of a play about Caesar'.[104] In these cases, there is strong cause to preserve the distinction between titles that have sometimes been conflated.

By contrast, the simple principle of erring on the side of caution and all-inclusiveness is probably what led Greg uniquely to propose 'Mark Antony (?)' as an Admiral's play, on the basis of Henslowe's record of having paid £2 on 10 November 1598 on behalf of the company 'to bye a sackebute of

[99] Foakes (ed.), *Henslowe's Diary*, 185 and 187; see Wiggins #1316 and 1318.

[100] White, 'The Admiral's and Worcester's Biblical Drama of 1602', paper for the SAA seminar 'Lost Plays and Their Contexts', Atlanta, GA, 6 April 2017.

[101] Foakes (ed.), *Henslowe's Diary*, 96 and 106; see Wiggins #1161 and 1177.

[102] See M. Teramura, 'Brute Parts: From Troy to Britain at the Rose, 1595–1600' in McInnis and Steggle (eds.), *Lost Plays in Shakespeare's England*, 127–147, esp. 131–132.

[103] See Greg #236, who thought the identification was 'beyond doubt'.

[104] Wiggins #1328; see Foakes (ed.), *Henslowe's Diary*, 202 and 201.

marke antoney' (subsequent critics have interpreted this as a reference to a character rather than a play).[105] In this vein, Greg also lists an entry for 'Bad May Amend' (the subtitle of Drayton and Dekker's 'Worse Afeared Than Hurt', 1598) but assigns it an '-a' suffix (#159a) in order to hedge his bets about whether it's a discrete title.[106] Carson omits 'Bad May Amend' and 'Mark Antony'.

Wiggins is significantly more thorough than previous critics in assessing the rationale for lumping and splitting of plays. Following Fleay's hint but offering a justification for the first time, Wiggins maintains a distinction between the titles Henslowe enters between 1595–1596 as 'Seleo and Olympo' (#994) and 'Olympio and Eugenio' (#995), noting that although it is tempting to follow Greg in assuming the titles refer to a single play because the performance records are continuous and 'the takings for the two titles dovetails neatly', Henslowe consistently records the 'similar proper names as Olympo and Olympio' respectively.[107] Likewise, as noted above, Wiggins splits the previously lumped 'Caesar's Fall' (#1329) and 'Two Shapes' (#1328). Wiggins alone distinguishes 'The French Comedy' recorded by Henslowe between 11 February and 24 June 1595 (#989) from 'A French Comedy' performed as a new play on 18 April 1597 and thereafter (#1066).[108] Wiggins also creates an entry (#1128) for a play for which Chapman received £3 10s in total, after an initial advance of £2 'in earneste of a boocke for the companye' on 16 May 1598.[109] Greg thought these payments were for 'The Iylle of a Woman', but the 15 June 1598 payment to Chapman for that play was specifically 'in earneste of his boocke', a phrasing which makes no sense if referring to the book which had already received the £2 advance the previous month.[110] Wiggins associates this untitled play with up to four quotations published in Allot's *England's Parnassus* (1600) which are attributed to Chapman but which have not been located in any of Chapman's surviving works. He further observes Meres' claim that Chapman was amongst the best for

---

[105] Greg #158a; Foakes (ed.), *Henslowe's Diary*, 101; see Wiggins #1156 and 1157 for plays that possibly included this character.

[106] See Wiggins #1146. Henslowe records 'Bad May Amend' but subsequently deletes the title and replaces it with 'Worse Afeared Than Hurt', the title he uses thereafter. See Foakes (ed.), *Henslowe's Diary*, 97.

[107] Wiggins #995; Fleay lists 'Olimpio and Hengenyo' (Anon. 143) separately to 'Seleo et Olympo' (Anon. 165) (*BCED* 2. 301 and 303) but does not explain his decision to split the titles.

[108] Further examples of Wiggins interpreting Henslowe's records as justifying discrete entries for lost plays include the play (tragedy?) by Chapman (#1128), the play for which Chettle received 10s in earnest of on 10 November 1599 (#1219), and the play being written by Chettle and Day in the summer of 1600 (#1255).

[109] Foakes (ed.), *Henslowe's Diary*, 89.   [110] Foakes (ed.), *Henslowe's Diary*, 91.

tragedies, and must therefore have written at least one tragedy by 1598 (the date of *Palladis Tamia*).

Wiggins too is the only scholar to explicitly list a '2 Fortunatus' play (#851). Greg suggested that 'a second part had been planned' as a sequel to Henslowe's '1 Fortunatus' play (1596), but refrained from declaring whether he thought it had been written ('in the confusion following on the inhibition of July 1597 the project was for a time abandoned').[111] Wiggins includes '2 Fortunatus', despite the lack of direct evidence (Henslowe never mentions it), on the grounds that Henslowe's record of '1 Fortunatus' as an old play means the appellation was retrospective (Henslowe already knew that a second part existed and wanted to differentiate the two). He further suggests that Dekker combined two old plays in 1599. In my edition of Dekker's play, I argue against both these propositions, noting that Henslowe occasionally made mistakes (but would not have corrected them during this period in the diary: the 'correction' feature only becomes common in the later, 1597–1603 series of entries) and that in a parallel case, when he begins recording entries for the two 'Tamar Cham' plays in 1596, he fails to designate part 1 as '1 Tamar Cham' despite demonstrably knowing of the existence of part 2, which he had recorded earlier in 1592 when it was still in the Strange's repertory.[112]

I am more easily persuaded by Wiggins' postulation of a '1 Henry Richmond' play (#1192) to make sense of Henslowe's reference to '2 Henry Richmond' (Wiggins #1213), as mentioned above. The complicating factor here is that Henslowe doesn't always label serial plays consistently. Famously, *The Blind Beggar of Bethnal Green* features a relatively incidental character named Tom Strowd, but Henslowe names the lost second part 'The Second Part of the Blind Beggar of Bethnal Green with Tom Strowd' and names the final part of the apparent trilogy simply '3 Tom Strowd'.[113] Although in theory the play that precedes '2 Henry Richmond' may well be lurking in Henslowe's records under an unobvious title, it is unlikely, for as Wiggins notes, '[t]here are no obvious candidates'.[114] Something similar occurs in the context of Day

---

[111] Greg #87.

[112] See T. Dekker, *Old Fortunatus*, D. McInnis (ed.) (Manchester: Manchester University Press, 2020), 4.

[113] See Knutson, *The Repertory*, 53.

[114] Wiggins #1192. Knutson has suggested that the lost 'Owen Tudor' play might be the missing first part of '2 Henry Richmond': R. L. Knutson, 'Toe to Toe Across Maid Lane: Repertorial Competition at the Rose and Globe, 1599–1600' in J. Schlueter and P. Nelsen (eds.), *Acts of Criticism: Performance Matters in Shakespeare and His Contemporaries* (Madison & Teaneck: Fairleigh Dickinson University Press, 2005), 23–24. Wiggins is cynical about the possibility. I discuss the 'Owen Tudor' play in Chapter 3.

and Haughton's lost '2 Tom Dough' play of 1601 (Wiggins #1301).
Here, Wiggins invokes the spin-off principle of the Tom Strowd example
to suggest that Tom Dough similarly grew out of an earlier play to
assume a greater status in the sequel. Following Fleay, he assumes
'Tom Dough' was the Tom Dove character from Thomas Deloney's
novel, *Thomas of Reading* (c.1599), which likely formed the basis of
'The Six Yeoman of the West' (Wiggins #1289), a play which may thus
have served as the precursor to '2 Tom Dough' despite not being known
as '1 Tom Dough'.[115]

Further plays might be attributable to the Admiral's repertory but are
not explicitly linked, and are known from additional sources of information. Wiggins is the first scholar to observe that Edmund Gayton's
reference (in *Pleasant Notes upon Don Quixote*, 1654) to having seen 'the
play of *Adam* and *Eve*' should be taken as a reference to recent English
drama, not medieval plays.[116] Furthermore, Henslowe's inventory of the
'Clownes Sewtes and Hermetes Sewtes, with dievers other sewtes' (10
March 1598) lists an otherwise unexplained 'Eves bodeyes' amongst the
Admiral's Men's properties.[117] Wiggins nevertheless resists ascribing this
play to the Admiral's repertory, noting the relative unsophistication of
such a topic for London audiences at the end of the 1590s, but Gayton
mentions it in the context of other known Admiral's plays, and I find
myself more convinced than Wiggins about the play's auspices. Wiggins
also lists a history play including the death of Percy (#1285), for which a
MS fragment in Day's handwriting survives on the verso of a note from
Samuel Rowley to Henslowe requesting payment for Day and Haughton's
'The Six Yeomen of the West'.[118] Again, Wiggins declines to associate this
play formally with the Admiral's, but the circumstantial evidence of the
'Six Yeomen' context is at least suggestive, and I have included it as a play
likely written for or offered to the Admiral's Men.[119]

---

[115] Fleay, *BCED*, 1.108 (Day 15).   [116] 'Adam and Eve' (Wiggins #1093).
[117] Foakes (ed.), *Henslowe's Diary*, 318.
[118] See MS I, article 35[v] in Greg, *Henslowe Papers*, 57–58.
[119] A counterexample, in which the evidence is simply too scant to assign an otherwise unknown
play to the Admiral's repertory, is Wiggins #1110 ('Play or Plays'), the evidence for which is three
fragments printed in *England's Parnassus* and attributed to Jonson. The fragments may or may
not be from a single dramatic work, but if they are, its identity remains unknown (it could
theoretically be any of the known lost Jonson plays of the 1590s, or an otherwise altogether
unknown play or plays). Jonson was writing for multiple companies, including 'The Isle of Dogs'
for Pembroke's, a series of collaborative plays (e.g. 'Page of Plymouth') for the Admiral's, and
Every Man In and *Every Man Out* for the Chamberlain's in the period leading up to Robert
Allot's publication of his miscellany. Wiggins's avoidance of assigning the play to any company's
repertory is eminently sensible.

Table 1.3 *Critical estimates of the size and loss rate of the Admiral's repertory*

	Greg	Gurr	Wiggins	McInnis
Extant plays	36	28	25	24
Lost plays	191 (84.14%)	177 (86.34%)	208 (89.27%)	211 (89.78%)
Total	227	205	233	235

Given the values Wiggins and I share vis-à-vis an inclination to split unless compelling documentary evidence necessitates lumping, it is somewhat unsurprising that I arrive at a very similar total number of plays and the same number of extant plays as him, but we do count differently in some specific cases, as noted above. We have 230 plays in common, but I follow Syme in splitting 'Joronymo' from *The Spanish Tragedy* in 1597; Wiggins includes two that I do not ('2 Fortunatus', plus he lists 'Pontius Pilate' and 'Judas' as discrete plays); and I tentatively assign four plays to the Admiral's that Wiggins stops short of ascribing (the untitled plays by Heywood and Hathway known through Meres, as well as the 'Adam and Eve' play and Day's history featuring the death of Percy). A revised table would thus read as above (see Table 1.3).

Even without significant archival discoveries, then, in the century since Greg's edition of Henslowe's diary was published, both the number (211, up from 191) and percentage (89.78 per cent, up from 84.14 per cent) of lost plays in the Admiral's repertory has increased. Coupled with the statistics above about the profitability of those plays that have not survived, it is simply not reasonable to infer either that lost plays were repertorial 'filler' or that the Admiral's Men's business strategy was to invest in a repertory whose size was inversely proportional to its quality. Instead, the calculations suggest that the size of the Admiral's repertory was commercially viable (perhaps even prudent),[120] and that although certain plays performed financially better than others, there is no reason to doubt the value to the company of the plays that have since been lost.

§

The foregoing conclusions have implications for our understanding of how Shakespeare's company likely operated. It should now be clear that

---

[120] In Chapter 3 I note that the Admiral's Men appear to have deliberately acquired more new plays than usual in anticipation of their move to the Fortune; here, it is simply worth noting that the number of purchases for discrete plays swells post-1598 to a far larger number than the pre-1597 playlists indicate.

Shakespearean biases distorted the conclusions of those scholars who were intent on emphasising the inferiority of the Admiral's commerce relative to the Chamberlain's, and who explained the size of the Admiral's repertory in terms of volume-based competition rather than quality-based competition. Perversely, the survival rate of documents (such as Henslowe's) *about* lost plays has exercised considerable influence over modern critical assumptions about the quality of early modern drama. Lacunae in the documentary records undoubtedly distort perceptions of attrition rates. The number of play-titles listed per calendar year in the *Lost Plays Database* changes markedly just after the turn of the century, but this does not mean the survival rates for play-texts improved. On 'the 14 daye of marche 1604', Henslowe tallied up 'all the acowntes from the begininge of the world' and ceased providing any information about theatrical activity.[121] Accordingly, theatre historians simply do not know what we have lost because the archive yields fewer clues; as Syme has acknowledged, '[a]n admission of ignorance strikes me as a more appropriate response to such lacunae than a confident assertion of certainty'.[122]

Whilst what we know from Henslowe about the incidence of loss in the Admiral's repertory might not hold true for every London company (presumably the smaller or shorter-lived companies such as Pembroke's had less opportunity to develop so extensive a repertory), it is reasonable to expect that the Chamberlain's Men – a company of comparable size, reputation, and means – would have had an analogous loss and survival rate, and a similarly sized repertory.[123] With the exception of possibly thirteen titles though, the lost Chamberlain's plays have sunk without a trace. It is therefore particularly hard to ascertain the relationship between the figure and ground in their repertory, or to understand the shaping effect of the contour that separates extant from lost plays, other than to posit that the surviving figure is almost certainly a distorted one. The thirteen plays known to be lost from the Chamberlain's repertory seems a gross underestimation of that company's real losses, which ought to be somewhere in the vicinity of 89.78 per cent of their repertory.

---

[121]   Foakes (ed.), *Henslowe's Diary*, 209.

[122]   Syme, 'The Meaning of Success: Stories of 1594 and Its Aftermath', 494.

[123]   Dismissing older suggestions by Greg that the companies associated with Henslowe were exceptional rather than typical in their financial affairs and repertories, Neil Carson has sensibly asserted that '[u]ntil new evidence is forthcoming we must conclude that the working condition of dramatists writing for the Admiral's Men were probably typical of the time' (see Carson, *A Companion*, 55).

If we adopt the conservative view that thirty-five extant plays can be confidently assigned to the Chamberlain's repertory, and assume that the loss rate for that company is analogous to the loss rate for the Admiral's Men (c.89 per cent), we might project an estimated total of 318 plays that ought to have been in the Chamberlain's repertory in the period under investigation. In this scenario, beyond the thirty-five extant and thirteen lost plays that we know about, there may have been a further 270 plays that have left no trace behind whatsoever.

Although my number-crunching above demonstrates the financial value to the company of plays that are now lost, my exploration of the attempts of various venerable scholars to trace the contour between figure and ground in the repertories of the Admiral's and Chamberlain's Men shows that there is a significant lack of clarity around the shape that those repertories took. Rubin suggests that in contrast to the 'substance-character' of the ground, the figure has a certain 'thing-character'; but that doesn't mean it must be recognisable: 'it may appear as something completely unknown and yet have thing-character, be characterized by features which define a thing. The ground, on the other hand, is characterized by its substance-like attributes'.[124] We might do well to content ourselves with acknowledging that the repertories of the Admiral's and Chamberlain's Men seem to possess a certain 'thingness', but that it is not necessarily recognisable beyond having a 'thing-character' that can be discerned through juxtaposition with the inherent 'substance-character' of the sprawling and amorphous ground that is the lost plays associated with these companies. What *is* clear is that the basis on which scholars have perceived the companies' repertories is more fragile, limited, and subject to alternative interpretations than has previously been acknowledged. The mental picture that we have of these companies' repertories is only possible through the rejection of sensory data: we have been seeing what we want to see (whether it's the figure or the ground, the vase or the faces) and not the possibilities of the entire picture. In the following chapter, I begin to retrace the contour that divides figure from ground in the Chamberlain's Men's repertory by reconsidering what we know about two seminal moments in the company's early years: their first documented performances (at Newington Butts) and their move from the Theatre to the Curtain (a less glamorous transition in playing venues than the company's more famous move to the Globe, but an important one).

---

[124] Pind, *Edgar Rubin*, 98.

CHAPTER 2

Early Shakespeare: 1594–1598

Any account of Shakespeare's career and the fortunes of the company with which he spent most of his professional life must include the eleven-day run of performances at Newington Butts, which is significant as the earliest documented glimpse of the Lord Chamberlain's Men in action.[1] Aside from scholarly interest in the presence of the 'ur-Hamlet' in that series of performances, little attention has been paid to the lost plays listed by Henslowe. Yet it is the lost plays – 'Hester and Ahasuerus' in particular – that provide the negative space that gives a meaningful shape to the Newington repertory and help make sense of the dramatic offerings at that venue. Attending to them reveals some surprising connections and duplication of motifs, interests, and dramaturgy that is otherwise missed. The fact remains, though, that the conditions under which the Chamberlain's Men played (somehow) in conjunction with the Admiral's Men at Newington made for a very unusual theatrical enterprise, one which differs in important ways from what we know of the London companies' commercial strategies throughout the 1590s. There is no evidence of sequels, spin-offs or serial plays at Newington, and only one (maybe two) of the play titles seem to refer to comedies despite the prevalence of comedies in company repertories throughout the rest of the decade. I call attention to these anomalies not in order to dismiss the significance of the Newington run, but to play this moment off against what I argue is an equally important 'formative moment' for Shakespeare's company: its eviction from what had become its regular venue – the Theatre – and the period of transition encompassing its tenancy of the Curtain and eventual move to the Globe.

Recent archaeological excavation work in Shoreditch paves the way for a reappraisal of the significance of the Curtain theatre as the company's

---

[1] See, most recently L. Johnson, *Shakespeare's Lost Playhouse: Eleven Days at Newington Butts* (New York: Routledge, 2017).

temporary venue at some point between 25 March 1597 (when their lease
on the Theatre expired) and May 1599 (when they moved into the
Globe). During this period the company was planning for the future.
They were looking to their new, purpose-built and permanent home on
the south bank of the Thames; and the Curtain itself (if excavation
evidence is a reliable indication) may have been more of a positive move
for the company in the interim than scholars have usually allowed.
Making a virtue of the necessary move from the Theatre to the Curtain
may have been easier than previously thought, and with plans for the
Globe's construction underway, this period should be limned in positive
terms. I argue that reconsideration of the physical and economic con-
straints faced by the Chamberlain's Men in this period, and attention to
lost plays in the Chamberlain's and in the Admiral's repertories for
additional context, stands to significantly revise scholarly opinion on
the conditions under which Shakespeare operated prior to his company's
move to the Globe. Together, these two temporary sites of performance
for the Chamberlain's Men (Newington Butts and the Curtain) provide
me with the opportunity to reconsider the theatrical context in which
Shakespeare was operating in the early part of his career. Attending to lost
plays and performance details from this period helps adjust our view of
the company's theatrical activity and enriches our understanding of the
company's formative years.

'Beginning at Newington': 1594

Henslowe's record of ten performances at Newington Butts in June
1594 is (as Knutson and others have noted) 'our earliest evidence' that
Henry Carey had given his patronage to the newly formed Lord
Chamberlain's Men.[2] Following a string of entries for the Earl of
Sussex's Men between 27 December 1593 and 6 February 1594, a brief
run of the Queen's Men and Sussex's performing together over the
Easter period (1 to 8 April 1594), and an even briefer three-day run of
the Admiral's Men between 14 and 16 May 1594, Henslowe recorded
these performances over eleven days in June:[3]

> In the name of god Amen begininge at newing
> ton my Lord Admeralle men & my Lorde chamberlen
> men As ffolowethe 1594

---

[2] Knutson, *The Repertory*, 1.   [3] Foakes (ed.), *Henslowe's Diary*, 21–22.

¶ 3 of June 1594   Rd at heaster & asheweros . . . . . .   viij s
¶ 4 of June 1594   Rd at the Jewe of malta . . . .   x s
¶ 5 of June 1594   Rd at andronicous . . . .   xij s
¶ 6 of June 1594   Rd at cvtlacke . . . . xj s
¶ 8 of June 1594   ne—   Rd at bellendon . . . x . . . . xvij s
¶ 9 of June 1594   Rd at hamlet . . . . viij s
¶ 10 of June 1594   Rd at heaster . . . . v s
¶ 11 of June 1594   Rd at the tamynge of A shrowe . .   ix s
¶ 12 of June 1594   Rd at andronicous . . . .   vij s
¶ 13 of June 1594   Rd at the Jewe . . . . iiij s

Because this string of performance records is the earliest pertaining to
Shakespeare's company, it is hardly possible to overstate its importance.
Yet precious little is actually known about these performances. The circumstances are highly unusual: two companies, 'not yet fully formed' (as
Holger Syme has reminded us) but destined to become powerhouses of the
late-Elizabethan theatrical scene, playing somehow together at a venue not
otherwise known to have been patronised by either, with a combined
repertory that seems on the surface to be 'hastily cobbled together'.[4] By
scholarly consensus, 'heaster & asheweros' ('Hester and Ahasuerus'),
'andronicous' (*Titus Andronicus*?), 'hamlet' (the 'ur-Hamlet'?) and 'the
tamynge of A shrowe' (*The Taming of A Shrew*, though some scholars
believe it was *The Taming of The Shrew*) belonged to the Chamberlain's
Men, for the simple reason that these titles do not reappear in Henslowe's
subsequent records of the Admiral's repertory.[5] The remaining three plays
belong to the Admiral's: 'the Jewe of malta' (Marlowe's *The Jew of Malta*),
'cvtlacke' ('Cutlack') and 'bellendon' ('Belin Dun').[6] Tragedies were
demanding to perform: the disproportionate number of tragic or tragicomic offerings in this short repertory (given the dominance of comedy at
the Rose throughout the 1590s) is presumably the product of having not
one, but two leading actors available to share the burden: one from each
company. This may have been one reason why some of the plays seem to
speak so directly to each other, as with the litany of abuses proudly claimed
by Marlowe's Barabas (here, on 4 June) only to be exceeded the next day

---

[4] H. S. Syme, 'Three's Company: Alternative Histories of London's Theatres in the 1590s',
Shakespeare Survey 65 (2012), 282; and R. L. Knutson, 'What's So Special about 1594?',
Shakespeare Quarterly 61.4 (2010), 467, respectively.
[5] See, e.g. Knutson, *The Repertory*, 59.
[6] The company attribution of 'Belin Dun' is helped by the presence in Henslowe's papers of
descriptions of props explicitly associated with the play: see Foakes (ed.), *Henslowe's Diary*, 320.

(5 June) by Shakespeare's Aaron. The 'Hamlet' play (presumed to be the Chamberlain's) and the 'Cutlack' play (Admiral's) may have afforded similar opportunities for inter-company correspondences, in that they both seem to have dramatised Danish kings.[7]

Most scholars assume that the companies are more likely to have alternated than collaborated in the performance of these seven plays at Newington, though joint performances were technically possible.[8] Collaboration or joint production can take many forms, however, and there are a number of curious features of these seven plays' repertorial scheduling at Newington that have received significantly less (if any) critical commentary but which suggest that the two companies scheduled their offerings with a close eye on what the other was performing. Whether the Admiral's and Chamberlain's came jointly to Newington in 1594 out of desperation caused by plague-induced closures of London theatres or by the 'extreme weather events' that flooded much of the city (but from which Newington, with its 'safe' geographical location on high ground, remained relatively immune), both companies would have had a commercial interest in reinvigorating the theatrical marketplace.[9] To this end, it is worth exploring the possibility that the two companies collaborated to a previously unrecognised extent in order to re-establish the basic platform for theatrical competition. Economists have a singularly unattractive neologism for this phenomenon: 'coopetition'. It applies to instances where competing companies in the same marketplace work together for the common good before distinguishing their offerings and competing for patronage. In what follows, I consider not only the repertorial logic of the two companies choosing these specific plays to perform on the same stage in June 1594, but also the extent to which these plays appear to have been selected strategically to make efficient use of significant stage properties available to both companies at this venue.

---

[7] See Steggle, *Digital Humanities*, 75–76.

[8] Henslowe had recently recorded performances of 'the Queenes men & my lord of Susexe to geather' the previous month (this list of plays also looks like alternation rather than joint production), and decades later Thomas Heywood noted in his address to the reader prefacing *The Iron Age, Part 1* (1632) that 'these were the Playes often (and not with the least applause,) Publickely Acted by two Companies, vppon one Stage at once'; see T. Heywood, *The Iron Age* (London: Nicholas Okes, 1632), sig.A4ᵛ. Laurie Johnson is atypical amongst recent scholars for suggesting that at least some of the Newington plays were performed by a combination of players from the two companies; see Johnson, *Shakespeare's Lost Playhouse*, esp. 145–146.

[9] Johnson, *Shakespeare's Lost Playhouse*, 140; see also W. Ingram, *The Business of Playing: The Beginnings of the Adult Professional Theater in Elizabethan London* (Ithaca: Cornell University Press, 1992), 234 on 'the plague of 1593/94' as 'a major watershed in the history of the playing companies, and a near disaster for playhouse owners'.

My point of entry into understanding the complexities of the repertorial offerings at Newington is the first play that Henslowe names for that venue: the lost 'Hester and Ahasuerus'. Because it belonged to the Chamberlain's Men, 'Hester and Ahasuerus' has received critical attention earlier than the many hundreds of other lost plays that are not associated with Shakespeare's company. Unfortunately, though, this was well before the recent advances in the study of lost plays. Despite Matthew Steggle's positivity about the fact that 'eponymous play-titles give a grip on the play's likely contents', this particular lost play has ironically fallen victim to that very phenomenon rather than benefitting from it, and the assumptions that were made by early critics have passed down from generation to generation largely without interrogation. According to Robert B. Sharpe (in an influential early twentieth-century study), 'Hester and Ahasuerus' is most notable for being the Chamberlain's only known biblical play.[10] It is therefore of interest to Sharpe in terms of ostensibly distinguishing the Admiral's subsequently high level of biblical plays from the Chamberlain's apparent avoidance of the subject matter. Both Gurr and Knutson have objected to Sharpe's inference.[11] Knutson has attended instead to the repertorial implications of scheduling 'Hester' in conjunction with Marlowe's *Jew of Malta* as instances of stage attitudes towards Jewishness.[12] More recently, Laurie Johnson uses the anonymous *Godly Queen Hester* play of 1561 to reconstruct the plot of the Newington 'Hester' play, and explores what he sees as the political topicality of such a play in 1594, rather than attending to its repertorial topicality.[13]

Because its subject matter is superficially 'knowable' without the need for a more probing investigation, an alternative source of information about the 'Hester and Ahasuerus' play, long-known to German scholars, has remained underutilised by Anglophone scholars. During Shakespeare's

---

[10] M. Steggle, *Digital Humanities and the Lost Drama of Early Modern England: Ten Case Studies* (Farnham: Ashgate, 2015), 6; R. B. Sharpe, *The Real War of the Theaters* (Boston: D. C. Heath, 1935), 28–29.

[11] A. Gurr, *The Shakespeare Company, 1594–1642* (Cambridge: Cambridge University Press, 2004), 130–131; Knutson rebuts Sharpe's suggestion on the grounds that so many plays have been lost from the company's repertory that it is imprudent to claim uniqueness of biblical subject matter (Knutson, *Repertory*, 66).

[12] See R. L. Knutson, 'New Directions: *The Jew of Malta* in Repertory' in R. A. Logan (ed.), *The Jew of Malta: A Critical Reader* (London: Bloomsbury, Arden Early Modern Drama Guides, 2013), 79–105, esp. 97–98: 'Side by side at Newington, and thereafter from the Rose in Southwark to the Theatre in Shoreditch, the continuing performances of "Hester and Ahasuerus" and *The Jew of Malta* dramatized a pernicious contradiction in Elizabethan attitudes towards biblical and contemporary Jews'.

[13] Johnson, *Shakespeare's Lost Playhouse*, 140.

lifetime, his plays and those of his contemporaries were translated into German and performed on the Continent by travelling English players, including the troupe led by Robert Browne and then John Green (the former having been Edward Alleyn's colleague in the early 1580s in the company of Worcester's Men), and another led by Thomas Sackville. These included plays by Marlowe, Shakespeare, Heywood, Dekker, Beaumont and Fletcher, Markham and Massinger.[14] Many of these German plays have been lost entirely and some exist in unique manuscript versions, but others were printed and even reprinted. Occasionally, a play written for the English commercial theatres survives, remarkably, only in German, thanks to this phenomenon. The German *Comœdia von der Königin Esther und Hoffertigen Haman* (*Comedy of the Queen Esther and the Haughty Haman*) is one such play; it seems to be a redaction of the 'Hester and Ahasuerus' play that was performed at Newington Butts in 1594. It was performed in Strasbourg on 7 August 1597 by Thomas Sackville's players and printed in *Engelische Comedien und Tragedien*, an octavo volume published in 1620 (and reprinted in 1624), probably at Leipzig, and probably edited by Friedrich Menius (1593–1659).[15] Martin Wiggins outlines the book's significance succinctly:

> [I]n the 1620 Leipzig volume, we have a small collection of English plays which paradoxically both survive and remain lost: their qualities as dramatic works, orchestrations of narrative and character, incident and staging, are still amply available, but not a word of their original spoken text. Somebody should set about translating them back into English.[16]

Here I am interested specifically in what a working knowledge of the German *Esther und Haman* play can tell us about the relationship of its

---

[14] See P. Drábek and M. A. Katritzky, 'Shakespearean Players in Early Modern Europe' in B. R. Smith (ed.), *The Cambridge Guide to the Worlds of Shakespeare* (Cambridge: Cambridge University Press, 2016), 2.1527–1533; S. Williams, 'Seventeenth-century beginnings: the English Comedians' in *Shakespeare on the German Stage, Volume 1: 1586–1914* (Cambridge: Cambridge University Press, 1990), 27–45; J. Schlueter, 'New Light on Dekker's *Fortunati*', *Medieval and Renaissance Drama in England* 67 (2013), 120–135; J. Schlueter, 'English Actors in Kassel, Germany, During Shakespeare's Time', *Medieval and Renaissance Drama in England* 10 (1998), 238–261; W. Schrickx, *Foreign Envoys and Travelling Players in the Age of Shakespeare and Jonson* (Wetteren: Universa, 1986); A. Cohn, *Shakespeare in Germany in the Sixteenth and Seventeenth Centuries* (London, 1865). Most recently, Lukas Erne has led a project at the University of Geneva (with Florence Hazrat, Kareen Seidler, and Maria Shmygol) which will make available new translations of four German Shakespeare plays: www.unige.ch/emgs. This project is supported by the Swiss National Science Foundation and will be published in two volumes by Arden Shakespeare.

[15] For the record of the 1597 performance see Schrickx, *Foreign Envoys and Travelling Players*, 197 and 330.

[16] Wiggins, 'Where to Find Lost Plays' in McInnis and Steggle (eds.), *Lost Plays in Shakespeare's England*, 265.

lost English predecessor to the rest of the plays in the Newington Butts performances.

'Hester and Ahasuerus' was not marked as 'ne' by Henslowe in 1594. Moreover, Wiggins argues that for a version of it to have been transmitted to the Continent and performed by 1597, it must antedate Robert Browne's departure from England in 1592.[17] Amongst English-speaking scholars, it was W. W. Greg who first suggested that 'Hester and Ahasuerus' might be a 'hypothetical lost original' of the German play, but his failure to explain his conjecture beyond footnoting the work (in German) of E. Herz meant that the identification has not received serious attention until recently.[18] In fact, Greg was relying on Herz's summary of the findings of the German play's nineteenth-century editor, Julius Tittman, who noted that although the play's dialect originated in lower Saxony, there is good cause to believe that the German is in fact a translation from an English original (Wiggins highlights a typical example from Tittman: a joke, made by the German clown, 'which turns upon the fact that the words "King" and "Queen" sound completely different; it falls quite flat when he says it in German with the words *koenig* and *koenigin*').[19]

Examination of *Esther und Haman* reveals a number of curious connections to the Newington Butts repertory. In the German play, the Persian King Ahasuerus's first queen (Vashti) refuses to be a literal trophy wife, showed off alongside Ahasuerus's wealth and other possessions; his favourite counsellor, Haman, suggests a royal decree requiring wifely obedience. (This is complemented by a comic plot in which a hen-pecked clown character has little luck taming his unruly wife). Ahasuerus issues the decree, banishes Vashti, and seeks a new wife. From a parade of eligible virgins, he finds a new wife in Esther. (The clown, empowered by the decree, sets about asserting his dominance over his wife, forcing her to accept ridiculous statements as the truth and beating her if she refuses.) Esther has a kinsman, Mardocheus, who serves as a counsellor to Ahasuerus; Mardocheus proves instrumental in thwarting an assassination

---

[17] Wiggins #801.
[18] W. W. Greg (ed.), *Henslowe's Diary, Part II. Commentary* (London: A. H. Bullen, 1908), 2.164, citing E. Herz in *Englische Schauspieler und englische Schauspiel zur Zeit Shakespeares in Deutschland* (Hamburg, 1903), 111. Wiggins (#801) takes seriously the possibility that the German play is an adaptation of the lost English original.
[19] J. Tittmann, *Die Schauspiele der Englischen Komödianten in Deutschland* (Leipzig: F.A. Brockhaus, 1880), esp. xxii–xxiii; Wiggins, 'Where to Find Lost Plays' in McInnis and Steggle (eds.), *Lost Plays in Shakespeare's England*, 265.

attempt by the king's chamberlains, Bightan and Theres, but is not rewarded for the life-saving intelligence he provides. Haman holds a grudge against Mardocheus; upon discovering Mardocheus's faith, he orders the massacre of all Jews, primarily in order to dispatch Mardocheus specifically. Haman's edict is to be effected without opportunity for appeal, even by Esther. The queen nevertheless finds an ingenious way to gain her husband's ear: she flatters Haman by inviting him to dine with her and the king. Honoured by the invitation, Haman plans to attend the banquet – but first arranges for a gallows to be constructed in his garden and Mardocheus to be hanged there. Over dinner, when Ahasuerus finally decides to honour Mardocheus for preventing the assassination attempt, Esther successfully petitions her husband to overturn the order to massacre the Jews (Esther is not known to be affected by the edict until she acknowledges her Jewish identity and pleads the case for the Jews). Ahasuerus consequently orders the hanging of the man responsible for the original order: Haman. The gallows Haman arranged for Mardocheus is instead used to hang Haman (whom the king knew to be secretly planning to betray the kingdom to the Macedonians). Haman duly recognises the ironic turn of events with his last breath: '*Wie sükt ist das leben, wie bitter ist der Tod!*' ('How sweet is life, how bitter is death!').[20]

Because the first recorded performance of the 'Hester' play is followed by an entry for Marlowe's *Jew of Malta*, scholars have focused exclusively on how the depiction of Jews in the lost play may have complemented other Jewish portrayals in the repertory.[21] Such repertorial topicality might shed light on the performance of 3 June; however, 'Hester' received a second performance, on 10 June,[22] this time followed by a performance of what Henslowe calls 'the tamynge of A shrowe' (which I take on face-value to be *The Taming of A Shrew*, published in 1594).[23] Though its title alone

---

[20] Tittman, *Comoedia Von der Königin Esther und hoffärtigen Haman* in *Die Schauspiele der Englischen Komödianten in Deutschland*, 40.

[21] Knutson observes that 'the presence of "Hester and Ahasuerus" in Henslowe's playlist for Newington suggests that a deeper and more complex cultural interplay was being exploited on London stages than the attitudes towards Jews invited by Marlowe's play'. See Knutson, 'New Directions', 97, responding to the observations made by S. Greenblatt in *Will in the World: How Shakespeare Became Shakespeare* (New York: Norton, 2004), 273–274.

[22] Though this second recorded performance of 'Hester' drew only 5s, that was more than *The Jew of Malta* on its second performance at Newington(4s), and we know that Marlowe's play went on to another nine performances at the Rose that same year alone. There is, in other words, no reason to believe the 'Hester' play should have been retired, or unprofitable to the company.

[23] Wiggins' case for thinking Henslowe meant *The Shrew* is uncharacteristically weak; he casts doubt on *A Shrew*'s title-page ascription to Pembroke's, whom he says 'no longer existed' in early 1594 (See Wiggins #916 and 955). But Holger Syme has argued instead that stationers 'seem to have

would not encourage such an identification, the subject matter of 'Hester' (judging from the German redaction) is a kind of shrew-taming play as much as a biblical play,[24] and playgoers at Newington would see obvious parallels between 'Hester' and *A Shrew*: both in the main plot, when King Ahasuerus summons his first wife but is defied by her (leading to the edict of wifely submission), and subsequently in the comic plot, where the clown struggles then succeeds in taming his own wife.

Moreover, a passage in the 'Hester' play conceivably forms the source for the exchange between Ferando/Kate in *A Shrew* (and Petruccio/Katherine in Shakespeare's play), in which the domineering suitor forces the shrewish character to concede that his patently absurd assertions have merit. In *Esther und Haman*, Hans (the clown) asks Frau (i.e. his wife) why the milk is so black ('*Aber, Frau, warumb ist die Milch so schwarz?*'); when she contradicts him – it is obviously white – he hits her ('*schlägt sie*') and reasserts his original, ludicrous observation ('*Ich sage, die Milch ist schwarz*'). An exasperated neighbour intervenes in aid of the wife, asserting that the milk is in fact white, prompting Hans to swear and explain that it is his will that the white milk be called black ('*ich wil es jetzo haben, daß die Milch sol schwarz seyn*'). The neighbour advises the wife to avoid further beatings by agreeing that the milk is black, which she subsequently does when Hans quizzes her again about the milk's colour.[25] In *A Shrew*, Ferando tells Kate that 'the Moone shines cleere to night methinkes' but she thinks he is 'deceiud' and that it is 'the sun', until he threatens 'it shall be / The moone ere we come at your fathers'.[26]

A key element of the 'Hester' play's plot is not legible in its title: the hanging of the treacherous Haman on stage. This execution would require a substantial stage property (described as fifteen cubits high; '*sünszig Ellen hoch*') and would constitute a memorable spectacle for playgoers.[27] (The

---

cared' about 'getting the initial claim to theatrical currency right' and suggested that 'we ought to feel more confident – and more obliged – to take first-edition title-pages at their word' ('Three's Company', 274; see also 283ff).

[24] The *LPD* entry for 'Hester and Ahasuerus' includes a helpful summary of the extant *Godly Queen Hester* play (registered for publication in 1561) which Sharpe was thinking of when he described the repertories of the Chamberlain's Men and Admiral's Men.

[25] Tittman, *Comoedia Von der Königin Esther und hoffärtigen Haman* in *Die Schauspiele der Englischen Komödianten in Deutschland*, 20–21.

[26] S. R. Miller (ed.), *The Taming of A Shrew, 1594. Malone Society Reprints 160* (Oxford: Malone Society, 1998), TLN 1225–1238, esp. 1223–1228 (sig.E4ᵛ in the quarto). The moon-sun parallel in *The Shrew* (where Hortensio takes the neighbour's role) is well known. See Shakespeare's *The Shrew*, scene 14, and Wiggins, 'Where to Find Lost Plays' in McInnis and Steggle (eds.), *Lost Plays in Shakespeare's England*, 265.

[27] Tittman, *Comoedia Von der Königin Esther und hoffärtigen Haman* in *Die Schauspiele der Englischen Komödianten in Deutschland*, 39.

German stage direction calls for Haman's body to hang, be cut down and carried offstage: '*Stürzet ihn herunter, ichneidet hernach ab, trägt ihn hinein*'.)[28] Here there is a clear, if unexpected connection to another Newington play. Despite the highly unusual circumstances of the two companies coming together at a venue neither is known to have otherwise used, the Admiral's (we assume) took the opportunity on 8 June to premiere their play about 'Belin Dun' – not a 'clown' as Gurr assumes, but rather one whom Matthew Steggle more accurately describes as 'an evil twin' of Robin Hood.[29] Steggle has provided the fullest survey of historical accounts of the legendary thief and highwayman who allegedly lived during the time of Henry I:

> In a typical episode, Dun and his men stay at an inn, kill the landlord, rape the landlord's wife, and then, when she refuses to tell them where the money is hidden … kill her as well.[30]

Dun hangs the sheriff's men when they attempt to arrest him, disguises himself and his men in their clothes to commit further robberies, and is for a great time 'seemingly untouchable by the law' until he is finally captured and is himself hanged.[31] Indeed, Stationers' Register entries for a chap-book and perhaps the play itself (or a prose narrative) both reveal that an indispensable feature of the Belin Dun legend was that he was allegedly '*the first thief that ever was hanged in England*'.[32] The sources and analogues that Steggle surveys are at pains to document Dun's execution, which in one account featured two hangman as well as a grisly dismemberment.[33] It is hard to imagine that a stage version of the Belin Dun legend would not dramatise the notorious culmination of Belin Dun's criminal activities. If it did, the gallows that hanged Haman in 'Hester' would have played a role in the new 'Belin Dun' five days later.

---

[28] Tittman, *Comoedia Von der Königin Esther und hoffärtigen Haman* in *Die Schauspiele der Englischen Komödianten in Deutschland*, 40.

[29] Gurr, *Shakespeare's Opposites*, 50; Steggle, *Digital Humanities*, 77. Although the significant investment in a 'ne' play yielded only 17s (modest by Rose takings; reasonable by the Newington standards exhibited in this short run of performances), the play was evidently a success inasmuch as there were sixteen subsequent performances at the Rose throughout 1594 (between 15 June and 15 November), one more in 1596 (11 July), and seven more in 1597 between 31 March and 25 June.

[30] See Chapter 4 in Steggle, *Digital Humanities*, 77–88. The quotation is from p. 81.

[31] Steggle, *Digital Humanities*, 81.

[32] Arber (ed.), *Stationers' Register*, 1.650, 3.54. On the 'Belin Dun' play see Steggle, *Digital Humanities*, 77–88.

[33] Steggle, *Digital Humanities*, 81–82.

Haman's death in the 'Hester' play might be profitably compared not just to Belin Dun's hanging, but – through poetic irony – to the fate of Barabas in *The Jew of Malta*, inasmuch as the fate intended for the Jew (Mardocheus) ultimately befalls Haman, just as in Marlowe's play the fate intended for the Turkish Selim Calymath instead falls to the Jew Barabas, thanks to the duplicity of the Christian governor of Malta (Ferneze). Haman's deception, undertaken with a view to self-advancement, is pivotal. Deceit/deception is thematically of interest to 'Hester' and *Jew of Malta*, more so perhaps than the more superficial investment in disguise which, Gurr argues, characterises the Admiral's repertory.[34] Deception is a trait common to *Titus Andronicus* too (if that's what is meant by Henslowe's 'andronicous' on 5 June), a play in which (amongst other things) Aaron the Moor tricks Titus into cutting off his own hand, and Titus tricks Tamora into eating her own sons.

The final banquet scene in *Titus* may also be noteworthy for its presumed use of a different but still substantial property: a large table. Shakespeare's text has no explicit stage directions to this effect, but Marcus urges the guests to take their 'places' and Titus is *'placing the dishes'* somewhere when he enters (12.24 and 25SD). The Leipzig volume containing *Esther und Haman* contains a redaction of *Titus* in which the banquet table is explicitly mentioned, and Titus is directed to walk up and down before the table.[35] This was not a small table in either version of *Titus*: the emperor and empress, tribunes and others, are all afforded a space. This significant stage property would also presumably have been used for the crucial scene in which Hester invited Haman to dine with her and Ahasuerus; a scene in which not only did she persuade the king to revoke the edict against Jews but in which the traitorous Haman's own fate was sealed. As with the final scene of *Titus*, the banquet would have been a decisive turning point in the play. The banquet table also serves as an important visual signifier of changes of fortune when it is used twice in *A Shrew*. In the play's second scene, two servants enter 'with a table and a banquet on it' whilst the sleeping drunkard, Sly, is brought on stage 'richlie apparelled' in preparation for the trick to be played on him.[36] Later, in the shrew-taming 'play' performed for his benefit, the table features again in the rescinded offer of a banquet: Ferando enters with Kate and complains

[34] Gurr, *Shakespeare's Opposites*, 2.

[35] See the stage directions in Ernest Brennecke's translation, 'A Very Lamentable Tragedy of Titus Andronicus and the Haughty Empress, Act VIII' [sic], lines 36–37 and 71–72 in *Shakespeare in Germany, 1590–1700* (Chicago: University of Chicago Press, 1964).

[36] Miller (ed.), *The Taming of A Shrew, 1594*, TLN 103-5SD.

that supper has not yet been prepared, beating the servants until *'They couer the bord and fetch in the meate'*; the starving Kate is deprived of the would-be feast, however, for Ferando subsequently 'throwes downe the table and meate and all, and beates them'.[37] The banquet table is thus fundamental to the world of the play's attempts to domesticate and control Kate.

The large banqueting table that focalised attention in important scenes of 'Hester', *Shrew* and *Titus*, like the gallows that seems to have been used on stage for 'Hester' and 'Belin Dun', points to the two companies' sharing of significant stage properties and perhaps even the deliberate construction of repertorial offerings based on the possibility of sharing such props.[38] Attending to the German *Esther und Haman* helps us see that 'Hester and Ahasuerus' appears to have had meaningful connections to a number of the Newington plays in both thematic and pragmatic ways. My identification of these connections and retracing the contours of the lost play gives a new shape to the repertory in the manner of the interplay between 'figure' and 'ground' in Rubin's Vase. Interestingly, Pind observes that 'it is possible that when a shape, which is experienced as figure, recedes and becomes ground, it may yet keep something of the characteristics of the figure. In fact, it may even happen that both areas of the stimulus are simultaneously experienced as figure'.[39] This strikes me as particularly pertinent to the mutually shaping influence of competing companies' repertories, most evident in the eleven-day run when Henslowe's diary provides a unique picture of what the Admiral's Men were offering alongside what the Chamberlain's Men were offering. In this instance, as my foregoing analysis suggests, rather than the figure and ground contrasting with each other to produce two alternative images, they seem to converge: the lost plays help us perceive a coherence in the companies' repertories that is less apparent when we

---

[37] Miller (ed.), *The Taming of A Shrew, 1594*, TLN 870-71SD and TLN 874-75SD; cf. scene 9 of Shakespeare's *The Shrew*, where Petruccio objects to the allegedly burnt meat and proceeds to starve Katherine.

[38] It is perhaps *just* worth mentioning that the only property that Henslowe lists in reference to 'Belin Dun' (in a March 1598 or 1599 inventory) is 'Belendon stable'. Although Steggle convincingly argued that it was an underground stable, much like the various tombs listed elsewhere in Henslowe's inventory, not a scenic representation of the town of Dunstable, as I had suggested previously, he – like all scholars – is relying on Malone's transcription of the lost Henslowe inventory list, not the original itself. Might Henslowe have actually meant 'Belendon's table'? See Foakes (ed.), *Henslowe's Diary*, 320; Steggle, *Digital Humanities*, 83–87; and D. McInnis, *Mind-Travelling and Voyage Drama in Early Modern England* (Basingstoke: Palgrave Macmillan, 2013), 155–156.

[39] Pind, *Edgar Rubin*, 96.

focus exclusively on the 'figure'. 'Hester and Ahasuerus' was more than simply a biblical play offering an alternative perspective on stage Jews to Marlowe's *Jew of Malta* (though it certainly did that too); it was a shrew-taming play, a play that thematised deception and duplicity, and a play that culminated in the spectacle of a public execution by hanging. This latter feature may even have played a role in the Admiral's Men's decision to debut their play about the first thief hanged in England, 'Belin Dun'. If each company's choice of offerings was governed in some way by an awareness of the other's repertory and staging possibilities, the analysis I have offered here may even prompt reconsideration of whether the repertorial competition at this venue was pre-planned or just highly responsive.

Moving to the Curtain: 1597–1598

The Chamberlain's brief appearance at Newington in 1594 is rightly recognised as a significant moment in the company's history, but it is their move to the Globe five years later that captures the imagination of most Shakespeare scholars. Accounts of the London theatre industry in the 1590s have understandably focused on the grossly embellished (but nevertheless entertaining) anecdote of the Lord Chamberlain's Men dismantling their former venue, the Theatre, transporting it across the (frozen, in some accounts) Thames, and using the materials to construct their new Globe theatre with improbable haste sometime around 28 December 1598.[40] In this narrative, the owner of the land on which the Theatre was originally built, Giles Allen, is the antagonist pitted against Richard Burbage, his brother Cuthbert Burbage, and several others as the heroes who – despite Allen's lawsuit against them – succeeded in appropriating the physical structure of the Theatre and establishing the company's flagship venue. But the Lord Chamberlain's Men occupied a third venue, the Curtain, for a time between vacating the Theatre and rebuilding it as the Globe, and it is the company's period at the Curtain that I wish to reconsider here.

Although the lease on the Theatre expired on 25 March 1597, allusions to the Chamberlain's occupying the Curtain do not commence until the

[40] According to popular tradition, it popped up overnight: see, e.g. J. Shapiro, *1599: A Year in the Life of William Shakespeare* (New York: Harper Collins, 2005); in reality it probably took closer to six months to assemble: see Alan H. Nelson's entry for the 'Allen v. Burbage' lawsuit of 1602 (NA STAC 5/A12/35) in *Shakespeare Documented* (available online at https://shakespearedocumented .folger.edu/exhibition/document/allen-v-burbage).

autumn of 1598, when Everard Guilpin referred to theatrical activity at the Curtain but characterised the Theatre as 'unfrequented'.[41] Traditional accounts of this series of events has characterised the company's period at the Curtain as a necessary evil; a pragmatic move. Gurr, for example, believes that '[t]he company struggled for the next two years, renting other play-houses while the Theatre stood empty'; painting a picture of the company characterised by 'desperation' during which 'cash-straitened years they sold *Romeo and Juliet*, *Richard II*, *Richard III*, *Loves Labours Lost* and *I Henry IV*, he regards the company's choice of a 'cheap thatch to top off the new Globe' (unlike the tiles used for the new Fortune theatre) as evidence that the company was struggling financially, their new theatre 'a distinctly cut-price job'.[42] (There is no evidence to suggest that playing companies sold their plays to stationers to raise quick cash.) More conservatively, Knutson has this to say of the company's acquisition of their first play by Jonson:

> The Chamberlain's men acquired *Every Man in His Humor* at a problematic time for them commercially. They had been closed out of the Theatre by the expiration of the Burbages' ground-lease, and (we assume) they had moved into the equally old but less commodious Curtain.[43]

Although the company's move to the Curtain was necessitated by their unanticipated eviction from the Theatre, and although long-term residency at the Curtain never seems to have been part of an intentional commercial strategy,[44] the move to this venue need not be viewed as a step backwards (or even sideways). The precise site of the original Curtain in Shoreditch was located in 2011, and excavation by Museum of London

---

[41] See G. Wickham, H. Berry and W. Ingram (eds.), *English Professional Theatre, 1530–1660* (Cambridge: Cambridge University Press, 2000), 375 (item 299) and 411 (item 328). Guilpin's *Skialetheia* (in which he makes these remarks; see sigs. D6 and B8ᵛ) was registered for publication on 15 September 1598.

[42] A. Gurr, *The Shakespearean Stage, 1574–1642*, 3rd ed (Cambridge: Cambridge University Press, 1994), 45; A. Gurr, *The Shakespearian Playing Companies* (Oxford: Oxford University Press, 1996), 284, 294. Stephen Greenblatt repeats these sentiments in *Will in the World: How Shakespeare Became Shakespeare* (New York: W. W. Norton & Co., 2004), 291.

[43] Knutson, *The Repertory*, 77–78.

[44] NB. The 'curious' financial arrangement entered into by James Burbage and John Brayne for seven years commencing Michaelmas, 1585, remains a 'puzzle'. The men approached Henry Laneman, the proprietor of the Curtain, with a profit-sharing proposition regarding their two theatres; they took the Curtain as an 'Esore' ('easer'? i.e. 'easement'; a form of contract of use for convenience) and decided to share the profits of it and the neighbouring Theatre. See Wickham, Berry and Ingram (eds.), *English Professional Theatre, 1530–1660*, 348 (item 276); see also Ingram, *The Business of Playing*, 227–236, esp. 231. Ingram assumes that Burbage sold shares in the Curtain around 1595/6 (*Business of Playing*, 235). Could the Chamberlain's Men have played at the Curtain even when the Theatre was available to them? The profit-sharing arrangements continued until at least 1592, possibly longer.

Archaeology (MOLA) began in 2016. Preliminary results indicated that 'the playhouse appears to be a rectangular building, measuring approximately 22 m × 30 m, rather than being polygonal', as previously assumed (this has subsequently been qualified to 22 m × at least 26 m (because the full width of the building fronting Curtain Road – possibly Curtain House – that the rest of the structure was built onto is not known).[45] It appears not, therefore, to have been comparable in shape to the Globe, the Rose, the Swan, the Theatre, and the Hope. Rather, it anticipated the much later Boar's Head and Fortune playhouses, and resembled the rectangular courtyards of inns, where much earlier (and indeed, much contemporary) drama had been staged.[46] So although probably still an unplanned move, the Chamberlain's Men's transfer to the Curtain was potentially a more positive one than has previously been allowed, in that it appears to have provided the company with a significantly larger stage and venue – a stage that was approximately 14 m long and 5 m wide,[47] and thus possibly about twice as large as its neighbour and the company's former home, the Theatre.[48] Such dimensions would be conducive to the Curtain's frequent hosting of fencing competitions, as on 25 August 1579, for example, when 'Richard Fletcher played his scholar's prize at the Curtain in Holywell ... at two weapons, the long sword and the sword and buckler'.[49] Such a space might accordingly have provided new opportunities for dramaturgy.

Moreover, the period during which the Chamberlain's occupied the Curtain might be re-read as a period of significance for the inter-company competition on par with the unique circumstances of the Newington Butts run of 1594 or the 1599–1600 period during which the Admiral's

---

[45] Heather Knight, Senior Archaeologist (MOLA), personal correspondence, 11 June 2019.

[46] Museum of London Archaeology blog, 'Initial findings from excavation at Shakespeare's Curtain Theatre revealed', 17 May 2016 (available online at www.mola.org.uk/blog/initial-findings-excavation-shakespeare%E2%80%99s-curtain-theatre-revealed).

[47] Heather Knight, Senior Archaeologist (MOLA), personal correspondence, 31 March 2018.

[48] Holger Syme estimated the Curtain's overall dimensions (not just the stage) as c.323 m², cf. 163 m² for The Theatre, 148–205 m² for the Rose and its expanded version, and 259 m² for the Globe. In a comment added to his blog post on 25 May 2016, Syme explained the basis of his calculations: 'The dimensions were reported on the MOLA blog (linked in the post). My area calculation assumes a standard gallery depth of 3.8 metres (as reported present at the Curtain after the initial dig). For all other theatres listed, the area calculations use the dimensions of those theatres as established in digs since the 1980s (for the Theatre, the Rose, the Globe, and the Hope). For the Boar's Head and the Fortune, I used documentary evidence as reproduced in Glynne Wickham, Herbert Berry, and William Ingram, eds. *English Professional Theatre, 1530–1660.* (Cambridge: Cambridge University Press, 2000)'. See H. S. Syme, 'Post-Curtain Theatre History', *dispositio*, 18 May 2016 (available online at www.dispositio.net/archives/2262).

[49] Wickham, Berry, and Ingram (eds.), *English Professional Theatre, 1530–1660*, 409 (item 323a).

occupied the Rose and the Chamberlain's established their adjacent Globe theatre across Maid Lane. Syme, diverging from the dominant theatre history paradigm that privileges the Globe as the culmination of playhouse-design improvements, has suggested that:

> [W]ith the appearance of a rectangular Curtain, we can now sketch out the influence of a competing paradigm, which produced just as many independent structures, and only one fewer than the round paradigm even if we count the Globe as an entirely separate building: the Curtain, in that view, spawned the Boar's Head, the Fortune, and the Red Bull.[50]

Guilpin's allusions to the Curtain were made by September 1598; on 8 January 1599/1600, Henslowe and Alleyn entered into a contract with the builder Peter Street to erect the square Fortune playhouse.[51] Even as the Chamberlain's were anticipating their move to the Globe, the Admiral's were anticipating a move to a new playhouse whose design seems to have been inspired by the Curtain. The Curtain may have been a substitute for the Chamberlain's Men, but something about its shape and size was evidently worth emulating. If frustration over the inability to renew the lease of the Theatre was a low-point in the company history of the Chamberlain's Men, things may have taken a turn for the better not just with the opening of their new Globe theatre around 16 May 1599, but with their temporary residence at the generously proportioned Curtain by September 1598.

Repertory studies and attention to lost plays can add a degree of nuance to our understanding of how Shakespeare's company operated whilst at the Curtain, from around September 1598 until May of 1599. Establishing a corpus of plays (from the Chamberlain's and other companies' repertories) for consideration is a vital first step. These fall into two categories: plays that appear to originate from the Curtain period,[52] and plays probably revived during this period. Some context can be provided through examination of the Admiral's better-documented repertory. Henslowe's surviving financial records at this time consist of his payments to playwrights and production expenses rather than his daily reckonings of plays in performance. The Admiral's acquired new plays to complement and extend their repertory at an increased rate throughout this period – some thirty-seven plays in 1598 alone, compared with the acquisition of a new play every two

---

[50] Syme, 'Post-Curtain Theatre History'.   [51] Foakes (ed.), *Henslowe's Diary*, 306–310.
[52] For convenience, consistency, and transparency, I use Wiggins' chronology, limiting this category to plays in the range of #1139 ('Hot Anger Soon Cold', summer-autumn 1598) to #1193 ('Cloth Breeches and Velvet Hose', 1599).

or three weeks in the immediately preceding years, 1594–1597.[53] In 1599–1600, the Admiral's acquired new plays in anticipation of their imminent move to the Fortune and the need to defray costs after the move: new plays cost more than revivals, both in terms of the payments to playwrights and the associated production expenses (including not just the acquisition of costumes and props, but the investment in actors preparing for performance of an entirely new play).[54] In 1598–1599 though, such high levels of acquisition may indicate the beginning of a long-term strategy to regain a foothold in the market (a strategy that culminated in the move to the Fortune), or it may reflect the relative stability enjoyed by the company, who had occupied the same venue (the Rose) for an extended period of time. A significant proportion of their repertory at this time had a historical focus: classical plays ('Catiline's Conspiracy'; 'Troilus and Cressida'; 'Agamemnon'), British mythological history ('Mulmutius Dunwallow'; 'The Conquest of Brute'; 'Conan, Prince of Cornwall'), and contemporary French histories ('1, 2 & 3 The Civil Wars of France'; 'The First Introduction of the Civil Wars of France') dominate, but there are also the occasional English histories ('The Spencers'; perhaps 'Pierce of Winchester').

Some of the histories were also tragic. A preoccupation with dynastic continuation, attempts to unify a kingdom, or the consequences of civil war dividing a kingdom are evident in a number of these. In available accounts of the 'Conan' story, King Octavius fails in his attempt to manage succession by marrying off his daughter; this ultimately leads to Conan becoming king of 'Little Britain' in Gaul.[55] In 'The Conquest of Brute' legend, after wars in France, Brutus landed at Totnes (a location that perhaps reinforces a repertorial link to the comic 'Tinker of Totnes' play of 1596?) and founded Britain, defeating giants including Gog and Magog in the process (on giants, see the discussion of 'the taner of denmarke' in the next chapter). To these can be added examples of the usual proverbially titled comedies ("Tis No Deceit to Deceive the Deceiver'; 'All Fools but the Fool'; 'Bear a Brain') and comedies of humours or city comedies ('Hot Anger Soon Cold', 'The Fountain of New Fashions'; 'The Two Merry Women of Abingdon' as a spin-off sequel to *The Two Angry Women of Abingdon* and '2 The Two Angry Women of Abingdon'). Subject matter need not necessarily dictate genre, of course:

[53] See Wiggins' discussion under #1099.   [54] See Knutson, *The Repertory*, 80.
[55] Wiggins #1157; see Holinshed, *The First and Second Volumes of Chronicles* (1587), bk 4, 65–67 (or the entry in the *LPD*).

the twelfth- and thirteenth-century crusades formed the backdrop for English history plays ('William Longsword') and for comedy (*Look About You*) in the company's repertory.

Given their uncertainty about venues it is possible that the Chamberlain's acquired new plays at a more conservative rate than the company at the Rose. Like the Admiral's, the Chamberlain's seemingly refrained from investment in new tragedies. Allusions to *Romeo and Juliet* in 1598 and the republication of *Titus Andronicus* with the company's name on the title-page in 1600 suggest they plausibly had these tragedies, and maybe others, in their repertory still. Another tragedy with a strong claim to being in the Chamberlain's repertory during their time at the Curtain is a domestic tragedy: *A Warning for Fair Women*. Like *Romeo* and *Titus*, *A Warning for Fair Women* may have been produced at the Curtain as an old play, rather than premiering there; Wiggins dates it to 1597.[56] Its printing in 1599, the same year as the republication of *Arden of Faversham*, suggests that the two may have competed repertorially, *Arden* in revival, its auspices uncertain. There is also an outside chance that, whilst still at the Curtain, the Chamberlain's may have staged *A Larum for London* (printed 1602), their dramatisation of the sack of Antwerp (1576) – perhaps in response to the Admiral's 'Civil Wars of France' quartet (Autumn 1598 – Spring 1599). As Wiggins notes, although it would have been imprudent to do so in 1598 when England and Spain were contemplating peace, it would have been distinctly more viable to perform this play around the summer of 1599 when it seemed that a Spanish invasion was imminent.[57] It might thus fit into the final months of the Curtain repertory and tie in with the vogue for contemporary continental history. There is no explicit documentary evidence, then, that the Chamberlain's acquired new tragedies whilst at the Curtain. Perhaps, though, as I suggest below, they focused their energy instead on adapting old tragedies to the new space.

The Chamberlain's responded to the Admiral's success with comedies of humours and disguises by strategically acquiring *Every Man in His Humour*: a play that trades in both these fashions, by a young but notorious playwright, Ben Jonson – co-author of the controversial 'Isle of Dogs' play (Pembroke's, 1597) that almost brought about a closure of all London theatres (Pembroke's, 1597) and recent contributor to the Admiral's own repertory ('Hot Anger Soon Cold', purchased by Henslowe on 18 August 1598). Jonson's comedy was possibly the first new play the Chamberlain's performed at the Curtain: a letter from Tobie

---

[56] Wiggins #1080.   [57] Wiggins #1191.

Mathew to Dudley Carleton dated 20 September 1598 helps date its performance run by relating that a German gentleman apparently 'lost 300 crowns at a new play called Every Man's humour'.[58] The company followed its investment in Jonson's humoral comedy with Shakespeare's apparently opportunistic response, *The Merry Wives of Windsor* (and subsequently, at the Globe, by Jonson's humorally and satirically – but not narratively – related play, *Every Man Out of His Humour*).

Around this time, Shakespeare appears also to have written the proverbially titled *Much Ado About Nothing*. This romantic love comedy, which plays on tropes of disguise and deception, might thus attract the kind of playgoer who also paid to see *The Two Angry Women of Abingdon* (and its two lost sequels) or *Look About You* at the Rose. It is unclear which company performed 'The Fair Maid of London', which was licensed for performance by Edmund Tilney on 24 May 1598 (but is known only through a record by Henry Herbert in 1662).[59] Wiggins's 'tentative hypothesis' that it was a Chamberlain's play is certainly possible, and the interest in a London setting would complement the London setting of *A Warning for Fair Women* in the company's repertory at the time.[60] If a parallel to the 'Fair Maid of London' play can be found in the ballad 'of the Princely wooing of the faire Maide of London by K. Edward', then the play's subject matter was probably not historical: the song does not clarify which Edward is meant, but he sings of having married and slept with two women prior to setting his eyes on the fair maid, and no historical King Edward of England fits this description.[61] If the maid in the play resembled the maid in the ballad in her attempts to deflect Edward's amorous advances, the play would complement *Much Ado*'s preoccupation with impediments to courtship. It would also speak to the final scenes of Shakespeare's *Henry V*, in which the English king tries his hand at courtship (see the following chapter for a discussion of the centrality of the Henry-Katherine relationship to that play). *Henry V* – perhaps without the Chorus, whose self-deprecating reference to the 'cock-pit' (Prol. 11)

[58] 'Sept. 20, London' in M. A. Everett (ed.), *Calendar of State Papers Domestic: Elizabeth, 1598–1601* (London, 1869), 97 via British History Online.

[59] N. W. Bawcutt (ed.), *The Control and Censorship of Caroline Drama: The Records of Sir Henry Herbert, Master of the Revels, 1623–73* (Oxford: Clarendon Press, 1996), items R29 and R33.

[60] Wiggins #1154.

[61] See the ballad in Richard Johnson, *The golden garland of princely pleasures and delicate delights* (1620), sig.D8v–E2v, where it is complemented by other songs that share subject matter with plays from the London commercial theatres, including 'A Princely song of King Richard Cordelion' (cf. Tilney's licencing of 'Richard Cordelyon' at the same time as 'The Fair Maid of London'); Wiggins #1154.

and 'wooden O' (Prol. 13) may not make sense in a rectangular Curtain – also appears to belong to the Curtain period. Dekker makes use of *Henry V* in scene 8 of *The Shoemaker's Holiday*, which was performed in the summer of 1599. However, *Henry V* was probably Shakespeare's last play to premiere at that venue: *Julius Caesar* is typically regarded as a Globe play, thanks in no small part to Swiss tourist Thomas Platter's account of seeing the play in performance in September 1599.[62]

James Roberts registered another proverbially titled play – a '*morall of Clothe breches and veluet hose*' – on 27 May 1600, two days before he registered another Chamberlain's play discussed above: *A Larum for London*.[63] Knutson suggests the company acquired 'Cloth Breeches and Velvet Hose' for the opening season at the Globe; Wiggins entertains the possibility that it had been staged at the Theatre or Curtain prior to any Globe productions and the mid-1600 registration for publication.[64] He does, however, follow Knutson in supposing that the subtitle of Robert Greene's *A Quip for an Upstart Courtier: or, A Quaint Dispute Between Velvet Breeches and Cloth-Breeches wherein is Plainely Set Downe the Disorders in All Estates and Trades* (1592) is at least a verbal source for the lost play's title. Greene's text consists of dream visions, including a final dream that enacts the interaction between Cloth and Velvet Breeches (two monstrous figures defined by their clothes and lacking their heads). These allegorical personae enter into a dispute and the dreaming narrator solicits a jury of passers-by to adjudicate (these jurors serve the additional function of forming the basis of an estates satire in the text: twenty-three types are listed, including a knight, grocer, printer, pewterer, rope-maker, sailor, shepherd and bellowsmaker, amongst others).[65] Knutson assumes the dramatist 'retained the dream structure of his source', citing *A Midsummer Night's Dream*, *The Old Wives Tale* and the *Shrew* plays as dramatic precedents, and further assumes that the dramatist 'characterized Cloth Breeches [a virtuous figure] and Velvet Breeches [a Vice figure] in

---

[62] It is technically possible that *Julius Caesar* was a continuation from the Curtain too.

[63] Arber (ed.), *Stationers' Register*, 3.161, 3.37. The registration of each was also noted on a flyleaf of Register C under the heading 'my lord chamberlens menns plaies Entred', but in that record, they appear to have been registered on the same day: 27 May. The first entry reads in full: '*morall of Clothe breches and veluet hose, As yt is Acted by my lord Chamberlens servants*. PROVIDED that he is not to putt it in prynte Without further & better Aucthority'.

[64] R. L. Knutson, 'Filling Fare: The Appetite for Current Issues and Traditional Forms in the Repertory of the Chamberlain's Men', *Medieval and Renaissance Drama in England* 15 (2003), 60; Wiggins #1193.

[65] Greene, *A Quip for an Upstart Courtier: or, A Quaint Dispute Between Velvet Breeches and Cloth-Breeches wherein is Plainely Set Downe the Disorders in All Estates and Trades* (1592), sig.F2ᵛ.

moral terms'.[66] The possibility that the play contained a dream structure and moral vision would also tie it stylistically to 'The Second Part of the Seven Deadly Sins' (discussed below).

This is very plausible, but I would add the possibility that another contrast may have driven the storyline: the subtitle of Greene's tract is 'Velvet *Breeches* and Cloth-Breeches' (my emphasis), but the more precise distinction between cloth breeches and velvet *hose* can be found elsewhere in a proverbial formulation delineating the differences between town and country. For example, Richard West's epigram on tobacco (published in 1608) sets up such a pastoral opposition:

> Things which are common, common men doe vse
> The better sort doe common things refuse,
> Yet Countries cloth breech, and Court veluet hose,
> Puffe both a like, Tobacco through their nose.[67]

Obviously there is insufficient material in a passing quip such as this to furnish an entire play with subject matter. But perhaps greater consideration should be given to the possibility that the lost play's satire points not to estates satire so much as to the kind of pastoral meditations espoused by Touchstone and Corin in *As You Like It* (3.2.11–68) – or in the lost 'God Speed the Plough' (Sussex's, 1593), if the surviving ballad is indicative of the play's subject matter.

'Love's Labour's Won', another pseudo-proverbially titled play, is probably the most tantalising of play titles associated with the period in which the Chamberlain's moved from the Theatre to the Curtain and thence the Globe.[68] Knutson acknowledges the potential for play titles to suggest a misleading sharing of subject matter between quite unrelated plays (e.g. *Every Man In / Out of His Humour* or the *Westward Ho / Eastward Ho / Northward Ho* plays) but notes that Shakespeare's 'usual habit' was to provide 'accurate and descriptive titles'; she therefore believes that 'Love's Labour's Won' was a narrative sequel to *Love's Labour's Lost*.[69] Knutson assumes the lost play 'ended with nuptial celebrations for the King of Navarre and the Princess of France along with the pairs of their attendant lords and ladies', and proceeds to note 'the novelty in turning a comedy into two parts', given that in comedies prior to 1595/6, 'there is not an instance

---

[66] Knutson, 'Filling Fare', 61.   [67] R. West, *Wits A.B.C. or A centurie of epigrams* (1608), sig.B2.

[68] The documentary evidence for this lost play is discussed in the introduction to this book.

[69] R. L. Knutson, 'Love's Labor's Won' in Repertory', *Publications of the Arkansas Philological Association*, 11(1) (1985), 49.

on record in which a love story is suspended over two plays'.[70] Such an interpretation leads to the conclusion that Shakespeare was undertaking 'an experiment in comedic form'. Citing subsequent serialised comedies such as 'The Two Angry Women of Abingdon' by Henry Porter and the three-part 'Blind Beggar of Bethnal Green' plays (only Part 1 of which is extant), she suggests that perhaps Shakespeare 'developed a standard commercial tactic in a way that other dramatists would subsequently imitate'.[71]

Quite what 'Love's Labour's Won' dramatised is anyone's guess, and in the absence of solid evidence there is little point in promoting one guess over another. In the interests of opening up possibilities for further investigation, however, I do wish to at least raise an alternative for consideration. Shakespeare may well have produced an imitable experiment in two-part comedy, but what if *Love's Labour's Lost* and 'Love's Labour's Won' were *not* planned as a pair that deliberately suspended the love story over two parts? Arguably the most notable feature of *Love's Labour's Lost* is that play's refusal to conform to genre expectations by deferring rather than culminating in marriage; a sequel that literally continued the first play's storyline through to nuptials would undermine the aesthetic success (or at least the novelty) of the first play, and may thus have been undesirable. Moreover, as H. R. Woudhuysen notes of the sequel, 'it is not easy to understand what the title means: it was proverbial to lose one's labour, but one wins a prize, not one's labour'.[72] The most important aspect of the opaque title, then, is its evident straining to engage with the earlier play's title. Clearly there was commercial value in having the title allude to its predecessor, but its lack of sense might suggest that the lost play was a spontaneous (or unplanned) sequel attempting to capitalise on the success of part one. Some spontaneous or unplanned sequels (*2 Tamburlaine*; '2 The Black Dog of Newgate'; *2 Fair Maid of the West*) fall under the 'more of the same' category.[73] Others, such as Marston's *Antonio* plays, which morph from comedy into gory revenge

---

[70] Knutson, *The Repertory*, 75.   [71] Knutson, *The Repertory*, 75.

[72] W. Shakespeare, *Love's Labour's Lost*, H. R. Woudhuysen (ed.) (London: Arden Shakespeare, 1998), 81.

[73] Wiggins suggests that as with *Tamburlaine*, the 'slight delay suggests that the sequel [to '1 Black Dog of Newgate'] was ordered as a consequence of the success of a play originally conceived as a standalone; the second part was therefore 'more of the same' rather than a continuation completing a narrative which was planned for disposition across two plays' (#1381). The relationship between Heywood's two *Fair Maid of the West* plays (c.1610, 1630) is initially unclear, Part 2 of which having been written twenty years after Part 1. But again, as with the *Tamburlaine* plays, the impetus for penning a sequel seems to have been that it was a response to the success of Part 1 – this time in the form of a revival of that first part that took place decades after the play was written (#2320).

tragedy, display marked differences in genre and tone.[74] Day and Chettle's
Blind Beggar of Bethnal Green (1600) spawned 'two *ad hoc* sequels' whose
titles increasingly emphasised the role of Tom Strowd; the sequels, in other
words, seemingly strayed from the original play's design, in response to
audience demand.[75] Shakespeare himself experimented with the spin-off
model in the late 1590s, straying from history and the Henriad long
enough to pen a comedy starring Sir John Falstaff: Wiggins thinks
Shakespeare may have 'temporarily suspended' work on *2 Henry IV* so as
to capitalise on the vogue for humoral comedy by hastily writing *Merry
Wives of Windsor* in 1597.[76]

Hence although there should be *some* relationship between *Love's
Labour's Lost* and 'Love's Labour's Won', it needn't entail reprising the
entire cast of characters, nor need it entail providing the marriages that
were deferred at the end of the first play. Indeed, this option seems to me
somewhat unlikely in that it would undercut the artistic originality of
Love's Labour's Lost as an experiment in comedic form that disavowed the
traditional comedic ending in marriage. Such a sequel might appear
bathetic (and from our vantage point in the present, could seem to sell
Shakespeare short). Of course, just as *2 Tamburlaine* provides the death of
the protagonist that was notably absent in *1 Tamburlaine*, it is *a priori*
possible that 'Love's Labour's Won' did indeed try to solve the lack of
marriages from the end of *Love's Labour's Lost* – and if it did, it is possible
that the sequel underscored rather than undercut the first play's innovations. I wonder, though, whether the lost play may simply have carried
over one or two characters, and provided a new narrative direction for
them.

There are also at least two examples in the Curtain repertory of
historical-tragical subject matter being refracted through the lens of other
genres. On 14 August 1600, the same day that he entered Jonson's *Every
Man In* in the Stationers' Register for publication, Cuthbert Burby also
entered something called '*The Famous Tragicall history, of ye Tartarian
Crippell Emperour of Constantinople*'.[77] Although described as a famous
tragical history, the item need not have been a play. But as Wiggins notes,
Burby did have 'an established relationship' with the Chamberlain's Men

---

[74] Wiggins #1218 & #1271. Marston's two Antonio plays may be separated by *Jack Drum's
Entertainment*, making them less immediately connected, but clearly they are related.

[75] W. Sharpe, 'A Critical Edition of *The Blind Beggar of Bethnal Green* by John Day and Henry
Chettle (1600)', unpublished PhD dissertation, University of Birmingham (2009), 4. See also
Wiggins #1250, #1279 and #1299.

[76] Wiggins #1079.   [77] Arber (ed.), *Stationers' Register*, 3.169.

(registering Jonson's play is one example), and the title's absence from Henslowe's records *prima facie* allows the possibility of it belonging to the Chamberlain's.[78] There is no consensus on the subject of this lost title: Wiggins observes that Stauracius was a crippled Emperor of Constantinople (but not Tartarian) and that Timur the Lame (i.e. Tamburlaine) was a crippled Tartarian (but not Emperor of Constantinople). Knutson, however, notes that Tamburlaine did have *some* association with the city.[79] According to Richard Knolles, the Greek emperor Emanuell was so grateful to Tamburlaine for indirectly saving Constantinople by defeating Bajazeth (who, as Marlowe relates, had been engaged in the 'dreadful siege / Of the famous Grecian Constantinople' at the time; 1 *Tam.* 3.1.5–6) that he offered Tamburlaine the Greek empire. Tamburlaine allegedly declined on the grounds of having empire enough, and the desire only for fame. Before departing the region altogether, though, he did have one favour to ask of the Greek Emperor, for he had 'conceiued a secret desire to see this so famous a citie as was CONSTANTINOPLE, from which he was not now farre, yet would he not goe thither as a conquerour, but as a priuat person'.[80] The Greek emperor obliged him, and provided a guided tour over the course of nearly a week. Unlike *Every Man In* and *Much Ado*, which build on the vogue for comedies of humours, this play had no exemplary comic precedent to model itself on; rather, it seems more likely to have engaged with one of the best-known tragic figures of the London stage and created a spin-off in a related genre (tragical *history*).

Duplication of successful offerings was a staple of the commercial strategies of the London repertory companies, who knew the value of the tried and true.[81] Rather than the straightforward cloning of a successful offering though, the 'Tartarian Cripple' example introduces an element of novelty by keeping a well-known protagonist but changing genres, transposing a pseudo-historical figure into the realm of comedy.[82] A comparable case of such genre innovation is found in 'The Second Part of the Seven Deadly Sins', the backstage plot of which survives in the Dulwich College archives (MS xix). Since David Kathman's groundbreaking article of 2004, the critical consensus has been to reassign the play from the Strange's repertory c.1590–1591 to the Chamberlain's

---

[78] Wiggins #1181.   [79] See Knutson's entry for the 'Tartarian Cripple' play in the *LPD*.

[80] R. Knolles, *The General History of the Turks* (1603), 222.

[81] See Knutson, *The Repertory*, 48–54.

[82] My argument here is complicated by the stationer Richard Jones having purposefully excised comic elements from *Tamburlaine* when he published the plays; possibly a comedy about the 'Tartarian cripple' (if Tamburlaine) may have actually continued a stage tradition that began with Marlowe.

repertory c.1597–1598 (placing it at the Theatre and/or the Curtain).[83] The plot reveals that although the play had an allegorical device (it commences with Envy, Sloth and Lechery jostling for primacy with Pride, Gluttony, Wrath and Covetousness, and emerging successful to have their stories portrayed on stage), it is framed by an historical personage: the plot calls for a tent to be placed on the stage and 'for Henry the Sixt [to] be in it A sleepe' (sc.1). As the Epilogue to Shakespeare's *Henry V* reminds playgoers, 'oft our stage hath shown' the story of 'Henry the Sixth, in infant bands crowned king' (13 & 9); seemingly an indication that *The First Part of the Contention betwixt the Two Famous Houses of York and Lancaster* (1591; Wiggins #888), *The True Tragedy of Richard, Duke of York and the Death of Good King Henry VI* (1591; Wiggins #902) and 'harey the vj' (1592; Wiggins #919) – subsequently known (respectively) as *2, 3, & 1 Henry VI* – had been performed 'oft' by 1599. The allegorical events of '2 Seven Deadly Sins', however, occur in a dream-like sequence presented by the poet John Lydgate whilst Henry is imprisoned in the Tower; the framing action thus corresponds to the historical period of 1465–1470 and overlaps with events dramatised in *The True Tragedy* (*3 Henry VI*), which take place between 1455–1471. At the end of the plot, the Earl of Warwick enters to Henry, the pursuivant and warders in the Tower, presumably to release Henry (sc.21). So again, a well-known stage character from one genre (history) is repurposed in another genre (morality), and the story-proper is not one traditionally associated with the character.[84]

The Chamberlain's '2 Seven Deadly Sins' play thus shares an interesting and potentially innovative feature with that company's 'Tartarian Cripple' play in that both turn to a new genre to create apocryphal adventures for a famous character. Inter-repertorial connections are also apparent: of the three inset plays representing Envy, Sloth and Lechery, two speak suggestively to plays in another company's repertory. Envy is depicted via the story of Gorboduc, who misguidedly divides his kingdom between his sons Ferrex and Porrex instead of leaving it in its entirety to the elder son, Ferrex. Porrex is driven to kill his brother, precipitating civil war. The Admiral's 'Mulmutius Dunwallow' play (the playbook was purchased in October 1598) would also have dramatised civil war and been set in post-

---

[83] D. Kathman, 'Reconsidering *The Seven Deadly Sins*', *Early Theatre*, 7(1) (2004), 13–44.

[84] The historical fantasy model featuring characters from the reign of Henry VI would subsequently form part of the Admiral's repertory when they acquired *The Blind Beggar of Bethnal Green* from Chettle and Day in May of 1600.

Gorboduc Britain but would have dramatised the opposite process: a divided kingdom being reunified. Likewise, the inset story of Lechery is depicted via the story of Philomel's rape and mutilation, and her use of a 'sampler' which is brought on stage (sc.20); this same Ovidian pattern informs the plot of *Titus Andronicus* (including, distinctively, mention of the 'tedious sampler', 4.39). By 1600, *Titus* (Q2) was advertised as having been played by the Chamberlain's Men.

The example of *Titus* – an old play, but one that apparently continued to be performed – raises interesting questions about how the company adjusted to their new playing environment at the Curtain if it really had such a significantly larger stage than their former venues. Could it be possible to consider the Chamberlain's response to the Curtain's dimensions as a kind of inverse-corollary to Leslie Thomson's argument about 'the relationship between staging requirements and conditions' for provincial touring?[85] Thomson refutes long-standing critical assumptions about the extent to which touring conditions curtailed performance possibilities – especially in terms of what W. W. Greg called the 'spectacular' or 'elaborate' elements of performance – and how this allegedly resulted in the so-called 'bad quartos' of plays.[86] Her survey of the thirty-five extant play-texts associated with companies who toured prominently between 1586–1594 demonstrates that merely ten or eleven demanded only 'a basic performance area' with doors and hand-held properties, and none of these showed signs of having cut out complex staging in order to be more easily performed at a provincial venue.[87] The majority of the surveyed play-texts called for the kind of elaborate staging that 'put the greatest demands on a performance space – action "above," ascents to or descents from an upper level, descents into or ascents out of a trap, discovery scenes, and the appearance of large properties such as a throne or bed'.[88] She suggests that it would be in a company's best interests to tour with plays that were successful in London, regardless of whether they were 'easy to stage', and that spectacular scenes using discovery spaces and large properties 'are very unlikely to have been eliminated on the road because their spectacular nature was surely one reason for their audience

---

[85] L. Thomson, 'Staging on the Road, 1586–1594: A New Look at Some Old Assumptions', *Shakespeare Quarterly* 61(4) (2010), 530.

[86] Thomson, 'Staging on the Road', 529. See W. W. Greg, *Two Elizabethan Stage Abridgements: 'The Battle of Alcazar' and 'Orlando Furioso'*, Malone Society, vol. 53 (Oxford: Oxford University press, 1922), 251–252 (cited in Thomson, 'Staging on the Road', 527).

[87] Thomson, 'Staging on the Road', 535 (see also 534).   [88] Thomson, 'Staging on the Road', 530.

appeal'.[89] Moreover, Thomson, drawing on John Astington's observations that a company could readily perform in a variety of spaces once
they knew their lines and blocking, astutely observes that 'to alter or cut
what the players had already memorized and acted would have done more
to jeopardize a successful performance than any differences or limitations
in the facilities they found on tour'.[90] In sum: elaborate spectacle (here
conceived in terms of stage business and properties) was a drawcard that
companies could hardly afford to cut for touring, and cutting chunks of
text in response to the perceived limitations of provincial conditions was
equally undesirable.

The Chamberlain's Men likewise faced a change in staging conditions
when they moved from the Theatre to the appreciably larger Curtain,
though in their case the new environment was at least semi-permanent,
unlike a provincial venue encountered on tour. The need to respond to the
demands and opportunities of the enlarged space had to be reckoned with.
Thomson argues compellingly that a company on tour 'would surely have
wanted to perform the more spectacular business if at all possible, and
would have found ways to do so'.[91] Barbara D. Palmer has likewise noted a
suggestive trend in the touring companies' preferences: 'Repeatedly the
records show professional companies' playing in the largest indoor space
they are permitted ... Because such spaces as moot halls, schoolhouses,
town halls, guildhalls, churches, church houses, and household great halls
are large, open, and sparsely furnished, they allow large audiences and
large-scale blocking'.[92] A significantly larger stage at the Curtain would
offer the Chamberlain's precisely this possibility of 'spectacular business'
and 'large-scale blocking'.

In the foregoing discussion I have attempted to establish a corpus of
'Curtain' plays, but as with Thomson's prudent caveats about how much
venue-specific information can be read into the printed play-texts of plays
associated with touring companies,[93] inferring Curtain-specific details
from the plays I've discussed above is more of an art than a science. Q2
of *Titus*, although published after the Curtain period (in 1600), derives
from a damaged copy of Q1 (1594), and the Folio text of 1623 differs
most significantly only in the addition of the fly-killing scene. The various
early printings do not therefore offer obvious clues to alterations for the

[89] Thomson, 'Staging on the Road', 532.   [90] Thomson, 'Staging on the Road', 532.
[91] Thomson, 'Staging on the Road', 533.
[92] B. D. Palmer, 'Early Modern Mobility: Players, Payments, and Patrons', *Shakespeare Quarterly*, 56
    (2005), 259–305, esp. 284.
[93] Thomson, 'Staging on the Road', 533–534.

physical environment, yet it is not hard to suggest moments that could easily be amplified for a play filled with hunting scenes, political rallying, empty wildernesses, and battle preparations. To pose the question slightly differently: what else is lost from early modern plays besides play-texts themselves? The move from one venue to a significantly larger one implies that dramaturgy must have changed, but the early textual witnesses of *Titus* do not document these consequences of changed performance spaces. It is entirely possible that no new lines would need to be learnt, but extensive alterations of choreography and blocking might require significant rehearsal or highly skilled negotiations of stage movement during performance, and such changes would remain inconspicuous in textual records.

The publication history of another Curtain play, *Romeo and Juliet*, is notoriously elusive, but given the pre- and post-Curtain dates of the earliest printings, I think it is worth examining for possible clues to Curtain dramaturgy. Q1, printed by John Danter in 1597, names Lord Hunsdon's Men as the company who performed the play; it therefore probably 'refers to early, if not the first, performances of the play', as the New Oxford Shakespeare editors note, since Shakespeare's company was only patronised by Lord Hunsdon between 22 July 1596 and 17 April 1597.[94] If so, it corresponds to a pre-Curtain period of the company's history. Its authority has been questioned, with memorial reconstruction or Chettle's editorial hand having been suggested as possible explanations for its significant differences from the '[n]ewly corrected, augmented, and amended' version published as Q2 in 1599 by Cuthbert Burby (who went on to register 'The Tartarian Cripple' and *Every Man In*). This second version of the play is about 700 lines longer than Q1 (though relies on Q1 as copytext in some passages). Accordingly, Jill L. Levenson notes with characteristic caution that 'the two earliest quartos of *Romeo and Juliet* represent two different and legitimate kinds of witnesses to two different stages of an ongoing theatrical event'.[95] It would be irresponsible to conjecture on the basis of current evidence as to whether one of the performances captured by the early quartos stemmed specifically from the environment and dynamics of the Theatre, the Curtain, or the Globe, but clearly a play that remained in a company's repertory did

[94] G. Taylor, J. Jowett, T. Bourus and G. Egan (eds.), *The New Oxford Shakespeare: Critical Reference Edition* (Oxford: Oxford University Press, 2017), 1.667.
[95] W. Shakespeare, *Romeo and Juliet*, J. L. Levenson (ed.) (Oxford: Oxford University Press, 2000), 127.

evolve over time, and available playing spaces must have factored into performance considerations. To that end, it is interesting that, as Levenson notes, Q1 has 'fewer party-goers (1.4), servants (1.4, 4.2, 4.4), and watchmen (5.3) than Q2', and Q1 occasionally 'reduces the minor roles to a single actor, avoiding the permissiveness of Q2: only one servant engages Capulet in 4.2 and 4.4 (H3^v, I1^r) where Q2 brings *'two or three'* and *'three or foure'* on stage (I4^r, K1^v)'.[96] In other words, Q1 would potentially suit a smaller stage or cast (Wiggins estimates between thirty-one and thirty-five speaking parts), whereas Q2's additional (superfluous?) bodies on stage might better accord with the need to fill out a larger performance space (Wiggins estimates up to forty-five speaking parts).[97] There is no significant difference in the number of weapons called for in each version, but about a dozen swords, blades, daggers or rapiers feature in what Levenson calls the play's 'striking outbursts of violence', and if a company were looking to capitalise on the dramaturgical possibilities afforded by a larger stage, fight choreography (brawl or battle scenes) would intuitively offer opportune moments for expansion at a venue that was demonstrably capable of hosting fencing competitions.[98]

As with *Titus*, a number of the plays mentioned above could easily accommodate expanded choreographies of battles and processions (virtually all the history plays meet this criteria). The masquerade balls in *Much Ado* and in *Romeo and Juliet* could similarly be enriched in spectacle if the space invited it: Capulet's welcome to his guests, 'A hall, a hall! Give room, and foot it, girls' (6.23) would take on a special resonance if accompanied by the sudden bursting forth of the full cast to dance, particularly if delivered in a performance venue approximating the shape of a hall. Tamburlaine's purported sightseeing in 'The Tartarian Cripple' would similarly be enhanced by the space afforded by a larger stage. Here it may be worth contemplating the uses of space in a much later Curtain play by Queen Anne's Men: George Wilkins, John Day and William Rowley's *The Travels of the Three English Brothers* (1607), a play whose wide-ranging geography takes in Persia, Russia, Rome, Venice, a Greek island and Constantinople. It concludes with an incredible split-screen effect wherein each of the three Sherley brothers (Robert, Anthony and Thomas) is given a prospective glass so that they can spy each other in Persia, Spain and England respectively:

[96] Levenson (ed.), *Romeo and Juliet*, 65   [97] Wiggins #987.
[98] Levenson (ed.), *Romeo and Juliet*, 36.

'*they seem to see one another and offer to embrace*'.[99] A scene like this would clearly be optimised if performed on a stage sufficiently large to accommodate the geographical conceit.[100] Presumably '2 Seven Deadly Sins' would also have made use of a large stage to create a split-screen effect of having Henry VI witness the depictions of Envy, Sloth, and Lechery from the relative safety of his tent in the Tower. In each of these examples, the challenge consists of trying to make appropriate use of the enlarged space, but there is no reason to think that the company itself had grown in size. By Wiggins' reckoning, *A Warning for Fair Women* has between forty-seven and forty-eight speaking parts, *2 Henry IV* forty-eight to fifty-one (cf. thirty-four to thirty-six for *1 Henry IV*), '2 Seven Deadly Sins' had forty or more speaking parts, *Henry V* had forty-seven to forty-eight, and *A Larum for London* had forty-seven to forty-eight. Only *Merry Wives* (twenty to twenty-one), *Much Ado* (twenty-four to twenty-five) and *Every Man In* (eighteen to nineteen) remain relatively smaller in speaking roles. The larger than usual number of speaking parts in many of the 'Curtain plays' has more to do with having more of the company on stage more often than with having more cast to deploy. As I have been at pains to stress, there is (frustratingly) no direct evidence for these kinds of modifications, but clearly some alteration to dramaturgy would be invited by the changed performance conditions produced by the company's move to the Curtain.

§

This chapter is about new beginnings for the Lord Chamberlain's Men: first at Newington Butts in 1594 and then at the Curtain, their unlooked-for but ultimately beneficial home from around September 1598. In the first section of this chapter, I explore the unique events of June 1594 that saw a form of 'coopetition' develop between the newly formed Admiral's and Chamberlain's companies as they attempted to stimulate the public's appetite for playgoing after a period of plague and extraordinary weather. By attending properly to the lost plays in that brief, eleven-day run, I make it possible to appreciate the full picture of how the companies'

---

[99] 'The Travels of the Three English Brothers' in A. Parr (ed.), *Three Renaissance Travel Plays. The Revels Plays Companion Library* (Manchester: Manchester University Press, 1995), Epilogue 13.6–7. On the use of prospective glasses, see L. Niayesh, 'Seeing and Overseeing the Stage as Map in Early Modern Drama' in C. Jowitt and D. McInnis (eds.), *Travel and Drama in Early Modern England: The Journeying Play* (Cambridge: Cambridge University Press, 2018), 39–54, esp. 47–48.

[100] In Robert Greene's much earlier *Friar Bacon and Friar Bungay* (1589), a similar split-screen effect divides the stage into two distinct geographical locations through the use of a prospective glass, but the Curtain's proportions evidently enabled a three-way division of the stage in *The Travels*.

short string of performances overlapped, intersected, and in some senses converged in their sharing of properties and thematic interests. Where older scholarship seized on the data contained in the Newington run as evidence that the two companies differed importantly in their repertorial offerings (the Admiral's allegedly favouring biblical plays, the Chamberlain's only having one: 'Hester and Ahasuerus'), my fresh perspective undermines such characterisations, showing that the Chamberlain's 'Hester' play was less biblical and more fully embedded in its repertorial moment than has previously been acknowledged.

In the second section, by prioritising the study of lost plays in the Chamberlain's Curtain repertory, I give a fuller picture of what the company's offerings looked like at that point in time, and by doing so offer a corrective to the standard assumption that this was a period of hardship for the company. The new archaeological evidence pertaining to the apparently large size of the Curtain stage prompts me to revisit and revise the received narrative in a substantially more positive light, and I regard the move to the Curtain as the (unlooked-for) beginning of a positive phase for the company. In the foregoing discussion I have proposed a number of variables that might invite alteration for a larger stage: fight scenes, processions, masquerades, and travel, in particular. None of these requires cuts or additions to dialogue, or even necessarily to physical features such as 'above' or 'below' spaces in order to maximise elaborate spectacle, but they would all require alterations to a larger-scale blocking and with that, additional rehearsal time and more stage time for the current company members.

By the logic of my negative space metaphor, our perception of the Curtain plays (the figure) has been shaped by loss (the ground) in two distinct ways. First, lost play-texts such as '2 Seven Deadly Sins' and 'The Tartarian Cripple' point to a trend for repurposing celebrated characters in new genres and contexts, while other lost plays (e.g. 'The Fair Maid of London', 'Cloth Breeches and Velvet Hose') help fill out the picture of what the repertory looked like. Second, the lost dramaturgy and choreography that I believe would have accompanied the move from the Theatre to a larger venue may have had an influence on the form taken by even the extant plays. Together, these losses have contributed to establishing the contour of the image we see today of dramatic activity whilst Shakespeare's company occupied the Curtain.

CHAPTER 3

Shakespeare at the Turn of the Century: 1599–1603

Shakespeare's company experienced significant changes at the turn of the century: as the 1590s drew to a close and conjecture about the nation's aging and heirless monarch loomed ever larger in the cultural imagination, the Chamberlain's Men were to move to a new playhouse. A number of companies experienced such change: the Admiral's Men temporarily lost their star actor, Edward Alleyn, to retirement, and moved from the Rose to their new Fortune theatre; the Earl of Pembroke's Men, who had vacated the Swan and toured regionally in the wake of the 'Isle of Dogs' fiasco and the associated inhibition of plays, turned up briefly at the Rose in October 1600; and the Earl of Worcester's Men appear to have replaced the Admiral's at the Rose for a time, before amalgamating with the Earl of Oxford's Men in 1602 and commencing playing at the Boar's Head. The greatest documentary evidence, however, pertains to the Chamberlain's and the Admiral's. Both companies, as Knutson notes, could 'anticipate the transfer of business' to their new venues and had time to 'prepare a suitable repertory'.[1] Knutson argues that the Admiral's Men (and infers that the Chamberlain's Men) stocked up on new plays ahead of their respective moves of venue, thereby 'saving themselves the expense of new productions (when their other costs were up)'.[2] Decisions around what kinds of new plays to acquire were presumably informed by theatrical activity of the period leading up to the move, but consideration of lost plays has not featured as prominently as it warrants in critical discussions.

A key feature of the Chamberlain's and Admiral's change of venues was the fact that the Globe and the Fortune were custom-built for these companies, with the promise of stability that this entailed. Andrew Gurr, Richard Dutton and others have detected celebratory references to the Globe and the Fortune in the plays performed at those new venues by the respective resident companies. For these scholars, Hamlet's reference to

[1] Knutson, *The Repertory*, 79. [2] Knutson, *The Repertory*, 80.

'this distracted globe' (5.96) and Jacques' conceit that 'All the world's a stage' (2.7.138) function as metatheatrical allusions to the venue's name and motto; Gurr attributes such sentiments to 'the new security the company sensed it now had at its new workplace'.[3] Elsewhere, he refers to 'post-*Hamlet* plays in the repertory', and suggests that '*Hamlet*, aided in complex ways by the evolution of Shakespeare's history plays, helped to push the repertory towards a more complex view of what drama can do' and thus represents a turning point in the company's history – a turning point associated with their move to the Globe.[4] It might even be argued that the very fact of Shakespeare creating a 'new' version of an old Hamlet narrative (known to playgoers since at least 1589, with versions appearing at Newington Butts in 1594 and at the Theatre in 1596) implicitly frames the play as forward-looking, announcing a conscious break with the past.[5]

In this chapter, I focus on two plays that have been traditionally associated with the Chamberlain's Men's move to their brand-new Globe theatre: *Henry V* and *Hamlet*. These two plays by Shakespeare have become synonymous with the Globe, but their association with this playwright and venue has, I argue, distorted our perception of their place in London's theatrical marketplace. An important finding of Edgar Rubin's psychological work on visually experienced figures is that through 'subjective' or 'relative localisation' it is possible for the observer to perceive the figure as closer to them than the ground; moreover, different observers can arrive at different estimations of how close the figure seems to be. In

---

[3] Gurr, *The Shakespearian Playing Companies*, 298; R. Dutton, '*Hamlet, An Apology for Actors*, and the Sign of the Globe', *Shakespeare Survey*, 41 (1989), 35–44. The corollary is Dekker's *Old Fortunatus* and the lost 'Fortune's Tennis' plays in the Admiral's repertory, which seem appropriate for performance at the Fortune theatre. For dissenting views, see T. Stern, 'Was *Totus Mundus Agit Histrionem* ever the Motto of the Globe Theatre?', *Theatre Notebook*, 51 (1997), 122–127; R. Lewis, *Hamlet and the Vision of Darkness* (Princeton: Princeton University Press, 2017), 163; and McInnis, '"2 Fortune's Tennis" and the Admiral's Men', *Lost Plays in Shakespeare's England*, 105–126, esp. 122. The Arden editors of *Hamlet*, Ann Thompson and Neil Taylor, steer clear of intention and focus on effect, cautiously noting only that such a meaning 'may have occurred to the earliest auditors at the Globe' (1.5.96–97n).

[4] A. Gurr, *The Shakespeare Company, 1594–1642* (Cambridge: Cambridge University Press, 2004), 147. See also Greenblatt, *Will in the World*, 307.

[5] Thomas Nashe referred to the old *Hamlet* play in his preface to Robert Greene's *Menaphon* (1589); a 'Hamlet' play was recorded by Henslowe in the Newington Butts run of performances on 9 June 1594 (Foakes (ed.), *Henslowe's Diary*, 21); and Thomas Lodge quoted the line, '*Hamlet, reuenge*' in *Wits Miserie* (1596). On 'the time being ripe for a new, improved version of *Hamlet*', see Stephen Greenblatt, *Will in the World*, 294. There are numerous examples of 'new' versions of 'old' plays: in 1599, Henslowe paid Dekker for a new Fortunatus play, having had at least one, maybe two Fortunatus plays in the Admiral's Men's repertory as recently as 1596; see the Introduction to my Revels Plays edition of T. Dekker's *Old Fortunatus* (Manchester: Manchester University Press, 2020).

other words, an unconscious bias affects such perceptions, and this is 'reflected in the fact that the ground is often termed the *back-ground* and the figure is often described as "stepping forward"'.[6] This phenomenon is particularly noticeable in the case of *Henry V* and *Hamlet* which have stepped forward to such an extent in the popular imaginary that the lost plays they once spoke to in repertory have been relegated to the background and a vital context for understanding these plays has been overlooked. Our unconscious biases and our ignorance of what is lost have shaped our perceptions.

By putting Shakespeare's plays into some unexpected dialogues with lost plays, I aim to defamiliarise *Henry V* and *Hamlet* and trace new sets of associations between their subject matter (and form) and the plays of other companies. Specifically, I argue that *Henry V* can potentially be seen as the culmination of Shakespeare's 1590s romance comedies as much as of the Henriad, and that it can thus be regarded as a continuation of the 1590s rather than a turn-of-the-century play intended for the Globe (and thus, by implication, a break with the past). Likewise, *Hamlet* – although described by Stephen Greenblatt and others in forward-looking terms as marking an 'epoch' in Shakespeare's professional life and having 'relaunched his entire career'[7] – can be seen as participating in a 'Danish matrix' of 1590s plays that playgoers would recognise as having its own set of expectations and concerns. Furthermore, the fact of the Danish prince having studied at Wittenberg seems to speak importantly to a hitherto underappreciated repertorial context preoccupied with theology in 1602. By retracing the contour dividing extant plays from lost plays, I argue that *Hamlet* can be understood as having an unexpected affinity with the lost Admiral's Men play, 'felmelanco', as well as with that company's *Doctor Faustus* (which was being reprised around this time). In the new picture that emerges from this reconceptualisation of the figure and ground, *Hamlet* is more firmly embedded in its repertorial moment than breaking from it.

Love and War: 'Owen Tudor' and *Henry V*

Shakespeare's 'last Elizabethan history', *Henry V*, has traditionally been historicised as a political mirror for Elizabethan England, a fantasy of national union or the culmination of English patriotism begun (in the

---

[6] Pind, *Edgar Rubin*, 99.   [7] Greenblatt, *Will in the World*, 323.

theatre) by the Queen's Men's brand of providential history.[8] *Henry V* was brought to the stage in the spring of 1599, its repertorial partners possibly including either or both parts of *Henry IV*. Furthermore, part of its appeal was no doubt its role as the culmination of the Henriad, completing the narrative arc begun in *1 Henry IV* and continued in *2 Henry IV*. *Henry V* was also to be the final instalment in the two tetralogies of Tudor history plays that Shakespeare had written or co-written throughout the 1590s. Serial and spin-off plays were a familiar feature of the repertories of London companies in the 1590s, but the extent of this practice is more apparent when surviving serials such as Shakespeare's first and second tetralogies are considered alongside such lost combinations of plays as 'Black Bateman of the North, parts 1 and 2' (Admiral's, 1598), 'Earl Godwin and his Three Sons, parts 1 and 2' (Admiral's, 1598), 'Fair Constance of Rome, parts 1 and 2' (Admiral's, 1600), or 'The Black Dog of Newgate, parts 1 and 2' (Worcester's Men, 1602–1603). Part of the appeal of *Henry V* was no doubt its narrative continuity, but its subject matter would also have made it an appropriate repertorial response to the offerings of other companies. Referred to by Catherine Alexander and others as being Shakespeare's 'best known "war" play', *Henry V* is typically remembered for what one of its source texts calls the 'victorious actes' of Henry against the French at Harfleur and Agincourt.[9] A French parallel to the formulaic serial plays on the Wars of the Roses offered by Shakespeare's company had been presented earlier in 1599 by the Admiral's Men, when they had been playing the final part of their own tetralogy on the 'Civil Wars of France' by Thomas Dekker and Michael Drayton. But whereas the Lord Chamberlain's Men had invested in Lancastrian history, the Admiral's Men had glanced across the Channel, and when they did dramatise English history, it was of earlier periods (the twelfth-century crusades) or mythological history (Britain in the time of Brute, or of King Arthur).[10]

---

[8] J. Clare, *Shakespeare's Stage Traffic* (Cambridge: Cambridge University Press, 2014), 163. See, e.g. Annabel Patterson's summary of the play's thematics ('popular monarchy, national unity, militarist expansionism', *Shakespeare and the Popular Voice* [Cambridge: Basil Blackwell, 1989], 72) or Richard Dutton's overview of the play's critical history in 'The Second Tetralogy' in S. Wells (ed.), *Shakespeare: A Bibliographical Guide* (Oxford: Clarendon Press, 1990), 359–363.

[9] C. Alexander, 'Shakespeare and War: A Reflection on Instances of Dramatic Production, Appropriation, and Celebration', *Exchanges: The Warwick Research Journal*, 1(2) (2014), 285; E. Hall, *The vnion of the two noble and illustre femelies of Lancastre [and] Yorke* (Londini, 1548), sig.Fi.

[10] See the chapters by David McInnis, Misha Teramura and Paul Whitfield White in McInnis and Steggle (eds.), *Lost Plays in Shakespeare's England*.

In the wake of the Chamberlain's *Henry V* play, though, the Admiral's acquired a play called the 'second part of Henrye Richmond' from Robert Wilson on 8 November 1599 (there is no record of their having acquired a first part, but the terminology requires that they did), and subsequently in January 1600 an 'Owen Tudor' play (about Richmond's ancestor), which was probably a prequel of sorts.[11] Owen Tudor was the second husband of Queen Katherine, whom playgoers had previously seen being wooed by Henry V in Shakespeare's play. Clearly, traditional textual analysis isn't possible in the absence of the play-text, but the methods of literary scholars remain relevant here inasmuch as some clue to the play's contents is offered by the fact that one of the playwrights responsible for the Admiral's play was Michael Drayton, whose own *England's Heroical Epistles* (1598) told, in poetic form, the love story of Katherine and Owen.[12] In Drayton's pair of epistles, Henry is dead and Katherine's eye is taken by the 'brave and gallant' Owen Tudor.[13] She writes to him to intimate her affection, in case he has felt daunted by her status, confiding that '[t]he British language, which sweet vowels wants, / And iars so much upon harsh consonants, / Comes with such grace from thy mellifluous tongue, / As do the sweet notes of a well set song'.[14] If the playwrights behind 'Owen Tudor' had been impressed by the final scene of Shakespeare's play, in which Henry woos Katherine in broken French, they may have been tempted in turn to dramatise this passage from Drayton's *Epistles*. I acknowledge the differing artistic demands of poetry and drama, but I also see strong grounds for conjecturing that Drayton's co-authored play on Owen Tudor recycled some of his own romance material from the *Epistles*, in an example of what Mark Houlahan calls 'self-sourcing'.[15] There is a relatively low incidence of

---

[11] See Roslyn L. Knutson's *LPD* entries for '2 Henry Richmond' and 'Owen Tudor'.

[12] Katherine Duncan-Jones, in her essay on Hugh Holland's *Owen Tudyr* poem of 1601 (published as *Pancharis* in 1603), calls attention to the rarity of literary focus on Owen Tudor on account of 'doubts about the legitimacy of his marriage to Henry V's widow'; see K. Duncan-Jones, 'A Feather from the Black Swan's Wing: Hugh Holland's Owen Tudyr (1601)', *English Manuscript Studies: 1100–1700*, 11 (2002), 95. Nevertheless, the existence of this poem points to a literary interest in the wooing of Katherine around the same time as the Admiral's Men's play. Duncan-Jones notes Drayton's poetic and dramatic treatment of the same theme and suggests that Holland, an avid theatre-goer who remains most famous for the prefatory verse he contributed to the Shakespeare First Folio, may have been inspired by 'Drayton's sympathetic and sentimental treatments of the Own Tudor legend' (97).

[13] Drayton, *Englands heroicall epistles. Newly enlarged, by Michaell Drayton. London : P. S for N. Ling, 1598)*, sig.G2ᵛ.

[14] Drayton, *Englands heroicall epistles*, sig.G4ᵛ.

[15] M. Houlahan, 'The Curious Case of Mr. William Shakespeare and the Red Herring: *Twelfth Night* in Its Sources' in D. A. Britton and M. Walter (eds.), *Rethinking Shakespearean Source Study: Audiences, Authors, and Digital Technologies* (New York: Routledge, 2018), 243.

plays (that we know of) whose authors had also previously treated the same subject matter in another format. The fact of Drayton's having written both a play and an earlier poem on the same topic at least tells us what the playwright knew about the subject matter at a minimum. (He may of course have deliberately distorted, enlarged or otherwise manipulated his earlier work when preparing it for the stage.)

If Drayton's previous work is reliable as a guide for content, what is particularly interesting about this lost play is not simply the fact that the Admiral's were encroaching on what we might now regard as the Chamberlain's territory vis-à-vis Tudor historical subject matter, but the fact that their repertorial response appears to have been made on the basis of the romance element of Shakespeare's play, not the wars.[16] Interestingly, a note on a flyleaf of Register C of the Stationers' Register, dated 04 August 1600, pertains to the publication of four Chamberlain's plays including *Henry V*, suggesting that the play had been in production recently.[17] If so, *Henry V* and 'Owen Tudor' may even have been in repertorial competition from early 1600. Repertory thus offers us a clue to the early modern frame of reference brought to Shakespeare's so-called 'war' play and encourages us to think more about the romance angle. As T. W. Craik observes, the Epilogue to Shakespeare's *2 Henry IV* promises that the 'humble author will continue the story with Sir John in it, and make you merry with fair Katherine of France', and Shakespeare repeats the phrasing 'Fair Katherine, and most fair' in the wooing scene that brings *Henry V* to a close.[18] 'Perhaps', Craik suggests, at the time that he was finishing the *Henry IV* plays Shakespeare 'was already composing the courtship dialogue [for *Henry V*], in his mind if not on paper'.[19] Ros King notes that Shakespeare's description of the king and his fleet leaving Southampton to fight at Harfleur recalls the passage from Thomas North's Plutarch describing the allure of Cleopatra; she asks 'Why should Shakespeare use one of the most extravagant seduction events in recorded history to describe Henry's expedition?'[20] His interest in Katherine and the romance dimension of the Henry V story may offer the beginnings of an

---

[16] It may be worth noting that Roger Boyle, Earl of Orrery's *History of Henry V* play (printed 1668) featured Owen Tudor as Henry's rival for Katherine's affections.

[17] Arber (ed.), *Stationers' Register*, 3.37; Knutson, *The Repertory*, 80.

[18] W. Shakespeare, *Henry V*, T. W. Craik (ed.) (Arden 3) (London: Thomson Learning, rpt. 2001), 6.

[19] Craik (ed.), *Henry V*, 6.

[20] *Henry V*, 3.0.4–13. The identification of Plutarch as source here was made by R King, 'Shakespeare and the Historians: The Writing of *Henry V* in A. Curry and M. Mercer (eds.), *The Battle of Agincourt* (New Haven, CT: Yale University Press, 2015), 241.

explanation. If the Admiral's choice of the love story between Owen and Katherine is any indication, perhaps Shakespeare's decision to introduce Katherine first in Act 3 – quite literally the centre of the *Henry V* play – didn't pass unnoticed by playgoers, or by his competition.

Denmark without Shakespeare

Few scholars would disagree that our perception of early modern drama has been distorted by veneration of the 'singularity' of Shakespeare (to borrow Gary Taylor's term).[21] Within the Shakespearean canon, *Hamlet* is often singled out for special importance. However influenced scholars now are about early modern perceptions of Denmark because of *Hamlet*, early modern playgoers' conception of Denmark and the Danes on stage would not have derived solely from Shakespeare. Recalling the art history metaphor of negative space, how should Shakespeare's nominally Danish setting in *Hamlet* be understood in light of a decade or more of representations of Denmark on the London stages? If we cease focusing on the 'figure' of *Hamlet* for a moment and attend instead to plays that do not survive (the negative space; the 'ground'), we may develop a richer sense of what Shakespeare's Denmark signified to early audiences, and reposition it as part of a consistent interest in Denmark on the early modern stage.[22]

In Shakespeare's *Hamlet*, 'something is rotten in the state of Denmark' (4.93). Laertes reluctantly returns to Denmark from France, where he enjoys greater autonomy (2.50–56), though his father takes care to proscribe his behaviours whilst abroad and even surveys his son's foreign activities for good measure. And to the melancholic prince, Denmark is a prison (in the Folio text, at least).[23] The Elsinore of Shakespeare's *Hamlet*

---

[21] See G. Taylor, *Reinventing Shakespeare: A Cultural History, from the Restoration to the Present* (Oxford: Oxford University Press, 1991).

[22] Cay Dollerup embarked on a related project of attempting to ascertain 'which authentic Danish features English audiences usually met with and to what extent works of fiction mirrored Danish history, culture, and social life', but I am less interested in purported authenticity than in how Denmark and the Danes signified for early modern audiences: see C. Dollerup, *Denmark, Hamlet, and Shakespeare: A Study of Englishmen's Knowledge of Denmark towards the End of the Sixteenth Century with Special Reference to Hamlet*, 2 vols. (Salzburg: Universität Salzburg, 1975), 1.48. On Britain as 'the product of a series of invasions' and the stage representations of not just the Romans but 'two of the other occupying nationalities – the Saxons and the Danes', see G. McMullan, 'The Colonisation of Early Britain on the Jacobean Stage' in G. McMullan and D. Matthews (eds.), *Reading the Medieval in Early Modern England* (Cambridge: Cambridge University Press, 2007), 119–140 (quotations from 122 and 125).

[23] *Mr. William Shakespeares comedies, histories, & tragedies Published according to the true originall copies* (London, 1623), sig.oo3ᵛ.

is also, of course, a foil for Elizabethan London, as Steven Mullaney, James Shapiro, and numerous others have observed, its crisis of succession eerily refracting *fin-de-siecle* English concerns.[24] But by contextualising *Hamlet* with lost plays we arrive at a different picture of its repertorial relationships. I argue that *Hamlet* might better be thought of as participating in a 'Danish matrix' alongside such lost plays as the anonymous 'Hamlet' performed during the Admiral's/Chamberlain's joint run at Newington Butts in June 1594. Other lost Denmark plays focused on the opaquely titled 'taner' of Denmark (Strange's Men, 23 May 1592); on Guichlac, king of the Danes ('Cutlack', Admiral's, 1594); on Earl Godwin's service on behalf of Denmark during Canute's reign, and the subsequent anti-Danish sentiment of Edward's reign (Admiral's, 1598); and on tragedy more generally in Henry Chettle's 'A Danish Tragedy' (Admiral's, 1602).

Let me begin with 'the taner of denmarke'. Play titles, as Matthew Steggle has argued, should be considered as very brief documents of performance, which, in the case of lost plays, is often the only substantive evidence there is to work with.[25] In Chapter 2, I draw attention to the tendency of critics such as F. G. Fleay to lump together titles of lost plays with surviving play-texts that they regarded as being a good fit for the subject matter. Reconsidering some of the more tenuous lumping of play titles can be amusing, but the habit points to a further bugbear of scholarship on lost plays: the tendency for traditional conjecture to ossify into ostensible 'fact' and be replicated with minimal pause by subsequent generations of scholars. To reframe this in a positive manner: the time is ripe for fresh approaches. Critical thinking on the lost play recorded by Henslowe on 23 May 1592 as the 'the taner of denmarke', for example, has largely stalled: this particular title demonstrates how previous critics defined the possibilities of this play without actually solving the mystery of its subject matter, and thereby essentially prevented further investigation.[26] While scholars don't know where Shakespeare was in 1592–1593, we do know where some of his fellows-to-be in the Chamberlain's Men were: learning the parts for 'the taner of denmarke' with the Lord Strange's Men.[27] At least three of them – George Bryan, Will Kempe and Thomas

---

[24] S. Mullaney, 'Mourning and Misogyny: *Hamlet, The Revenger's Tragedy*, and the Final Progress of Elizabeth I, 1600–1607', *Shakespeare Quarterly*, 45(2) (1994), 139–162; J. Shapiro, *1599: A Year in the Life of William Shakespeare* (London: Faber and Faber, 2005), chs 13 and 14, e.g. 313, 323.

[25] Steggle, *Digital Humanities*, 14.   [26] Foakes (ed.), *Henslowe's Diary*, 18.

[27] On the relationship between Lord Strange's company and the Lord Chamberlain's Men, see L. Manley and S.-B. MacLean, *Lord Strange's Men and Their Plays* (New Haven, CT: Yale University Press, 2014).

Pope – had had first-hand experience of Denmark when they performed for the Danish court at Helsingør (Elsinore) in 1586.[28] Although the play returned £3 13s 6d for its single recorded performance in Henslowe's diary on 23 May 1592, the performance comes at a time when the company (Strange's Men) was launching a tour into the country. As a new play with high receipts, it was probably performed on tour with them, but no documentary evidence has been found to confirm this.

Somewhat uncharacteristically, Fleay did not hazard a guess as to the identity of this play; Greg, however, noted that '[t]he only tanner known to dramatic history is, I believe, the tanner of Tamworth in [Heywood's] *Edward IV*'.[29] Subsequent criticism has accepted Greg's implicit suggestion that this must, therefore, be a 'craft play', a species of drama most famously exemplified by Dekker's *Shoemaker's Holiday*, though as Knutson cautiously notes, the most we might infer is that 'the taner of denmarke' *could* be '[a]n early example' of such a type.[30] Cay Dollerup, in her study of English knowledge of Denmark in the 1590s, noted in passing that '[f]or all we know, the tanner in question may have been English'.[31]

Lawrence Manley is the first critic to challenge the orthodoxy of the 'taner' in Henslowe's title being a 'tanner' and offer a genuinely alternative interpretation.[32] Manley's argument rests on a conjectural premise that Henslowe meant to write the letter 'm' but his hand gave him an 'n' – that the play should be known as the 'tamer of Denmark', and that the extant manuscript play, *Edmund Ironside*, is a candidate for its true identity.[33] Inasmuch as the fully searchable component of *Early English Books Online* doesn't offer an alternative to the propositions currently being canvassed by scholars, one might be inclined to think the mystery will always remain insoluble; a 'dead end' as Manley and MacLean dub it.[34] Steggle has carefully delineated the most useful search strategies for raiding *Early*

---

[28] P.l Drábek and M. A. Katritzky, 'Shakespearean Players in Early Modern Europe' in B. R. Smith (ed.), *The Cambridge Guide to the Worlds of Shakespeare* (Cambridge: Cambridge University Press, 2016), 2.1527.

[29] Fleay, *BCED*, 2.298; W. W. Greg (ed.), *Henslowe's Diary, Part II. Commentary* (London: A. H. Bullen, 1908), 156.

[30] R. L. Knutson, 'Playing Companies and Repertory' in A. F. Kinney (ed.), *A Companion to Renaissance Drama* (Malden: Blackwell, 2002), 185; Knutson, *The Repertory*, 43.

[31] Dollerup, *Denmark, Hamlet, and Shakespeare*, 1.48; see also her 'A Shakespeare Allusion to a Lost Play ("Hamlet", V.i.162)?', *Notes & Queries*, 23(4) (1976), 156–157.

[32] See Manley and MacLean, *Lord Strange's Men*, 149–156; Manley presented this material earlier at the Shakespeare Association of America's 2013 meeting in Toronto.

[33] Manley and MacLean, *Lord Strange's Men*, 151.

[34] Manley and MacLean, *Lord Strange's Men*, 149.

English Books Online (*EEBO*) for clues about lost plays,[35] including the use of basic searches (for example, **tanner of**), proximity searches (which in this case could be **tanner NEAR.4 denmark**), search strings to decipher the word 'taner' (**tan***) and 'select from a list' searches in which **tane** or **tanne** are entered and related words identified.[36] None of these yields a solution to the present crux, but as Ian Gadd and others have gently reminded us, *EEBO* should be treated as a very fine library of texts, not a complete representation of everything printed.[37] Not everything that is in *EEBO* has been transcribed by the Text Creation Partnership branch of the project: John Baret's *An Alvearie* (1580) is one such text that is not fully searchable. This dictionary includes a headword entry for 'tanner' explaining its proverbial use as applied to 'those that are of hautie behauiour, and vaunt of their doings, a though they had harrowed hell'. The etymology is suggested by Randle Cotgrave in his *Dictionary of the French and English Tongues* (1611, also not yet in EEBO-TCP), where the French 'taner' is glossed as 'To tanne … also, to trouble, irke, molest, harrie, ouertoile'.[38]

If I expand our purview by adding to the mix this definition of 'tanner' as one of 'hautie behauiour', at least two additional possibilities for subject matter become worth considering in relation to the extant drama. Rather than advocate either of these possibilities over the more traditionally accepted alternative (or even over Manley and MacLean's preferred solution), what I want to do here is to suggest that when dealing with the amorphous mass of lost plays, it can be more beneficial to keep options open than to shut them down. Pending the discovery of new information that might confirm the subject matter of this play, the most responsible

---

[35] Steggle, *Digital Humanities*, 22–24, and see his principles for using EEBO-TCP on p. 26.

[36] Entering **tane** yields such options as **'taner' OR 'Taner' OR 'tanern' OR 'Tanerne' OR 'Tanernes'** to enter as search terms (the last two being errors for 'tavern', the most interesting of the others being Welsh words or the name of a river – the Tanaro, known in ancient times as the Tane – in north-western Italy; nowhere near Denmark), which produces twenty-one hits in seventeen records. Entering **tanne** in the 'select from a list' search menu yields such variants as **'Tanne' OR 'tanne' OR 'Tannè' OR 'tanné' OR 'Tanné' OR 'Tanner' OR 'tanner' OR 'TANNER' OR 'Tanner' OR 'Tanneras' OR 'tannere' OR 'Tannere'**, producing 1865 hits in 722 records, most of which are unhelpful. A villain named John Tanner who tried to pass himself off as the son of Edward I; Jesus's disciple Peter lodged in Joppa with a tanner named Simon; and 'ta'en' (a variant of 'taken') as the true referent of 'tane' are the more common hits.

[37] I. Gadd, 'The Use and Misuse of *Early English Books Online*', *Literature Compass*, 6(3) (2009), 680–692.

[38] *Lexicons of Early Modern English*. Ed. Ian Lancashire. Toronto, ON: University of Toronto Library and University of Toronto Press, 2006. http://leme.library.utoronto.ca/lexicon/entry.cfm?ent=298-43366

thing to do is to survey the possibilities and thereby make them available to future scholars to build upon.

The first of the possible candidates for subject matter is none other than Hamlet's father in Danish legend: the pirate king, Horvendile. There may be a topical allusion to him in drama performed around the time of the 'taner of denmarke' play. In Marlowe's *Edward II* (1592), Mortimer Junior tells Lancaster that '[t]he haughty Dane commands the narrow seas'.[39] The Revels Plays editor observes that '[t]he notion of Denmark's controlling the English Channel ("the narrow seas") in Edward II's reign is totally unhistorical',[40] so the identity of the 'haughty Dane' of Marlowe's allusion has remained untraced. If our 'taner' or 'tanner' (one of 'hautie behauiour') were a pirate and Danish, an obvious candidate would be Hamlet's father, Horvendile, who was king of Denmark and 'the most renoued [sic] pirate that in those dayes scoured the seas and havens of the north parts' according to François de Belleforest's account of the Hamlet legend in *Histoires Tragiques*.[41] A play about Hamlet's father would provide Strange's Men with repertorial competition for the lost 'Hamlet' performed by the Admiral's Men in 1594 but dating to an earlier season (c.1587–1589).[42] One explanation for why Marlowe might allude to '[t]he haughty Dane' without elucidation is that playgoers might be expected to recognise an allusion to the eponymous protagonist of a now lost play, if Marlowe had 'the taner of denmarke' in mind.

The prospect that the 'haughty Dane' line refers to a lost play is marginally improved by the likelihood that at least one other lost play seems to be the subject of an allusion in *Edward II*: Mark Hutchings has recently suggested that when Lancaster uses the term 'Greekish strumpet' pejoratively to describe Gaveston, he is not necessarily repurposing the Helen of Troy allusion from *Faustus* (Gaveston becoming the cause of destruction as well as being beautiful); rather, Hutchings proposes that the young Greek girl, Irene (or Hiren) – who captured the heart of Sultan Mehmed II at the capture of Constantinople in 1453 – is a better fit for the subject of the reference.[43] Hutchings does not seem to notice that the

---

[39] Marlowe, *Edward II*, C. R. Forker (ed.) (Revels Plays) (Manchester: Manchester University Press, 1994), 2.2.167.

[40] Marlowe, Edward II, 2.2.167n.

[41] The quotation is the English translation, *The Hystorie of Hamblet* (London: Imprinted by Richard Bradoke, for Thomas Pavier, 1608) as reproduced in Sir I. Gollancz, *The Sources of Hamlet, with an Essay on the Legend* (London: Frank Cass & Co. Ltd, 1967), 181.

[42] On the dating of 'old' Admiral's plays in the 1594 repertory, see Wiggins' discussion under entry #785.

[43] M. Hutchings, 'Marlowe's "Greekish Strumpet"', *Notes and Queries*, 62(1) (2015), 66–69.

allusion, if indeed to Irene, most likely invoked Peele's lost play of c.1588–1589, 'Turkish Mahomet and Hiren the Fair Greek'.[44]

I am just guessing about this Horvendile suggestion, of course, and to forcefully insist on this guess would be analogous in some ways to the hastiness of early critics in closing down options when the situation calls for possibilities to be kept in play. I therefore want to explore the alternative possibility that the Dane of 'haughtie behauiour' could instead be associated with Colebrand, the proud giant from the Guy of Warwick story. The legend of Guy circulated widely in the fifteenth century and was 'the best known of English popular romances', as Helen Moore notes.[45] The subject was treated by such authors as Michael Drayton in his *Poly-Olbion* (1612) and mentioned by Stow and Holinshed.[46] A ballad on the topic was registered at Stationers' Hall on 5 January 1592, but is now lost.[47] One early version from 1600 relates 'the proud disdain of Colbrond', the Danish giant who boldly challenged any Englishman to combat, 'calling the English cowardly Dogs, & that he would make their Carcasses meat for Crows and Ravens'.[48] The English King Athelstan and his men could not best the giant until a champion came to their aid in the form of Guy of Warwick, his greatness disguised by the palmer's weeds he wore. In the anonymous *Guy of Warwick* play, printed in 1661 but almost certainly of sixteenth- or early seventeenth-century origins, the giant has only a small but memorable part, taunting Guy towards the end of Act 4: 'Must *Colbron* Fight with such a withered Ghost, / a very shrimp, a worm, a gnat, a fly, / I scorn him and will spurn him at my feet'.[49]

Although it might seem unlikely that a play would be named for a giant rather than the giant-killer, it is possible that another lost play encapsulates precisely this phenomenon: on 6 April and then 8 May 1592 – the latter only a fortnight before Henslowe recorded the 'taner of denmarke' performance – Henslowe entered in his diary a play he called 'brandymer' (or 'brandimer').[50] As Wiggins notes, this ambiguous title might refer to 'King Brandimort' from Ariosto's *Orlando furioso*, but it might alternatively refer

---

[44] Wiggins #803; see also the *LPD* entry.

[45] H. Moore (ed.), *Guy of Warwick. Malone Society Reprints*, vol. 170 (Manchester: Manchester University Press, 2007), xxiii.

[46] Drayton, Song 12, *Poly-Olbion* (London, 1612), 195; J. Stow, *The chronicles of England from Brute vnto this present yeare of Christ. 1580* (London, 1580), 131; R. Holinshed, *The First and Second Volumes of Chronicles* (London, 1587), Bk 6, 156.

[47] Arber (ed.), *Stationers' Register*, 2.601.

[48] S. Smithson, *The Famous History of Guy Earl of Warwick* (London, 1600), sig.[B3]v.

[49] Moore (ed.), *Guy of Warwick*, TLN 977–79.   [50] Foakes (ed.), *Henslowe's Diary*, 17–18.

to 'Brandimore', another giant killed by Guy of Warwick.[51] Wiggins refers to a ballad published in 1612 which states that Guy 'slew the Giant Brandimore', suggesting that a mistake has possibly been made for the giant 'more commonly called Colbrand, or perhaps Amarant'. In fact, Brandimore appears to have been a giant in his own right, existing outside the story of Guy's slaying of Colebrand and Amarant, but added to the Guy legend at some point prior to 1675 when printers combined *Guy of Warwick* and *The Seven Champions of Christendom*, making Guy the eldest son of Saint George and Guy's brother Alex the slayer of Brandimore.[52] The 1612 ballad may indicate that this merging of legends occurred significantly earlier however. Two carved statues adorning the Guild Hall prior to the Great Fire of 1666 were variously referred to as the indigenous British giants Gog and Magog or less commonly as Colebrand and Brandimore.[53] It is not inconceivable that the moderate success of 'brandymer' encouraged the company to indulge in a related play about another giant-slaying. It is tempting to imagine the famously tall Edward Alleyn, who was probably cast as both Longshanks and Long Meg in plays performed together in 1595,[54] having earlier played the Danish giant Colebrand.[55]

To summarise: the 'taner of denmarke' may have referred to one who is haughty in behaviour rather than one who tans hides for a living. Either of the options that I explore above, involving sea-faring piracy or giant-slaying would accord well with the penchant for spectacle in the Lord Strange's Men's repertory.[56] Moreover, a play in which the English were pitted against the Danish (or a Dane, at least) would complement what

---

[51] Wiggins #897.

[52] 'Amarant' is the name given to the giant killed by Guy in Samuel Smithson's *The Famous History of Guy Earl of Warwick* (London, 1600). The details of Brandimore's defeat (at the hands of Sir Alex) are preserved in expanded late-seventeenth-century editions of Richard Johnson's *The famous history of the seven champions of Christendom* (1596–1597), e.g. the London, 1696 edition, 27–29; see V. Bourgeois Richmond, *The Legend of Guy of Warwick* (New York: Garland Publishing, Inc., 1996), 199.

[53] The ballad is *Saint Georges commendation to all Souldiers* (London, 1612), *English Broadside Ballad Archive* #20041. On Colebrand and Brandimore as distinct giants see Anon., *A Dialogue between the Two Giants in Guildhall, Colebrond and Brandamore, concerning the Late Election of Citizens to Serve in Parliament for the City of London* (London, 1661).

[54] R. L. Knutson, 'What Was James Burbage Thinking?' in P. Kanelos and M. Kozusko (eds.), *Thunder at a Playhouse* (Selingsgrove: Susquehanna University Press, 2010), 122. She refers to 'Longshanks', marked 'ne' on 29 August 1595 in the Admiral's repertory, and 'Long Meg of Westminster', introduced the previous February but not marked 'ne'.

[55] Alleyn also appears to have played the Danish king Cutlack, a role recalled by Everard Guilpin in his reference to '*Allens Cutlacks* gate'; see E. Guilpin, *Skialetheia. Or, A shadowe of truth, in certaine epigrams and satyres* (London, 1598), sig.B2ᵛ.

[56] Manley and MacLean, *Lord Strange's Men*, 188.

I see as a general trend in lost Danish plays of the 1590s, which are notable for apparently dramatising events in which Denmark's fate is closely entwined with England's, the two countries sharing political ties and even rulers. Taken together, these lost plays constitute a stage history of Anglo-Danish interactions from the pre-Norman era in which Denmark is frequently twinned with England's fortunes.

This phenomenon is abundantly evident in the second example I want to discuss: the story of Earl Godwin and his three sons, which was dramatised by Chettle, Dekker, Drayton and Wilson as a two-part play for the Admiral's Men in the spring to summer of 1598. The subject matter, which is preserved in Foxe amongst other sources, is related to that of a number of other plays from the period. Earl Godwin's story takes place in the generation after the confrontation and amicable resolution of King Edmund and King Canute with which the anonymous manuscript play *Edmund Ironside* (c.1597) concludes.[57] Edmund has been killed and Canute has reigned as the sole monarch for twenty years or more until his death. His sons Harold and Hardicanute were kings of England and Denmark respectively, but Harold died after four years and the Danish Hardicanute became King of England too, thus uniting the two countries.

Hardicanute reigned only briefly. A short time into his reign, he was suddenly struck dumb, fell to the ground, and died within eight days, leaving no heirs. He thus became the last Danish king of England. (A 'Hardicanewtes' play appears in the list of playbooks in Henslowe's inventory in 1598: it was performed by Pembroke's Men, and must have become part of the Admiral's repertory when some of the players from Pembroke's joined the Admiral's Men in October 1597.[58])

With Canute and now his two sons dead, the potential successors included the two sons of Canute's second wife, from her former marriage: Alfred and Edward. Matters are further complicated though: owing to his military exploits on behalf of Denmark against Norway, the English Earl Godwin had previously been in great favour with Canute and had even married Canute's sister (or daughter; the sources are unclear). Godwin, seeing a claim to the throne for his own family, intercepted Alfred and Edward as they prepared to return to England from Normandy. He blinded Alfred and sent him to an abbey at Ely, where he died shortly thereafter. Edward survived and became Edward the Confessor. When the Lords of England learned of Godwin's treachery, they determined that he

---

[57] Wiggins #1064; the play is found in British Library MS Egerton 1994, fos. 96ᵣ–118ᵣ.
[58] Foakes (ed.), *Henslowe's Diary*, 324; Wiggins #1069.

should be put to death; but by that stage, Godwin had already fled to Denmark, where he remained for more than four years, forfeiting his lands in England as a result.

Godwin's service on behalf of the Danes placed his progeny in line for the English throne; and when events took a turn for the worse, Denmark became a place of refuge for Godwin. Later, Godwin returned to England and was accepted by King Edward. Edward even married Godwin's daughter but he did not consummate the marriage (hence, Foxe tells us, his reputation as 'Holy K. Edward, a virgine in maryage').[59] Edward's reign is characterised by anti-Danish sentiment: as a king, he was notably a 'mere [i.e., pure] Englishman', and he 'discharged the Englishmen of the great tribute called Dane gelt, which before time was yerely leuied to the great impouerishing of the people'.[60] Shakespeare evokes Danegelt when he has Claudius send Hamlet 'with speed to England / For the demand of our neglected tribute' (8.163–164), and it is clearly England's recent conquest by the Danes (the English scars are 'raw and red / After the Danish sword', 13.54–55) and the debt England subsequently owes to the Danes ('thy free awe / Pays homage to us', 13.55–56) that Claudius believes will secure English cooperation in executing Hamlet.[61] Godwin, though, straddles the national divide, embracing both Denmark and England; when he finally fell out of favour with Edward the Confessor, he died by an apparent *deus ex machina*: over dinner, Edward asked Godwin whether he had murdered Edward's brother Alfred; Godwin swore that just as he could eat this morsel of bread, he was guiltless of the deed. He ate the bread and promptly choked. Edward eventually named Godwin's son Harold his successor, and it is this Harold who is well-known as having been vanquished by William the Conqueror. Sussex's Men had performed a 'William the Conqueror' play at the Rose in December 1593.[62]

The picture that is beginning to emerge, then, is of a stage history of Anglo-Danish interactions from the pre-Norman era, in which Denmark is figured almost as England's uncanny Other. England resists Danish rule and resents Danish influence, but the two countries' fortunes are interlinked at various points of succession crisis. Englishness is seemingly depicted through emergence from the Danish shadow, via direct

---

[59] J. Foxe, *Actes and Monuments* (London, 1583), 1.164.   [60] Foxe, *Actes and Monuments*, 1.164.
[61] I thank Douglas McQueen-Thomson for pointing out this connection.
[62] William the Conqueror is also a character in the anonymous *Fair Em* play, which is sometimes conflated with the lost 'William the Conqueror' play.

engagement with the Danish challenge. In 'the taner of denmarke' and 'brandymer' this may even have symbolically involved the slaying of a Danish giant. The Hamlet legend had been dramatised since at least the 1580s, and may even (at a stretch) have involved a prequel play about Hamlet's father, the pirate king Horvendile (if my alternative conjecture about the haughty Dane who controls the sea, the 'tanner' of Denmark, turns out to have merit). When Shakespeare was writing his *Hamlet*, probably at the turn of the century, the parallel between Denmark and England was already familiar and well established; his Elsinore as foil for Elizabethan London didn't come from nowhere, but rather tapped into a stage history of the two nations' shared fortunes and England's progression towards independence. To grasp the full picture of Anglo-Danish relations as a context for *Hamlet*, the 'ground' of Denmark needs to be valued for its shaping effect on the 'figure' of *Hamlet* when we look at early modern drama.

Hamlet and 'felmelanco'

Just as 'Owen Tudor', as a repertorial response to *Henry V*, prompts reconsideration of the early reception and commercial identity of Shakespeare's play, it is possible that 'felmelanco' (Admiral's, 1602) might provide a helpful context for understanding *Hamlet*.[63] This section, then, is not so much about *Hamlet* occupying a pivotal position in the Chamberlain's repertory as it is about 'felmelanco' and how that lost play may have participated in a vogue for theological subject matter with which *Hamlet*, to a lesser extent, also engages. My argument here is necessarily more tentative than it was for 'Owen Tudor'/*Henry V* because 'felmelanco' is notorious amongst theatre historians for refusing to yield any clues to its identity. As such, it represents an extreme test case for working with lost plays. The question that interests me most here is: What sort of evidence would scholars require in order to take a proposed subject matter seriously?

If sense could be made of the apparently mangled title, the subject matter might be judged as 'possible' according to the taxonomy of claims proposed by Terence Schoone-Jongen (the possible, the plausible, and the probable).[64] If there were a timely availability of a relevant source

---

[63] Henslowe refers to the play as 'felmel*a*nco', 'felmela*n*co', 'felmelanco' and 'felmel*anco*'; see Foakes (ed.), *Henslowe's Diary*, 205. For convenience I choose to use the version without italics.

[64] T. G. Schoone-Jongen, *Shakespeare's Companies: William Shakespeare's Early Career and Acting Companies, 1577–1594* (Farnham: Ashgate, 2008), 4.

text, or if the subject matter were complemented by other plays in the company's repertory, the identification might proceed to at least 'plausible', because it can be justified (though not proven) in some way. To become 'probable' would require the explanation being stronger than the alternatives, such that those alternatives might be safely discarded: an eyewitness account of the performance of a play featuring the proposed subject matter – or better yet, an account which explicitly mentions the title and enables us to interpret it confidently as either an error or as an invented name – would be required. But such things are exceptionally rare: the diary of Frederic Gerschow, tutor to Philip Julius, Duke of Stettin-Pomerania, is one such example, for it contains eyewitness accounts that have enabled scholars to identify Henslowe's 'Albere galles' with 'The Capture of Stuhlweissenburg' and the play about 'A Royal Widow of England' with *Sir Giles Goosecap*.[65] Unfortunately, if Gerschow saw 'felmelanco' in performance, he does not mention it. I therefore offer the following as 'plausible' and potentially more compelling than previous hypotheses, but still in need of further evidence.

Here is the evidence Henslowe provides: on September 9, 1602, Henslowe lent Humphrey Jeffes £3 as partial payment to 'm^r Robensone' for an enigmatically named tragedy whose title Henslowe recorded as 'felmelanco'. A week later, on September 15, Henslowe lent Thomas Downton a further ten shillings to pay Henry Chettle for the same 'tragedie of felmelanco', and on a subsequent, undated occasion he made a final payment of fifty shillings to Chettle (via Downton), again consistent in his naming of the play as 'felmelanco'.[66] No performance records exist, but the £6 total fee advanced to Robinson and Chettle is on par with the usual payment for a complete play and there is no reason to think the play was not produced. Critics have remained baffled both by the subject matter of this lost play (who or what was 'felmelanco'?) and by Chettle's otherwise unknown collaborator, 'Mr Robinson'.

Fleay, who misread the entry in Henslowe as 'Femelanco', doubted the existence of Henslowe's 'Mr Robinson' as co-author: 'Robinson was, I think, to Chettle what Mrs. Harris was to Mrs. Gamp' (Harris being a product of Gamp's imagination in Charles Dickens' *Martin Chuzzlewit*).[67] W. Carew Hazlitt, following Fleay's misreading of the title, interpreted

---

[65] See Steggle, *Digital Humanities*, 104–105; A. H. Tricomi, 'The Dates of the Plays of George Chapman', *English Literary Renaissance*, 12(2) (1982), 247.
[66] Foakes (ed.), *Henslowe's Diary*, 205.   [67] Fleay, *BCED*, 1.70.

'Femelanco' as 'The Female Anchoress'.[68] In his index entry for Robinson, Hazlitt added the forename 'Richard' but did not provide dates to clarify which Richard Robinson he had in mind. Greg assumed that Hazlitt meant 'an obscure miscellaneous writer of the time', namely the poet active from 1573 to 1589.[69] (Chambers however, following George McGill Vogt, noted that '[d]ates make it improbable' that he was the poet Richard Robinson.[70]) Harold Jenkins, in a biography of Chettle, has nothing to add about the title, but dismissed four candidates for Chettle's co-author: a Richard Robinson who wrote 'The ruefull Tragedie of Hemidos and Thelay' by 1569, a later Richard Robinson who 'wrote chiefly on subjects of theological interest', and two actors who are not heard of until after 1611 and 1616 respectively.[71] Greg dismissed Fleay's fanciful conjecture that 'Mr Robinson' was a 'fictitious character', suggesting instead that Chettle had pawned a play (as he subsequently did on 07 March 1603) and that Robinson was involved in the financial transaction rather than having 'any hand in the play'.[72] Regarding the title, Greg preferred to think Henslowe meant 'Fell Melanco', but declined to explain what he thought that might mean.[73] Most recently, Wiggins surveys the various suggestions for interpreting the title (noting the 'especial desperation' of the 'Female Anchoress' suggestion, with its 'redundant adjective').[74] With 'equal lack of conviction', he raises the possibility of 'a deaf or confused Henslowe mangling the word *calamanco* (meaning a type of fine chequered cloth)' or the possibility of 'the title as the worn-down remnants of *Philip the Melancholy*' (but dismisses this possibility on the grounds that Henslowe 'would then have bought the play twice over' within the space of about a month). The 'nearest long-shot' he offers is 'Philomela', which he notes 'fails to account for the last three letters'. Wiggins concludes that 'felmelanco' might 'just as well be an invented proper name, and therefore unlikely to be traceable'.

Wiggins may well be right, and in what follows I do not claim to have solved the 'felmelanco' riddle conclusively, by any means; but in keeping

---

[68] W. Carew Hazlitt, *A Manual for the Collector and Amateur of Old English Plays* (London, 1892), 84.

[69] Greg, *Henslowe's Diary, Part II: Commentary*, 224. See also Brian Cummings, 'Robinson, Richard (fl. 1573–1589)', *Oxford Dictionary of National Biography*, Oxford University Press, 2004 (www.oxforddnb.com/view/article/23865, accessed 11 July 2017).

[70] Chambers, *Elizabethan Stage*, 3.471; see also G. McGill Vogt, 'Richard Robinson's "Eupolemia" (1603)', *Studies in Philology*, 21(4) (1924), 629–648.

[71] H. Jenkins, *The Life and Work of Henry Chettle* (London: Sidgwick & Jackson Ltd, 1934), 241.

[72] Greg, *Henslowe's Diary, Part II: Commentary*, 224.

[73] Greg, *Henslowe's Diary, Part II: Commentary*, 224.   [74] Wiggins #1354.

with my methodology throughout this book, I see value in exploring alternatives that might one day yield new conclusions even if they currently remain inconclusive. Let me begin with the one clearly readable name: 'Robinson'. What if Hazlitt meant not Richard Robinson the poet, who disappeared from public view too early (by 1589) to be of any use to Chettle in 1602, but Richard Robinson (1544/5–1603), scribe, translator, and freeman of the Leathersellers' Company, who published between 1576–1600 and was sometimes styled 'Citizen of London' on the title-pages of his books?[75] This was the Robinson that Jenkins dismissed, perhaps too hastily, on the grounds of his theological interests; he was in fact the Robinson who translated the *Gesta Romanarum* (1577; revised in 1595 and with further editions in 1600 and 1602). It was his translation that Shakespeare appears to have relied upon for the caskets episode of *Merchant of Venice*.[76]

This Robinson was by no means a successful writer; G. E. Bentley uses Robinson's account of his literary receipts (his *Eupolemia*; British Library, Royal MS 18 A LXVI) as primary evidence of literary income from patronage and publication in the period. He notes that Robinson 'tried for a gift from a patron in connection with each publication between 1577–1596, but he was only intermittently successful'.[77] Amongst his patrons were Sir Philip Sidney and the Earl of Rutland, the dedicatees of Robinson's translations of Phillip Melanchthon's *Prayers* (1579) and his *In defence of Gods church, and of his worde* (1580).[78] Nevertheless, eking out an existence through solicited patronage was far from lucrative; Bentley juxtaposes Robinson's total earnings from non-dramatic literature over

[75] See R. C. L. Sgroi, 'Robinson, Richard (1544/5–1603)' in *Oxford Dictionary of National Biography*, Oxford University Press, 2004 (www.oxforddnb.com/view/article/23866, accessed 11 July 2017).

[76] See, for example, R. Krug, 'Shakespeare's Medieval Morality: *The Merchant of Venice* and the *Gesta Romanorum*' in C. Perry and J. Watkins (eds.), *Shakespeare and the Middle Ages* (Oxford: Oxford University Press, 2009), 243; Shakespeare, *The Merchant of Venice*, J. Drakakis (ed.) (London: Arden Shakespeare, 2010), 60–61; and G. Bullough (ed.), *Narrative and Dramatic Sources of Shakespeare*, vol. 1 (London: Routledge and Kegan Paul, 1957), 459–460.

[77] G. E. Bentley, *The Profession of Dramatist in Shakespeare's Time, 1590–1642* (Princeton, NJ: Princeton University Press, 1971), 90.

[78] See Vogt, 'Richard Robinson's "Eupolemia" (1603)', 632–633. The texts are: *Godly prayers meete to be vsed in these later times: collected out of the workes of that godly and reuerende father, Doctor Philip Melancthon and others: Now newly translated into Englishe. Seene and allowed, according to the order appointed. Imprinted at London: By [Henry Denham, being] the assigne of W. Seres, 1579.* (STC (2nd ed.)/17790.5); *A godly and learned assertion in defence of the true church of God, and of His Woorde written in Latine by that Reuerend Father D. Philip Melancthon, after the conuention at Ratisbona, anno 1541; translated into English by R.R. [London]: Imprinted at London at the three Cranes in the Vinetree by Thomas Dawson, 1580.* (STC (2nd ed.)/17790).

nineteen years (£52 17s 5d) with Chettle's receipt of £123 17s 6d for dramatic writings in just five and a half years working for Henslowe; the annual average for Robinson was less than £3, whilst Chettle averaged close to £25.[79] If Richard Robinson were Henslowe's 'Mr Robinson', it is little wonder he might have been tempted to abandon subsistence by patronage and try his hand at earning a playwright's fee. My thesis would be greatly strengthened of course if there were some clearly documented connection between Robinson and Chettle to improve the likelihood of their collaboration in 1602. Chettle was apprenticed to the printer Thomas East (or Est) in 1577 for a period of eight years, becoming a freeman of the Stationers' Company in 1584.[80] It was East who published Robinson's revised edition of the *Gesta* in 1595 (and again in 1600 and 1602), but the East connection is far from a smoking gun in terms of attempting to establish some kind of material connection between the two writers.

Now to the apparently garbled title: what might the title 'felmelanco' mean? A promising approach might be to follow Matthew Steggle's method for solving the textual crux of another opaquely titled lost play, 'albere galles' by using the 'Select from a list' feature of EEBO-TCP.[81] This function generates a list of every key term in the EEBO-TCP database, sorted alphabetically. It enables users to locate every possible term beginning with the first element of their search term. The longest string of letters from 'felmelanco' for which the database returns hits, however, is 'felme'; and these hits are either mis-transcriptions (of 'Anselme' or 'Flemish'), or variant spellings of 'film'. Selecting keywords from a list does not provide an obvious solution to what Henslowe may have meant.

Previous attempts to explicate this opaque noun have assumed that the title as Henslowe recorded it was a bastardisation of a vaguely similar sounding name ('calamanco', 'Philomela'); they have assumed that Henslowe combined two words into one ('felmelanco' actually stands for 'Fell Melanco' or the 'Female Anchoress'); or they have relied on extrapolation and inference (the misread 'femelanco' became 'Female Anchoress'; the correctly read 'felmelanco' became 'Philip the

---

[79] Bentley, *The Profession of Dramatist*, 104.

[80] E. Smith, 'Chettle, Henry (d. 1603x7)', *Oxford Dictionary of National Biography*, Oxford University Press, 2004 (www.oxforddnb.com/view/article/5245, accessed 11 July 2017).

[81] Steggle, *Digital Humanities*, 104–105. The title 'albere galles' turns out to be 'Alba Regalis', an alternative name for the besieged city of Stuhlweissenberg.

Melancholy').[82] Drawing on all three approaches, I propose a hitherto unconsidered alternative that relies on Henslowe mis-recording or mishearing two words in an abbreviated form, whereby 'felmelanco' might actually mean not 'Philip the Melancholy' but 'Phil[ip] Melanc [hth]o[n]'. The process whereby 'philip' might be abbreviated to 'phil' and written as 'fel' is plausible enough: Henslowe uses 'ph' and 'f' interchangeably, as in his varied spelling of 'fayeton' and 'phayeton' on a single page of the diary (15 and 26 January 1598, respectively), and his use of 'e' in lieu of 'y' or 'i' is evident in his recording of 'allece perce' for 'Alice Pierce', 'pethageros' for 'Pythagoras', and both 'bendo' and 'byndo' for one of the titular characters of a lost Strange's Men play.[83] Working on the premise that the '-thon' in 'Melanchthon' might be misheard as an 'o' sound (or even written as such, with a tilde representing an absent 'n': 'Melanchthõ'), I conducted a keyword search for **phil.melanc*** in EEBO-TCP, using the wildcard symbol (*) to allow for variant endings. This search currently yields thirty-seven hits in twenty-one records between 1570–1602, every single one of which point to variants of 'Phil.Melanchthon'.[84]

Serendipitously – though quite possibly by a complete coincidence – the Richard Robinson who died a year after Henslowe's 'felmelanco' references, and whose literary receipts were analysed by Bentley, was intimately acquainted with the work of Phillip Melanchthon – perhaps uniquely so, having translated not one but two of his works:

> *Godly prayers meete to be vsed in these later times: collected out of the workes of that godly and reuerende father, Doctor Philip Melancthon and others: Now newly translated into Englishe. Seene and allowed, according to the order*

---

[82] 'Philip the Melancholy' is perhaps an unlikely extrapolation from Henslowe's '-melanco' for the simple reason that when Henslowe elsewhere records the word 'melancholy' as part of a play title, his preferred spelling entails a double-l: 'mellencoley' and 'mallencoley' (Foakes (ed.), *Henslowe's Diary*, 23, as part of 'Tasso's Melancholy' on 11 and 18 August 1594). Perhaps coincidentally though, 'Philomela' is an apt guess in that Melanchthon's student Johann Major referred to Phillip Melanchthon as 'Philo Mela' (the nightingale) on account of Melanchthon's poetry; see M. P. Fleischer, 'Melanchthon as Praeceptor of Late-Humanist Poetry', *Sixteenth Century Journal*, 20 (1989), 559–580, esp. 570, citing A. Blaschke, 'Wittenbergische Nachtigall: Sternstunden eines Topos', *Wissenschaftliche Zeitschrift der Martin Luther Universitat Halle-Wittenberg, Gesellschafts-und Sprachwissenschaftliche Reihe*, 4 (1961), 897–908.

[83] See Foakes (ed.), *Henslowe's Diary*, 86 ('fayeton'/'phayeton'), 73 ('allece perce'), 34 ('pethagoras'), and 16–17 (for the 'Bendo and Richardo' play). The records of a play variously spelled 'barnado & philameta' (32; or 'phiameta', 34) and 'barnado & fiameta' (36) provide a further instance of interchangeable 'ph'/'f' spellings in Henslowe's diary.

[84] A keyword search for a more abbreviated form, **phil.mela***, does not yield any other possibilities either; it generates forty hits in twenty-two records for the same timespan, all of which point to variants of 'Phil.Melanchthon'.

appointed. Imprinted at London : By [Henry Denham, being] the assigne of W. Seres, 1579 (STC 17790.5)

and:

A godly and learned assertion in defence of the true church of God, and of His Woorde written in Latine by that Reuerend Father D. Philip Melancthon, after the conuention at Ratisbona, anno 1541 ; translated into English by R.R., [London] : Imprinted at London at the three Cranes in the Vinetree by Thomas Dawson, 1580 (STC 17790).

If my proposal that 'felmelanco' were about Melanchthon is correct, it possibly explains the collaboration between an established playwright and an otherwise unknown amateur playwright who was, in Jenkins' phrase, characterised by his 'theological interest': Chettle may have been motivated to consult Robinson for biographical information about the play's subject matter.[85]

Phillip Melanchthon (1497–1560) is not necessarily an intuitive choice for the subject matter of an early modern commercial play. However, Shakespeare's contemporaries would have known him as 'a famous learned man' (in Lodowick Lloyd's words) and a champion of Erasmus's work.[86] Alongside Martin Luther and John Calvin, Melanchthon was considered one of the founders of Protestantism and his Wittenberg 'the cradle of the Reformation'.[87] Melanchthon might even have been a better choice to depict in a stage play than his now more famous peers given the failure of Lutheranism in the English Reformation and, by contrast, Melanchthon's theological impact on it (as John Schofield has argued). Schofield pithily characterises Melanchthon and England's Queen Elizabeth as 'soulmates who never met', suggesting that in the alignment of their particular brand of Protestant values, Elizabeth might best be described as 'Melanchthonian'.[88] In 1594, Thomas Nashe demonstrated a keen interest in the ferment of Reformation in northern Europe when he had his unfortunate traveller,

---

[85] A perhaps comparable case is the lost 'Strange News Out of Poland', for which Henslowe paid William Haughton and a certain 'Mr. Pett' in May to June 1600; here, as Sharpe has suggested, it appears that an established commercial playwright sought '[d]etails for dramatic use' from someone outside the theatrical world of London, thereby creating 'an interesting experiment in journalism'; see R. B. Sharpe, *The Real War of the Theaters* (Boston: D. C. Heath, 1935), 177, 179. Sharpe proposes that Henslowe's Pett was part of the Deptford shipbuilding family – probably Peter Pett (younger brother to Phineas), who came to London in November 1599 and died in June 1600 (178).

[86] L. Lloyd, *The first part of the diall of daies* (London, 1590), 57; C. G. Nauert, *Humanism and the Culture of Renaissance Europe* (Cambridge: Cambridge University Press, 1995), 165.

[87] S. H. Stein, 'Hamlet in Melanchthon's Wittenberg', *Notes and Queries*, 56(1) (2009), 56.

[88] J. Schofield, *Philip Melanchthon and the English Reformation* (Aldershot: Ashgate, 2006), 204.

Jack Wilton, visit Wittenberg and witness theological disputes between Martin Luther and Andreas Karlstadt, as well as a Faust-like conjuration performed by Cornelius Agrippa.[89] Suzanne H. Stein has noted that Shakespeare overtly altered his source texts by making Hamlet a student at Wittenberg specifically (it is mentioned four times in the play's second scene). She argues that he did this in order to explore his own 'ambivalence about Reformation humanism' and relied upon Melanchthon's reputation to do so.[90]

There remains the not inconsiderable problem of what a play about Philip Melanchthon would actually dramatise. Certainly he was an important scholar of international repute, and if Stein and others are correct, he may have indirectly influenced Shakespeare's *Hamlet* in some ways (which is to say, he held relevance to the London stage). Melanchthon's earliest and most influential biographer, Joachim Camerarius, is responsible for perpetuating a largely biased account of the reformer's life that would influence historians for centuries to come. Published in Leipzig in 1566, Camerarius's biography has been carefully analysed by Timothy J. Wengert in terms of its rhetorical mythologising of Melanchthon. Nevertheless, some of the details are interesting: 'Camerarius describes Melanchthon in terms of his great sorrow and perturbations of soul, which he bears with great patience and understanding'; that is, he is a stoic figure suffering from a melancholic disposition.[91] The depiction of Melanchthon's childhood is dimly reminiscent of Faustus's accomplishments and aspirations, tempered by Christian grace: 'We discover a child prodigy and polymath who had mastered all the liberal arts including rhetoric, physics, and astrology, a deeply religious individual, and a Christian of impeccable virtue'.[92] Camerarius creates a foil for Melanchthon in the figure of Matthias Flacius Illyricus: 'Flacius, the gnesio-Lutheran from Croatia who trained under Melanchthon and who began his attack on Melanchthon over his stand on the so-called

---

[89] Nashe, *The Unfortunate Traveller* (1594), sigs. E4ᵛ–F3ᵛ.

[90] 'Humanism came to Wittenberg and evolved into the reigning orthodoxy primarily through the determined efforts of one figure, Phillip Melanchthon, *Praeceptor Germaniae*, complex and brilliant, considered by Reformation scholars more influential in some features of Lutheran German life than Luther himself, and occasionally suggested as Shakespeare's model for Hamlet' (Stein, 'Hamlet in Melanchthon's Wittenberg', 56).

[91] T. J. Wengert, '"With Friends Like This …": The Biography of Philip Melanchthon by Joachim Camerarius' in T. F. Mayer and D. R. Woolf (eds.), *The Rhetorics of Life-Writing in Early Modern Europe: Forms of Biography from Cassandra Fedele to Louis XIV* (Ann Arbor, MI: University of Michigan Press, 1995), 118.

[92] Wengert, 'With Friends Like This', 118.

Leipzig Interim in 1548, serves as a counterpoint to all of Melanchthon's personal characteristics'.[93] He might serve as an appropriate antagonist on stage. Robinson was demonstrably familiar with Camerarius's biography of Melanchthon.[94]

The 'cause célèbre' of Melanchthon's life was his failed attempt to intervene in a notorious theological dispute between clergy and professors in Heidelberg over the question of the transubstantiation (or otherwise) of Christ's body in the Last Supper and 'bridge the gap' between the parties.[95] Melanchthon sent a letter to Elector Frederick of the Palatinate on 01 November 1559, stating his position vis-à-vis Christ's presence in the Supper; it generated a flurry of lengthy attacks and defences and earned Melanchthon the disparaging moniker of 'old fox', one who slinks 'around in the bushes waiting to attack some defenseless rabbit'.[96] Inherently timid or mild in nature, Melanchthon was grieved by the unwelcomed attention received from rival theologians throughout the last years of his life (he described it as the 'rage of theologians').[97] Camerarius's biography was written 'as a massive attack against Melanchthon's opponents', and 'portrays a Stoic hero, beset by cares, labors, solicitudes, sorrows, and finally miseries'.[98] Possibly such material might furnish a 'tragedy', as Henslowe records it, but 'tragedy' could also simply mean a play that included the protagonist's death (or even, perhaps, 'not a comedy'). I do not think that the term 'tragedy' is used by Henslowe specifically to refer to classical conceptions of genre.[99] Furthermore, in guessing at the kind of material that may have been depicted in this lost play, this could be an instance where, by privileging our expectations of extant early modern drama, we inadvertently try to fit a square peg into a round hole. Extant plays aren't always a reliable indicator of dramatic possibilities. Other lost Admiral's plays seem to have been improbable biographical dramas: what exactly was dramatised in the play named after the Greek philosopher 'Pythagoras'

[93] Wengert, 'With Friends Like This', 119.

[94] R. Robinson (trans.), *A godly and learned assertion in defence of the true church of God, and of His Woorde written in Latine by that Reuerend Father D. Philip Melancthon, after the conuention at Ratisbona, anno 1541; translated into English by R.R.* (London, 1580), sig.*5ᵛ.

[95] Wengert, 'With Friends Like This', 120–121.

[96] Wengert, 'With Friends Like This', 121, 123.   [97] See Schofield, *Philip Melanchthon*, 193.

[98] Wengert, 'With Friends Like This', 122, 123.

[99] As Matthew Steggle reminds me (personal correspondence), Henslowe also has a habit of entering plays in his diary according to the names of their most interesting characters (e.g. 'The Guise' for *The Massacre at Paris*); so perhaps Melanchthon could be a significant character in a play about (say) the Anabaptist revolt, which he was tangentially connected to, and which Nashe wrote about in *Unfortunate Traveller*.

(1596)?[100] Or in 'the play*e* of tasso' (about the Italian poet), which Dekker was paid to revise in January and November 1602, a few months before and after 'felmelanco' was paid for?[101] The Strange's Men play about the mendacious English traveller 'Sir John Mandeville' (1592) was similarly regarded as an unpromisingly biographical topic until Lawrence Manley and Martin Wiggins each independently noticed a possible redaction of the lost play in an apocryphal romance story involving Mandeville that appeared in William Warner's *Albion's England* (1596).[102] Perhaps a similarly lively but unhistorical or anecdotal account of Melanchthon lurks in the archive, awaiting rediscovery.

From the point of view of repertory studies, there are grounds for believing that the Admiral's Men may have thought it desirable to acquire a play about Wittenberg and theological dispute (whether scholarly or physical): 'felmelanco' was purchased in September 1602, weeks before Henslowe paid Bird and Rowley for additions to another play about a Wittenberg scholar, *Doctor Faustus* (22 November). Other famous scholars and theological disputes featured in plays around this time. The Dutch humanist scholar Erasmus joined the English Reformer Sir Thomas More in the manuscript play named after the latter (*Sir Thomas More*) – which, incidentally, Chettle co-authored, as Hand A (Jowett says that 'Henry Chettle may well have shared with Munday in the writing of the Original Text', for which he proposes a late date of around 1600; Wiggins opts for a 1601 date).[103] Subsequently, the Chamberlain's Men produced *Thomas, Lord Cromwell*, a play about another prominent advocate of the English Reformation, and one which had been 'lately acted' at the time of registration at Stationers' Hall on 11 August 1602. (The historical Melanchthon referred to Henry VIII as the 'English Nero' in light of Henry's execution of Cromwell and divorce from Anne of Cleves.)[104] Between June 1601 and May 1602, Chettle contributed to and then revised two Admiral's Men's plays about Cardinal Wolsey that may similarly have dramatised events important to the rift between

---

[100] Foakes (ed.), *Henslowe's Diary*, 34–37, 47–48, 89 and 324.

[101] Foakes (ed.), *Henslowe's Diary*, 187, 206. Henslowe refers to it elsewhere as 'Tasso's Melancholy', and Wiggins identifies '[c]ontemporary accounts of his personal story' that may have served as source material, suggestive of unrequited love and consequent dejection and 'Hamlet-like madness' (#963). Such a biographical account might pave the way for the dramatisation of the sorrows of Melanchthon's later years.

[102] L. Manley and S.-B. Maclean, *Lord Strange's Men and Their Plays* (New Haven, CT: Yale University Press, 2014), 134; Wiggins #911.

[103] J. Jowett (ed.), *Sir Thomas More* (Arden 3) (London: Methuen Drama, 2011), 15; Wiggins #1277.

[104] Schofield, *Philip Melanchthon*, 145.

Catholicism and Protestantism as experienced by the English.[105] Earlier in
1602, the year that 'felmelanco' was written, Henslowe paid Alleyn for
three playbooks including 'the massaker of france' (18 January); probably
Marlowe's *Massacre at Paris*, which famously included the murder of
another notable reformer and scholar, Peter Ramus.[106]

Further circumstantial support for the conjecture that 'felmelanco' took
a founder of Protestantism for its subject matter might be found in the
Admiral's Men's notable acquisition of a 'flurry' of biblical plays around
the turn of the century (Andrew Gurr calls it '[t]he most conspicuous
innovation of [Alleyn's] return').[107] In short succession, the company
acquired plays about 'Judas' and 'Pontius Pilate' (January 1602);
'Jephtha' (July 1602); 'Samson' (summer 1602); the Apocryphal 'Tobias'
(summer 1602); and 'Joshua' (autumn 1602). Robert B. Sharpe thought
this biblical series was the company's repertorial response to 'the current
vogue of satire'; their response being a 'harking back to the religious-ethical
type and justifying their scurrilities to their relatively unsophisticated
audience by uttering them as jeremiads'.[108] In the absence of explicit
archival evidence of biblical plays in the Chamberlain's repertory, Sharpe
believed a significant point of difference between these two companies was
that '[a]pparently the Chamberlain's company did not feel that plays on
Bible subjects would appeal to their clientele'.[109] He implied that the
Admiral's Men's 'great piety' at that date was political, and an implicit
response to the future King James I 'having done a great deal of coquetting
with Rome'.[110] John Astington also thought the biblical plays offered
thinly veiled political commentary as the 'virtues of the Old Testament
heroes and patriarchs were to be hoped for in a new monarch who would
maintain the political and religious integrity of the nation'.[111] Gurr, by
contrast, cites Alleyn's turn-of-the-century religiosity as a possible motivation for the company's biblical investments, going so far as to candidly
suggest: 'I suspect that he felt he needed this rush of biblical stories because
he was trying to downplay his own durable fame as the voice of that great

[105] See Wiggins #1293 and #1309.
[106] See J. Guillory, 'Marlowe, Ramus, and the Reformation of Philosophy', *English Literary History*, 81
(3) (2014), 693–732.
[107] Gurr, *Shakespeare's Opposites*, 41.
[108] R. B. Sharpe, *The Real War of the Theaters* (Boston: D. C. Heath, 1935), 136.
[109] Sharpe, *The Real War of the Theaters*, 28.   [110] Sharpe, *The Real War of the Theaters*, 29.
[111] J. H. Astington, 'A Jacobean Ghost, and Other Stories', *Medieval and Renaissance Drama in
England*, 17 (2005), 51.

downfaller, Faustus' – a reprised role for which Alleyn had famously taken the precaution of adorning himself with a prominent cross pendant.[112]

A play about one of the fathers of Protestantism – and a Wittenberg scholar who, far from abandoning his Christian faith, actively advanced its cause – would serve both Alleyn and the company well for all the reasons noted above. It would be consistent with the apparent ideological agenda (whether it be the company's or Alleyn's specifically), and it would offer an attenuated version of the *Faustus* premise, which Alleyn might find personally more agreeable. It would also suggest a closer alignment of these two companies' repertories than Sharpe allowed, an alignment that would be consistent with the repertorial competition that transpired two years earlier when the companies occupied the playhouses 'toe to toe across Maid Lane', as analysed by Knutson.[113] If the Admiral's put 'felmelanco' into production at their Fortune playhouse in late 1602, it may have competed for playgoer patronage with Shakespeare's *Hamlet* and its Wittenberg-educated prince, which had been 'latelie Acted by the Lord Chamberleyn his servantes' by 26 July 1602, when the first quarto was entered in the Stationers' Register.[114]

These new connections between *Hamlet* and its cross-company repertorial rivals in the form of *Faustus*, 'felmelanco', *The Massacre at Paris* and others, have implications for how literary critics might understand Shakespeare's play. Studies of *Hamlet* in terms of theological disputes (purgatory, the ghost of Old Hamlet) or in terms of biblical imagery (Genesis / the unweeded garden; the primal elder's curse / Cain and Abel imagery) could be revisited in terms of the apparent topicality of Reformation theologians. New connections might be made between the dramatisation of *ennui* in Faustus's boredom and Hamlet's 'stale and unprofitable' seeming world. So too studies of Shakespeare's protagonist as philosopher-student and of the nature of perception (being versus 'seeming' for Hamlet; transubstantiation for Melanchthon) are lent a fresh vibrancy when considered in the context of repertorial competition that activated or emphasised these dimensions of *Hamlet* for an early modern playgoer. It is tempting to think that *Hamlet* has been

---

[112] Gurr, 'What is lost', 57; see Samuel Rowlands, *The Knave of Clubs* (1609), sig.D3[r]: 'The Gull gets on a surplis, / With a crosse vpon his breast, / Like *Allen* playing *Faustus*'.

[113] R. L. Knutson, 'Toe to Toe Across Maid Lane: Repertorial Competition at the Rose and Globe, 1599–1600' in J. Schlueter and P. Nelsen (eds.), *Acts of Criticism: Performance Matters in Shakespeare and His Contemporaries* (Madison & Teaneck: Fairleigh Dickinson University Press, 2005), 21–37.

[114] Arber (ed.), *Stationers' Register*, 3.212.

approached from every conceivable scholarly angle, but here I have attempted to show how attention to lost plays might produce new intertextual connections or contexts for consideration – in terms of specific plays, this might entail comparative studies with *Doctor Faustus*, *The Massacre at Paris*, and of course 'felmelanco', but in more general terms it might mean treating *Hamlet* as a kind of English history play rather than a Danish tragedy.

§

Throughout this chapter, I focus on the distorting effect of Shakespearean bias and the role it plays in shaping our perception of how performances of *Henry V* and *Hamlet* at the Globe related to other plays performed in the London commercial theatres. In the case of *Henry V*, I argue that the contour we have traced between the extant and lost plays of its historical moment needs retracing because we may have misunderstood, at least in some measures, how early moderns conceived of the play's relationship to other drama. We do not know why the 'Owen Tudor' play did not survive; we do not have grounds for presuming its inferiority; we do have good cause to let its repertorial engagement with *Henry V* be the impetus to reconsider Shakespeare's play afresh. Critics tend to see *Henry V* as heralding a new phase in the company's trajectory, looking forward to its new home at the Globe and (though the company couldn't have known it at the time) their elevation to royal patronage. Perhaps, though, *Henry V* is equally backward-looking in its apparent emergence out of 1590s romantic comedies, at least in some regards.[115]

Although playgoers may have found much in *Hamlet* that was new and exciting, that play too is more of a piece with the 1590s, and a stage tradition of figuring Denmark as England's uncanny Other, than is commonly allowed by scholars who insist on seeing it as a radical break from dramatic tradition. *Hamlet* does also anticipate (or participate in) concerns more relevant to the turn of the century, including the

---

[115] There is a remote possibility that another lost play (if indeed it were a play) has some unlikely relevance here: 'The Tartarian Cripple, Emperor of Constantinople'. As I discussed in the previous chapter, there is reason to suppose that the subject matter essentially consisted of Tamburlaine being on vacation in Constantinople with the Greek emperor Emanuell. If the Chamberlain's Men did have a play that explored these events, Tamburlaine's turn from his usual military incursions to what is essentially a sightseeing excursion would be a particular type of genre-shifting spin-off. It would be consonant with the plausible turn from war to romance that pivots on Katherine's roles in *Henry V* and 'Owen Tudor', and with Falstaff's shift from history in the *Henry IV* plays to comedy in *The Merry Wives of Windsor* for that matter.

emergence of an inter-company engagement with theological interests. There is not yet any direct, primary evidence that 'felmelanco' was a play about 'phil melanc[hth]ō' (hence my suggested identification remaining 'plausible' rather than 'probable'), but the circumstantial repertorial evidence is suggestive. To invoke my negative space metaphor, the fuzzy edges of a distinctly Melanchthonian gap are beginning to appear in the 1602 theatrical season, perception of which encourages us to see an alternative figure taking shape in the repertory of the adult playing companies around that time.

CHAPTER 4

Courting Controversy – Shakespeare and the King's Men

On 19 May 1603, the Lord Chamberlain's Men became the King's Men when King James I declared via royal patent that he had 'licenced and authorized'[1] the company to use his name as their patron when playing 'Comedies, Tragedies, Histories, Enterludes, Moralles, Pastoralles, Stageplayes and such like' in public 'when the infection of the plague shall decrease'.[2] The prevalence of plague which James alluded to in his patent led to an indefinite extension of the ban on public performances that the Privy Council had imposed on 19 March 1603 (in anticipation of Elizabeth's imminent death). The ban was not lifted officially until Easter Monday 1604. Although there are records of occasional performances by the company at court during this period (one play on 2 December 1603, and eight plays between 26 December 1603 and 19 February 1604), the opportunities for public performances were severely limited.

One of the most puzzling aspects of how the now royal company conducted its business following these uncertain times is their decision to acquire 'the tragedie of Gowrie' – a play about an attempt to assassinate their new patron – for performance sometime in the late autumn of 1604. In this chapter, I ask whether that decision might be understood better in the context of a performance choice made two months later in that Christmas season, when the King's Men offered a play called 'The Spanish Maze' at court. No scholar has attempted to offer an educated guess about the specific subject matter likely dramatised in this lost play performed on 11 February 1605 (Shrove Monday), but the possibility I propose – though highly conjectural – is appealing in that it offers a kind

---

[1] A. H. Nelson and Folger Shakespeare Library staff, 'King James establishes the King's Men: warrant under privy seal,' *Shakespeare Documented* (available online at https://doi.org/10.37078/125).
[2] E. K. Chambers and W. W. Greg (eds.), 'Dramatic Records from the Patent Rolls. Company Licences' in *Malone Society Collections*, vol. 1.3 (Oxford: Oxford University Press, 1909), 264.

of 'missing link' between 'Gowrie' and *Macbeth* as plays that engage with political controversy and the king's interests. *Macbeth* seems designed to appease the patron of Shakespeare's company, with its favourable (though historically inaccurate) portrayal of James's ancestor Banquo, its oblique allusions to Gunpowder plot associates such as Father Garnet (and the Jesuit practice of equivocation), and its interest in witchcraft (a subject of personal concern for James who, amongst other things, wrote at great length about witches in his *Daemonologie*, 1597). But *Macbeth* was not the company's first or only attempt to capitalise on the identity of their new patron by dramatising highly personal stories that related to him. Shakespeare scholars have credited *Macbeth* with innovations that had actually been developing over a period of time and a number of plays in the company's repertory. The lessons from Rubin's psychological experiments are instructive here, in that often the figure and the ground are distinguished by the fact that 'the figure tends to "dominate consciousness" and is more memorable than the ground'; Rubin describes the figure as seeming 'more impressive and dominant' to his test participants.[3] Clearly, it is easier to describe and work with extant plays, and specifically Shakespeare's plays, than with lost plays, hence the political topicality of *Macbeth* and its allusions to the Gunpowder Plot are well known, but the ground that gives a form to Shakespeare's play – 'Gowrie', 'The Spanish Maze' – fade into the background and seem to lose their shape.

The chronological period covered by this chapter ends with another significant change to the company's practices, namely the acquisition of an additional playing venue: the Blackfriars playhouse. Here it is important to recognise that alongside George Chapman's controversial *The Conspiracy of Charles, Duke of Byron* and his *Tragedy of Charles, Duke of Byron* (1608), a lost play referred to by scholars as 'The Silver Mine' also played a key role in the circumstances of March 1608 that led to the Children of the Queen's Revels vacating the Blackfriars playhouse and the King's Men being able to lease the venue. Repertorial records associated with the company's commencement at the indoor playhouse are insufficient to make confident claims about how the company planned for and anticipated the change in playing conditions, but the dearth of obviously new plays in the first period of the company's Blackfriars tenancy at least suggests that the cost-mitigation strategy deployed for the move to the Globe may have been recycled. Facing the prospect of managing two playhouses simultaneously, the King's Men may have concentrated their

---

[3] Pind, *Edgar Rubin*, 100.

energies on adapting existing repertory to the new space (much as, I argue, they adjusted the plays they transferred from the Theatre to the Curtain) before they set about actively acquiring new plays. But here, unlike in previous chapters, there is a paucity of documentary evidence about if or how the venue in question (the Blackfriars) affected the company's repertory. Accordingly, I reflect here on the limitations inherent in working with lost plays. Noting the propensity for scholars to interpret the limited evidence differently, I suggest that it is prudent to resist the temptation to use the features specific to an indoor theatre and its capabilities as the basis for making assumptions about what kinds of plays have been lost from the company's repertory. The simple truth is that we do not actually know how the King's Men's repertory was (or was not) affected by the company's simultaneous use of the Blackfriars and Globe playhouses. Recognising such limitations in our knowledge is vital if my larger project of demonstrating the utility and necessity of lost-plays research is to have integrity.

'[T]he tragedie of Gowrie'

The inhibition on public playing was lifted in early April 1604, and by the late autumn of that year, the King's Men had evidently acquired a new play that contrasted strikingly with the vast majority of their extant plays in that it was steeped in recent history. It is the first new history play acquired by the company in their first five years under their new patron for which there is any kind of documentation, and it was played during the company's second Christmas as the King's Men (1604–1605; the first Christmas had of course been disrupted by plague). A letter by John Chamberlain to his close friend, the diplomat Ralph Winwood at The Hague, dated 18 December 1604, provides the documentary evidence:

> [T]he tragedie of Gowrie with all the action and actors hath ben twise represented by the Kings players, with exceeding concourse of all sortes of people, but whether the matter or manner be not well handled, or that yt be thought unfit that princes should be plaide on the stage in theyre life time, I heare that some great counsaillors are much displeased with yt: and so is thought shalbe forbidden.[4]

There is no corroborating evidence to confirm that the play was subsequently censored, but neither is there any evidence of further

---

[4] J. Chamberlain, *The Letters of John Chamberlain*, N. E. McClure (ed.) (Philadelphia: American Philosophical Society, 1939), 1.199.

performances, despite the apparent popularity of the two recent productions noted by Chamberlain.

The narrative, which was well known to all, must have depicted the kidnapping and failed assassination attempt of James VI of Scotland at Gowrie House in Perth on 5 August 1600.[5] John Ruthven, third earl of Gowrie (henceforth referred to as 'Gowrie'), had earned James's ire by opposing the Scottish king's request for money in parliament earlier that year. Then, on the morning of 5 August, as James prepared to go hunting in Falkland, the king was approached by the earl's younger brother, Alexander Ruthven, who held a private conversation with the king. At the conclusion of the hunt, James spoke once more with Alexander, again out of earshot of any witnesses. The king subsequently told the Duke of Lennox that Alexander had shared tantalising news about the location of a hidden treasure. Lennox mistrusted the news as unlikely but agreed to follow the king in stealth, as the king had agreed both to keep the treasure a secret and to follow Alexander to Gowrie House to view the treasure.

At Gowrie House, after the king had dined, Lennox and other members of the king's household were invited to eat; as they finished their meal, they saw the king and Alexander Ruthven walk through the hall and up the main stairs of the house. Lennox attempted to attend the king; however Gowrie prevented him with an excuse about the king needing to perform a quiet errand and it being the king's will that the courtiers remained in the hall. At the conclusion of the meal, Gowrie led Lennox and some of the others to the garden. One of the king's party, John Ramsay, turned to the Laird of Pittencrieff (John Moncrieff) and inquired after the king's present whereabouts, but after a fruitless search of the dining chamber and courtyard, the laird was unable to provide an answer. Another of Gowrie's household (Thomas Cranstoun), however, came to the garden to announce that the king had gone riding. According to Lennox, Gowrie called for his own horse and studiously ignored his servants when they pointed out that his horse was in Scone (another village in Perth), as Gowrie himself ought to have known. Worse, when Lennox asked the porter whether the king had gone riding, the porter was adamant that the king had not left and certainly not through the back gate (for the porter himself had the key). Gowrie nevertheless continued to contradict the porter and assert that the king had gone riding that way;

---

[5] In what follows, I summarise the thorough account provided by W. F. Arbuckle in 'The "Gowrie Conspiracy": Part I' and 'The "Gowrie Conspiracy": Part II', *The Scottish Historical Review*, 36 (1957), 1–24 and 89–110.

ascending the stairs, he claimed to be able to verify that the king had departed thence by horse.

No sooner had the party walked through the gate to the street in search of the king than Lennox heard the king's own voice emanating from a window in the turret above, where James could be seen crying, red in the face, 'I am murtherit! Treassoun! My Lord of Mar, help! help!'[6] One witness reported seeing James forcibly pulled back into the room from the window. Lennox led most of the party back up the stairs to the room where the king was apparently held hostage, but could not gain entry. Two of the king's men (Sir Thomas Erskine and his brother James) detained Gowrie and accused him of orchestrating the attack. John Ramsay, who had left earlier for his horse, heard the king's cries independently of the rest of the group and gained access to the chamber via an alternative approach; once inside, he discovered Alexander Ruthven wrestling with the king whilst another man stood poised behind the king. Ramsay stabbed Ruthven in the face and neck, and James hurled him down the stairs. Erskine and the others rushed up the stairs, where they stabbed Ruthven again, giving him his death wound. Gowrie, who had escaped Erskine and initially fled, now returned to the scene with two swords drawn, but Ramsay overcame and killed him.

The mysterious other man in the turret seems to have slipped away quietly. Numerous candidates for that accomplice's identity emerged, including one 'Younger' who was conveniently slain in a cornfield as he was on his way to proving the charges false. Eventually Andrew Henderson, chamberlain to the earl of Gowrie, wrote to the royal chaplain to confess that he had been present in the turret that fateful day but that he had not had foreknowledge of the plot and that he actively resisted the attempted murder, to the point of assisting James. The chaplain conveyed this information in a sermon preached from the Market Cross in James's presence on 11 August but failed to persuade the sceptical crowd. Henderson surrendered himself on 20 August, confirming key details of much of the happenings in his deposition – but not, it seems, of Gowrie's allegedly treasonous role. Indeed, in the aftermath, none of Gowrie's household or relations were able to provide any evidence of treasonous intentions, but on 15 November 1600 the earl and his brother Alexander were nonetheless deemed guilty of treason (posthumously) by parliament.

These are the state-sanctioned details of the narrative. Interpretation of reported events is another matter, and a great deal turns on what Alexander

---

[6] Quoted in Arbuckle, 'The "Gowrie Conspiracy": Part I', 7.

allegedly said to the king during their private conversation before the hunt, and on what transpired in the locked turret before the king appeared at the window crying murder. The king's own account of the affair was published in early September 1600.[7] He elaborates on the details to which only he was privy (including that Alexander professed 'that he was sure that now the kings conscience was burdened for the murthering of his father'),[8] and largely confirms the publicly known details, with the exception of down-playing Henderson's claims of having tried to assist more than harm the king. Both the earl and his brother Alexander were no longer alive to defend themselves or offer alternative narratives. Louis A. Barbé sets out the argument that, far from being the ruthless and treasonous conspirators that King James would have them remembered as in his version of events, the Ruthvens were the political (and actual) victims of James's scheming.[9] James's version of events met with significant scepticism at the time, as Arbuckle summarises, but the alternative – that James manufactured an excuse to have the Ruthvens killed – is also distinctly problematic.[10] The possibility that the Ruthvens would devise such a preposterous conspiracy on slender motivation is as improbable as the possibility that a Scottish king should concoct such a series of fabrications in a plot to rid himself of a noble family. Indeed, Sir William Bowes, in a letter to Cecil dated 2 September 1600, expressed an altogether simpler view: that an initially amicable interview in the turret became heated when conversation touched on the execution of Ruthven's father, whom James denounced as a traitor. (Ruthven's father was a Protestant nobleman, William Ruthven, who in 1582 had kidnapped James and unlawfully detained him to prevent James from accepting Catholicism.[11]) James, worried and finding himself unarmed, resorted to crying 'treason', thus precipitating the whole calamity.[12] Whatever the truth of the matter, the seeming rashness of the alleged Gowrie conspiracy, coupled with the improbability of luring the king (unarmed and unattended) to his confinement with the vague promise of hidden treasure – to say nothing of the extraordinary conve-nience of the Ruthven brothers being killed before they could offer a

---

[7] *Gowreis conspiracie a discourse of the vnnaturall and vyle conspiracie attempted against the kings majesties person at Sanct-Iohnstovn vpon Twysday the 5. of August. 1600* (Edinburgh: Printed by Robert Charteris, 1600).

[8] *Gowreis conspiracie*, B4.

[9] L. A. Barbé, *The Tragedy of Gowrie House: An Historical Study* (London, 1887).

[10] Arbuckle, 'The "Gowrie Conspiracy": Part II', 89–90.

[11] This earlier attack on James is known as the 'Ruthven Raid'; William was beheaded in 1584 as a direct consequence.

[12] See Arbuckle, 'The "Gowrie Conspiracy": Part II', 97.

counter-narrative – combined to rouse deep suspicion amongst the general populace. As if to cement his version of events as the official and inviolable account, James (whilst still in Scotland) initiated an annual commemoration of the failed conspiracy, declaring 5 August a national holiday.

To return to the London theatres in December 1604: why would the King's Men acquire a Gowrie play? For one thing, within the history genre, its subject matter would have been cutting-edge for its timeliness.[13] The dramatisation of Elizabethan succession anxieties had peaked at the turn of the century in anticipation of the queen's imminent death (e.g. *Hamlet*, c.1600), and some playwrights had already begun mining the pre-history of the Stuart dynasty for stage-worthy material in anticipation of James's possible succession (e.g. the 'Robert II, King of Scots' play in the Admiral's repertory in September 1599).[14] 'Gowrie' was breaking important new ground by covering much more recent material and portraying events immediately preceding the Scottish king's accession to the English throne. The King's Men had invested heavily in Tudor history plays throughout the 1590s; they were now complementing and continuing this investment by turning to Stuart history. At the same time, it was also an important departure for the company inasmuch as (based on known play titles) they had rarely attempted to bring contemporary events to life on stage: their *A Larum for London* (c.1599) had renewed topicality in light of the threat of Spanish invasion in 1599, but it actually portrayed events of 1576; their *A Warning for Fair Women* is presented as contemporary but dramatised events of 1573.

A stage adaptation of the 'Gowrie' story also had the potential for sensation in a different way: through the unexpected revelation of necromancy. The *Gowreis Conspiracie* pamphlet published in Edinburgh in 1600 (and reprinted in London in 1603) made special mention of the fact that after the conspiracy had been thwarted and the earl killed, 'His Maiesteie … caused searche the saide Earle of Gowries pockets in cace anie letters that might further the discouerie of that conspiracie, might bee found therein'. No such evidence was found to incriminate the earl in the conspiracy plot, but something far more astonishing was discovered in his pocket: 'a little close parchment bag, full of Magicall characters, and words of inchātment, wherein it seemed that he had put his confidence, thinking

---

[13] Cf. Marlowe's dramatisation of the St. Bartholomew's Day massacre of 1572 in his *Massacre at Paris* (1593).

[14] See I. Donaldson, 'Robert II, King of Scots (lost play)' in D. Bevington, M. Butler and I. Donaldson (eds.), *The Cambridge Edition of the Works of Ben Jonson* 7 vols. (Cambridge: Cambridge University Press, 2012), 1.232.

himself neuer safe with out them, and therefore euer carried them about with him'.[15] This quasi-Kabbalistic enchantment device, said to guard its possessor from harm, is in some ways analogous to a motif in *Macbeth*, in which the eponymous character is led to believe that he bears 'a charmèd life, which must not yield / To one of woman born' (5.10.13–14).

'Gowrie' also related to a different subset of repertorial offerings in that it was in some sense a true-crime play, whose closest theatrical relatives might be those domestic tragedies that dramatised conspiracies and intrigues culminating in murder motivated by personal grievances: *Arden of Faversham*, or *A Warning for Fair Women*, for example. A stock device in domestic tragedy – the corpse that bleeds in the presence of the murderer – could have been given a new twist in the lost 'Gowrie' play. The *Gowreis Conspiracie* pamphlet provides haunting, preternatural details after the magical enchantments are discovered on the earl's body:

> [W]hile they were vpon him, his wound wherof he died, bled not, but incontinent after the taking of them away, the blood gushed out in great aboundance, to the great admiration of al the beholders.[16]

Perhaps audience members would not notice or care how long ago the events billed as 'contemporary' had actually taken place (in the case of *Arden* the events occurred in 1551; for *Warning*, 1573).[17] But if sensational contemporary events were proving popular in the theatres, a 'Gowrie' play that was genuinely timely might have seemed like an attractive proposition to the King's Men. Perhaps part of its appeal for the company was the fact that a dramatisation of the King's own experiences served as a kind of reminder that the company had a significant new patron: this story, it may have been implied, was the exclusive domain of the King's Men.

And yet, as Gustavo Turner laments, the lost 'Gowrie' play is usually mentioned by scholars only 'in a cursory manner or as a footnote'.[18] More than a century ago, John Tucker Murray thought 'Gowrie' was a nonevent, hardly worthy of scholarly comment: 'as nothing more is heard of the matter, and during the Christmas festivities of 1604–1605 the king's

---

[15] *Gowreis conspiracie*, C3.   [16] *Gowreis conspiracie*, C3.

[17] A counterpoint is Richard Brome and Thomas Heywood's *The Late Lancashire Witches*, written in August 1634, which draws on contemporary legal records of sensational events that occurred in 1633–1634, suggesting that playgoers might indeed find very recent events of interest.

[18] Gustavo Secchi Turner, 'The Matter of Fact: *The Tragedy of Gowrie* (1604) and Its Contexts', unpublished PhD dissertation, Harvard University (2006), 3.

company often acted at court, the offence could not have been very serious'.[19] More recent scholars have examined the play in considerably more detail. In *Shakespearian Playing Companies* (1996), Gurr wrote the play off as an aberration in the otherwise confident repertorial programming of the King's Men:

> Tilney as censor must have approved it for staging, and as a play about an event from the new king's earlier career it may even have been designed for higher things altogether. Its staging in December not long before the court season was under way may indicate that the company, and conceivably in the first place Tilney, thought of it as a new play suitable for presentation at court. If so, they miscalculated disastrously.[20]

Just as he comes close to acknowledging the ease with which offence could have been made – even a seasoned Master of the Revels could approve 'Gowrie' for performance before any offence was detected in it – Gurr simultaneously offers what is arguably an unduly harsh conclusion that the performance decision was a disastrous miscalculation. In a subsequent treatment of the play, Gurr's criticisms hardened. He now conceived of 'Gowrie' as part of the company's deliberate attempt 'to get closer to the royal sentiment' in their 'second season of royal junketing', but deemed that attempt a 'fiasco' that 'in 1604 misplayed the role that *King Lear* filled much better at court in 1606'.[21] Gone is any sense of the play being 'designed for higher things', and gone too is the charitable spreading of the blame to include the Master of the Revels. Turner offers an evaluation of 'Gowrie' that is more respectful of the company's business acumen, noting that the play 'was chosen and devised to ensure the success of the incipient company' and that it was 'a calculated decision' by 'seasoned players' who were already familiar with controversy via the performance of a Richard II play for supporters of the Earl of Essex's attempted revolt: 'Their main intention was probably neither to flatter nor to offend James, but to create a spectacle that would have caught his fickle attention'.[22]

I share Turner's more positive valuation of the company's commercial shrewdness, but I query the investment that previous scholars have placed in the nature of the political and representational offences. In a 1992 biography of Shakespeare, Dennis Kay remarks on the lost 'Gowrie' play in

---

[19] J. T. Murray, *English Dramatic Companies, 1558–1642* (London: Constable, 1910), 150.
[20] A. Gurr, *The Shakespearian Playing Companies* (Oxford: Clarendon Press, 1996), 290.
[21] A. Gurr, *The Shakespeare Company 1594–1642* (Cambridge: Cambridge University Press, 2006), 171, 172, 177.
[22] Turner, 'The Matter of Fact: *The Tragedy of Gowrie* (1604) and its Contexts', 239.

terms of 'the temptation of staging the king and his known interests' and the 'limits of such representation'. He considers the 'Gowrie' episode 'a useful caution' against 'excessive realism', going so far as to declare that a 'line was drawn at *Gowrie*, at direct representation of the king in an unmediated, unambiguous form'. In Kay's view, after this watershed moment, if the company wanted to perform 'plays which touched the king closely', they would need 'a more oblique, suggestive approach' to guard against 'charges of excessive directness'.[23] Stephen Greenblatt, echoing Kay's thoughts on the limits of representation, ascribes a quasi-hubristic quality to the newly patronised company: 'Buoyed by the monarch's patronage and secure in their place as the premier company, they evidently decided to test the conventional limits of representation'.[24] But both these comments dwell on John Chamberlain's pondering of whether it 'be thought unfit that princes should be plaide on the stage in theyre life time'. Ben Jonson had certainly found himself in hot water over the depiction of a living prince when he had a boy actor impersonate Queen Elizabeth in the final catastrophe of his *Every Man Out of His Humour* at the Globe just a few years earlier.[25] Chamberlain's explicit mention of 'exceeding concourse of all sortes of people' attending the two performances of 'Gowrie' tends to suggest performances at a public theatre, presumably the same venue (because the same company) as the *Every Man Out* performance: the Globe. But the problematic depiction of living royalty is not the first thought that occurred to Chamberlain. Indeed, it is difficult to ascertain when, precisely, it became officially unacceptable to depict certain classes of living people on stage. A Privy Council Minute dated 10 May 1601 records a complaint made against certain players at the 'Curtaine in Moorefeildes' who 'do represent upon the stage ... the persons of some gentlemen of good desert and quallity that are yet alive under obscure manner'.[26] In 1624, in response to the controversial depiction of James I as well as the Spanish king and others on stage in Middleton's *Game at Chess*, James invoked memory of a 'commaundment

---

[23] D. Kay, *Shakespeare: His Life, Work and Era* (London: Sidgwick & Jackson, 1992), 264.

[24] S. Greenblatt, *Will in the World: How Shakespeare Became Shakespeare* (New York: W. W. Norton & Co., 2004), 339.

[25] See H. Ostovich, '"So Sudden and Strange a Cure": A Rudimentary Masque in *Every Man Out of His Humour*', *English Literary Renaissance*, 22(3) (1992), 315–332.

[26] Chambers, *Elizabethan Stage*, 4.332.

and restraint given against the representinge of anie modern Christian kings in those Stage-plays'.[27] This restraint was presumably made during James's reign, so would differ from the one alluded to in the Privy Council Minute of 1601. It seems rather to have been issued in 1608 in response to Chapman's *Byron* plays and the lost play, 'Silver Mine' (see below).[28] The more important point is that Chamberlain seems most concerned with 'whether the matter or manner be not well handled'. In the case of 'matter', this implies a failure in the way the narrative of the lost play was presented.

Greenblatt comes closer to the mark, in my opinion, when he notes that the King's Men 'may have noted that the king had gone out of his way to reward anyone who actively supported his version of the bloody events at Gowrie House'.[29] One of the most distinctive elements of the cultural reception of the Gowrie Conspiracy is its polarising effect on public sentiment: James had insisted (and the promulgated prayers, pamphlets and declaration of a public holiday had reinforced the sentiments) that the Ruthvens' deaths had resulted from a treasonous attempt to assassinate the king; the general populace were not entirely convinced. Chamberlain says nothing of James's own response to news of the 'Gowrie' play, but it would be surprising if the King's Men elected to limn the Ruthvens in a positive light and risk undermining the official state line about the events. Was it an incredible, verging on propagandistic interpretation of the sensational events in Perth that Chamberlain referred to when he queried 'whether the matter or manner be not well handled'? Obviously there are limits to how much can be inferred from the scanty evidence, but I think it is helpful to move away from the established critical position of assuming that the likely portrayal of a living prince onstage is the primary reason for the 'Gowrie' play generating concern amongst counsellors; moreover, as I will suggest in the next section, it may be possible to see the imprudent decision (whoever's it was) to depict a royal assassination attempt onstage in 'Gowrie' as more than a regrettable aberration in the company's repertory during the early years of James's reign.

[27] R. Dutton, *Mastering the Revels: The Regulation and Censorship of English Renaissance Drama* (Basingstoke: Macmillan, 1991), 187.
[28] Quoted in Dutton, *Mastering the Revels*, 242; see also 187.
[29] Greenblatt, *Will in the World*, 341.

'A Tragidye of The Spanishe Maz:'

Although 'Gowrie' has recently garnered significant scholarly attention, a play performed by the King's Men at court less than two months after John Chamberlain's letter to Ralph Winwood remains neglected. The Accounts of the Office of the Revels show that during the 1604/5 Christmas season, the King's Men performed eleven plays, including 'On Shroumonday A Tragidye of The Spanishe Maz:'.[30] For obvious reasons, scholarly attention has been fixated on the plays explicitly attributed to 'Shaxberd' (i.e. Shakespeare), including two performances of *The Merchant of Venice*, before and after 'The Spanish Maze'. A result of this Shakespeare focus is that scholars have not paid attention to the lost play by an unknown author (or authors) or hazarded a guess as to its subject matter. Gurr, for example, does not mention 'The Spanish Maze' except to list it in the appendices of repertorial acquisitions and court performances.[31] Perhaps the scholarly reluctance to engage with this lost play is at least partially fuelled by an awareness of how historical events may have limited the dramatisable options available to the playwright(s). Six months prior to the Shrove Monday performance at court, the King's Men had served their new patron in a non-theatrical context when they were summoned to Somerset House, in their royal livery, to attend upon the Spanish delegation during crucial diplomatic talks that culminated in The Treaty of London and the end of the Anglo-Spanish conflict that had precipitated the Armada of 1588.[32] Given this historic peace accord and the King's Men's presence at (and implicit role in) the ambassadorial visit, Wiggins notes that the lost play is 'unlikely to have presented generalised anti-Spanish sentiment, and therefore also unlikely to have been a product of the Elizabethan war years'.[33] An assumption of neutral or pro-Spanish sentiment rules out a number of options for subject matter drawing on recent geopolitical events, though Lois Potter has suggested that perhaps

---

[30] National Archives, AO 3/908/13, reproduced in W. R. Streitberger (ed.), 'Declared Accounts of the Office of the Revels' in *Malone Society Collections XIII* (Oxford: Oxford University Press, 1986), 9.

[31] Gurr, *The Shakespearian Playing Companies*, 304, 387; *The Shakespeare Company*, 284, 303.

[32] I.e. between 9 to 26 August 1604. See National Archives AO 1/388/41, digitised and transcribed in *Shakespeare Documented* as 'Audit Office, Declared Accounts, Treasurer of the Chamber recording the King's Men as attending on the Spanish ambassador', (available online at https://shakespearedocumented.folger.edu/exhibition/document/audit-office-declared-accounts-treasurer-chamber-recording-king-s-men-attending).

[33] Wiggins #1449.

the play 'recalled the recent peace negotiations' themselves.[34] Knutson cautiously observes that '[b]ecause the title of *The Spanish Maze* implies a play of intrigue, I am tempted to add it to the list of revenge tragedies, but there is no evidence of its subject matter and form'.[35]

What if the King's Men hadn't quite given up on the prospect of appealing to royal sentiment and capitalising on sensational news after their problematic 'Gowrie' play, though?[36] The title, 'The Spanish Maze', is both vague and, I suggest, possibly very specific. It could invoke a labyrinthine structure such as a hedge maze, popular throughout England and Europe. (One such garden was created for Emperor Charles V in the sixteenth century in Alcazar, Seville.)[37] By metaphorical extension, 'maze' could apply to any situation that could be characterised as knotty, complicated or confusing. For example, John Lyly's *Sappho and Phao* (1584) subtly associates itself with mazes by including an epilogue that expresses a concern that the play has been somewhat circular:

> They that tread in a maze walk oftentimes in one path, and at the last come out where they entered in. We fear we have led you all this while in a labyrinth of conceits, diverse times hearing one device, and have now brought you to an end where we first began.[38]

This play implies bewilderment or confusion, more than the comforting circularity associated with Shakespearean comedy's resolution of social discord. Indeed, as Mary Moore observes, 'the labyrinth symbolized both conscious craft and perplexity during the Renaissance'.[39]

But I would like to explore the possibility that the 'maze' of the play's title could have evoked something much more precise for Londoners and courtiers: namely, 'The Maze', the Copley family's manor house in

---

[34] L. Potter, *The Life of William Shakespeare: A Critical Biography* (Malden, MA: Wiley-Blackwell, 2012), 309.

[35] Knutson, *The Repertory*, 120.

[36] James Shapiro posits such a trajectory from 'Gowrie' to *Macbeth* but does not mention 'The Spanish Maze': 'Though they could no longer perform this play ['Gowrie'], the King's Men knew how popular, if controversial, its subject matter was. Shakespeare took note of two things in the aftermath of the suppression of *The Tragedy of Gowrie*, a play that had failed to recoup the company's investment: audiences had flocked to see the story of the plotted assassination of a Scottish king; and the King's Men had to be careful about sailing too close to the political winds': see J. Shapiro, *1606: Shakespeare and the Year of Lear* (London: Faber & Faber, rpt 2016), 242.

[37] W. H. Matthews, *Mazes and Labyrinths: A General Account of Their History and Developments* (London: Longmans, 1922), 125–126.

[38] J. Lyly, *Sappho and Phao*, Epilogue 1–5, in G. K. Hunter and D. Bevington (eds.), *Campaspe, Sappho and Phao* (Revels Plays) (Manchester: Manchester University Press, 1991).

[39] M. Moore, 'The Labyrinth as Style in *Pamphilia to Amphilanthus*', *Studies in English Literature, 1500–1900*, 38 (1998), 109.

Southwark. The reference is oblique to us but would not have been to audiences in 1603/4. Such a play might focus on Sir Thomas Copley (1532–1584), who converted from Protestantism to Catholicism in 1563, was imprisoned for his recusancy, and subsequently fled England without licence in 1570 (though he claimed to remain loyal to Elizabeth and continued to correspond with her, William Cecil, and others from abroad, despite his new faith). During Copley's time on the Continent, King Philip II of Spain gave him a Spanish pension and ennobled him with the title 'grand master of the Maes' (i.e. the Maze in Southwark): a title or office that is explicitly linked to the family's manor house. The Spanish king's bestowing on Copley of a title that references the 'Maze' thus provides an unexpected conjunction of the terms 'Spanish' and 'Maze'.[40] As an exiled Catholic in the employ of the Spanish king, Copley would make an interesting subject for drama at a time when recusants still hoped that James would restore the old faith.

Such events of the 1560s and 70s, though neither recent nor topical, would furnish a playwright with an oblique means of broaching contemporary concerns about Catholicism in England. However, topicality would have been provided by the subsequent generation of the notorious Copley family of the Maze, who continued to fuel controversy. 'The Spanish Maze' might have been about more recent controversies connected with Thomas's third son, Anthony (b. 1567, d. in or after 1609), who was caught up in the Bye Plot to kidnap James and force him to grant toleration to Catholics in July 1603. These events, which took place about eighteen months before the performance of 'The Spanish Maze' at court, were well-known to Londoners, including the aforementioned letter writer John Chamberlain, whose missive to Winwood provided the details of the 'Gowrie' play's performances (more on this below). The same people who took an interest in 'Gowrie' took a natural interest in the Bye Plot: both attempts on the king's life were sensational news.

Anthony Copley played a role in what was a highly sensitive religious moment in England, when the Catholics themselves were hopelessly divided and driven often to self-denial. Born in England but having stolen

[40] M. A. R. Graves, 'Copley, Thomas (1532–1584)' in *Oxford Dictionary of National Biography* (Oxford: Oxford University Press, 2004); online ed, January 2008. Contemporaneous sources give the alternative title, 'Lorde of the Maze' or 'graund Lorde of the Maze'; see W. Fulke, *A reioynder to Bristows replie in defence of Allens scroll of articles and booke of purgatorie* (London, 1581), 15 and Anon., *Certein letters vvherin is set forth a discourse of the peace that was attempted and sought to haue bin put in effecte by the lords and states of Holland and Zelande in the yeare of oure Lorde 1574* (London, 1576), sig.b5.

away to Rouen to join his exiled parents when he was fifteen years of age, this Copley spent two years in Rome with a Jesuit kinsman before returning to Flanders with a pension to serve the King of Spain's interests in war (according to his own admission), which led to his arrest in England.[41] Whilst under arrest, he proved his loyalty to the English crown by disclosing the location and identities of English Catholic fugitives. Furthermore, '[i]n a dramatic role reversal the former Spanish pensioner besought God to favour queen and kingdom against Philip II', but he never quite rose altogether above suspicion.[42] He was fiercely anti-Jesuit but an advocate for Catholic toleration.[43] It was by siding with secular priests against the Jesuits (including William Watson and William Clark) that he became involved with the failed 'Bye Plot' attempt to capture James at Windsor Castle and forcibly extract a promise of toleration.[44] The plot was thwarted on 24 June 1603 when Jesuits (including Henry Garnet) informed the government, and armed Catholic support failed to materialise. On 2 July 1603, James issued a royal proclamation for the apprehension of Anthony Copley, noting that he 'hath dealt with some to be of a conspiracie to vse some violence vpon our Person' with the likely result being 'perill to our life, or danger of innouation in our State'. James further observes that Copley had been sought for but not found, 'So as it seemeth he lurketh very closely, awayting opportunitie to attempt his treasonable purposes, or to procure other of our Subiects to conspire with him in so disloyall a fact'.[45] When his own sister refused to harbour him, Copley confessed to his role in the plot and implicated the other conspirators, his testimony leading to their convictions and, ultimately, executions.

James's remarkable handling of the conspirators seems ready-made for theatrical representation. On 11 December 1603, the diplomat and letter writer Dudley Carleton provided John Chamberlain with details of the events following the plot's failure. The priests, Watson and Clark, were 'very bloodily handled' and 'cut down alive' before finally being killed,

---

[41] M. A. R. Graves, 'Copley, Anthony (b. 1567, d. in or after 1609), writer and conspirator' in *Oxford Dictionary of National Biography*, Oxford University Press, 2004; online ed, September 2004.

[42] Graves, 'Copley, Anthony (b. 1567, d. in or after 1609), writer and conspirator', *ODNB*.

[43] A. Shell, *Catholicism, Controversy, and the English Literary Imagination 1558–1660* (Cambridge: Cambridge University Press, 1999), 134.

[44] The name 'Bye Plot' distinguishes these actions from the so-called Main Plot – funded by Spain, and led by Henry Brooke, Lord Cobham, Sir Walter Raleigh and others – which was to install Lady Arbella Stuart on the throne.

[45] *Although it cannot be without griefe to vs to publish, that in this our kingdome we should finde any subiect so contrary to all the rest of our louing people*, ... (London, 1603), STC 8323.

their quarters and heads displayed publicly.[46] George Brooke was beheaded next. Sir Griffith Markham, the Lord Grey and the Lord Cobham (in that order) were subsequently named in warrants for execution, but here James began to orchestrate an extraordinary series of events. As Peter G. Platt observes, 'Carleton clearly saw the theatrical nature of the event'.[47] Carleton relates that '[a] fouler day could hardly have been picked out, or fitter for such a tragedy'; he proceeds to describe how each of the three men were led to the scaffold in turn. Whilst Markham made his devotions and 'prepared himself to the block', the executioner conferred aside with a mysterious Scotsman, John Gib (Gib had received a warrant from James, stipulating that the previously warranted executions were not to go ahead). Returning to the scaffold, the executioner informed Markham that 'since he was so ill prepared, he should yet have two hours' respite', and led him away to the Great Hall. Grey was then brought out for execution, but when he finished his confession and prayers, 'the sheriff stayed him and said he had received orders from the king to change the order of the execution and that lord Cobham was to go before him'. Grey, too, was led away, confused. Cobham, 'who was now to play his part', similarly made his final preparations and was similarly stayed and led away.[48]

Finally, the three conspirators, ignorant of each other's fates, were brought together onto the scaffold, and 'looked strange one upon the other, like men beheaded and met again in the other world':

> Now all the actors being together on the stage (as use is at the end of a play), the sheriff made a short speech unto them, by way of the interrogatory of the heinousness of their offences, the justness of their trials, their lawful condemnation, and due execution there to be performed, to which they assented; then, saith the sheriff, see the mercy of your prince, who of himself hath sent hither a countermand and given you your lives.

The audience erupted into applause and 'experience was made of the difference of examples of justice and mercy'.[49] That James was pleased with his theatrical strategy is evident from the fact that he subsequently called all three men to his presence, where he explained to them his rationale, which again drew applause from those present to hear it.

---

[46] D. Carleton, 'Salisbury, December 11, 1603' in M. Lee, Jr. (ed.), *Dudley Carleton to John Chamberlain, 1603–1624: Jacobean Letters* (New Brunswick: Rutgers University Press, 1972), 47.

[47] P. G. Platt, *Shakespeare and the Culture of Paradox* (Farnham: Ashgate, 2009), 133.

[48] Carleton, 'Salisbury, December 11, 1603', 50.

[49] Carleton, 'Salisbury, December 11, 1603', 51.

Carleton concludes by noting how close the plan came to inadvertent catastrophe: 'But one thing had like to have marred the play, for the letter was closed and delivered him unsigned, which the king remembered himself and called for him back again'.[50] In relating these astonishing events, Carleton alluded to previous correspondence and noted that 'this was a part of the same play and that other acts came betwixt to make up a tragical comedy'.[51] Platt calls it 'a description of the theatricality of mercy and equity'.[52] Apparently because his confession had secured the conviction of his fellow conspirators, Anthony Copley was pardoned on 18 August 1604. If the 'Spanish Maze' play dramatised these events, it would have been an auspicious selection for performance on Shrove Monday (justice/mercy being an appropriate *topos* for Lent) and audience members would have noticed a neat complement to the two performances of *The Merchant of Venice*, with that play's culmination in Portia's distinction between justice and the 'quality of mercy' (4.1.178).

The King's Men's 'Spanish Maze' was performed at court on 11 February 1605. The Master of the Revels approved it for court performance, after which there is no suggestion (as there was with 'Gowrie') that it would be banned. Even though both plots that I have discussed in this chapter were historical attempts to assassinate the reigning monarch, the Bye Plot differed from the Gowrie Conspiracy in a number of significant ways that would make censorship less likely. The Presbyterian William Ruthven had kidnapped James in 1582 to prevent the king embracing Catholicism, and the implicit suggestion from those who accepted the king's official narrative about the Gowrie Conspiracy of 1600 was that William's sons Alexander and perhaps even John (the earl of Gowrie) had harboured similar desires when they had the opportunity for a private interview with the king eighteen years later. Anthony Copley, by contrast, though anti-Jesuit, was in favour of Catholic toleration, and his father, Sir Thomas Copley, was famously a recusant; if 'The Spanish Maze' was about nefarious dealings of the pro-Spanish family who occupied 'The Maze' in Southwark, the religious affiliation of the antagonists would be less controversial. Perhaps more importantly, the official accounts of the Bye Plot had not attracted the kind of aspersions that hung over the Gowrie Conspiracy, and the actions of Copley and his associates were roundly condemned. If the King's Men sought to express support for their

---

[50] Carleton, 'Salisbury, December 11, 1603', 52.
[51] Carleton, 'Salisbury, December 11, 1603', 47.
[52] Platt, *Shakespeare and the Culture of Paradox*, 133.

patron through valorising his deliverance from conspirators, this was an altogether safer way to do so, building on the 'Gowrie' precedent but cautiously so.

A dramatisation of the Bye Plot would not require the depiction of the king himself onstage in order to showcase the king's benevolence in issuing pardons, or in order to celebrate the successful aversion of a serious attempt at a political and religious coup. It would retain the company's apparent interest in aligning with 'royal sentiment' (as Gurr calls it in the context of 'Gowrie'), but with reduced risk of it becoming a 'fiasco'. Although audiences in the Christmas season of 1604/5 could not yet have known it, Anthony's younger brother John Copley (aka Luttrell, 1577–1662) was soon to be entangled in the Gunpowder Plot, ensuring that the family's notoriety continued. In short, the Copley family was filled with colourful characters, and their association with the Maze in Southwark (as well as their labyrinthine pro- and anti-Catholic contrivances) would have given delicious point to the play's title.

All this is highly conjectural. What it offers is a plausible interpretation of the otherwise opaque noun 'maze' and a subject matter that makes sense of the adjective 'Spanish' without running into the political problems that Wiggins notes would make a dramatisation of 'generalised anti-Spanish sentiment' impossible at this date. Much more evidence is required before I could place my proposed subject matter on Terence Schoone-Jongen's taxonomy of the possible, plausible, or probable with any degree of confidence.[53] A further encouragement for even entertaining my conjecture, beyond the plausible interpretation of the key terms in the play's title, is that it works as part of the 'negative space' shaping the repertory, joining with what is already known about 'Gowrie' to form a contour that gives shape to the company's most successful handling of a Jacobean assassination attempt fuelled by religious controversy – the Gunpowder Plot – in Shakespeare's *Macbeth*.

There is even some slight evidence that there was another King's Men play that was more explicitly concerned with the Gunpowder Plot than is *Macbeth*. In 1606, Oliver Ormerod condemned the anti-Catholic pamphlet *The Double PP* (1606) and 'another that was thrown abroad vpon the stage at the late execution of the traitors, together with many other toyes lately printed against the Papists', adding in a marginal note that 'It is a very vnfit thing, that histrionicall iesters and stage players should bee

[53] T. G. Schoone-Jongen, *Shakespeare's Companies: William Shakespeare's Early Career and Acting Companies, 1577–1594* (Farnham: Ashgate, 2008), 4.

suffred to writ books of such matters'.[54] Ormerod may simply have been referring to a pamphlet 'written by a player and distributed at a playhouse', as Wiggins notes (#1490), but William Hubbard, writing in the wake of the Gunpowder Plot, independently mentions how 'the Theater and English *Roscius* himselfe hath pourtrayed this work of God, and set it aloft'.[55] William C. Woodson first drew attention to the two historical records implying the one-time existence of this play; he suggested that Hubbard, who was Chaplain to the King, intended an allusion to the King's Men player Richard Burbage with the reference to 'Roscius'.[56] Apparently subscribing to a belief in the inherent superiority of the King's Men relative to other professional playing companies, Woodson was troubled by the reputation of this lost play and resisted assigning it to the King's Men.[57] He nevertheless situated the lost play in relation to Shakespeare's work: 'the existence of the topical play on the Gunpowder Plot may help explain the limited topicality of Shakespeare's *Macbeth*, on grounds that it was not the first play to allude to the Gunpowder Plot'.[58]

But critics who emphasise *Macbeth*'s dramatisation of 'thwarted conspiracy' with a view to establishing the Gowrie Conspiracy (and perhaps even the lost play, specifically) as a source for Shakespeare's play have, I think, missed the mark in their too rigid hunt for direct influence in the manner required of older modes of source study.[59] Stanley Kozikowski was right to note 'a resurgence of interest in the King's wondrous gift of royal survival' at the time that Shakespeare was writing *Macbeth*, but if I am right about the subject matter of 'The Spanish Maze', there may have been a wider interest (almost a vogue) for such conspiracy/survival stories on the Jacobean stage, in which case *Macbeth* grew out of the company's sustained interest in their patron's close escapes, just as Shakespeare's *Hamlet* (as I argue in the previous chapter) engaged with a dramatic interest in Denmark that had been established by multiple companies in London.[60]

---

[54] *The Picture of a Papist* (1606), sig.A4[v].
[55] *Great Brittaines resurrection: or the Parliaments passing bell By vvay of psalmodie, against the tryumphing of the Papists, in their seuen psalms* (London, 1606), sig.A3[v].
[56] 'Since Richard Burbage, of the King's Men, was identified by Camden with the flattering title alter Roscius, and since that name is otherwise given to Burbage in the seventeenth century, there is a possible connection between this lost play and the King's Men': see W. C. Woodson, 'A Lost Play on the Gunpowder Plot', *Notes and Queries*, 222 (1977), 529.
[57] 'Ormerod's easy contempt for the merit of the play makes the connection difficult' (529).
[58] Woodson, 'A Lost Play on the Gunpowder Plot', 529.
[59] S. J. Kozikowski, 'The Gowrie Conspiracy Against James VI: A New Source for Shakespeare's *Macbeth*', *Shakespeare Studies*, 13 (1980), 198.
[60] Kozikowski, 'The Gowrie Conspiracy Against James VI', 211.

The Blackfriars: 1608

Not all companies courted controversy and survived unscathed. The Children of the Queen's Revels, for example, misjudged the fine line between the sensational and the salacious. They had played at the Blackfriars playhouse since 1600, when Henry Evans acquired the lease from Richard Burbage (whose father had purchased the relevant rooms in the Blackfriars building in 1596). Early in 1608, the company performed Chapman's *Conspiracy of Charles, Duke of Byron* and his *Tragedy of Charles, Duke of Byron*, both of which plays were about recent (1598–1601) French political intrigue culminating in the execution of the treasonous Charles Gontaut, Duke of Byron (Biron). Edmund Tilney, Master of the Revels, accused the company of having performed passages that he had previously ordered excised as a condition of licensing the *Byron* plays. Antoine Lefèvre de La Boderie, the French Ambassador, duly took offence at the representation of his country's recent history and attempted to have the plays banned. His intervention was at least partially successful, for in a letter dated 11 March 1608, Sir Thomas Lake, Clerk of the Signet, wrote to Robert Lord Salisbury, Secretary, stating that 'His ma' was well pleased with that which your lo. aduertiseth concerning the committing of the players y^t haue offended in ye matters of France' and adds that the Lord Chamberlain would act 'to dissolue' the Blackfriars company and 'punish the maker [of the play] besides'.[61]

Yet the Children of the Queen's Revels proceeded to compound their offence. Waiting until the court was absent from London, they defied the ban on performing Chapman's *Byron* plays. They aggravated the insult further by including additional scandalous material. La Boderie, in his report to the French secretary of state, Pierre Brulart de Puisieux, marquis de Sillery, provides the evidence of this new *Byron*-related offence:

> About mid-Lent those very actors whom I had had barred from playing the history of the late Marshal de Biron, noting all the court to be away, did so nonetheless, and not only that but introduced into it the Queen and Madame de Verneuil, the former treating that lady very ill verbally and giving her a slap on the face.[62]

---

[61] Sir Thomas Lake, quoted in 'Four Letters on Theatrical Affairs' in E. K. Chambers (ed.), *Malone Society Collections II.ii* (Oxford: Oxford University Press, 1923), 149.

[62] Trans. John Margeson in his Revels Plays edition of *The Conspiracy and Tragedy of Charles, Duke of Byron by George Chapman* (Manchester: Manchester UP, 1988), 276; for the French, see J. J. Jusserand, 'Ambassador La Boderie and the "Compositeur" of the *Byron* Plays', *Modern Language Review*, 6 (1911), 203–205 and Chambers, *Elizabethan Stage*, 3.257–258.

A few days after learning of this fresh offence by the players, La Boderie complained to the earl of Salisbury, who 'sent orders to arrest them'. Only three players were found and imprisoned, while 'the principal culprit, the author, escaped'.[63] Chapman's plays, thus verifiably notorious for damaging international diplomacy, served as a caution to playing companies against the dramatisation of contemporary political events.

However, subsequent remarks in La Boderie's letter make clear that in the lead-up to a defiance of the ban on the *Byron* plays, the company had taken yet a further risk by satirising King James I on stage in a play that is now lost:

> A day or two before, they had slandered their King, his mine in Scotland, and all his Favourites in a most pointed fashion; for having made him rail against heaven over the flight of a bird and have a gentleman beaten for calling off his dogs, they portrayed him as drunk at least once a day.[64]

I will return to the confusing reference to James's 'mine in Scotland' below; the main point here is that on this occasion, La Boderie assumed that the king's ire would be sufficiently raised by these actions of the players that no further diplomatic intervention would be necessary. Sure enough, the king was 'greatly annoyed with the scoundrels and commanded that they be punished', especially the author.[65] He 'forbade the further performance of any plays whatsoever in London', prompting 'four other companies' in London to offer the equivalent of 'a hundred thousand francs, which could well restore permission to them'.[66] Although La Boderie implies that the king's ban was thus unlikely to be upheld, an important condition would nevertheless be imposed: 'that they should no longer perform any modern histories nor speak of contemporary affairs on pain of death'.[67] Echoing widely held opinion, John Margeson asserts that Chapman's *Byron* plays provided the impetus for the prohibition against depicting living princes on stage.[68] As I noted above, no such official dictate survives, but insomuch as it can be inferred from James's public musings in the wake of the *Game at Chess* controversy of 1624, the circumstances of 1608 offer the likeliest occasion for such a commandment

---

[63] *The Conspiracy and Tragedy of Charles, Duke of Byron*, Trans. Margeson, 276.   [64] Ibid.
[65] Ibid.   [66] Ibid.
[67] *The Conspiracy and Tragedy of Charles, Duke of Byron*, Trans. Margeson, 277.
[68] Margeson deduces that the Master of the Revels 'objected to the presentation of Queen Elizabeth in her own person' in a scene portraying Byron's embassy to England; Richard Dutton concurs. See Margeson (ed.), *The Conspiracy and Tragedy of Charles, Duke of Byron*, 9, referring to 4.1 of *The Conspiracy*; Dutton, *Mastering the Revels*, 187.

to have been issued.[69] Nevertheless, it is telling that La Boderie exercised restraint in prosecuting the offence against his country made by Chapman in the belief that the offence against James in the lost play would suffice to trigger punishment for the players (he explicitly reasoned that 'it would be better to attribute their punishment to the irreverence they had shown him than to what they might have said of the afore-mentioned Ladies'). It is James's displeasure at the report of being satirised on stage which leads, in La Boderie's account, to the exclusion of 'any modern histories' or 'contemporary affairs' from the public stages.

The letter by Sir Thomas Lake about the king's reaction to the punishment of the players offers corroboration that it was indeed this lost play that caused the king to take grave offence and to order that 'ye others who haue offended in ye matter of ye Mynes and other lewd words which is ye children of ye blackfriers ... should neuer play more but should first beg their bred'.[70] The 'matter of ye Mynes' is clearly distinct from any offence caused by Chapman's plays. A ciphered letter from the Florentine diplomat Ottaviano Lotti corroborates that the lost play caused offence and that the playwright fled in the wake of the scandal:

> A comedy has been acted here by the public players which has given a good deal of displeasure, because it made fun of the new fashion found in Scotland. One expects to see the players banned, and the author of the play has run off in fear of losing his life, probably because he mingled ideas that were too wicked, in which so much was concealed.[71]

---

[69] Quoted in Dutton, *Mastering the Revels*, 242; see also 187. The injunction against depicting living princes may be related to (or identical with) an injunction alluded to in the Privy Council Minute of 10 May 1601 (Chambers, *Elizabethan Stage*, 4.332).

[70] Sir Thomas Lake, quoted in 'Four Letters on Theatrical Affairs' in E. K. Chambers (ed.), *Malone Society Collections II.ii* (Oxford: Oxford University Press, 1923), 149.

[71] 3 April 1608 (24 March 1607/8 O.S.), quoted in J. Orrell, 'The London Stage in the Florentine Correspondence, 1604–1618', *Theatre Research International*, 3 (1978), 164. The identity of the author continues to elude scholars. Chambers and others proposed John Marston as the playwright in question, on the grounds that a 'John Marston' was imprisoned in Newgate on 8 June 1608, as F. P. Wilson first noticed; see F. P. Wilson, 'Marston, Lodge, and Constable', *Modern Language Review* 9 (1914), 99–100. Scholars who took this as a hint that Marston had been imprisoned for anti-Scots satire as a result of this lost play include Chambers, *Elizabethan Stage* 2.54; P. J. Finkelpearl, *John Marston of the Middle Temple: An Elizabethan Dramatist in His Social Setting* (Cambridge, MA: Harvard University Press, 1969), 256–257; M. P. Jackson and M. Neill (eds.), *The Selected Plays of John Marston* (Cambridge: Cambridge University Press, 1986), xv; and G. Wickham, 'Part One: Documents of Control, 1530–1660' in *English Professional Theatre, 1530–1660*, ed. G. Wickham, H. Berry and W. Ingram (Cambridge: Cambridge University Press, 2000), 126–127.

Wiggins, however, points out that the playwright responsible for the 'Silver Mine' fiasco pointedly fled rather than being imprisoned (#1586), and Lucy Munro argues that Marston left London three years before being ordained as a deacon in 1609 (meaning he couldn't have written

The reference to the 'new fashion found in Scotland' is rather opaque. From the context that Lotti provides, it seemingly refers to the alleged affectations of James and his courtiers, including their habits whilst hunting and the king's fondness for drink.

This lost play has been named by scholarly convention 'The Silver Mine' following E. K. Chambers, who suggested that the mine in question 'was no doubt the silver mine discovered at Hilderston near Linlithgow in 1607, and worked as a royal enterprise with little success'.[72] In the entry for 'The Silver Mine' in the *Lost Plays Database*, Misha Teramura has pointed out several problems with positing the silver mine as a viable topic for a play in mid-Lent, 1608. He instead proposes that the play may have concerned the project to locate gold mines in Scotland and James's alleged mercenary offer to dub twenty-four investors as 'knights of the golden mine':

> If James's mercenary creation of knights could be the subject of satire in a Blackfriars play like *Eastward Ho* – featuring the ridiculous Sir Petronel Flash as one of James's "thirty-pound knights" – then perhaps the subject of mines might have provided a similar opportunity for joking about the purchase of "golden" knighthoods.

Richard Dutton offers another interpretation. Taking Lake's conjunction of 'the Mynes and other lewd words' as significant, he suggests that because 'mine' was 'bawdy for female genitalia', the play may have satirised sexual, even homosexual, activity amongst James's courtiers.[73] If the play focused thus on the relationships between James and his male courtiers, this would arguably make better sense of Lotti's otherwise opaque mention of 'the new fashion found in Scotland' and of La Boderie's suggestion that the play 'slandered their King, his mine in Scotland, and all his Favourites'.[74] The picture that emerges is of a play that depicted James

---

the play in 1608); see L. Munro, *Children of the Queen's Revels: A Jacobean Theatre Repertory* (Cambridge: Cambridge University Press, 2005), 182. She suggests that John Day is a more likely candidate for authorial ascription (at p. 176).

[72] Chambers, *Elizabethan Stage*, 2.53n; he indexes the lost play under the name 'Silver Mine' in *Elizabethan Stage*, 4.421, and Gertrude Marian Sibley accordingly enters the play's information under an entry by that name in her *Lost Plays and Masques, 1500–1642* (Ithaca, NY: Cornell University Press, 1933). Margeson suggests it was 'perhaps a reference to James's handling of monopolies for silver mines in Scotland' (*The Conspiracy and Tragedy of Charles, Duke of Byron*, 276).

[73] Dutton, *Mastering the Revels*, 188.

[74] Wiggins resists using the invented title bestowed on the play by scholars, preferring the generic 'Satirical Play' as his descriptor for entry #1586 of the *Catalogue*; but he still specifies the 'silver mine' as forming part of the likely plot. I find myself persuaded by Dutton's alternative interpretation, but because I recognise that readers will likely search for the name 'Silver Mine' in

cavorting with his male favourites and neglecting his wife, and of such homosocial or homosexual cavorting being the fashion in Scotland.

Satire of this kind was surely ill-advised in light of the fallout from the anti-Scots sentiments in *Eastward Ho* (1605), also staged by the Children of the Queen's Revels, that saw Chapman and Jonson imprisoned. Even more recently, in May 1607, another lost play was said by Ottaviano Lotti to have included the imprudent denigration of bagpipes. According to Lotti, '[a] poet's work almost caused a very grave scandal, because several players who were acting it on the stage performed it so that when one of the characters wanted to make a serenade to a lady he went and gathered various sorts of music', bringing on stage a great variety of musicians (and their differing instruments), 'each one of them claiming to come from one part or another of the provinces of England'. Together they produced delightful music until a further musician arrived 'with a bagpipe which, besides being toneless, made such a noise that it stunned and ruined all the music'. At length he identified himself as a Scotsman and 'he was bundled out and told that he had very little judgment if he thought that so villainous an instrument could harmonize and unite with others so noble and so worthy'. Lotti reports that the 'Scots knights who were present to hear the play thought about making their resentment plain right there, but they refrained, and hoped that the king would be greatly moved to anger'.[75] In light of this anti-Scots offence, perhaps we might conjecture that the offence caused by the Children of the Queen's Revels in 'The Silver Mine' differed categorically from the offence reportedly caused by the King's Men in 'Gowrie' in the sense that the depiction of the Scots, not just the monarch, was problematic. Both plays appear to have brought a personation of James on stage explicitly, but only one company was ordered to be dissolved in the aftermath. Or perhaps 'The Silver Mine' might not, on its own, have brought the company into complete disrepute if the brazen offences of the *Byron* plays' repeated performances had not already occurred.

Whatever the case, the lost 'Silver Mine' play proved pivotal in precipitating the circumstances that culminated, on 08 August 1608, in Richard Burbage's reacquiring the lease on the now vacant Blackfriars stage for the benefit of the King's Men. If the King's Men had hoped to commence this

order to learn more about this play, I am reluctant to arbitrarily change the name, which I continue to use out of convenience more than any conviction that it accurately reflects the lost play's subject matter.

[75] Quoted in Orrell, 'The London Stage in the Florentine Correspondence, 1604–1618', 162. See also Wiggins #1538, 'Play with a Serenade Scene'.

new phase in their history with a bang, they were to be thwarted, for plague returned to London with unfortunate timing. The company toured most of the autumn, and if they did perform in winter (at court or publicly), their commerce at the Globe and Blackfriars was not sustained, for they were touring again in May and throughout the summer of 1609. Knutson tentatively assumes the company continued to acquire new plays even under these trying circumstances, though 'far fewer than their norm', and that they continued more old plays from the previous year than would ordinarily be the case.[76] The plague did not appreciably dissipate until Easter 1610, at which time the company recommenced more regular performances in London, their repertory including such new plays as Beaumont and Fletcher's *Philaster* (1609), Fletcher's *The Woman's Prize* (1610; though Wiggins casts doubt over whether the King's Men were the original owners of the play), Jonson's *The Alchemist* (1610), Shakespeare's *Cymbeline* (1610), plus revivals of *Othello* and *Mucedorus*.[77] When Simon Forman visited the Globe in the spring of 1611, he saw performances of *Macbeth* (20 April), *Cymbeline* (between 21 to 29 April; carried over from the previous season), a new, lost 'Richard the 2' play (on 30 April), and *The Winter's Tale* (on 15 May; new in 1611). Knutson conjectures that amongst the older plays available to the company, *Pericles*, *Troilus and Cressida*, and *Romeo and Juliet* – all printed or reprinted in 1609 – were probably revived too, and that the reprinting of *The Miseries of Enforced Marriage*, *Hamlet*, *Titus Andronicus*, and *The Troublesome Reign of King John* by 1611 may also reflect recent revivals on stage (though she argues that Shakespeare's *King John* is the likelier play to have been revived by the King's Men around the time that the Queen's Men play was reprinted).[78]

From the limited information available, I cannot confidently assert the company's repertorial strategy in the lead-up to and wake of their acquisition of the Blackfriars as a second venue. Given how few new plays we know of, it is tempting to posit that the King's Men replicated the practice they adopted when anticipating their move to the Globe and stocked up on new plays before adjusting to the new playing circumstances. Possibly, as I have suggested in the context of the move from the Theatre to the larger Curtain, the company expended energy in adapting their existing repertory for what they expected to be the stable playing conditions of the

---

[76] Knutson, *The Repertory*, 137.

[77] Performances of *Othello* were witnessed by Prince Louis Frederick of Württemberg at the Globe in April, and by Henry Jackson in Oxford in September 1610. Knutson infers the revival of *Mucedorus* from the title page ascription on the newly reprinted quarto (*The Repertory*, 138).

[78] Knutson, *The Repertory*, 137–139.

future. But possibly this is all completely wrong. The negative space metaphor works best when there is a contour to trace, however faint or counterintuitive; I have appreciably fewer dots to join in 1608 than for the 1590s, and I think it highly probable that the company may have acquired many more new plays that have disappeared without leaving an archival trace. One of the greatest challenges of working with lost plays is the capriciousness of the documentary record: no document for the Blackfriars period is comparable to Henslowe's diary.

I am reluctant to attempt to fill in the negative space surrounding the known repertory of the King's Men through venue-based conjecture and assumptions about what kind of plays were performed once the Blackfriars playhouse became available to the King's Men. It was G. E. Bentley, in an otherwise admirable attempt to have scholars conceive of Shakespeare as 'above all else a man of the theatre', who influentially painted the picture of the Blackfriars as a 'private theatre' with 'superior audiences' and 'sophisticated drama'.[79] Bentley believed that the company members 'were well aware of the Blackfriars and the type of performance it required, or specialized in, long before they came to lease the theatre'.[80] Specifically, he cited Harley Granville-Barker's suggestions that acting in the indoors theatre would have to be quieter and would use candlelight for emphasis; and on the basis of such venue-specific conjecture (and his positing of a different playgoing clientele for each of the two theatres), Bentley thought it was self-evident that *Mucedorus* 'was clearly one of the Globe plays which might be laughed at by a Blackfriars audience' (as was *The Merry Devil of Edmonton*), but that Jonson's *Every Man In* and *Every Man Out*, though old, would be 'suitable' for the indoors venue.[81] He proposed that the company would have turned to Jonson as a writer on account of his social status and court connections (again, the argument rests on the assumption of an elite audience), but to Bentley's credit, he acknowledged that his conjecture amounted to nothing more than the recognition that 'if *I* had been participating in the conferences about the Blackfriars I should have argued long and lustily for Ben Jonson'.[82]

Yet he persisted with the argument that Shakespeare 'should write henceforth with the Blackfriars in mind and not the Globe', and that

---

[79] G. E. Bentley, 'Shakespeare and the Blackfriars Theatre', *Shakespeare Survey*, 1 (1948), 40.
[80] Bentley, 'Shakespeare and the Blackfriars Theatre', 41.
[81] Bentley, 'Shakespeare and the Blackfriars Theatre', 43, citing H. Granville-Barker, *Prefaces to Shakespeare* (second series) (London: Sidgwick & Jackson Ltd, 1947), 249–250.
[82] Bentley, 'Shakespeare and the Blackfriars Theatre', 44 (original emphasis).

'the Globe could be left to take care of itself with an old repertory'.[83] Knutson, citing the work of Ann Jennalie Cook as a salient reminder that social class and aesthetic tastes are not necessarily correlated, responds that '[t]he evidence on performance venues supports an offering of one repertory, regardless of playhouse'.[84] Both Knutson and John Astington have expressed scepticism over the possibility that stagecraft might differ between performance at the Globe and at the Blackfriars, Astington noting explicitly that '[p]lays which we may think of as being inspired by the new intimacy possible in Blackfriars were freely moved by the King's Men between the two houses' and '[t]he requirements dictated by the physical conditions at Blackfriars did not essentially differ from those at the Globe'.[85] This is true of the court as a venue for performances too, of course. That Barnabe Barnes' rabidly anti-Catholic farce, *The Devil's Charter*, could be played at court (on 2 February 1607) after public performances at the Globe is a sign that court tastes were not inherently more 'sophisticated' than the tastes of the playgoing public. Likewise, it is notable that Bentley pronounced that *The Merry Devil of Edmonton* (with its lowbrow antics including a fake friar, fake ghost, comical switching of inn signs, and thwarted diabolical pact) 'was not a good Blackfriars prospect'; yet this play is amongst the eighteen performed at court (an indoor venue for the elitest of the elite) by the King's Men in 1612–1613. '[T]aste and intelligence' are not easily correlated, as Knutson reminds us.[86]

Recent developments in historically inspired recreations of early modern playhouses have encouraged scholars to pursue performance-based research to glean insights into the effects of material playing conditions on repertory and stagecraft. Drawing on insights from the modern Globe and Sam Wanamaker Playhouse in London for a study of the King's Men's repertory in the Globe and Blackfriars playhouses, Sarah Dustagheer writes: 'Rather than arguing Shakespeare (and other King's Men's playwrights)

[83] Bentley, 'Shakespeare and the Blackfriars Theatre', 46.
[84] Knutson, *The Repertory*, 141. See A. J. Cook, *The Privileged Playgoers of Shakespeare's London, 1576–1642* (Princeton, NJ: Princeton UP, 1981), esp. 132–139.
[85] J. H. Astington, 'The Popularity of *Cupid's Revenge*', *SEL: Studies in English Literature, 1500–1900*, 19 (1979), 217. He adds: 'The only play in which the peculiarities of private theatre performance are incorporated in the dramaturgy, Beaumont's *The Knight of the Burning Pestle*, missed its mark in performance, and its failure should give pause to any attempt to differentiate too simply between the ambiance of the private and that of the public theaters', and concludes with his belief that 'there were no important differences in the stage and stage equipment between the two types of theater'.
[86] R. L. Knutson, 'What If There Wasn't a "Blackfriars Repertory"?' in P. Menzer (ed.), *Inside Shakespeare: Essays on the Blackfriars Stage* (Selinsgrove, PA: Susquehanna University Press, 2006), 57.

entirely embraced or rejected writing for the Blackfriars after they acquired this new space in 1609 I contend that something more nuanced occurred: a combination of spatial practices that gave the repertory a performance duality'.[87] According to Dustagheer, both on account of the proximity of the Blackfriars to the church and residences of the local community, and the architecture of the auditorium itself (where 'sound bounced and travelled around the auditorium'), 'deploying a series of loud sound effects was unsuitable for such a live space'. Instead, 'the acoustic effect which dominated the repertory at the Blackfriars and other indoor playhouses was music', and a feature of such indoor spaces was that they were conducive to 'a wider selection of more subtle instruments' than their amphitheatre counterparts permitted.[88] Moreover, she points to the fact that amongst the surviving drama, the Children of the Queen's Revels Blackfriars plays (1599–1608) featured some thirteen masques, whereas the King's Men at the Globe only staged two masques. Music, she argues, 'became far more than just an incidental or discrete presence … it was integral to the dramaturgy of many indoor plays as playwrights began to weave music into narrative and character development'.[89] Lighting, too, may have made a difference: 'at the Blackfriars, the candlelight and the highly fashionable audience gave the playhouse a particular visual aesthetic which, in turn, meant that the Children of the Queen's Revels produced the stage as a site for the display of clothing, jewellery and other props'.[90]

Such technological features, according to Dustagheer, in turn make it more likely that playwrights at the Blackfriars would explore specific subjects: if she is right that 'like the Children of the Queen's Revels' playwrights before 1609, the King's Men begin a particular examination of links between materiality, decadence and corruption at the Blackfriars', we might expect to find more plays in the King's Men's repertory that resemble such topics.[91] But such performance-based observations, born from experience in modern recreations of early modern venues, are not without their complications. Dustagheer herself acknowledges the difficulty of there being a four-century 'gap' between the original and reconstructed early modern theatres, but points to the acknowledgment by Farah Karim-Cooper that such performance-based research can help reshape and refocus thinking even if it does not necessarily offer definitive

[87] Dustagheer, *Shakespeare's Two Playhouses*, 7.
[88] Dustagheer, *Shakespeare's Two Playhouses*, 111.
[89] Dustagheer, *Shakespeare's Two Playhouses*, 112.
[90] Dustagheer, *Shakespeare's Two Playhouses*, 27.
[91] Dustagheer, *Shakespeare's Two Playhouses*, 6.

answers.[92] This is a sensible and attractive proposition when working with staging practices (Karim-Cooper's comments pertain to the application of cosmetics, for example), but we should exercise extreme caution if using such methods to extrapolate the likely subject matter or form of lost plays from the surviving Blackfriars offerings. Candlelight certainly would create a specific aesthetic effect, and a candlelit performance of a quintessentially 'dark' play such as *Macbeth* (most scenes of which take place under cover of night) would intuitively produce heightened affect in the candlelit spaces of indoor venues like the Blackfriars or Hampton Court (thought by many to be the site of the play's first performance), but we know from Simon Forman's notes that *Macbeth* was also performed at the open-air Globe. So, too, music – and complicated, sophisticated music at that – may have been integral to the dramaturgy of many plays performed at the Blackfriars, but counterexamples hint that this observation may be slightly overstated: Thomas Dekker's *Old Fortunatus* (1599), an Admiral's Men play written for performance at an outdoor theatre (the Rose), appears to be one of the most musical plays of the period, including what Elizabeth Ketterer called 'the longest continuous musical performance evidenced in the extant repertory of the company'. Ketterer in fact argues that '[t]he plays the company performed at the first Fortune allowed musically gifted players to show off their talents'.[93] And of course, the plays that survive (as I have been at pains to emphasise throughout this book) may not be typical, or even representative of a Blackfriars performance, given the time that lapsed between first performance and first publication (an interval of years, even decades sometimes, and with that the opportunity for changes to have been made to the play-text).[94]

A safer approach, in my view, is to follow the lead of John Astington, who also comments on the features Dustagheer observes in the post-1608 King's Men's plays but avoids ascribing their presence to an indoor-playhouse hypothesis. He argues that the 'descent scenes', 'special effects', 'strange costumes' and 'masque scenes' in the King's Men's plays of the early Blackfriars years 'are all to be understood in terms of an attempt . . . if

[92] Dustagheer, *Shakespeare's Two Playhouses*, 11, citing F. Karim-Cooper, 'Cosmetics on the Globe Stage' in C. Carson and F. Karim-Cooper (eds.), *Shakespeare's Globe: A Theatrical Experiment* (Cambridge: Cambridge University Press, 2008), 68.

[93] E. Ketterer, '"Govern'd by stops, aw'd by dividing notes": The Functions of Music in the Extant Repertory of the Admiral's Men, 1594–1621', unpublished PhD dissertation, University of Birmingham (2009), 231, 298.

[94] Knutson makes a similar point in 'What if there wasn't a "Blackfriars repertory"?' in Menzer (ed.), Inside Shakespeare: Essays on the Blackfriars Stage, 56.

not to rival then to imitate as closely as possible, the newly fashionable scenic effects of the court masques'.[95] Bentley's two-audiences theory of tailored stagecraft strikes me as an unsound basis from which to extrapolate details of lost plays from the period, for the reasons I outlined in the context of Leslie Thomson's work on touring. When London companies toured the provinces, part of the appeal for audiences was surely to see London plays in their full spectacular glory; actors were adept at performing a play in a variety of spaces (see Chapter 2). Positing different tastes and thus an entirely different dramaturgy at the Blackfriars leads to similarly distorted conclusions.

§

Our understanding of the repertorial offerings of the London companies has been distorted by an inherent bias towards Shakespeare's work at the expense of lost plays within his own company's repertory. Within the five-year period covered by this chapter, I have argued that although *Macbeth* has attracted scholarly attention for its topical allusions to the Gunpowder plot, these seem to have been part of a consistent interest of the King's Men in dramatising controversies affecting their patron. Their handling of the 'Gowrie' conspiracy may have been unsuccessful because of the approach they adopted to what was a polarising event, rather than because they had deigned to represent a living king. If further evidence could be found to support my conjecture that the 'Spanish Maze' play similarly engaged with conspiracies against the king, a picture of the company's propensity to indulge in risky or sensational material would emerge.

In the context of the company's move to the Blackfriars playhouse, sounding a note of caution about inferential license is the key message I want to communicate. Armed with an awareness of how an observer's biases can affect their perception of an ambiguous image like the visually experienced figures that so fascinated Rubin, I suggest that there is insufficient material in the stimulus here from which to draw conclusions about the interplay between figure and ground. Sometimes, as Rubin's extensive testing with homemade stimuli demonstrated, it is not possible to establish a fundamental difference between figure and ground, and 'the contour has no shaping effect on either area in which case no figure is perceived'.[96]

Various scholars have been tempted to deduce characteristics of the Blackfriars repertory from features of the venue (or features that would

---

[95] Astington, 'The Popularity of *Cupid's Revenge*', 226.   [96] Pind, *Edgar Rubin*, 97.

presumably suit the venue well), but the risk here is that what is nominated as the figure (tragicomedies) may not have been shaped by the nominal ground (the venue) at all, or at least not exclusively. In Figure 4.1 – which is taken from Rubin's work – two distinct interpretations are possible: 'When the concentric lines form the ground, one can easily experience the lines as extending behind and being joined behind the sectors with the radially extending lines', but the same is not true if the concentric lines form the figure.[97]

If the Blackfriars is thought to give shape to the repertory, the radial sector lines are the plays (tragicomedies, primarily) and the concentric lines are the venue that lurks in the background and gives rise to them; but if, as I am suggesting (following Astington), there is an independent reason why tragicomedies flourished around the time the King's Men moved to the Blackfriars, the picture changes.

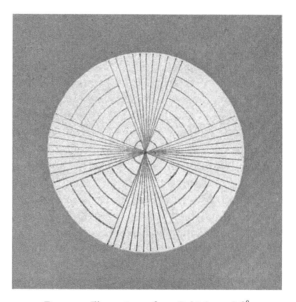

Fig. 4.1   Illustration 5 from Rubin's work.[98]

[97] Pind, *Edgar Rubin*, 97.
[98] Illustration 5 from the German edition of Rubin's work, *Visuell Wahrgenommene Figuren* (Copenhagen: Gyldendalske Boghandel, 1921) (out of copyright) (available online at https://archive.org/details/visuellwahrgenomo1rubiuoft).

Now the concentric line segments, corresponding to what we know of the Blackfriars plays, stand out and the radial lines, which are a more general vogue for tragicomedy that operates independently of the venue-specific requirements or possibilities, lie behind them.

Bentley went so far as to attribute the development of tragicomedy as a genre at the end of Shakespeare's career to the notional imperative to write exclusively for the Blackfriars' space and audience. In doing so, he confused correlation with causation when he observed a shift in Shakespeare's writing style, evident in the late romances, that coincided with the company's commencement at the Blackfriars, and he ignored the simpler explanation that stage romances were in vogue again.[99] Noting similarities between Shakespeare's *Cymbeline* and Beaumont and Fletcher's *Philaster*, he concluded that '[i]t is their common purpose and environment [i.e. to please the sophisticated audience at the Blackfriars], not imitation of one by the other, which makes them similar'.[100] There are indeed numerous similarities between *Philaster* and *Cymbeline* (for example, the revelation that Bellario is really a girl in disguise, just as Imogen's true identity is disclosed at the denouement of Shakespeare's play), but in the following chapter I discuss at length the relationship between *Cymbeline* and a lost play (the 'Play of Oswald') to make a very different argument that does not rely on playhouses to explicate the relationship between plays.

[99] Bentley, 'Shakespeare and the Blackfriars Theatre', 47.
[100] Bentley, 'Shakespeare and the Blackfriars Theatre', 48.

CHAPTER 5

Late Shakespeare: 1609–1613

In previous chapters, I demonstrate that the more scholars attend to lost plays, the more we realise just how closely related the plays of early modern London were in terms of recurring subject matter, popular genres and forms, plot devices, and other dramatic features that might otherwise be assumed to have been unusual or distinctive if our attention were restricted to the extant drama alone. Every extant play is deeply embedded in its repertorial moment, influencing and reacting to the other commercial offerings available on the London stages. (Sometimes, the relationship involves an active distancing from, rather than emulation of, another play or plays, in which case the relationship can be obscured.) In this chapter I re-examine Shakespeare's final plays in terms of their relationship to other drama in the repertory of the King's Men but also in competition with that repertory, but to do so I must grapple with some venerable Shakespearean biases.

Rubin, again, can help us rethink these biases. In an account of Rubin's experiments with visually experienced figures, Jörgen Pind says of the famous vase image specifically:

> While in general it is easy to realize the great difference associated with seeing a particular area as figure or ground, it sometimes can happen that this difference is muted. This occurs particularly when we focus on the fact that we are in both cases dealing with one and the same "objective item."

The striking figure of the vase is so pronounced and the face-shaped contours of the ground so inextricably part of the viewer's experience of the overall figure, that it can be hard to let the vase recede into the background and to direct due consideration to the faces. Pind's advice: 'Here, it is necessary to make clear to oneself that one is not to judge the item as such but only the visual experiences which it gives rise to'; he cites Rubin (in translation): 'One must as far as possible discard from consciousness one's knowledge about the objective item'.[1] I can see a direct analogy between this example and scholars' experience of the final phase of Shakespeare's professional career. Taking my cue from Rubin, I suggest that we need to discard as far as possible our preconceptions both of Shakespeare's influence on the repertory and of his infamous lost play, 'Cardenio'. Instead, I want to reassess the dramatic output of the repertory companies without privileging the distorting effect that Shakespeare (the vase) exerts on our perception of the theatrical marketplace. The Shakespearean 'figure' that we have grown accustomed to seeing has dominated our sense of the playgoing industry, producing significant distortions in our perception.

Specifically, two distortions in our understanding of these plays have resulted from the name 'Shakespeare' being attached to them. The first kind pertains to genre. The plays at the end of Shakespeare's career defy the generic classification instituted in the 1623 folio. *Pericles, Cymbeline, The Winter's Tale, The Tempest* and *The Two Noble Kinsmen* differ in form from Shakespeare's earlier drama. Surveying these and similar plays by other dramatists, Cyrus Mulready describes a vogue for dramatists to 'invoke a distant past through a genre that is definitively old-fashioned to engage with present concerns about travel, cross-cultural contact, and overseas expansion'.[2] The Victorian critic Edward Dowden coined a label for these plays. Noting that '[t]here is a romantic element' in *Pericles, Cymbeline, The Tempest* and *The Winter's Tale*, he accordingly dubbed them 'romances'.[3] As Mulready and others have noted, this use of the romance appellation by Dowden has misleadingly produced a perception of the term being inextricably linked to these Shakespearean examples, which have thus come to define the genre rather than be defined by it.[4] More recently, the fashion of deploying Dowden's categorisation has largely subsided in favour of attending to Shakespeare's 'late style', but this has only heightened the prioritisation of Shakespeare over his peers by conceiving of his plays purely in relation to the playwright's own *oeuvre* rather than the plays' generic kin. Charles Moseley has urged scholars to return to the romance appellation, calling attention to an underappreciated value in the term:

---

[1] Pind, *Edgar Rubin*, 95.
[2] C. Mulready, *Romance on the Early Modern Stage: English Expansion before and after Shakespeare* (Basingstoke: Palgrave Macmillan, 2013), 26.
[3] E. Dowden, *Shakspere. New Edition* (London: Macmillan & Co., 1877), 54–55.
[4] Mulready, *Romance on the Early Modern Stage*, 50–51.

It was once fashionable to call the late plays 'romances', a label more helpful than modern sneers might suggest. For the frequent editions suggest that popular taste for the now neglected narrative chivalric romances, like *Amadis de Gaul*, *Bevis of Hampton*, *Guy of Warwick* or the works of Malory, eventually deriving from medieval romance Arthurian or not, was consistent and influential, and affected dramatic writing.[5]

In the first section of this chapter, then, I focus on the romance intertexts of two of Shakespeare's late plays, *Cymbeline* and *The Tempest*, in order to prompt reconsideration of how they relate to other dramatic offerings of the period. Subsequently, I revisit the series of plays performed at court in 1612–1613 by Shakespeare's company and others, paying particular attention to what this season looks like if we 'discard from consciousness' Shakespeare's assumed pre-eminence.

The second distortion produced by a Shakespeare-centric approach is evinced by the coterie industry of publications pertaining to that Holy Grail of Shakespeare studies, the lost Fletcher and Shakespeare play, 'Cardenio' (1612). Almost all of the scholarship on this lost play is fixated on attempts to recover the play-text itself. By convention, scholars now widely (though not unanimously) agree that the play that Lewis Theobald presented to the world as *Double Falsehood* in 1727 is in fact a redaction of (a Restoration adaptation of) the lost Fletcher-Shakespeare play. Presented with the gift of a complete play, at second- or third-hand remove from the 1612 original, scholars have debated how best to glimpse a palimpsestic sight of the underlying Shakespearean content. Because the subject matter of *Double Falsehood* derives from no less an eminent source than Miguel de Cervantes' acclaimed Spanish novel, *Don Quixote* (1605), textual detectives have both been attracted to and able to reverse engineer the lost 'Cardenio' by drawing on the famous source text, the Theobald play text, knowledge of how Fletcher collaborated with Shakespeare, and knowledge of how Fletcher's and Shakespeare's plays were adapted throughout the seventeenth and early eighteenth centuries. At least four attempts have been made to write new versions of 'Cardenio': a creative response by Charles Mee and Stephen Greenblatt (2003);[6] an ambitious attempt by Gary Taylor to strip the Theobald out of *Double Falsehood* and leave a

---

[5] C. Moseley, 'The Literary and Dramatic Contexts of the Last Plays' in C. M. S. Alexander (ed.), *The Cambridge Companion to Shakespeare's Last Plays* (Cambridge: Cambridge University Press, 2009), 47.

[6] The Mee/Greenblatt script is available online via their 'Cardenio Project' site at https://sites.fas .harvard.edu/~cardenio/us-script.html

Fletcherian/Shakespearean 'unadaptation' or residue (2011);[7] and attempts by Bernard Richards (2009) and by Gregory Doran and Antonio Alamo (2011) to reconstruct missing scenes from the Theobald text via recourse to Cervantes.[8] The *New Oxford Shakespeare* included 'Fragments of *The History of Cardenio*', a version of *Double Falsehood* in which the editors removed 'everything demonstrably or probably written, or overwritten' by anyone other than Fletcher and Shakespeare, the resultant text being full of clearly identified lacunae.[9] Rather than adding to this abundance of critical energy devoted to recovering or reanimating the play-text, I ask a different question about 'Cardenio': How did this play relate to other commercial plays being performed in London? By attempting to answer this, and by understanding 'Cardenio' in relation to the other plays performed in repertory with it at court, I clarify the picture of the company's commercial offerings during the final phase of Shakespeare's career.

Recycling Romance

Scholars generally date Shakespeare's *Cymbeline* to 1610, and the play was certainly written by 1611, when Simon Forman saw it performed (probably at the Globe) sometime in April. Scholars have noted that Shakespeare, in writing *Cymbeline*, drew on suggestive details from Holinshed's *Chronicles* (1577) and a prose romance (*Frederyke of Jennen*, 1518), yet it has also been proposed that Shakespeare (as the Arden 2 editor summarises it) 'refashioned an old play of which all record has been lost'.[10] No direct evidence of such a pre-*Cymbeline* play has been offered by those scholars who seek 'an evasion of the source problems'; the postulation of such an Ur-play is what Knutson calls 'little more than a "get out of jail

---

[7] The term 'unadaptation' is used frequently to describe Taylor's project, e.g. by D. Carnegie, 'Introduction' in D. Carnegie and G. Taylor (eds.), *The Quest for Cardenio: Shakespeare, Fletcher, Cervantes, & the Lost Play* (Oxford: Oxford University Press, 2012), 3. Taylor's play is published in full in T. Bourus and G. Taylor (eds.), *The Creation & Re-Creation of Cardenio: Performing Shakespeare, Transforming Cervantes* (New York: Palgrave Macmillan, 2013), 241–316.

[8] Richards describes his writing process in 'Reimagining *Cardenio*' in Carnegie and Taylor (eds.), *The Quest for Cardenio*, 344–351; it is critiqued by Richard Proudfoot in the next chapter of that collection, 'Will the Real *Cardenio* Please Stand Up? Richards's *Cardenio* in Cambridge', 352–355. The Doran script is found in his *Cardenio: Shakespeare's 'Lost Play' Re-imagined* (London: Nick Hern Books, 2011) and an account of the writing process in his *Shakespeare's Lost Play: In Search of Cardenio* (London: Nick Hern Books, 2012).

[9] J. Fletcher and W. Shakespeare, 'Fragments of The History of Cardenio' in G. Taylor (ed.), *The New Oxford Complete Works of Shakespeare*, 3136.

[10] W. Shakespeare, *Cymbeline*, J. M. Nosworthy (ed.) (Arden 2) (Surrey: Thomas Nelson & Sonse Ltd., rpt 1998), xxvii.

free" card for puzzled textual scholars'.[11] Such scholarship was born of an era that craved straightforward source/adaptation relationships between texts; even rebuttals, such as Nosworthy's attempt 'to demolish the pre-*Cymbeline* theory' still proceeded on the assumption that plays need sources that could influence an entire plotline or furnish a key scene with highly specific details.[12] There may not be an Ur-*Cymbeline* play that lives up to these criteria, but what I want to explore in the first part of this chapter is the extent to which we can use an alternative model of source and influence to help us appreciate the contributions of lost plays in shaping the surviving drama of the period: the concept of theatergrams. As Louise George Clubb has noted in a study of early modern English borrowings from the Italian performance tradition, the creation of drama entailed drawing on pre-texts in such a way that 'demanded the interchange and transformation of units, figures, relationships, actions, *topoi*, and framing patterns, gradually building a combinatory of theatergrams that were at once streamlined structures for svelte play making and elements of high specific density, weighty with significance from previous incarnations'.[13] Accordingly, when looking for sources, we could be looking for variation and synthesis, not necessarily similitude, and we could be looking at scenarios rather than scenes. The fragmentary records pertaining to lost plays frequently offer us this 'outline' level of detail.

British Library, MS Egerton 2623, ff.37–38 – the 'Oswald fragment' (as Paul E. Bennett called it) or the 'Play of Oswald' (as Wiggins prefers) – is comprised of only four pages (two folio leaves).[14] Water-damaged, the manuscript may have suffered further in the hands of John Payne Collier, who allegedly forged an allusion to Shakespeare at the end of the manuscript, and who certainly failed to record the provenance of the text before 'sticking the leaves into his scrap-book the wrong way round', as Greg observes, 'so that in each case the text begins on the verso'.[15] The fragment

---

[11] Nosworthy, *Cymbeline*, xxvii; Knutson, 'Ur-Plays and Other Exercises in Making Stuff Up' in McInnis and Steggle (eds.), *Lost Plays in Shakespeare's England*, 32.

[12] Nosworthy, *Cymbeline*, xxviii.

[13] L. G. Clubb, *Italian Drama in Shakespeare's Time* (New Haven, CT: Yale University Press, 1989), 6. Material from this section appeared in an earlier version in my chapter, 'Lost Plays and Source Study' in D. A. Britton and M. Walter (eds.), *Rethinking Shakespearean Source Study* (New York: Routledge, 2018), 297–315, and is reproduced by permission of the publisher.

[14] P. E. Bennett, 'The Oswald Fragment and "A Knack to Know a Knave"', *Notes & Queries*, 196 (1951), 292–293; Wiggins #1260. The digitised fragment is available on the *LPD* entry for the play.

[15] W. W. Greg, 'A Dramatic Fragment', *Modern Language Quarterly* 7(3) (1904), 148. Greg is in fact slightly equivocal about whether Collier introduced a forgery and Arthur Freeman and Janet Ing Freeman do not believe there to be a Collier forgery in this particular manuscript; see A. Freeman and J. Ing Freeman, *John Payne Collier: Scholarship and Forgery in the Nineteenth Century*, 2 vols.

belongs to the end of the play and resolves two plot lines. In one, it is revealed that Genissa has defied her father Toogood by marrying Count Coell instead of her father's proposed match, Sir Ingram, precisely in the manner of Shakespeare's Imogen, who avoids her father's attempt to have her marry Cloten by pre-emptively marrying Posthumous (whom her father resents and subsequently banishes). (Curiously, in Holinshed's *Chronicles*, Genissa is the daughter of the Roman emperor Claudius, and is given in marriage to Cymbeline's son Arviragus.[16]) In the other plotline, the Duchess enters astonished, holding the hand of a young man named Oswald, ostensibly unknown to the court. The Duchess's husband, Duke Ethelbert, examines the man closely, especially his distinctive jewels. This prompts Ethelbert to recount how his ambitious uncle had attempted to seize power for himself by killing Ethelbert's first-born son:

> My wife had a first son, but my lewd [uncle],
> Should I die heirless, thinking mine his own,
> Poison'd that child; a second blest her womb;
> That too was marked for death ere it knew life;
> He meeting with the world was in one night
> Secretly in the swathing clathes conveyed
> Into Northumberland out of Mercia;
> To mock the tyrant she gave out it died,
> The nurse that kept it likewise lived not long,
> But how nurse jugled, how my boy was lost,
> I'm sure this cock and crucifix I tied
> To a small chain of gold about his neck
> With my own fingers . . .[17]

In the lead up to the imminent revelation of Oswald's true identity as the Duke's son, students of *Cymbeline* may already be recalling Belarius's 'dangerous speech' in the denouement of that play (5.6.314), in which he reveals that 'his' sons Polydore and Cadwal are really Cymbeline's sons, the princes Guiderius and Arviragus. In both *Cymbeline* and the 'Play of Oswald', a dangerously ambitious family member plots and attempts the murder of the rightful heir: the Queen plans to poison Imogen and kill Cymbeline in order to install Cloten, her own son from a former marriage, on the throne; Ethelbert's 'cunning' and 'lewd' uncle poisoned Ethelbert's firstborn son, resulting in the second-born (Oswald/Eldred) being 'Secretly

(New Haven, CT: Yale University Press, 2004), 2.1038. Citations from the 'Play of Oswald' are from Greg's modernised transcription.

[16] Holinshed, 'Arviragus' in 'The Historie of England', *Chronicles* (1577), sig. vij (p. 51).

[17] Greg, 'A Dramatic Fragment', 154.

in the swathing clathes conveyed / Into Northumberland out of Mercia',[18] much as Cymbeline's sons were wrapped '[i]n a most curious mantle' and removed from their true family's custody (5.6.362).

In both plays, the inherent nobleness of the unsuspectingly high-born exiles is readily discernible however; Imogen meditates on the greatness of spirit possessed by the men who are ultimately revealed to be her brothers, likening their cave to a court (3.6.80); and Belarius continues to be surprised by the irrepressible regality of the boys he knows to be princes: ''Tis wonder / That an invisible instinct should frame them / To royalty unlearned' (4.2.178–180). Oswald's insight into inherent nobility is expressed more crudely, and with bathos, but remains a variation on the theme:

> I knew there was noble
> blood in me, for I am in debt, and full of
> other such noble qualities, can drink hard,
> spend bravely, and love a sweet girl.[19]

This sentiment is actually something of a commonplace in the period. Will Sharpe draws a parallel between *Cymbeline* and another romantic comedy, Henry Chettle and John Day's *The Blind Beggar of Bethnal Green* (Admiral's, 1600) in precisely this regard, noting that in that play, '[t]he daughter, Bess, must venture out alone into the world until she is taken pity on and cared for by the mysterious "Blind Beggar", who, like Belarius in *Cymbeline*, knows of the child's true identity, and observes her noble nature manifesting itself even in the humblest circumstances'.[20] Simon Forman, who also saw *The Winter's Tale* at the Globe in 1611, commented in his diary on how a royal child in that play (Perdita) was raised in exile by shepherds and was eventually recognised for her nobility.[21]

Other, less commonplace parallels between 'Oswald' and *Cymbeline* continue, however, with the circumstances and criteria for positive iden-tification in *Cymbeline* closely resembling those in the 'Oswald fragment':

---

[18] Greg, 'A Dramatic Fragment', 154.   [19] Greg, 'A Dramatic Fragment', 154.

[20] Will Sharpe, 'A critical edition of *The Blind Beggar of Bethnal Green* by John Day and Henry Chettle (1600)', unpublished PhD thesis (University of Birmingham, 2009), 72.

[21] See the digitisation and transcription for 'Forman's account of seeing plays at the Globe: *Macbeth, Cymbeline, Winter's Tale*' in the Folger's *Shakespeare Documented* site (https://shakespearedocumented .folger.edu/resource/document/formans-account-seeing-plays-globe-macbeth-cymbeline-winters-tale). This conceit whereby a noble youth is raised rustically is reversed in a play offered by the King's Men at court in 1612–1613: in Beaumont and Fletcher's *A King and No King*, a false heir to the throne (Arbaces) is installed after having been raised as if he were royal, despite actually being the son of the Lord Protector (hence he is both a king and not really a king).

CYMBELINE　　　　　Guiderius had
　　Upon his neck a mole, a sanguine star.
　　It was a mark of wonder.
BELARIUS　　　　　　　　　This is he,
　　Who hath upon him still that natural stamp.
　　It was wise nature's end in the donation
　　To be his evidence now.

(5.6.364–369)

Guiderius has a birthmark that matches the 'cinque-spotted' one Giacomo so famously spies on Imogen's left breast earlier in the play (2.2.38). Siblinghood is thus established on the basis of the analogous moles. In the recognition scene from the 'Play of Oswald', the Duchess recognises Oswald as the son she had named Eldred, and Ethelbert confirms Oswald's identity to his own satisfaction by examining not just the distinctive jewels (the 'cock and crucifix' that he tied to 'a small chain of gold' about the boy's neck; presumably a Catholic device in the play's pre-Reformation England), but also his distinctive birthmarks: 'the print / Of a ripe mulberry' on his neck and '[t]he talon of an eagle on this arm'.[22] Oswald compares his eagle birthmark with one that his mother also apparently has, exclaiming, 'A whole eiry of eagles! So, so, sire; 'tis here, / [. . .] *et haec Aquila*, both he and she!'[23] The revelation of identity was fortuitously timed, for it turns out that the woman Oswald was about to marry was actually his sister. No such accidental incest is likely in *Cymbeline* – Imogen is a woman (unlike the wandering Oswald/Ethelred) and therefore prudently disguises herself as a boy (Fidele) whilst travelling to Milford Haven. It is in this guise as a boy that she

[22] Greg, 'A Dramatic Fragment', 154. The cock and crucifix likely allude to Peter's repeated betrayal of Jesus in the garden of Gethsemane and the crucifixion that followed as a direct consequence; that the pendant includes a crucifix rather than a cross suggests Catholicism. William Winstanley, for example, notes these specific connotations in his *The new help to discourse or, Wit, mirth, and jollity. . .* (1680):
　　Qu. Wherefore on the top of Church-steeples is the Cock set upon the Cross, of a long continuance?
　　An. The Papists tell us, it is for our instruction; that whilst aloft we behold the Cross, and the Cock standing thereon, we may remember our sins, and with *Peter* seek and obtain mercy. (60)
　　The significance of the imagery may well have been established earlier in the play, in the lost portion.
[23] Greg, 'A Dramatic Fragment', 154. Matthew Steggle has positively identified this garbled Latin tag as a quotation from the popular Renaissance teaching text, Lily's *Short Introduction to Grammar*, where 'aquila' (eagle) is given as an example of gender-ambiguous or 'epicene' nouns: '[T]he joke is clear – Oswald lapses into Latin, and then spoils the effect by observing that 'Haec aquila' could denote a male or a female eagle. It is a bathetic scrap of schoolboy learning, puncturing the seriousness of this recognition-scene'. See the 'For What It's Worth' section of the 'Play of Oswald' entry in the *Lost Plays Database*.

unwittingly meets her brothers. Nevertheless, the potential for disguised and dispersed siblings to form a sexual attraction *is* registered on an almost metatheatrical level when Guiderius declares, 'Were you a woman, youth, / I should woo hard' (3.6.66–67).

Beyond the similarities in the structure and details of the recognition scene (a theatergram popular in the commercial theatre, and a device that Shakespeare also exploited in *The Winter's Tale, The Tempest* and elsewhere), the generic experimentation of the 'Oswald fragment' is noteworthy as a precursor to Shakespeare's late plays. Shakespeare scholars have long noted that the collaboratively written *Henry VIII, or All is True* revisits historical material through the lens of romance and thus marks a turn in Shakespeare's handling of history away from the *Henry V* model (which itself had been developed in response to the providential, chronicle history form associated with the Queen's Men in the 1580s). The 'Oswald fragment' mixes *Cymbeline*-style romance (the prince raised pseudonymously in exile, eventually returning and being identified) with ostensibly Anglo-Saxon history. There are several pseudo-historical personages in the plot described above, which occupies the bulk of fol.37. An Ethelbert was king of Kent, a convert to Christianity, and uncle to 'Sigebert kyng of Essex' (there is a 'Sibert' listed in the stage directions), with whom he began the foundations of St. Paul's cathedral in London. After he was killed in battle, his daughter married Edwin, the first Christian king of Northumberland. After his grandson was killed, Osricus and Eufridus reigned until they were succeeded by their brother Oswald, who reigned in Northumberland for twenty-two years, his son becoming the last king of the Britons. Even with so limited a textual fragment surviving, the 'Play of Oswald' enlarges our pool of historical romance plays and our number of identity-revelation theatergrams.

Although it is not yet possible to confirm the date of the Oswald play with any certainty, scholars have tentatively assigned it to the turn of the century (i.e. preceding Shakespeare's *Cymbeline*). If this is true, the roughness and bathos with which 'Oswald' treats the components of the identity-revelation theatergram would help us to clarify Shakespeare's refinement of those elements in his own play. One reason for seeing the 'Oswald fragment' as sharing a theatergram with *Cymbeline* rather than necessarily being a source is that perceptions of the fragment's crudeness and dating of its distinctive words cannot guarantee that it preceded Shakespeare and was available to him as a source in the traditional sense. But creating a dialogue between the two moments remains a worthwhile enterprise because it creates a more vivid dramatic context for each and is mutually illuminating. We may not yet know which company performed 'Oswald' (if it was performed), who wrote it, or when, but the parallels between it and *Cymbeline* suggest they were related to each other and that the formulaic ending was worth repeating and varying. A company may have repeated its own successes with the theatergram, or it may have attempted to emulate the success of a rival.

Other Shakespearean romances may be reconsidered in light of the theatergrams they share with lost plays. *The Tempest*, which stubbornly refuses to yield clues to its primary source text, is a good example. Although Shakespeare came to writing romances relatively late in his career, his (and his audience's) familiarity with the genre stretched back decades. Cyrus Mulready has begun to call attention to the extent to which playgoers' expectations would have been conditioned by the large group of plays he calls 'stage romances' (to distinguish them from their prose counterparts) and draws on the suggestion of Helen Cooper that audiences were 'deeply familiar with the tropes and motifs of a 500-year-old tradition' of romance writing.[24] Mulready contends that 'the continued attention to Shakespeare's "late plays" as romances has led to neglect for the rich history of romance adapted to the stage in the sixteenth and seventeenth centuries'.[25] Although Mulready chooses Robert Greene's *Orlando Furioso* (c.1591) and the relatively recently rediscovered *Tom a Lincoln* (c.1613) as the basis for 'evidence of what audiences saw (and perhaps expected) when romance came to the stage', he makes mention also of lost stage romances such as 'Herpetulus the Blue Knight and Perobia' (1574) and 'The History of the Solitary Knight' (1577).[26] Recovering the likely narratives of such lost plays increases our awareness of the variables at play in the romance theatergrams deployed by Shakespeare in *The Tempest*. The entries in Henslowe's diary show, for example, that an anonymously authored 'Chinon of England' was performed as a new play by the Admiral's Men on 3 January 1596, receiving fourteen performances in total.[27] W. W. Greg and others have suggested that the lost play may have been based on Christopher Middleton's *The famous historie of Chinon of England*

[24] C. Mulready, 'Romance on the Early Modern Stage', *Literature Compass*, 6(1) (2009), 114.

[25] Mulready, 'Romance on the Early Modern Stage', 116.

[26] Mulready, 'Romance on the Early Modern Stage', 116.

[27] Foakes (ed.), *Henslowe's Diary*, 33–37, 47 and 54. The title also appears in the booksellers Richard Rogers and William Ley's list, 'An exact and perfect Catologue of all Playes that are Printed', appended to Thomas Goffe's *The Careless Shepherdess* (London, 1656). See the *LPD* entry for 'Chinon of England'.

(London, 1597) whilst still in manuscript form.[28] Amongst other things, Middleton's romance includes a witch (Europa, not Sycorax), an 'ayrie Spirit' (cf. the airy Ariel), a beautiful daughter (Cassiopea, rather than Miranda) exiled to a wilderness 'far from the resort of men', a fool (Chinon) imprisoned in a rock (cf. Caliban styed in a 'hard rock,' 1.2.344), a cannibal in the Arabian desert, and an island where harpies (cf. Ariel, clad 'like a harpy', 3.3.52SD) guard a golden book.[29] Traditional source study is unlikely to regard the lost 'Chinon' as a source for *The Tempest*, but as Clubb observes, source studies are typically 'resistant . . . to historicizing synthesis', whereas a focus on theatergrams potentially enables us to place 'Chinon' on a continuum of stage romances including Shakespeare's play.[30] Other variants of the use of magicians, witches, rocky imprisonments, and exiles to barren locations might turn up in the narratives of lost plays; if they do, they will undoubtedly help us better appreciate Shakespeare's unique reconfiguration of such elements.

Shakespeare and the King's Men at Court: 1612–1613

I lamented in earlier chapters that there is no King's Men equivalent of Henslowe's records to help us reconstruct the repertory of Shakespeare's company in the same vivid detail as was possible for companies at the Rose. However, there *is* a tremendously useful source of historical information for the final phase of Shakespeare's career in the form of the court records of performances; specifically, the Declared Accounts of the Treasurer of the Chamber (Bodleian, MS Rawlinson A 239). Two Chamber Account warrants dated 20 May 1613 together provide details of twenty performances at court by the King's Men.[31] The first of these warrants is a list of fourteen performances:

> Itm paid to Iohn Heminges vppon the Cowncells warr' dated att Whitehall xx° Die Maij 1613 for presenting before the Princes Highnes the La: Elizabeth and the Prince Pallatyne Elector fowerteene several playes viz one called † Pilaster, One other called the Knott: of Fooles, One other Much adoe abowte nothinge, The † Mayeds Tragedy, The merye Dyvell of

[28] Greg (ed.), *Henslowe's Diary, Part II*, 178.

[29] C. Middleton, *The famous historie of Chinon of England . . .* (London, 1597), sig .H2; sig. H3.

[30] Clubb, *Italian Drama*, 3. The theatergrams apparently present in 'Chinon' may in turn have been inspired by Italian pastoral as traced by Robert Henke in *Pastoral Transformations*, 56–60.

[31] D. Cook and F. P. Wilson (eds.), 'Dramatic Records in the Declared Accounts of the Treasurer of the Chamber 1558–1642' in *Malone Society Collections VI* (Oxford: Oxford University Press, 1961), 56 and 55.

Edmonton, The Tempest, A Kinge and no Kinge The Twins Tragedie The Winters Tale, Sr Iohn Falstafe, The Moore of Venice, The Nobleman, Caesars Tragedye And one other called Love Lyes a bleeding, All wch Playes weare played wth in the tyme of this Accompte, viz p^d the some of iiij^xx xiij^li vj^s viij^d

The second, better-known of these warrants is famous for including Fletcher and Shakespeare's 'Cardenio' amongst the six performances it records:

Itm paid to the said Iohn Heminges vppon the lyke warr': dated att Whitehall xx° die Maij 1613 for presentinge six severall playes viz one playe called a badd † beginininge makes a good endinge, One other called ye Capteyne, One other the Alcumist. One other Cardenno. One other The Hotspurr. And one other called Benidicte and Betteris All played wth in the tyme of this Accompte viz p^d Fortie powndes, And by waye of his Ma^tes rewarde twentie powndes In all lx^li

Leaving 'Cardenio' (here entered as 'Cardenno') to one side for now, as I return to it in detail in the sections below, I would like to ponder some of the more curious inclusions in the company's broader repertory at the time and explore how our picture of court performances changes if we focus on lost plays.

Eighteen discrete plays by the King's Men are listed in these warrants (*Philaster* and *Much Ado* are entered twice using alternative titles). The vast majority (thirteen) are comedies or tragicomedies. Only three are obviously tragedies ('The Twins' Tragedy', *The Maid's Tragedy* and *Othello*) and only two are clearly histories (*Julius Caesar* and *1 Henry IV*). The plays associated with Shakespeare account for less than half the offerings and account for almost all of the old plays performed by the company: *1 Henry IV* (1597), *Merry Wives* (1597), *Much Ado* (1598), *Julius Caesar* (1599) and *Othello* (1604), plus the apocryphally Shakespearean *Merry Devil of Edmonton* (1603). Beaumont and Fletcher's *Philaster* dates from around 1609 but the remaining eleven plays seem to have been written in 1611 or even more recently. As romances, the more current Shakespeare plays (*The Tempest*, *The Winter's Tale* and 'Cardenio') are typical rather than exceptional within the repertory. In sum: the company relied on Shakespeare for the old favourites but most of their offerings at this time were recent tragicomedies (Shakespeare's contributions being very much on trend rather than exceptional).

Two of the lost plays offered by the King's Men provide little clue to their subject matter. 'The Twins' Tragedy' is unusual in that twins more

usually feature in comedies; rare exceptions include the King's Men's own
Duchess of Malfi by John Webster (1613) and possibly their much later *The
Cruel Brother* by William Davenant (1627) (the twinship of the siblings
Foreste and Corsa is uncertain).[32] These two examples produce horror
through 'the potential for incestuous inclinations within the twin relation-
ship'.[33] By featuring one or more twins who came to a 'sticky end' (as
Wiggins puts it), the play is noteworthy for its apparent generic innova-
tion.[34] The subject matter of 'The Nobleman' is also ambiguous.
Stationers' Register entries reveal that the play was a tragicomedy by
Cyril Tourneur, which is in itself interesting in that – like the author of
'The Twins' Tragedy', entered merely as 'Niccolls' in the Stationers'
Register – Tourneur was hardly a resident playwright for the King's Men
in the manner of Shakespeare, Beaumont or Fletcher (who together
dominate this repertory).[35] The only earlier play certainly by Tourneur
is *The Atheist's Tragedy* (1611), but its company auspices are uncertain. His
biographer, David Gunby, describes Tourneur as a man who had 'written
for gain only when not employed in his chosen profession of soldier'.[36]
'The Nobleman' may well have been his first and only play for the King's
Men. A consequence of this is the recognition that playgoers at court seem
not to have been overly concerned with authorship, and were perfectly
content with the dramatic offerings of lesser-known playwrights (the
precedent of Barnabe Barnes in 1607 is worth recalling here). A musical
setting for this play survives, suggesting that the play perhaps included a
masque, but so too did plays as diverse as *The Tempest* and *The Revenger's
Tragedy*.[37] Both 'The Twins' Tragedy' and 'The Nobleman' were contin-
uations from 1611–1612, having been performed at court previously.

These King's Men's plays were offered at court alongside plays from
other companies, a number of which remain identifiable. We know from
other Privy Council warrants that the Children of the Queen's Revels
performed Fletcher and Beaumont's *The Coxcomb* (October 1612) and
Cupid's Revenge (1 and 9 January 1613), and Chapman's *The Widow's*

---

[32] On the tragic representation of twinship in these plays, see Daisy Murray's study, *Twins in Early Modern English Drama and Shakespeare* (New York: Routledge, 2017).

[33] Murray, *Twins*, 24.   [34] Wiggins #1640.

[35] The authorship of 'The Nobleman' is confirmed by *Stationers' Register* entries on 15 February 1612 (Arber (ed.), *Stationers' Register*, 3.478) and 9 February 1653 (Eyre et al. (eds.), *A Transcript of the Registers*, 1.429). The authorship of 'The Twins' Tragedy' is given in the entry dated 15 February 1612 (Arber (ed.), *Stationers' Register*, 3.478).

[36] David Gunby, 'Tourneur, Cyril (d. 1626)', *ODNB*.

[37] An audio recording (using modern copies of historical instruments) of the music preserved in British Library Add. MS 10444, no. 55 can be found on the *LPD* entry for 'The Nobleman'.

Tears (27 February 1613). The Lady Elizabeth's Men performed Marston's *The Dutch Courtesan* ('Cockle de Moye') on 25 February and the lost 'Raymond Duke of Lyons' on 1 March 1613. Although this last title sounds like a history, there is no known Duke of Lyons named Raymond (the duchy itself only existed for about seventy years). Wiggins is likely to be correct that the play's subject matter is 'irrecoverable' because unhistorical and therefore probably 'imaginary'.[38] Its title suggests a French setting but the play could just as easily have featured a French character elsewhere (just as the other play performed by Lady Elizabeth's Men, *The Dutch Courtesan*, is actually set in London). Finally, the Prince's Men performed a pair of lost plays, 'the first parte of the knaues' and 'the second p^te of the knaues' on 2 and 5 March 1613 respectively.[39]

These last plays by the Prince's Men (or Duke of York's Men, if before November 1612), '1 & 2 The Knaves', are particularly interesting for their opaque titles. Usually such characters are found in the context of 'parasites, knaues, & fooles' (as Dekker lists them in a play published in 1612) or 'Knaues, and Baudes, and Whores' (as Jonson lists them in a play performed at court that season).[40] Wiggins hedges his bets, suggesting that the knaves in question 'might have been the four knaves from a pack of cards, or their knavery may have been more naturalistic', but does not elaborate on what either possibility might entail.[41] Regarding Wiggins' first suggestion, I find it striking that the satirist Samuel Rowlands (fl. 1598–1628) published a series of pamphlets between 1609 and 1613 that exemplify how a pack of cards might furnish a playwright with material for the stage. Beginning with *The Knave of Clubbes* in 1609 (a reprinting of the lost 'A Mery Metinge', which had been destroyed in 1600 after bishops Whitgift and Bancroft objected to its satirical content), Rowlands provided vignettes of a 'Whoor-monger', a 'Pander', a 'Gull', a 'Cuckold' and many more.[42] (The sketch of a 'Gull' is the source of the anecdote about Edward Alleyn wearing a cross whilst playing the role of Faustus on stage.)[43] *Clubbes* concludes with the promise that subsequent instalments featuring the knaves of hearts, diamonds and spades will follow, and in *Roome, for a messe of knaues* (1610), he delivered on this promise, offering witty

[38] Wiggins #1685.
[39] Cook and Wilson (eds.), *Malone Society Collections VI*, 56, item 47b; 57, items 47b and 48a; 55, item 47a; 54, item 46b.
[40] Dekker, *If it be not good, the Diuel is in* it (London, 1612), sig. F4^v; B. Jonson, *The Alchemist* (London, 1612), sig. E3.
[41] Wiggins #1677.   [42] S. Rowlands, *The Knave of Clubbes* (London, 1609).
[43] Rowlands, *The Knave of Clubbes*, sig. D3.

caricatures of the knaves of hearts, diamonds, spades and clubs. These could readily provide the impetus for a humoral comedy: the first example Rowlands gives is of 'A Melancholy knaue, & a Chollericke: A Sanguine knaue, & a Flegmaticke'.[44] His *Knave of Harts* (1612) and *More Knaues yet: The Knaues of Spades and Diamonds* (1613) continued the theme, the respective knaves (who seemingly curate each pamphlet as fictional authors) competing to get their stories into print next.

The abundant material provided by Rowlands' humoral vignettes seems to me ripe for dramatisation. Comedies of humours had peaked in the late 1590s, but humoral plays including *Merry Wives of Windsor* and *Much Ado About Nothing* were apparently experiencing a revival at the time of the 1612–1613 revels season. It is occasionally suggested that Jonson's *Every Man in His Humour* may have been revised around this time too,[45] lending further credibility to the likelihood that the 'Knaves' plays were humoral comedies. Rowlands had a difficult relationship with the stage, professing hostility but also nostalgia for the days of Tarlton and evident familiarity with staging practices (as in the Faustus example).[46] I cannot rule out Wiggins' second guess of more 'naturalistic' knavery, but the timeliness of Rowland's material being published and the King's Men reviving their humoral comedies encourages me to favour the 'pack of cards' hypothesis.

In addition to *Much Ado* and *Merry Wives*, the King's Men had another comedy on offer in the form of Jonson's *The Alchemist*; but they may have had a variation of the knavery theme in their repertory also: the lost play referred to as 'The Knot of Fools'. Wiggins does not hazard a guess as to the subject matter, but lists 'Fools' as the only inferable characters. What does the phrase 'knot of fools' mean? Fortunately, a text from 1624 offers a very clear model for how early moderns might understand the phrase: *A knot of Fooles. But, Fooles, or Knaues, or both, I care not, Here they are; Come laugh and spare not*, by Thomas Brewer (fl. 1605–1640). It consists of a short dialogue between various kinds of fools (a 'knot' or group, in the sense of being bound together; a collective noun), beginning with the direction 'The Crew meet and salute: For their Characters, take them as

---

[44] S. Rowlands, *Roome, for a messe of knaues Or, a selection, or a detection, or, a demonstration, or a manifestation. of foure slaues. Or, a conuiction, or a comiction, or, a combination, or a copulation of foure varlets. Or, a reperition, or a repetition. Or, a replication, or a recapitulation. of foure harlets* (London, 1610), sig. B.

[45] See, e.g. Knutson, *The Repertory*, 146.

[46] See Reavley Gair's entry for 'Rowlands, Samuel (fl. 1598–1628)' in the *Oxford Dictionary of National Biography*.

you find them in *their owne phantasticall prating*'. Each type of fool (they are assigned numbers, not names) reveals their particular humour in the course of conversing. This is followed by a series of satirical verses attributed to the Greek philosopher Democritus, famous for his love of folly, whose name became 'shorthand for a whole mode of satirical discourse' in early modern England.[47] The topics of the verses are mostly proverbial, ranging from 'A Foole and his money is soone parted' and 'Better lost than found' to 'All is not gold that glisters' and 'Much adoe about nothing'. Towards the end of the pamphlet, the sequence of verses is interrupted and the reader is told that '[t]his old Abderite', i.e. Democritus, is 'gone to sleepe, tyred with this Knot of incurable Fooles'. The remaining four pages consist of verses on 'Pride teaching Humility', in which the Egyptian king Sesostris (or Sesoösis) is reprimanded by one of the rulers who drags the conqueror's chariot.[48]

In his address to the reader, Brewer likens his work to stage entertainments: '*I will not call't a* Puppit-show: / *Though those and these, come something neare* . . .'.[49] The title-page's woodcut features six men and a woman variously attired as kinds of fools alluded to in the verses of the text, engaging with each other in active dialogue, almost in the manner of a stage play. Interestingly, Brewer had a track record of taking inspiration from the stage: his prose tract on 'the lyfe and deathe of the Merry Devill of Edmonton', entered in the Stationers' Register on 5 April 1608, was 'doubtless influenced by' the *Merry Devil of Edmonton* play (1603) performed by the King's Men at court in 1612–1613.[50] I am tempted to imagine that if Brewer's *Knot of Fools* is in any way indicative of what the King's Men may have staged at court, the lost play – apart from chiming with the Prince's Men's 'Knave' plays in their dramatisation of fools – might take the form of an elaborate series of jests or paradoxes, or have some analogy with the framed playlets of the Chamberlain's earlier '2 Seven Deadly Sins' play (see Chapter 2), perhaps with Democritus instead of John Lydgate commenting on the short episodes he witnesses.[51]

[47] M. Steggle, *Laughing and Weeping in Early Modern Theatres* (Aldershot: Ashgate, 2007), 22.

[48] The anecdote was well known, as Elizabeth Tavares has shown, and probably provided the model for Tamburlaine's debasement of his enemies in 2 *Tamburlaine*: see E. Tavares, 'The Chariot in "2 Tamburlaine", "The Wounds of the Civil War", and "The Reign of King Edward III"', *Notes & Queries* 63(3) (2016) 393–396.

[49] Brewer, *Knot of Fools*, sig. A1ᵛ.

[50] Arber (ed.), *Stationers' Register*, 3.374; E. Haresnape, 'Brewer, Thomas [T. B.] (fl. 1605–1640)', *ODNB*.

[51] Henslowe recorded as 'ne' a play called 'Paradox' for the Admiral's Men on 1 July 1596: see Foakes (ed.), *Henslowe's Diary*, 47.

Attending to lost plays helps recalibrate our picture of the dramatic offerings at court in 1612–1613. Alongside the obvious vogue for tragicomedy (evident in the surviving plays), there seems to be a previously unappreciated nostalgia for older comedies of humours in '1 & 2 The Knaves' and 'The Knot of Fools'. There may have been some imaginary engagement with history in 'Raymond, Duke of Lyons', perhaps in the model that Fletcher and Shakespeare would later develop in their *Henry VIII, or All is True*. In 'The Twins' Tragedy' there seems to have been generic innovation involved in staging a pointedly tragic tale of twins. And there is evidence both in the form of that lost play and 'The Nobleman' that a greater variety of playwrights (here, the otherwise unknown 'Niccolls' and Cyril Tourneur respectively) than is usually thought had their work selected for court performances.[52] As far as the evidence confirms, both of these lost plays were their authors' first and maybe only offerings for the King's Men, yet both were selected for multiple performances at court, in 1611–1612 and 1612–1613.

What Was 'Cardenio'?

The court documents that I have been working with above constitute the earliest evidence of that most notorious of lost plays, Fletcher and Shakespeare's 'Cardenio'. In this section, I want to first address the question of what 'Cardenio' actually was, before contemplating why the company might have invested in such a play at this point in time. Theatergrams remain a useful tool for thinking about what narrative elements of the playwrights' likely source text would have fired their imaginations and may, therefore, have featured in the play as performed.

But first: What is documentable about 'Cardenio' and its authorship? Two early manuscript accounts pertaining to performances of the play have an indisputable claim to authority: the Declared Accounts of the Treasurer of the Chamber and the imperfect copies of these in the Pipe Office collection of the Declared Accounts (E351/544). These manuscript sources offer documentation of two separate performances, but only the version in the Chamber Accounts names the play. It does not use the name 'Cardenio' in the form now familiar to scholars, nor does it nominate a playwright by name, but it does specify that on both occasions the play was

---

[52] Bentley's theory of a distinct and elitist Blackfriars repertory is further undercut by the company's presenting such 'common' fare at court by what he would have regarded as second- or third-tier dramatists.

performed by the King's Men. The first of the records from the Chamber Accounts records details of a performance of the play at Court before King James in 1613:

> Itm paid to the said Iohn Heminges vppon the lyke warr': dated att Whitehall xx° die Maij 1613 for presentinge sixe severall playes viz one playe called a badd † beginininge makes a good endinge, One other called ye Capteyne, One other the Alcumist. One other Cardenno. One other The Hotspurr. And one other called Benidicte and Betteris All played wth in the tyme of this Accompte viz p^d Fortie powndes, And by waye of his Ma^tes rewarde twentie powndes In all lx^li

This warrant is dated 20 May 1613, but the court performance took place earlier that year in the Christmas season.

An alternative spelling of the play's title is provided in a second record in the Chamber Accounts, which documents a private performance for the Duke of Savoy's ambassador:

> Item paid to Iohn Heminges vppon lyke warr': dated att Whitehall ix° Die Iulij 1613 for him self and the rest of his fellowes his Ma^te servauntes and Players for presentinge a playe before the Duke of Savoyes Embassadour on the viij^th Daye of Iune 1613 called Cardenna the some of vj^li xiij^s iiij^d

Here, the version in the Pipe Office collection specifies two or more 'Ambassado^rs' (plural).[53] This performance took place on 8 June 1613; letters by John Chamberlain offer confirmation that the location was the private house of the Lord Mayor, Sir John Swinnerton in the parish of St Mary Aldermanbury. The audience probably included Sir Giovanni Battista Gabaleone and the Marquese Francesco Villa, ambassadors of the Duke of Savoy, as well as Sir Robert Rich and Sir Henry Wotton.[54] Gary Taylor has offered cogent suggestions for why 'Cardenna' may have been performed for this particular diplomatic contingent, including the possibility of heightened audio and visual spectacle to offset any lack of proficiency in the playgoers' English; the 'recycling of a Spanish novel with a pan-European reputation'; and the political prudence of adapting 'a recent Catholic novel' for an audience who were attempting to arrange a

---

[53] Cook and Wilson (eds.), *Malone Society Collections VI*, 56 and 55. Cook and Wilson provide transcriptions from both manuscripts, with the Pipe Office version appearing first, separated by a horizontal line from the Chamber Accounts version below it.

[54] Taylor, 'The Embassy, The City, The Court, The Text: *Cardenio* Performed in 1613', 286–288, citing Chamberlain's letter to Sir Dudley Carleton dated 10 June 1613 in N. E. McClure (ed.), *The Letters of John Chamberlain*, 2 vols (Philadelphia: American Philosophical Society, 1939), 1.457.

dynastic marriage of the Duke's daughter with one of James's sons.[55] My purpose in this chapter, though, is to focus on the repertory context before James at court.

These records of performance are complemented by a third variant of the play's title in a document that dates from a much later period but nonetheless has a claim to authority. On 9 September 1653, Humphrey Moseley entered 'The History of Cardenio, by M[r]. Fletcher. & Shakespeare' into the Stationers' Register, thereby providing a third variation of the title and this time an authorship attribution.[56]

It was not until 1727 that Lewis Theobald announced that his *Double Falsehood*, which rehearses the Cardenio story, was based on an old Shakespearean play. As I noted above, the tantalising possibility that Fletcher and Shakespeare's 'Cardenio' may be recoverable to a substantial extent by engaging with Theobald's professed adaptation has meant that the overwhelming majority of scholarship on this lost play has been geared towards textual recovery. The picture (or 'figure') of 'Cardenio', then, is limned in relation to the background of Shakespeare's career usually, or very occasionally Fletcher's career, both in terms of textual recovery and authorial style. Focusing on the play in relation to the King's Men's repertory can change the way we conceive the negative space, and the relationship between figure and ground.

Theobald's ostensible redaction of a lost Shakespearean play has inevitably shaped the perception of 'Cardenio', but several scholars (including Harriet C. Frazier, Jeffrey Kahan and Tiffany Stern) have accused Theobald of forgery.[57] Although theirs remains the minority opinion and scholars continue to debate the nature and extent of Theobald's purported borrowings, I want to make an altogether simpler point: that the one thing we know with certainty is that Theobald's play – by his own

[55] See Taylor, 'The Embassy, The City, The Court, The Text: *Cardenio* Performed in 1613', 286–293.

[56] The terminal punctuation mark after Fletcher's name is not always noticed or reproduced by scholars, yet it may be read as evidence that Shakespeare's name was added to the entry as an afterthought. See Eyre et al. (eds.), *A Transcript of the Registers*, 1.428, but NB. Eyre's edition omits the punctuation after Fletcher's name, which is clearly visible in the digitised manuscript available via *Literary Print Culture: The Stationers' Company Archive, 1554–2007* (see *Register of entries of copies: Liber E, 3 Dec 1645–27 Feb 1657*, p. 285).

[57] H. C. Frazier, *A Babble of Ancestral Voices: Shakespeare, Cervantes, Theobald* (The Hague: Mouton, 1974), 146; J. Kahan, *Shakespeare Imitations, Parodies and Forgeries: 1710–1820*, vol. 1 (London: Routledge, 2004), 163; T. Stern, '"The Forgery of some modern Author"?: Theobald's Shakespeare and Cardenio's *Double Falsehood*', *Shakespeare Quarterly*, 62(4) (2011), 555–593.

acknowledgment – differs from whatever the King's Men performed in 1613.[58] Putting *Double Falsehood* to one side, then, I proceed as I have throughout this book by interrogating the title as it is given in the two performance records and Moseley's Stationers' Register entry before considering how a play based on the available source material may have related to the rest of the King's Men's repertory at this point in time.

I agree with those scholars who have assumed, based on Theobald's play, that 'Cardenio' derived from Cervantes, but I reach that conclusion via a different approach and independent support. In keeping with my methodology throughout this book (and in the *Lost Plays Database*), I see value in exploring alternative subject matter systematically. Let's rule out the alternatives. Noting the spelling of the play's title as 'Cardenna' in the second record, Stern proposes that the title invokes 'Cardena' (Cardeña) in Spain, 'or a hero from there'.[59] As a scholar who has worked with lost plays for a decade or more, I struggle to think of commercial plays whose titles consists solely of a geographical location; usually titles involving place names take the form of 'conquest of ~', 'king of ~', and the like.[60] Stern's suggestion, though technically not impossible, strikes me as remote; and it is more so because a search for 'cardenna' or 'cardena' in the fully searchable Text Creation Partnership branch of *Early English Books Online* produces only a handful of references to Cardeña in Spain (none of which provides a narrative to dramatise). An imaginative leap to 'Cardenia' (which approximates 'Cardeña' in the absence of the tilde) provides further unhelpful references to Spain, as well as to a nymph or shepherdess of that name and Faustus, the lover who spurned her (thus

---

[58] Here I differ importantly from Richard Wilson, who largely equates *Double Falsehood* with 'Cardenio' (he calls it a 'transcription') and performs close textual analysis on Theobald's play as though it were a reliable record of 1613 performance, with a view to conducting a historicist reading of pro-Catholic sympathies and the Howard faction's influence at Court. See R. Wilson, *Secret Shakespeare: Studies in Theatre, Religion and Resistance* (Manchester: Manchester University Press, 2004), 231.

[59] Stern, 'The Forgery', 556–557.

[60] Only very occasionally will a title be recorded in the abbreviated manner that fits Stern's paradigm: 'The Conquest of the West Indies' by John Day, William Haughton and Wentworth Smith (Admiral's, 1601), for example, *is* noted by Henslowe as simply 'the weaste enges' ('The West Indies'), though not initially. See the relevant passages from Henslowe in the *Lost Plays Database* entry for 'The Conquest of the West Indies'; I have quoted the version of the title as Henslowe gives it on the fifth occasion that he refers to the play (Foakes (ed.), *Henslowe's Diary*, 178/f.92). Another example is the play Henslowe records as 'al*be*[*l*]*re* galles' (Foakes (ed.), *Henslowe's Diary*, 215) and which Steggle has identified as referring to the city of Alba Regalis (as it is known in Latin) or Stuhlweissenberg (in German) (Steggle, *Digital Humanities*, 104). The play of 'Troy' entered as 'ne' by Henslowe on 22 June 1596 (Foakes (ed.), *Henslowe's Diary*, 47) is an ambiguous case in that it may invoke the war as much as the geographical location.

demonstrating the potential pitfalls of this sort of work: there is a danger inherent in assuming a particular name brings with it a particular story. Marlowe's Doctor Faustus was never a shepherd). Searching 'Cardenno' (as the other performance record lists the play) yields no hits and 'Cardeno' (as a variant) results in references to a type of iris or to something coloured black and blue.[61]

The titles as preserved in the documents of performance from 1613 are therefore of limited value for understanding the lost play. What of the name as Moseley gives the play in 1653: 'Cardenio'? There are mercifully few instances of the name 'Cardenio' and its variants in EEBO-TCP; they are confined to just ten records, containing 555 hits. Almost all of these hits (378 of them) occur in four editions of Cervantes (1612, 1652, 1687 and 1712). Two of the other records that feature a large number of hits are Thomas D'Urfey's *The comical history of Don Quixote* (1694) and a related volume of songs from his play (thirty-seven hits). Gayton's *Pleasant Notes Upon Don Quixot* (1654) contains fifty-seven hits. A translation of French letters by Monsieur de Voiture (1657) includes a single reference to '*Sierra Morena*, the place where *Cardenio* & *Don Quixot* met'.[62] The only outliers are the eighty-one hits in Edward Phillips' *The Illustrious Shepherdess* (1656), a translation of a Spanish novel that post-dates the English play of 1613,[63] and a single mention of the French *Les Folies de Cardenio* in a book-seller's catalogue from 1640.[64] Taking this brute-force approach to searching the EEBO-TCP corpus strongly suggests that whatever the truth about Theobald's play, the King's Men play

[61] Using EEBO's 'Select from a list' function to browse all keywords in the database beginning with the letters 'card . . .' offers little inspiration for variant spellings with potential. A 'Cardino' yields multiple hits in Munday's *Palmerin D'Oliva* (1588) and his *Palmendos* (1589), translations of the French and Spanish *Palmerin* romances, where the name is assigned to an insignificant squire and an ineffective knight respectively. Both are incidental to the main plots. A celebrated Milanese physician, Girolamo Cardano (1501–1576), predicted a long life for the young Edward VI, but the king died shortly after at the age of fifteen. Such subject matter would be grossly inappropriate given that the eighteen-year-old Prince Henry had become gravely ill himself by the start of the winter season and would die during the course of the playing period.

[62] John Davies, trans., *Letters of affaires love and courtship. Written to several persons of honour and quality* (1657), 70.

[63] Juan Pérez de Montalbán uses 'Cardenio' as the name assumed by a character in disguise in *La villana de Pinto*, the fifth novel from his *Sucesos y prodigios de amor* (1624; translated by Phillips as *The Illustrious Shepherdess* in 1654). But de Montalbán was born in 1602 and was thus only 10 or 11 years of age when the English 'Cardenio' play was written and performed; if the lost play has any analogy to the Spanish romance, it would have to be via a common, as yet untraced source. For a plot summary, see L. A. Daniel, 'Selected Dramas and Novelas of Juan Pérez de Montalbán', unpublished MA dissertation, University of North Texas (1972), 95–101.

[64] Robert Martin, *Catalogue des diverses liures francoises recueillées dans la France* (1640).

performed in 1613 was most likely based on Cervantes.[65] Having this confirmed quantitatively by a thorough search of EEBO (with its acknowledged limitations) is helpful because what interests me is the subject matter and the related question of why the King's Men might want to acquire a play like this, at this point in time, given the rest of their repertory.[66]

The Cardenio story in Cervantes has three main parts: Don Quixote's initial meeting with Cardenio (in which Cardenio begins his tale), the continuation of Cardenio's tale for the benefit of the Curate and Barber, and Dorotea's tale, culminating in the collective conclusion of their interspersed stories at an inn or tavern.[67]

In the first phase of the narrative, we learn that Cardenio has loved Luscinda since they were young. Her father approved of the union but kept the young lovers separate: Cardenio likens the situation to Thisbe being denied access to her lover (Pyramus), 'which hinderance serued onely to adde flame to flame, and desire to desire', leading to the couple exchanging love letters.[68] (Here we have a kind of *liebestod* theatergram with a history of stage success: the pattern of tragic love familiar to playgoers from the examples of Shakespeare's Pyramus and Thisbe in *Dream*, his Romeo and Juliet, Troilus and Cressida, and Antony and

---

[65] In Spanish Golden Age literature, the name was frequently used as a pastoral disguise and given to shepherds or rustic fools (perhaps with malicious or untrustworthy character traits). See A. F. G. Bell, 'Who was Cardenio?', *Modern Language Review*, 24(1) (1929), 67–68. Lope de Vega has a Cardenio in his play, *La Arcadia* (1602), which is based on one of Lope's own prose pastorals (one of his most popular works). It was not translated into English, but Lope's work was known in England: James Mabbe sent a copy of Lope's *Rimas* from Madrid to his friend William Baker in Oxford in 1613, inscribed with a note by Leonard Digges comparing Lope to Shakespeare. I am grateful to Alexander Samson for advising me that the only Lope de Vega translation from before 1640 is *El peregrino en su patria*; see P. Morgan, '"Our Will Shakespeare" and Lope de Vega: An Unrecorded Contemporary Document', *Shakespeare Survey*, 16 (1963), 118–120, and a digitisation and transcription at the *Shakespeare Documented* site in the entry for 'Rimas de Lope de Vega Carpio'. Kenneth Muir pointedly avoids suggesting that Shakespeare read Lope, but finds it 'difficult to doubt that Digges, who loved both dramatists, would have discussed Lope with Shakespeare', 'Lope de Vega and Shakespeare' in J.-P. Maquerlot and M. Willems (eds.), *Travel & Drama in Shakespeare's Time* (Cambridge: Cambridge University Press, 1996), 240. Recent work by José A. Pérez Díez strongly suggests that sources from Spanish drama could have circulated in England regardless of publication or translation: ('What the Quills Can Tell: The Case of John Fletcher and Philip Massinger's *Love's Cure*', *Shakespeare Survey* 70 (2017), 89–98. He argues that the play was based on Guillén de Castro's recent *La fuerza de la costumbre*, which the English dramatists encountered in manuscript.

[66] There *is* a surviving German play that features the name 'Cardenio' in its title – Andreas Gryphius's *Cardenio und Celinde* (1649) – but unlike the 'Hester' example that I discussed in Chapter 2, this German play is a red herring which does not correspond to anything originating in England. See M. E. Gilbert, 'Gryphius's "Cardenio und Celinde"', *Modern Language Review*, 45(4) (1950), 488.

[67] Thomas Shelton, trans., Cervantes, *The history of the valorous and vvittie knight-errant, Don-Quixote of the Mancha Translated out of the Spanish* (1612).

[68] Shelton, trans. *Don-Quixote*, 3.10.221.

Cleopatra.) Cardenio seeks permission to marry Luscinda; her father agrees on the condition that Cardenio's father also bestow his blessing on the union. Before Cardenio can ask, he is called away to court to serve as a companion to Duke Ricardo's eldest son, Don Fernando.

Don Fernando quickly takes Cardenio as his confidant, confessing his love for Dorotea, a rich farmer's daughter. Fernando insists they adjourn to Cardenio's father's house while Fernando gets over his infatuation with Dorotea (actually, Fernando and Dorotea have already consummated their union; he forced himself on her and she only ceased resisting when she extracted from him a promise of marriage; however, what had seemed love was actually lust, and now Fernando is desperate to avoid having to marry her).[69] Unfortunately for Cardenio, Fernando soon falls for Luscinda. He cunningly sends Cardenio away on the pretext of an errand. After four days, Cardenio receives a letter and a ring from Luscinda.[70] The letter reveals Fernando's treachery: he has persuaded Luscinda's father to give Luscinda's hand to *him* in marriage, to take place in secret, within two days. Cardenio flees, arriving home to find Luscinda in her wedding dress, her father and Fernando waiting for her in the great hall. She confides that she is carrying a hidden poniard and plans to kill herself. Cardenio hides behind a tapestry in the hall (playgoers familiar with Polonius's fate in *Hamlet* might be worried at this point), hoping (but failing) to spring out at the opportune moment to stop the ceremony. Instead, he witnesses first Luscinda then Fernando declare '*I will*', whereupon Luscinda faints 'in a trance'.[71] (The apparent death of a heroine or hero features as a standard device in a number of romances and comedies from the period, including *Much Ado About Nothing*, *Cymbeline* and *The Winter's Tale*; I return to this below). Cardenio sneaks out of the hall, unnoticed, and so does not witness Fernando finding a letter in Luscinda's clothes; it states 'that she could not be *Don Fernandoes* wife, because she was already *Cardenioes*'.[72] He seizes her hidden poniard and tries to kill her with it, but is prevented and flees. While this is happening, Cardenio rides off into the night, cursing Luscinda's covetousness (for he believes she chose Fernando's money over his own love). After a period of days, he finds himself in the most remote part of the wilderness, where he hopes to end his life. His is a kind of self-imposed exile in a barren place, but it chimes with the fate of Prospero and others from stage romances well enough.

---

[69] Shelton, trans. *Don-Quixote*, 4.1.291.   [70] Shelton, trans. *Don-Quixote*, 3.13.270.
[71] Shelton, trans. *Don-Quixote*, 3.13.275.   [72] Shelton, trans. *Don-Quixote*, 4.1.296.

Cardenio's exile is complemented by another character's: we soon learn that the dejected Dorotea has been roaming the Sierra Morena mountain range disguised as a shepherd this whole time. When word reached her that Fernando had married Luscinda, she was furious. She had tried to find Luscinda's family home, but in asking for directions, soon learned what happened at the wedding after Cardenio fled. (What she doesn't know is that when Luscinda recovered, she exiled herself to a nunnery to spend the rest of her life, until Don Fernando and three associates eventually found and kidnapped her.) Despondent and defeated, Dorotea has thus lived in exile for months, lamenting her sad state. The hermit-like Cardenio stumbles upon Doretea by chance as she is washing her feet. Here, we might have some of Dorotea's actual lines of lament preserved: scholars have proposed (persuasively, in my opinion) that a genuine fragment of writing from the original Fletcher-Shakespeare play may survive in the form of a song by Robert Johnson, a composer associated with the King's Men. The song consists of two verses of lyrics beginning, 'Woods, rocks, and mountains', the earliest surviving setting of which is dated c.1620:[73]

> Woods, rocks, and mountains, and ye desert places
> Where naught but bitter cold and hunger dwells,
> Hear a poor maid's last will killed with disgraces.
> Slide softly while I sing, ye silver fountains,
> And let your hollow waters like sad bells
> Ring, ring to my woes, while miserable I,
> Cursing my fortunes, drop, drop, drop a tear and die.
>
> Griefs, woes, and groanings, hopes and all such liars
> I give to broken hearts that daily weep;
> To all poor maids in love, my lost desires.
> Sleep sweetly, while I sing my bitter moanings,
> And list may hollow lovers, that ne'er keep
> Truth, truth in their hearts, while miserable I,
> Still cursing my fortunes, drop, drop, drop a tear and die.

In tone and content, it agrees well with Dorotea's plight, lied to and abandoned by Don Fernando and now wandering the Sierra Morena

---

[73] The identification was first proposed by Michael Wood in an unpublished manuscript, 'A Sound from Heaven: Lost Music from *Cardenio*' (2001) cited by B. Hammond in his Arden edition of *Double Falsehood* (London: Methuen Drama, 2010), 328–335 and by G. Taylor, 'A History of *The History of Cardenio*' in Carnegie and Taylor (eds.), *The Quest for Cardenio*, 27–33. Both the music and the lyrics of the song survive in five seventeenth-century musical manuscript collections. The versions in British Library Add. MS. 11608, fols. 15ᵛ–16ʳ and Christ Church MSS Mus 56–60, no. 56 have been digitised and appear with an audio recording on the *Lost Plays Database* entry for 'Cardenio'.

ranges in desolation. It would correspond perfectly with this particular moment of Dorotea's imminent encounter with Cardenio. The two exiles talk to each other and Doretea supplements Cardenio's knowledge of Luscinda's fate.

Hearing all this brings Cardenio to his senses. At this point in Cervantes's narrative, the Don Quixote plot interrupts the Cardenio story: his return is important to the story simply in the sense that it provides the impetus for Cardenio and Dorotea to travel to an inn.[74] At length, four masked men and a nun in white arrive at the inn; Dorotea and Cardenio hide, but when the nun speaks, Cardenio recognises the voice as Luscinda's instantly.[75] (Already we have the beginnings of a recognition-scene theatergram, but this one will be exceptional in its nature and the extent of its revelations.) Luscinda hears Cardenio's voice and recognises it too, rising but being restrained by one of the masked men (Don Fernando); in the ensuing struggle they each lose their masks and are recognised. Dorotea falls in a trance at the sight of Don Fernando. All four lovers stand dumb and amazed. Dorotea recovers and reminds Fernando that she is rightfully his wife; Fernando, 'full of confusion and maruell', relinquishes Luscinda and takes back Dorotea. Luscinda now falls in a trance, but Cardenio steps forward to catch her. With the couples reunited according to their original pairings, Don Fernando gives thanks 'vnto heauen for hauing dealt with him so propitiously, and vnwinded him out of the intricate Labyrinth, wherein straying, he was at the point to haue lost at once his soule and credite'.[76]

Cervantes' 'Cardenio' narrative must have seemed a gift to dramatists seeking material: merely consider its premise of tragic love; the seeming death but unexpected survival of Luscinda after she has been coerced into marriage; the made-for-stage business of Cardenio hiding behind a tapestry and misconstruing the events he witnesses; the double exile of Cardenio and Dorotea to live amongst the shepherds and the self-imposed exile of Luscinda who takes herself to a nunnery; and the spectacular recognition scene that reunites four disguised lovers with their rightful partners. A play based on the 'Cardenio' story would be a welcome addition to the company's repertory in a number of important ways. Another King's Men dramatist, Thomas Middleton, had set a precedent by adapting an

---

[74] Don Quixote's servant, Sancho, interrupts Dorotea and Cardenio and solicits their help to cure Don Quixote of his madness. The party (consisting of Cardenio and Dorotea, Sancho, Don Quixote, and his friends the Curate and Barber) sets off to an inn, where Quixote sleeps and the Curate tells a story of the 'Curious Impertinent'.

[75] Shelton, trans. *Don-Quixote*, 4.9.401.   [76] Shelton, trans. *Don-Quixote*, 4.10.411.

episode from Cervantes' novel as a standalone play: *The Second Maiden's Tragedy*, which is usually connected instead, via a misnomer, to the unrelated *Maid's Tragedy* performed at court by the company that winter.[77] Two of the King's Men's dramatists, Francis Beaumont and John Fletcher, had produced noteworthy experiments with the tragicomic form: the parodic *Knight of the Burning Pestle* and the self-declared novelty of *The Faithful Shepherdess*; an adaptation of Continental (in this case, Spanish) romance – by a novelist of international renown – would be a desirable investment for the company. Moreover, the 'Cardenio' story is not as parodic of the genre as Beaumont's 'famous failure',[78] yet also not as serious as Fletcher's earlier, notoriously unsuccessful play, which was a purer form of the genre – the 'Cardenio' material offered the company (and perhaps Fletcher specifically) an opportunity to strike a happy medium between those two extremes, retaining humour but also the cultural cachet of what had by now become the trendy Continental style, thanks in part to Fletcher's own pioneering work.

How, though, might such a play complement other plays performed at court by the King's Men in 1612–1613?

'Cardenio' at Court: 1612–1613

We know from one of the Chamber Accounts records cited above that 'Cardenio' was played at court during the 1612–1613 Christmas season alongside five other plays paid for by James: the anonymous 'A Bad Beginning Makes a Good Ending', Fletcher and Beaumont's *The Captain*, Jonson's *The Alchemist*, and Shakespeare's *1 Henry IV* ('The Hotspurr') and *Much Ado About Nothing* ('Benidicte and Betteris'). That particular Christmas season was historically significant in two ways. Prince Henry fell ill around 25 October, just as the revels season was commencing, and died suddenly on 6 November. His death prompted 'an unprecedented display of grief on the streets of London'.[79] The funeral took place on 7 December and burial on 19 December; the official mourning period extended into late January. This tragic and unexpected development was

---

[77] Incidentally, Beaumont and Fletcher's *The Coxcomb*, performed by the Children of the Queen's Revels in October 1612, also relies on Cervantes' tale of 'The Curious Impertinent' for its source. (The relevant plotlines from each play begins with the premise of a man being encouraged to seduce his friend's wife.)

[78] E. Price, 'Why Was *The Knight of the Burning Pestle* Revived?', *Shakespeare Bulletin*, 37(1) (2019), 47.

[79] Wilson, *Secret Shakespeare*, 230.

complemented by the more expected and welcome news of the betrothal of Frederick, Elector Palatine and Princess Elizabeth, which took place on 27 December 1612. Their wedding – the first royal wedding in England since Henry VIII married Catherine Parr in 1543 – followed on 14 February 1613.

What we don't know is how these plays were selected for performance. Possibly the Master of the Revels considered each play's suitability for court when he first read the texts before licensing them for public perfor-mance or saw them in public playhouses. Subsequently, when entertain-ment was required at court, he probably summoned the relevant companies to wherever the Revels were scheduled to take place and requested that some of those plays be rehearsed. (In his *Apology for Actors* (1612), Thomas Heywood refers to 'the office of the Revels, where our court plays have been in late days yearly rehearsed, perfected, and corrected before they come to the public view of the prince and the nobility'.[80]) The Master of the Revels might then require improvements or alterations to meet court tastes; as Dutton has argued in the context of Tilney apparently collaborating with Shakespeare on the production of *Lear* at court in 1606/7, the Master 'would not have been a passive gatekeeper in such matters' and some negotiation with the Master (if not explicit requirements by him) must have taken place.[81] When Dutton focuses on the King's Men's performances of *Lear* and of Barnabe Barnes' *The Devil's Charter* at the 1606–1607 revels season at court, he sees in those plays 'features in common' that are 'surely not accidental', including both plays' preoccu-pation with devils and devilry, a subject close to the heart of James, author of *Daemonologie* (1597). Although only two King's Men's plays are known to have been performed at court that season, Dutton sees potential for reading significance into the selection:

> It could hardly have been pure chance that two plays on that subject were chosen for the same Revels season. Was this a result of the players antici-pating the court taste? Or might Tilney have prompted them, and if so at what point in the writing/revision process?[82]

Dutton provides additional evidence in the form of examples from 1604–1605, 1631 and 1633 court performances to illustrate 'the court revels season being structured or thematised beyond what could reasonably have been expected if the Masters of the Revels had simply trawled

---

[80] Heywood, *Apology for Actors* (1612), sig. E1ᵛ, quoted in R. Dutton, *Shakespeare, Court Dramatist* (Oxford: Oxford University Press, 2016), 6.
[81] Dutton, *Shakespeare, Court Dramatist*, 64.   [82] Dutton, *Shakespeare, Court Dramatist*, 65.

whatever happened to be in the repertoire of the current "allowed" companies'.[83]

The Masters in this account function as 'impresarios' for the court.[84] From the limited evidence available, it seems possible that the companies, for their part, were obliging, as for example when the King's Men revived an old play, *Love's Labour's Lost*, at court in 1604 because Queen Anne had already seen all their more recent fare and Richard Burbage thought this play had 'wytt & mirthe' that would 'please her exceedingly'.[85] It is not clear whether Burbage means that the company had revived *Love's Labour's Lost* specifically to please the queen, or merely that they happened to have recently revived it and it might be the most appropriate to offer the queen. Evidently its suitability, as judged by Burbage and others, motivated the decision to perform the play before her in 1604.

It is also possible that the Master of the Revels might consciously *avoid* certain titles if he perceived a risk in allowing them – for example, a play that could be deemed inappropriate in the unexpected context of mourning. The decision, whoever's it was, to stage Shakespeare's *1 Henry IV* is interesting from that point of view, because it seems like an odd choice. If Gary Taylor is right that the only play performed by the King's Men before the young Prince Henry died in November was 'A Bad Beginning Makes a Good Ending', then *1 Henry IV* must have been performed after Prince Henry died.[86] Yet the Master of the Revels must have deemed it uncontroversial to stage *1 Henry IV* even though it featured three characters named Henry, each flawed in their own way: Henry Percy (Hotspur) is a hot-headed knight; Prince Henry (Hal) is a 'prodigal son'-type who shirks his responsibilities; and King Henry (Bolingbroke) has never truly outstripped the notoriety of having come to the crown by deposing his cousin, Richard II. (Indeed, we know from Simon Forman's diary accounts that the King's Men had a 'Richard the 2' play in production

---

[83] Dutton, *Shakespeare, Court Dramatist*, 65.   [84] Dutton, *Shakespeare, Court Dramatist*, 65.

[85] Sir Walter Cope, letter to Viscount Cranborne [Robert Cecil], c.1604. Hatfield House, MS CP 189/95. Digitisation available online through the Folger's *Shakespeare Documented* website: https://shakespearedocumented.folger.edu/resource/document/sir-walter-cope-letter-viscount-cranborne-robert-cecil-describing-loves-labors

[86] Taylor has argued that 'Henriquez', the name given to Cervantes' 'Fernando' in *Double Falsehood*, could not possibly belong to the lost 'Cardenio' play as performed in 1613: 'Henriquez' would 'inevitably have suggested Prince Henry', hardly a prudent association given that Fernando/Henriquez is 'the play's most despicable character'. A court audience, Taylor observes, 'could hardly have applauded a play with a villain whose name mocked the deceased' (Taylor, 'The Embassy, The City, The Court, The Text: *Cardenio* Performed in 1613', 304).

at the Globe in April 1611.[87]) Everyone in the audience at the court performance would be familiar with the trajectory of Hal's character as he became the 'the mirror of all Christian kings' (*Henry V*, 2.0.6), so in that sense a performance of *1 Henry IV* did not run the risk of vilifying the recently deceased Prince Henry; at the same time, the focus on three Henries strikes me as somewhat unfortunate at a time when Prince Henry's death would have dominated the court's mood.

As I say, strictly speaking we don't know how plays were chosen or not chosen for performance at court, but I concur with Dutton that some evidence of curation is apparent in the handful of instances in which play names are recorded in the official documents. Three court masques celebrating the royal wedding were offered at Shrovetide (Thomas Campion's *Wedding Masque of Stars and Statues Made Human*, Chapman's *Wedding Masque of the Princes of Virginia* and Beaumont's *Wedding Masque of Olympian Knights*).[88] Planning for these had begun as early as 23 October 1612.[89] The current Master, George Buc, may therefore have looked favourably on fare appropriate to the celebratory mood.

What do we know about the plays that were performed at court that season and how might they complement each other if indeed the repertory had been curated by the Master of the Revels or someone else? Gary Taylor has observed that if the company performed 'A Bad Beginning Makes a Good Ending' on 31 October 1612, it 'would have been a suspiciously prescient title, for a season in which an unexpected royal death was followed by a royal wedding', and if the performance took place in January or February, 'its title would have been self-evidently appropriate to the court's situation'.[90] With its generic title, apposite to comedy, tragicomedy or romance, it may have set the agenda for the genre of plays that dominated the season. It is worth noting, however, that the more common formulation, often found in sermons, is actually that 'a *good* beginning makes a good ending'. A play title along those lines is ascribed to John Ford in a Stationers' Register entry of 29 June 1660 and in Warburton's list of unprinted manuscript plays in his possession at the

---

[87] Bodleian MS Ashmole 208, fol.201[r-v]; see the *LPD* entry for 'Richard the 2' for a digitisation and transcription of Forman's account. Reprising a play about Bolingbroke would be an obvious choice if the company had 'Richard the 2' in production recently.

[88] For convenience, I have used the names that Wiggins assigns these masques in *Catalogue* entries #1698–1700.

[89] See Wiggins #1698.

[90] Taylor, 'The Embassy, The City, The Court, The Text: *Cardenio* Performed in 1613', 298.

end of the seventeenth century.[91] It has been noted (e.g. by Dent) that the unusual take on the proverb, as encapsulated in the title recorded in 1612–1613, is indebted to John Heywood.[92] It is less commonly noted (if at all) that Heywood uses it with irony:

> Of a harde beginning, comth a good endyng:
> Truth, on this terme is not alway dependyng.
> Some hardely begin, by the feete to syt fast:
> That ende with harde hangyng, by the neckes at last.[93]

The twist in the play's title (its substitution of a 'bad' beginning for a 'good' one), coupled with Heywood's ironic inflection of the proverb, leaves open the possibility that for all we know, the play's interest may have lain in its interrogation of the proverbial title rather than its adherence to it.

Shakespeare's *Much Ado About Nothing* (1598), like *1 Henry IV*, was quite an old play by 1612–1613, yet it was performed twice at court that season: once for the king and once for Princess Elizabeth and the Elector Palatine.[94] The play is generically of a piece with repertorial offerings in 1612–1613: like the tragicomedies popular at that time, it is a romantic comedy that looks poised to slide into tragedy with Claudio's appalling treatment of the maligned Hero at their wedding (4.1). Intriguingly, as Richard Wilson notes, just as 'Cardenio' appears to have been 'one of the few Jacobean plays with sympathetic Spanish characters', so too, 'tellingly, was ... *Much Ado*, with its Aragonese Prince and Spanish troops'.[95] As would befit a revels season that included a royal wedding, marriage is the

---

[91] For 'An ill begining has a good end, & a bad begining may have a good end. a Comedy ... by Iohn fforde', see Eyre et al. (eds.), *A Transcript of the Registers*, 2.271; for 'A good beginning may have A good end by Jon. Ford' see British Library, Lansdowne MS 807, fo.1ʳ, in the *LPD* entry, 'Warburton's List'.

[92] R. W. Dent, *Proverbial Language in English Drama Exclusive of Shakespeare, 1495–1616: An Index* (Berkeley: University of California Press, 1984), B260, 'A hard (ill) BEGINNING has (makes) a good ending'.

[93] Heywood, 'Of beginning and ending. xxi', *Two hundred epigrammes, vpon two hundred prouerbes* (1555).

[94] Item 47b in Cook and Wilson, *Malone Society Collections VI*, 55.

[95] Wilson, *Secret Shakespeare*, 235. It would be convenient to associate the revival of *Much Ado* with a renewed vogue for humoral comedy at this time, but Knutson's suggestion (*The Repertory*, 140, based on Herford and Simpson's scholarship on Jonson), that *Every Man In His Humour* may have been revived around 1612 (thus explaining the alterations made to that play's quarto text when it appeared in the folio of 1616) is now less certain than it once appeared; David Bevington concludes (at 4.621) in his recent work (D. Bevington, M. Butler and I. Donaldson (eds.), *Cambridge Edition of the Works of Ben Jonson* (Cambridge: Cambridge University Press, 2012)) that: 'On balance, there appears to be no compelling reason to place all of the folio revisions as late as 1610–1612, even if some revising work does indeed seem to have continued into the printing process'.

central theme of *Much Ado*, beginning with the undermining of Hero and Claudio's relationship (and Claudio's humiliating rejection of Hero at their wedding) and culminating in not only Claudio's surprise wedding, sight unseen, to Leonato's 'brother's daughter' (5.4.37; actually Hero in disguise) but also in the wedding of Benedick and Beatrice. Beyond noting the analogy of Claudio's rejection of Hero at their wedding with Luscinda and Fernando's failed wedding in the Cardenio story, a playgoer familiar with the company's repertory would recognise the emergence of a recurring theme in Hero's surprising resuscitation at the end of *Much Ado*. I would describe this as a development of the 'recognition scene' theatergram, incorporating miraculous revival. *The Winter's Tale* (performed at court that season) has the most explicit and magical version of such restorations and reunions with the reanimation of Hermione-as-statue, but *The Tempest* (also in repertory that season) contains a further variation on the theme too. When Prospero, left for dead by the Neapolitans who exiled him, confronts his enemies, the recognition scene theatergram takes the form of an allusion to the Doubting Thomas episode in the Gospel of John. Prospero presents himself as the 'wrongèd Duke of Milan' to the shocked Neapolitans and says to Gonzalo, 'For more assurance that a living prince / Does now speak to thee, I embrace thy body' (5.1.107–109), just as Jesus offered tactile proof to his disciple. Beyond these resonances with *The Winter's Tale* and *The Tempest*, Claudio's shock at the seemingly impossible resuscitation of Hero in *Much Ado* would potentially find parallels in 'Cardenio': Luscinda, since falling in a trance at her wedding to Don Fernando, has for all intents and purposes been dead to Cardenio, and Dorotea has likewise been at least metaphorically dead to Fernando, but in the denouement of Cervantes' story, all four lovers are miraculously reunited.

I can also see some reasons why a playgoer at court could think that Fletcher and Beaumont's *The Captain* (c.1612), a play that ends with marriage but also moral unease, might resonate with the interests of other plays being performed at court. It includes a tavern scene (4.2) reminiscent of those in *1 Henry IV* (and imitated in the 'Tapster fragment'),[96] just as the Cardenio story in Cervantes culminates in an all-important tavern scene. As with the generic conventions of Cervantes' work, *The Captain* draws on tragicomedy – specifically in the form of experiments from the King's Men's own dramatists (Beaumont's Children of the Queen's Revels

---

[96] For a digitisation and commentary, see the *LPD* entry, 'Play of Thieves and a Gullible Tapster'; see also Wiggins #1470.

play, *The Knight of the Burning Pestle* in 2.2 and Fletcher's *Faithful Shepherdess* in 1.3)[97] – and professes to defy generic categorisation in its Prologue: 'This is nor *Comody*, nor *Tragedy*, / Nor *History*, nor any thing that may / (Yet in a weeke) be made a perfect Play' (Prol.6–8). *The Captain* thus integrates well enough with tragicomic romance and the history of this repertory but is noteworthy for its generic innovation: its content is somewhat darker than usual for tragicomedies. This deeply disturbing play is rife with misogyny, exceeding that of Don Fernando in Cervantes, and features a bizarre spectacle of imminent incest between the widow Lelia and her father,[98] in which she lures him into her home through provision of a banquet and musical seduction (reminiscent of Ariel's banquet of harpies in another King's Men play that had recently been performed at court: *The Tempest*). The Father's response speaks to the company's repertorial interests in romance: 'What's here? a Banquet? and no mouth to eate, / Or bid me do it? this is something like / The entertainment of adventurous Knights / Entring enchanted Castles' (4.4.76–78).

The commentary on marriage in *The Captain* is peculiar but a potentially interesting addition to the Revels season: the eponymous Captain (Jacamo) marries Franck after a Benedick / Beatrice awkwardness is resolved; Lelia marries Signor Piso but only after Piso's friend Ludovico is tricked into paying for the wedding because he thinks he will be the groom; and Julio marries Clora in great haste at the denouement, causing another character to remark: 'If a marriage should be thus slubberd up in a play, er'e almost any body had taken notice you were in love, the Spectators would take it to be but ridiculous'.[99] Implicitly drawing a connection with another play in repertory, *1 Henry IV* (see above), Knutson notes that Jacamo is 'a Hotspur in his relish for war, who complains bitterly about the tedium of peace'.[100] Indeed, one of the greatest oddities of *The Captain* is precisely that the play pushes beyond the common comic resolution of (in this case a triple) marriage to conclude with the news, welcomed by Jacamo, that war has returned.

The scheduling of Jonson's *The Alchemist* is perhaps the hardest to make sense of in the selection of plays produced at court that season: its presence

---

[97] See Wiggins #1665.

[98] I.e. scene 4.4, which includes Lelia's defense of such a sexual union, a *reduction ad absurdum* devoid of irony or self-awareness, at 4.4.185–197.

[99] J. Fletcher and F. Beaumont, *The Captain*, L. A. Beaurline (ed.) in *The Dramatic Works in the Beaumont and Fletcher Canon*, vol.1, F. Bowers (gen. ed.) (Cambridge: Cambridge University Press, 1966), 5.5.32–34.

[100] Knutson, *The Repertory*, 146.

in this group of six may simply be attributable to it being an excellent play. Its take on marriage differs markedly from what we know of the rest of the plays offered at court that season in that marriage is perfunctory and has a non-focal role in the narrative (I'm thinking here of Face and Subtle wanting to marry the widow, and Lovewit actually marrying her). Surly's posing as a Spanish count constitutes a further example of Hispanic-themed comedy in the repertory. It also offers a complement to supernaturally themed plays named in the other warrant pertaining to that season, including *The Tempest* and *The Merry Devil of Edmonton*, and it recreates farcically the exile, recognition and winding paths of the other plays performed at court that year.

For Richard Wilson, the great question about the performance of 'Cardenio' at court is 'how this drama of a reluctant bride could possibly have been thought appropriate to the wedding of a Stuart princess'.[101] This characterisation of 'Cardenio' as featuring a 'reluctant bride' and her 'unswerving resistance to an arranged alliance' is misrepresentative, however.[102] If Shelton's translation is a reliable indicator of the lost play's contents, the peculiar (if generically satisfying) closure of the Cardenio narrative, with its reunion of two betrothed couples (Cardenio and Luscinda, Fernando and Dorotea) may have tallied very nicely with the resolution of *The Captain* with its three marriages (each complicated in its own way) and the felicitous matrimonial conclusion to *Much Ado*, in which Claudio is unaware that he will in fact be marrying his beloved Hero despite his appalling treatment of her, and Benedick and Beatrice marry after discovering that they love each other. It may even have complemented an older play performed by the company that year: *The Merry Devil of Edmonton*, a play in which Millicent Clare and Raymond Mounchensey hatch an elaborate scheme to marry in defiance of her father's wishes, including Millicent entering a nunnery and the resolution occurring in the setting of an inn. Collectively, these plays depict not just the resistance of strong-willed female characters to arranged marriages (as Wilson would have it), so much as the overcoming of odds, the triumph of love, and a perhaps undeserved but appreciated reprieve for badly behaved husbands-to-be (offering the chance for redemption before a worse error is made). Luscinda resists a marriage arranged badly, on short notice, and for apparently mercenary reasons (Cardenio himself likens it to the sin of covetousness, or the love of riches), and stays true to her childhood sweetheart. Dorotea deserves better than the villainous Fernando, but

[101] Wilson, *Secret Shakespeare*, 235.   [102] Wilson, *Secret Shakespeare*, 233.

playgoers would register her virtue as a defining characteristic and would potentially admire the determination that sees her avoid the fate of a 'fallen woman' and instead married to a man of means and influence. (Despite Don Fernando's ignoble personality, there is, I think, some hint that we are meant to see him as reformed as a result of his experiences: he praises divine providence for delivering his soul from a labyrinth of sin.) As such, 'Cardenio' would not be out of place in a repertory selected – by whom, we cannot be sure, but most probably the Master of the Revels – for performance in a season that coincided with the betrothal of a royal couple in England.

§

Throughout this chapter I retrace the contours of the image we have of the repertory theatre during Shakespeare's final years, where our perception of the commercial offerings of London theatres has been distorted through the assumption of older scholarship that Shakespearean examples of stage romances are exemplary of what the industry was doing. In this chapter, I redraw the contour between extant and lost plays of this late period in Shakespeare's career in order to reshape our perception of how the repertory of the King's Men was constructed. Shakespeare's late plays exhibit stylistic and generic differences to his earlier plays to some extent, but they are far more closely intertwined with other playwrights' commercial plays than is usually acknowledged. In the context of stage romances, I argue that these similarities are most evident at the level of the numerous theatergrams shared by plays from the 1590s through to the 1610s.

Our picture of these last years of Shakespeare's career is further distorted when 'Cardenio' is conceived of purely in terms of Shakespeare's career rather than as a commodity offered by the King's Men. 'Cardenio' is almost exclusively contextualised within Shakespeare's oeuvre (his 'late style') and in relation to Theobald's play, but my focus on 'Cardenio' in repertory at court in 1612–1613 paints a different picture. Establishing through a systematic search of EEBO-TCP that the Cervantine Cardenio remains the most plausible subject matter for the 1612 play regardless of Theobald's claims, I focus on Shelton's English translation to better understand the narrative material available to Fletcher and Shakespeare. Rather than trying to reconstruct an authentically Shakespearean (or Fletcherian) play-text, I instead establish how the 'Cardenio' play related to the company's other offerings, specifically those of their plays selected for performance before the king in the winter of 1612–1613. Regardless of how the six plays came to be the ones chosen for performance for James during that winter, a playgoer at court who saw all six could have drawn certain connections between the offerings. 'Cardenio' potentially shared 'exile' and 'recognition' (or 'miraculous survival') theatergrams and recurring motifs with *Much Ado*, *The Winter's Tale* and *The Tempest*, and – like *The Captain* and *Much Ado* – it probably dramatised the winding paths its four lovers took to reach their final unions in marriage. My analysis shows the play enmeshed in a network of European-inspired tragicomic romances, rehearsing and complicating the typical comic ending of marriage with auspicious timing in light of the impending royal marriage; and it suggests that the play makes sense as a logical refinement of and intertextual companion to Fletcher's (and to some degree, Beaumont's) experiments in a romance genre with strong Continental influences, that owes little to Shakespeare.

CHAPTER 6

Loose Canons
The Lost Shakespeare Apocrypha

Even a dramatic historian can be confident that
Shakespeare wrote nothing after his death . . .

—G. E. Bentley[1]

My account of Shakespeare and lost plays does not end with the playwright's
death in 1616. Seven years later the Shakespeare 'First Folio' was published,
and in the decades to come further attempts were made to enlarge the canon
by ascribing plays to Shakespeare that we now no longer credit as being his.
When C. F. Tucker Brooke brought together what he called such 'waifs and
strays of the Elizabethan drama' as *Arden of Faversham, Locrine, Edward III,
Mucedorus, Fair Em*, and nine other 'pseudo-Shakespearian plays . . . with no
common bond but that mighty name, beneath whose broad influence they all
seek shelter', he recognised that the critical juncture at which his study was
produced (1918) uniquely placed to use the term 'Apocrypha' to describe
these plays.[2] During Shakespeare's lifetime and the seventeenth century more
generally, Brooke observes, ascription of authorship was determined by 'purely
unliterary attribution. Plays were stated on title-pages, on the Stationers'
Registers, or in book-lists to be by William Shakespeare, and there, for a
time, the matter ended'.[3] The concept of a playwright's 'literary works',
conventionally thought to originate with the publication of Jonson's First
Folio in 1616, and the related concept of the author itself (conventionally
associated with the publication of Shakespeare's First Folio in 1623), were
emerging categories but not necessarily standard principles for conceiving the
relationship between plays.[4]

---

[1] Bentley, *The Jacobean and Caroline Stage*, 5.1048–1049.
[2] C. F. Tucker Brooke, *The Shakespeare Apocrypha: Being a Collection of Fourteen Plays Which Have Been Ascribed to Shakespeare* (Oxford: Clarendon Press, 1918), vi.
[3] Brooke, *The Shakespeare Apocrypha*, viii.
[4] On the collection of vernacular writers' works, see (for example) the excellent overview provided by Jeffrey Todd Knight in *Bound to Read*, especially Chapter 5, 'The Custom-Made Corpus: English Collected Works in Print, 1532–1623', 150–179.

Subsequently, in the eighteenth and nineteenth centuries, with the revaluation of Shakespeare and the rise of the modern editor, the unscientific impressions of eighteenth-century editors including Edmond Malone, Edward Capell and George Steevens formed the basis for ruling what was canonical and what non-canonical. '[T]hey and their followers', writes Brooke, 'took a purely literary point of view'; a method unavailable to me in the present chapter, in the absence of texts to analyse.[5] At the time Brooke was writing, not only had 'Shakespeare' emerged as a revered category in its own right, laden with cultural capital, but early attempts at metrical analysis and quantifiable results were being deployed as litmus tests for what had become a highly politicised need for authorial ascription. We live with the legacy of those interests and methodologies today, with the recent flourishing of stylometric analyses, both digital and manual.[6] Then, as now, the deployment of these tests was a far from neutral act of classification, free from value judgment; it was more precisely an ostensible separation of the chaff from the grain. It is in this context that the biblical term 'Apocrypha' became associated with those quasi-Shakespearean texts that fail to convince us of any genuinely Shakespearean content. It is for intellectual, cultural and social reasons, then, that the doubtful Shakespearean plays have been subjected to a terminology of religiosity not accorded to their Marlovian or Jonsonian analogues.

But the London commercial theatre that Shakespeare was writing for did not privilege authorship as an organising principle; collaboration was the norm not the exception, and plays were more often uncredited than they were assigned to playwrights by name. Although he titled his recent book *Shakespeare and the Idea of Apocrypha*, Peter Kirwan has helpfully problematised the use of the term, appealing to the 'historical realities of playmaking' in a collaborative-authorship, commercial repertory context, and noting that '[a]n 'Apocrypha' has inescapably Biblical connotations in that it subsists as the inverse of the Authorised Canon; but when that Authority is itself dispersed [as it is in the case of collaborative playwriting], an Apocrypha ceases to carry its meaning'.[7] Kirwan challenges the appropriateness of the term 'Apocrypha' whilst continuing 'to use it throughout

---

[5] Brooke, *The Shakespeare Apocrypha*, viii.

[6] See, e.g. H. Craig and A. Kinney (eds.), *Shakespeare, Computers, and the Mystery of Authorship* (Cambridge: Cambridge University Press, 2009); M. P. Jackson, Determining the Shakespeare Canon: *Arden of Faversham* and *A Lover's Complaint* (Oxford: Oxford University Press, 2014); and B. Vickers, *Shakespeare, Co-Author: A Historical Study of Five Collaborative Plays* (Oxford: Oxford University Press, 2002).

[7] P. Kirwan, 'Canonising the Shakespeare Apocrypha: Shakespeare, Middleton and Co-Existent Canons', *Literature Compass*, 9(8) (2012), 538–548, 540.

in recognition of the still-current negative associations attached to these plays'.[8] He uses it as 'a starting point for exposing the limitations of a study which restricts itself by maintaining boundaries between authorial canons', in part because:

> [t]ogether, these plays form a deeply problematic group on the fringe of Shakespeare studies, tying Shakespeare to a range of collaborators, genres, themes and sensibilities that pollute the purity of the approved canon. Collectively, they highlight the indeterminacy of the canon, posing a threat to Shakespeare's ideological unity.[9]

But if the fourteen plays identified by Brooke as lurking on the fringe of the Shakespeare canon are accorded little literary value by the current generation of critics, there is a class of drama whose reputation has fared even worse: the lost plays in the Shakespeare Apocrypha. Here I focus on a mere six of these lost plays: half a dozen titles distinguished from the others on the basis of their ascription to Shakespeare. In doing so, I find myself forced (like Kirwan) to continue using the bardolatrous term 'Apocrypha' for the simple reason that, even though my objects of inquiry are lost and therefore necessarily beyond the pale of textual canonicity, some terminology is required to differentiate 'canonically lost' plays like 'Cardenio' and 'Love's Labour's Won' from the 'non-canonical' lost plays under examination here.

As Bentley so eloquently reminds us, it is unlikely that Shakespeare had anything to do with the lost plays examined in this final chapter, but my interest lies not in discovering a 'new' Shakespeare play so much as in asking what we might learn, if anything, from the posthumous attribution to Shakespeare of plays that are now lost. The 'figure' in Rubin's Vase becomes distorted – bloated – when lost plays are assigned to Shakespeare and fill out the contours of his known canon. In what follows, I examine six titles – 'Henry I', 'Henry II', 'Duke Humphrey', 'Iphis and Ianthe', 'King Stephen' and 'Eurialus and Lucretia' – in the hope that understanding the reasons for ascribing these *dubia* to Shakespeare might produce new knowledge about how Shakespeare was perceived after his death.

'Henry I' and 'Henry II'

On 10 April 1624, the Master of the Revels, Sir Henry Herbert licensed 'The Historye of Henry the First, written by [Robert] Damport [i.e. Davenport]'

---

[8] P. Kirwan, *Shakespeare and the Idea of Apocrypha* (Cambridge: Cambridge University Press, 2015), 4.
[9] Kirwan, *Shakespeare and the Idea of Apocrypha*, 5.

for performance by the King's Men.[10] It was not until almost thirty years later, when Humphrey Moseley entered the play in the Stationers' Register on 9 September 1653, that Shakespeare's name became associated with it, and just as surprisingly, a sequel or companion piece emerged: Moseley entered it as 'Henry ye first, & Hen: ye 2^d. by Shakespeare, & Davenport'.[11] Critics are divided about whether Moseley's entry refers to one play or two. Alfred Harbage points out that 'as Moseley in 1653 was saving fees by entering two plays as one, it is fairly obvious that he was doing so in the present instance'.[12] Gary Taylor, by contrast, has recently treated it as referring to a single play, even whilst observing that '[l]ike publishers of most masterpieces of early English literature, Moseley sometimes broke, bent, or evaded bureaucratic regulations. Seventeen of the forty-two plays in his 1653 list have subtitles, and in at least nine cases those subtitles are demonstrably the titles of other plays'.[13]

The 'Hen: ye 2^d' companion piece, but not Shakespeare's co-authorship, subsequently disappeared from historical records after John Warburton (1682–1759) listed 'Henry ye 1st. by Will. Shakespeare & Rob. Davenport' in his list of unprinted play manuscripts supposedly in his possession.[14] To W. W. Greg, Warburton's story of his play collection's destruction at the hands of his clumsy/philistine cook – 'they was unluckily burnd or put under Pye bottoms' – seems suspiciously convenient, leading him to believe that Warburton may have owned a few of the manuscripts named, but the remainder were *desiderata* known from Moseley's list and other sources.[15] Bentley, too, was sceptical, repeatedly cautioning that '[t]he fact that the title appears in Warburton's list is no assurance that he ever had the manuscript' but noting, by contrast, that 'Moseley certainly had a manuscript, and he must have had some reason for assigning it as he did'.[16] Davenport is not known to have been writing early enough to collaborate with Shakespeare, and Herbert's licensing fee is that of a new play, which discourages any suggestion of an older play being revised.[17] Harbage thought that 'Shakespeare's name could have become

---

[10] N. W. Bawcutt (ed.), *The Control and Censorship of Caroline Drama: The Records of Sir Henry Herbert, Master of the Revels, 1623–73* (Oxford: Oxford University Press, 1996), 151 (entry #95).

[11] *Register of entries of copies: Liber E, 3 Dec 1645–27 Feb 1657*, p. 286 via *Literary Print Culture: The Stationers' Company Archive, 1554–2007* (cf. Eyre et al. (eds.), *A Transcript of the Registers*, 1.429).

[12] A. Harbage, 'Elizabethan-Restoration Palimpsest', *Modern Language Review*, 35 (1940), 287–319, 310.

[13] Taylor, 'A History of *The History of Cardenio*', 13.

[14] British Library, MS Landsdowne 807, fol.1.

[15] W. W. Greg, 'The Bakings of Betsy', *The Library*, 3rd series, 7(11) (1911), 232, 259.

[16] Quoted from Greg, 'The Bakings of Betsy', 232; Bentley, *The Jacobean and Caroline Stage*, 3.230.

[17] Bentley, *The Jacobean and Caroline Stage*, 3.230–231.

attached to the manuscript of *Henry the First* merely because it was evident that it was an adaptation of a play dating from Shakespeare's time', but was the late-Elizabethan and Jacobean period thought of as the 'period of Shakespeare' in 1653?[18] Just a few months after Moseley ascribed 'Henry I' and 'Henry II' to Shakespeare and Davenport, he ascribed 'A comedie called The Maiden's Holiday' to Marlowe and Day for similarly opaque reasons.[19] Taken together, these two examples might at least suggest an alternative possibility: that Moseley was attaching big name playwrights to hitherto unknown manuscripts, possibly with a view to sales. Emma Depledge implicitly concurs, citing Moseley's entry of the 'King Stephen', 'Duke Humphrey' and 'Iphis and Ianthe' plays (discussed below) as evidence not only that 'Shakespeare's name [was] ... deemed marketable at the start of the Restoration, but also that stationers were willing to expand the Shakespeare canon in order to exploit such a market'.[20] Heidi C. Craig is more direct in her evaluation of Moseley: 'Moseley was interested in *new* Shakespeare, or whatever he thought of as Shakespeare, or could pass off as Shakespeare'.[21] Warburton appears to have accepted both of Moseley's spurious ascriptions, listing not just 'Henry I' by Shakespeare/Davenport, but 'The Mayden Holaday by Chris. Marlowe' (note the less glamorous Day's conspicuous absence). What would make a 'Henry I' (or 'Henry II') play appear Shakespearean?

The life of Henry I (AD 1068/9–1135) informed the subject matter of a number of plays during Shakespeare's lifetime, but they belonged to the repertories of rival companies rather than Shakespeare's own. *Fair Em* (Strange's, c.1590) and a lost 'William the Conqueror' play (Sussex's, c.1594) are relevant inasmuch as Henry was the youngest son of William the Conqueror and Matilda of Flanders. Henry was responsible for the introduction of strict new laws against thieves and felons, as most famously encapsulated in the case of Belin Dun (the first thief hanged in England, during Henry's reign) whose story was dramatised by the Admiral's Men in 1594 (see Chapter 2). An anonymous 'Life and Death of Henry I' was acquired by the Admiral's Men in 1597, and Henry

---

[18] Harbage, 'Palimpsest', 311.

[19] *Register of entries of copies: Liber E, 3 Dec 1645–27 Feb 1657*, 307 via *Literary Print Culture* (cf. Eyre et al. (eds.), *A Transcript of the Registers*, 1.445). See also M. Steggle, 'Marlowe's Lost Play: "The Maiden's Holiday"' in K. Melnikoff and R. L. Knutson (eds.), *Christopher Marlowe, Theatrical Commerce, and the Book Trade* (Cambridge: Cambridge University Press, 2018), 243–257, for a discussion of Marlowe's early reception.

[20] E. Depledge, *Shakespeare's Rise to Cultural Prominence: Politics, Print and Alteration, 1642–1700* (Cambridge: Cambridge University Press, 2018), 41.

[21] H. C. Craig, 'Missing Shakespeare, 1642–1660', *English Literary Renaissance*, 49(1) (2019), 133.

Chettle, Michael Drayton and Thomas Dekker evidently exploited Henry's military campaigns in their lost 'The Famous Wars of Henry I and the Prince of Wales' (Admiral's, 1598). Malone thought Davenport's 'Henry I' play might have been a remodelling of this Admiral's play and explained the addition of Shakespeare's name as the work of 'some knavish bookseller'.[22] F. G. Fleay, ever the 'lumper' of discrete play titles, concurred with Malone. Bentley, however, poured cold water over Malone and Fleay's lumping of titles by querying why 'the King's men in 1624 would have needed to make use of such an old and obscure piece' and asking (moreover) why 'they would have had one of Henslowe's manuscripts' at all.[23] Finally, during Henry's reign, work was begun on the hospital of St. Bartholomew in Smithfield; a project that was finished by Richard Whittington (c.1350–1423), mayor of London and subject of a play by Prince Henry's Men ('The History of Richard Whittington', c.1604). There were, therefore, reasonable grounds for someone like Moseley to associate a play about Henry I with a period of dramatic activity during which Shakespeare was still alive, and perhaps even a temptation to assume that Shakespeare's own company would have responded to the competitions' offerings by adding a Henry I play to their own repertory – but there is no evidence for this, and there is (moreover) reliable documentary evidence for ascription to Davenport and dating to 1624, in the form of Herbert's licensing. Whatever the allure of ascribing the lost 'Henry I' play to Shakespeare, it is not supported by evidence.

Harbage thought there definitely was a discrete play on 'Henry II' by Shakespeare and Davenport. He points out that '[s]ince the long reign of King Stephen intervened between those of the two Henrys, *Henry the First and Henry the Second* seems an extremely unlikely title for a play' and deduces from Warburton's reference only to 'Henry ye 1st' that 'the *Henry the Second* manuscript had evidently become separated from its fellow'.[24] He argues that the anonymous *Henry the Second, King of England; With The Death of Rosamond* (published by the actor William Mountfort in 1693) is a palimpsest containing traces of the lost 'Henry II' play, but his argument does nothing to advance the case for Shakespearean authorship.[25] Moseley's unverified ascription in the Stationers' Register remains the only basis for including 'Henry II' in the lost Apocrypha.

---

[22] E. Malone, 'Additions: Historical Account of the English Stage' in *The Plays and Poems of William Shakespeare*, vol. 3 (London, 1821), 319.

[23] Fleay, *A Biographical Chronicle of the English Drama*, 1.104); Bentley, *The Jacobean and Caroline Stage*, 3.231.

[24] Harbage, 'Palimpsest', 310.   [25] Harbage, 'Palimpsest', 311.

'Duke Humphrey', with a Note on 'King Stephen' and 'Iphis and Ianthe'

Seven years after registering 'Henry I' and 'Henry II', Moseley registered the following titles at Stationers' Hall on 29 June 1660:[26]

The History of King Stephen.
Duke Humphrey. a Tragedy.
Iphis & Iantha, Or a marriage
without a man. a Comedy.
⎱ by Will: Shakespeare.

By 1660 Moseley, described by David Scott Kastan as being more responsible for the 'invention of English literature' than any other stationer of the period, had made a name for himself by publishing collections of plays including those by John Suckling (*Fragmenta Aurea*, 1646), Francis Beaumont and John Fletcher (*Comedies and Tragedies*, 1647), William Cartwright (*Comedies, Tragicomedies* ..., 1651), Richard Brome (*Five New Plays*, 1653), James Shirley (*Six New Plays*, 1653), Thomas May (*Two Tragedies*, 1654) and Philip Massinger (*Three New Plays*, 1655) amongst others, as well as numerous individual play-texts.[27] The registration of three 'new' Shakespeare titles gives the appearance of another planned collection, but nothing eventuated from it.[28] The dubiousness of the authorial ascription may itself be the reason these manuscripts never made it to print: Moseley may have staked his hopes on unsupportable claims of Shakespearean authorship as his planned marketing strategy. In his comments on all three of these titles, Bentley applies variations of the formula, '[i]t is quite unlikely that Shakespeare wrote the tragedy of Duke Humphrey, for no other reference to the title has been found. I know of no evidence as to the date or authorship of the manuscript Moseley had in 1660'.[29] The one-time existence of the manuscripts is not in doubt, only their ascription to Shakespeare.

Perhaps 'Duke Humphrey' should not be treated precisely the same way as its neighbours though. Bentley's comments are biased here, for by his own admission, there *is* a second historical document that names Shakespeare as

---

[26] *Register of entries of copies: Liber F, 2 Mar 1657 –24 Jan 1683*, p. 196, via *Literary Print Culture* (cf. Eyre et al. (eds.), *A Transcript of the Registers*, 2.271).

[27] D. S. Kastan, 'Humphrey Moseley and the Invention of English Literature' in S. Alcorn Baron, E. N. Lindquist and E. F. Shevlin (eds.), *Agent of Change: Print Culture Studies after Elizabeth L. Eisenstein* (Amherst, MA: University of Massachusetts Press, 2007), 105–124, especially 113.

[28] Heidi Craig independently arrived at a similar conclusion in an article that she was kind enough to share with me prior to publication: see 'Missing Shakespeare', 133.

[29] Bentley, *The Jacobean and Caroline Stage*, 5.1323. See also the parallel constructions deployed in entries for 'King Stephen' (5.1361) and 'Iphis and Ianthe' (5.1355).

the author of the play: Warburton's list. The sceptical position regarding Warburton has been outlined above; more recently, John D. Freehafer and Wiggins have each drawn attention to plays named on the list that Warburton could not have known from the Stationers' Register or else-where, and Freehafer in particular has called for a reappraisal of the list's status as an historical document, noting that 'a new examination of Warburton's list, memorandum, sale catalogue and surviving manuscripts suggests that Warburton's list and memorandum record plays that he owned and information that he believed to be correct' and that 'skepticism about Warburton's motives and veracity might well give way to a further study of his statements and collection that could add considerably to existing knowledge'.[30] Whether Warburton possessed the plays he listed or merely desired them, it is striking that of the three titles entered by Moseley in 1660 as being by Shakespeare, only 'Duke Humphrey' appears in Warburton's list. Why? What singled this play out from its pseudo-Shakespearean relations? Assuming the most conservative view of Warburton – that he drafted a wish-list rather than a genuine inventory – what he chose to include might form some kind of early modern response to Shakespeare's posthumous reputation. What about a 'Duke Humphrey' play might lend it the veneer of the genuinely Shakespearean?

Although it might sound like a potentially common name, 'Duke Humphrey' refers almost exclusively in the early modern period to Humphrey of Lancaster, Duke of Gloucester (1390–1447), also known as Good Duke Humphrey. The youngest son of King Henry IV, brother to Henry V, and uncle to Henry VI, he fought at Harfleur and Agincourt (where Henry V saved his life) and although denied the regency upon Henry V's death, he was made protector to his nephew, Henry VI.[31] Duke Humphrey appears as a minor character in Shakespeare's *2 Henry IV* and *Henry V* and has a more substantial role in *1 Henry VI* and *The First Part of the Contention*, the quarto text of which advertises 'the death of the good Duke Humphrey' prominently on its title page and, unlike its folio counterpart (*2 Henry VI*), includes Humphrey's onstage murder.[32]

[30] J. D. Freehafer, 'John Warburton's Lost Plays', *Studies in Bibliography*, 23 (1970), 155–165, esp. 164; see also (e.g.) Wiggins #485, "'Tis Good Sleeping in a Whole Skin' ('a presumptive case that he really did own this one').

[31] G. L. Harriss, 'Humphrey, duke of Gloucester (1390–1447)' in *Oxford Dictionary of National Biography* (Oxford University Press, 2004; online edition, May 2011).

[32] See Shakespeare, *The first part of the contention betwixt the two famous houses of Yorke and Lancaster with the death of the good Duke Humphrey: and the banishment and death of the Duke of Suffolke, and the tragicall end of the proud Cardinall of VVinchester, vvith the notable rebellion of Iacke Cade: and the Duke of Yorkes first claime vnto the crowne.*, London: Printed by Thomas Creed,

Although it might be tempting to associate this *First Part of the Contention* quarto version of *2 Henry VI* with the lost 'Duke Humphrey' play, such an identification falters on the fact that *2 Henry VI* was apparently transferred from Robert Bird to Richard Cotes as 'Yorke and Lancaster' on 08 November 1630 (as part of Thomas Pavier's 1619 publication of both *The First Part of the Contention* and *The True Tragedy of Richard, Duke of York* as *The Whole Contention*) and remained in Cotes' possession until his widow transferred the rights to John Martin and Henry Herringman on 6 August 1674.[33] There is no room in this chain of transfers between stationers for Moseley to have acquired the play in 1660, when he registered 'Duke Humphrey'.

In his study of Humphrey's historical and literary reputation, Samuel M. Pratt emphasises the significance of Shakespeare's contribution to the duke's mythology:

> To Shakespeare must go the credit of developing the image of Humphrey in the greatest detail. Some of this credit is due to his use of dramatic form, which gave him a distinct advantage in characterization over [George] Ferrers, using the complaint [in *The Mirror for Magistrates*, 1578], and Drayton, using the epistle [in his *Englands Heroicall Epistles*, 1598].[34]

It is not impossible that Duke Humphrey may have become the subject of a 'spin-off' play associated with the cluster of Wars of the Roses plays in vogue in the 1590s, much like Knutson has suggested the lost 'Buckingham' play (1593) may have been, given that it was being performed by Sussex's Men when Shakespeare's *Richard III* was new.[35] Such a spin-off may date to a later period: Wiggins persuasively dates the manuscript play *Thomas of Woodstock* to c.1611 (#1647) and notes the 'striking' fact that the King's Men had performed a 'Richard the 2' play at the Globe that year (#1635). From a repertory studies perspective, 'the existence of more than one play on the same narrative is thoroughly consistent with the commercial strategy of the companies to duplicate the popular offerings of their competitors'.[36] Did Duke Humphrey emerge, Falstaff-like, from his original dramatic context and assume the lead role in his own spin-off? (The subject of my implicit reference here was intended to be *The Merry Wives of Windsor*, but it is intriguing that something called the '. . .nd part

    for Thomas Millington, and are to be sold at his shop vnder Saint Peters Church in Cornwall, 1594. (STC (2nd ed)/26099), sig.E2.

[33] See Arber (ed.), *Stationers' Register*, 4.208; and Eyre et al. (eds.), *A Transcript of the Registers*, 2.488.

[34] S. M. Pratt, 'Shakespeare and Humphrey Duke of Gloucester: A Study in Myth', *Shakespeare Quarterly*, 16(2) (1965), 201–216, esp. 215.

[35] Knutson, *The Repertory*, 70.   [36] Knutson, *The Repertory*, 71.

of Falstaff is listed by Sir George Buc, Master of the Revels, in the fragments of Revels Office wastepaper (c.1619) that he repurposed for the drafting of his own *History of Richard III*).[37] Companies demonstrably acquired 'one or more additional plays on popular subject matter' (hence the 'Richard the 2' play at the Globe in 1611) but which repertory would a Duke Humphrey play belong to and resonate with?[38]

The case for Shakespearean authorship or the play's candidacy for direct engagement with the tetralogies of the 1590s would be strengthened had there been an explicit reference to this title during Shakespeare's lifetime. However, Moseley's designation of 'Tragedy' is suggestive of an alternative repertorial possibility that may be worth considering. Although some early chroniclers perceived tragedy in Humphrey's own biography, suggesting he met with foul play, another tragic possibility is presented by Michael Drayton, whose *Englands Heroicall Epistles* (1603) includes an epistolary exchange between Humphrey and his mistress, Eleanor Cobham.[39] Humphrey's first marriage, to Jacqueline of Hainault, saw him pursue Jacqueline's claims to Holland, Zeeland and Hainault, but his enemies conspired against him and a Papal verdict determined that Jacqueline's earlier marriage to John of Brabant remained valid (he had, however, died by this time). Humphrey elected to marry his mistress, Eleanor, rather than remarry his wife, Jacqueline. Eleanor reportedly became obsessed with Humphrey succeeding his nephew, Henry VI, as King of England and consulted astrologers on the matter. Their predictions of illness befalling the current king (opening the way for Humphrey to succeed) led to charges of necromancy being brought against Eleanor in 1441, chiefly on the basis of her confession that she had procured fertility potions (to secure Humphrey an heir) from Margery Jourdemayne, the Witch of Eye (Ebury; near Westminster).[40] Eleanor was publicly humiliated, being forced to walk barefoot through London on November market days, carrying a candle; was forcibly divorced; and was ultimately imprisoned at Chester, Kenilworth, the Isle of Man, and eventually Beaumaris, where she died

---

[37] See the image and transcription of the Revels Office waste paper, British Library (at the time, British Museum) Cotton MS. Tiberius E. X., fo.211[v] in F. Marcham, *The King's Office of the Revels 1610–1622: Fragments of Documents in the Department of Manuscripts, British Museum* (London: F. Marcham, 1925), 32–33.

[38] Knutson, *The Repertory*, 48.

[39] See, e.g. E. Hall, *The vnion of the two noble and illustre famelies of Lancastre [and] Yorke...* (London, 1548), sig.Bbiii[v]; M. Drayton, *The barrons vvars in the raigne of Edward the second. VVith Englands heroicall epistles* (London, 1603), fol.49[v]–58.

[40] G. L. Harriss, 'Eleanor, duchess of Gloucester (c.1400–1452)', *ODNB*.

in 1452. Much of this material is dramatised in Shakespeare's *First Part of the Contention* (*2 Henry VI*), but as Matthew Steggle has cautiously noted, it may also have been the subject matter of another lost play: 'The White Witch of Westminster, or Love in a Lunacy'.[41] This play is known only through the book collector Abraham Hill's list of plays from a bookseller's stock, most of which are Jacobean or Caroline in date; the subject matter would complement witch plays of the Jacobean period (e.g. *The Witch*, c.1616, and also *The Witch of Edmonton* c.1621, the latter entered in the Stationers' Register in 1658, two years before 'Duke Humphrey'). If 'Duke Humphrey' were part of a 'commercial cluster or loose serial' in repertory, its connection may have been to English chronicle history but alternatively it may have been to witchcraft narratives (in which case the closest living Shakespearean relative might be *Macbeth*).[42]

By contrast, the other two titles registered by Moseley in 1660 have only slender Shakespearean connections. The tale of Iphis and Ianthe from Book 9 of Ovid's *Metamorphoses* bears the slightest of superficial resemblances to tropes found in Shakespeare's *Twelfth Night*, but no explicit connection to this or any genuinely Shakespearean text. In Ovid, Telethusa gives birth to a girl but tells the father, Ligdus, that it's a son to avoid his wrath. Iphis (a deliberately gender-neutral name) is thus raised as a boy, with only the mother and nurse knowing the truth. When Iphis turns thirteen, Ligdus arranges a marriage to the beautiful maid Ianthe. Iphis finding herself attracted to Ianthe and on the verge of marriage, bemoans her untenable situation, 'herself a Mayden with a Mayd (ryght straunge) in loue became'.[43] She laments having ever been born, noting that even the unnatural pairing of Pasiphae with the bull was a female-male union, and queries why Juno and Hymen would come to solemnise such an unnatural wedding 'where no brydegroome you shall see / But bothe are Brydes that must that day tooghter coupled bee?'[44] Iphis prays to the

---

[41] See Steggle's entry for 'The White Witch of Westminster' in the *LPD*. This play is undated and its authorship unknown; it appears as the twenty-fifth item on Abraham Hill's list of plays, apparently a bookseller's inventory created between 1677 and 1703, and pertaining chiefly to Jacobean and Caroline-era titles (Bentley, *The Jacobean and Caroline Stage*, 5.1283); see also J. Quincy Adams, 'Hill's List of Early Plays in Manuscript', *The Library*, 4th Ser., 20(1) (1939), 71–99.

[42] R. L. Knutson, 'The History Play, *Richard II*, and Repertorial Commerce' in J. Lopez (ed.), *Richard II: New Critical Essays* (London: Routledge, 2012), 76.

[43] Ovid, *The. xv. bookes of P. Ouidius Naso, entytuled Metamorphosis, translated oute of Latin into English meeter, by Arthur Golding Gentleman, a worke very pleasaunt and delectable* (Imprynted at London, by Willyam Seres, 1567), fol.122.

[44] Ovid, fol.122ᵛ.

goddess Isis, who is so moved by the maiden's plight that she turns him into a boy, and '[t]he vowes that Iphys vowd a wench he hath performd a Lad'.[45] It may be only the distinctly Ovidian flavour of the names 'Iphis' and 'Ianthe' that encouraged any association with Shakespeare, in whom 'the sweete wittie soule of *Ouid* liues' (as Francis Meres famously noted).[46] It is extremely unlikely that the extant MS play *Iphis*, by Henry Bellamy, could ever have been mistaken for a Shakespeare play, as it is written in Latin.[47] However, whilst its clear indebtedness to Ovid for subject matter is Shakespearean (given his explicit use of Ovid when the *Metamorphoses* is produced on stage in *Titus Andronicus*, for example, and the device of gender confusion and transgressive unions that featured so prominently in *Twelfth Night*), the specifics of this example also make it very un-Shakespearean, for as Jonathan Bate observes, Shakespeare 'always resolves the apparent need for a sex-change naturalistically, he does not resort to direct divine intervention in the Ovidian manner'.[48]

The reign of King Stephen, as mentioned briefly above, links the stories of King Henry I and Henry II, and would thus complete a chronological trilogy with the two Henry plays entered in the Stationers' Register seven years earlier in 1653. Shakespeare had enjoyed success with the serial play format, not only in the first and second tetralogies, but most likely with 'Love's Labour's Won' and *Love's Labour's Lost*, and *Merry Wives* as a spin-off to the *Henry IV* plays that shared 'a central character but not a chronological narrative'.[49] Moreover, a trilogy dramatising the reigns of Henry I, Stephen, and Henry II would accord with Chamberlain's/King's Men preference for English chronicle history (as opposed to the Admiral's notable investment in English mythological history).[50] But the place of a 'History of King Stephen' play in this imagined trilogy depends on knowledge of the lost Henry I and II plays (which, it should be noted with a degree of circumspection, their earlier registration by Moseley in

[45] Ovid, fol.123.

[46] F. Meres, *Palladis tamia. Wits treasury being the second part of Wits common wealth* (London: Printed by P. Short, for Cuthbert Burbie, 1598), fol.281ᵛ.

[47] Bodleian Library MS. Lat. Misc. e.17; Bentley reproduces Moseley's registration in his entry for the comedy from St. John's, Oxford, on the grounds that the Thomas Percy sale catalogue had suggested the lumping of the MS with the lost 'Shakespeare' play (Bentley, *The Jacobean and Caroline Stage*, 3.19–20).

[48] J. Bate, *Shakespeare and Ovid* (Oxford: Clarendon Press, rpt. 2001), 37. Bate's point of contrast is Lyly's *Gallathea*.

[49] Knutson, *Repertory* 51.

[50] See M. Teramura, 'Brute Parts: From Troy to Britain at the Rose, 1595–1600' and Paul Whitfield White, 'The Admiral's Lost Arthurian Plays' in McInnis and Steggle (eds.), *Lost Plays in Shakespeare's England*, 127–147 and 148–162 respectively.

1653 conveniently provides) rather than on any external, let alone contemporaneous, evidence of Shakespearean authorship or association.

'Eurialus and Lucretia'

A generation of scholars raised on New Historicism has been trained to read between the lines and assume that '[a]bsence of evidence cannot be taken as evidence of absence'.[51] What happens, though, when the *presence* of evidence does not constitute evidence of presence?

'Eurialus and Lucretia' was never a play, let alone one by Shakespeare, yet the so-called evidence comes from an authoritative source: the Stationers' Register. The process by which a non-Shakespearean, non-dramatic text is transformed into a lost play by Shakespeare can be clearly observed in a string of entries beginning on 4 August 1626, when Thomas Pavier's widow assigned her late husband's rights and interests in certain titles (including 'Mr Paviers right in Shakesperes plaies or any of them') to Edward Brewster and Robert Bird. The list included over sixty titles of diverse genres and authorship, amongst which are 'The historye of Hen: the fift and the play of the same', 'Sr John Old Castle a play', 'Tytus & Andronicus', 'Historye of Hamblett' and 'Euriolus & Lucretia'.[52] Four years after the Pavier transfer, on 8 November 1630, Bird transferred his interest in the following titles to Richard Cotes:

> . Henrye the fift
> Sr John Oldcastle
> Titus and Andronicus.
> Eureolus & Lucretia
> Yorke and Lancaster
> Agincourt.
> Persiles
> Hamblet.
> Yorkshire Tragedie[53]

'Eureolus & Lucretia' is clearly grouped with plays associated with Shakespeare in this entry, at least two of which (*Oldcastle* and *A Yorkshire Tragedy*) were among the 'seven Playes never before Printed

---

[51] Manley and MacLean, *Lord Strange's Men*, 46; they invoke this dictum in the context of perceptions of a period of suspension in the activity of the Lord Strange's players in November 1589.
[52] *Register of entries of copies: Liber D, 10 Jul 1620–1 Dec 1645*, p. 127 via *Literary Print Culture* (cf. Arber (ed.), *Stationers' Register*, 4.164–165).
[53] *Register of entries of copies: Liber D, 10 Jul 1620–1 Dec 1645*, p. 208 via *Literary Print Culture* (cf. Arber (ed.), *Stationers' Register*, 4.208).

in Folio' advertised in the second imprint of the Third Folio of
Shakespeare's works in 1664. The association of 'Eureolus & Lucretia'
with Shakespeare's works is consolidated in the subsequent transfer of
6 August 1674 (from Richard Cotes' widow Elinor to John Martin and
Henry Herringman), where 'Eureolus & Lucretia' is included in an
expanded list of twenty-five Shakespearean titles.[54] Herringman retained
his rights and went on to publish the Fourth Folio of Shakespeare's works
(1685), but on 21 August 1683 John Martin's widow Sarah transferred his
rights to Robert Scott; the entry at Stationers' Hall reproduces the precise
list of the previous transfer, but explicitly places the titles (including
'Eurialus & Lucretia') under the heading, 'Shakespeare'.[55]

Although the explicitness of this final entry makes 'Eurialus and
Lucretia' look like a lost play by Shakespeare, the chain of Stationers'
Register transfers strongly suggests that the text in question is *The historie
of Eurialus and Lucretia*, Charles Aleyn's English translation of the
fifteenth-century erotic prose romance by Aeneas Sylvius (later Pope Pius
II), which does not even superficially resemble a play-text.[56] None of the
other extant print editions of the romance resemble drama either, and
Richard Cotes, who acquired the title in 1630 does not appear to have
been tempted to include it in the Second Folio, which his brother Thomas
printed in 1632: the Cotes brothers instead preferred to wait until 1639 to
publish the romance by itself.[57] Whilst critics such as Gertrude Manley
Sibley who thought 'Eurialus and Lucretia' was a lost play have simply
misunderstood the reasons for its place in the Stationers' Register lists,
more sceptical critics such as Greg or Harbage and Schoenbaum have

---

[54] *Register of entries of copies: Liber F, 2 Mar 1657–24 Jan 1683*, p. 458 via *Literary Print Culture*
(cf. Eyre et al. (eds.), *A Transcript of the Registers*, 2.488).

[55] *Register of entries of copies: Liber G, 29 Jan 1683–29 Apr 1710*, p. 72 via *Literary Print Culture*
(cf. Eyre et al. (eds.), *A Transcript of the Registers*, 3.188). Herringman was associated with all three
versions of F4: Wing S2915, S2916 and S2917.

[56] Aleyn's translation was entered in the Stationers' Register on 03 October 1638 (*Register of entries of
copies: Liber D, 10 Jul 1620–1 Dec 1645*, p. 412 via *Literary Print Culture*; cf. Arber (ed.), *Stationers'
Register*, 4.438) and was published the next year as *The historie of Eurialus and Lucretia. Written in
Latine by Eneas Sylvius; and translated into English by Charles Allen, Gent.* (London: By Tho. Cotes,
for William Cooke, 1639).

[57] There is also a little-known version of the story in verse, held by the Library at Deene Park, which
may be the 'boke intituled of *ij lovers EURYALUS and LUCRESSIE plesaunte and Dilectable*'
entered by William Norton in 1569–1570 (Arber (ed.), *Stationers' Register*, 1.189). According to
Pollard and Redgrave (STC 19972.5), this octavo is the only translation in verse; it has twenty-eight
lines per page. Deene Park has two imperfect copies of sheet E only, their whereabouts currently
uncertain (the current owner, Mrs Charlotte Brudenell, suggests, on advice from the estate's Book
Trustee, that the fragments are probably 'binders' waste used as endpapers in a book in the library,
and therefore not catalogued'; personal correspondence, 19 January 2015).

overlooked the importance of its relationship to genuinely Shakespearean drama in those lists, and in the process, have ignored an interesting aspect of Shakespeare's posthumous reception.[58]

The first-named stationer in this string of entries, Thomas Pavier, may be the key to understanding the early interest in this romance. Pavier, of course, is the publisher notorious for having produced a series of play quartos, ostensibly taking Shakespearean authorship as their organising principle, in 1619. Variously referred to as the 'Pavier Quartos' or the 'False Folio', this publishing endeavour was not entirely above-board: traditional scholarship holds that although Pavier genuinely had the rights to publish some of the titles, he rounded out his collection by illegally reprinting other titles and falsifying their title page dates to pass them off as original, unsold copies.[59] The Lord Chamberlain's letter to the Court of the Stationers' Company seeking to prevent publication of King's Men's plays in May 1619 has thus typically been read as a direct response to Pavier's activities. However, Sonia Massai has been instrumental in recuperating Pavier's reputation, arguing that Pavier did not seek to deceive the King's Men nor his fellow stationers, but merely to produce quartos with the appearance of 'a nonce collection gathering seemingly older and newer editions' so as to 'whet, rather than satisfy, readers' demand for a new collection of Shakespeare's dramatic works'.[60] She suggests that instead of 'literary piracy', Pavier's activities in 1619 should be seen as 'a pre-publicity strategy devised by Isaac Jaggard to boost his chances of getting the Folio project off the ground'.[61] Tara L. Lyons has further complicated our perspective on Pavier's activities by tracing his acquisition habits in the first decade of his career and suggesting that 'seriality and historicity' rather than Shakespearean authorship 'largely guided the stationer's accumulation of playbooks and thereby influenced the selection of titles in the 1619 project'.[62] She argues that, as an organising principle, '"Shakespeare," with

---

[58] G. M. Sibley, *The Lost Plays and Masques, 1500–1642* (Ithaca, NY: Cornell University Press, 1932), 48–49; W. W. Greg *A Bibliography of the English Printed Drama*, vol. 2 (London: Bibliographical Society, 1939–1959). Harbage and Schoenbaum gave little credence to the Stationers' Register entries, recording 'Eurialus and Lucretia' as 'sometimes incorrectly listed as a play': see A. Harbage, *Annals of English Drama*, rev. S. Schoenbaum (Philadelphia: University of Pennsylvania Press, 1964), Index, 248. Martin Wiggins will be relegating the title to his Appendix 2 (Works Excluded), in a forthcoming volume of his *Catalogue*.

[59] Knight, *Bound to Read*, 151.

[60] S. Massai, *Shakespeare and the Rise of the Editor* (Cambridge: Cambridge University Press, 2007), 115, 107–108.

[61] Massai, *Shakespeare and the Rise of the Editor*, 121, 119–120.

[62] T. L. Lyons, 'Serials, Spinoffs, and Histories: Selling 'Shakespeare' in Collection before the First Folio', *Philological Quarterly*, 91(2) (2012), 185–220, 193.

his close affiliations with serial and historical drama, did not supplant these other principles in 1619, but emerged for booksellers and readers as an additional or even optional framework for collection'.[63] Focusing on Pavier's publication of a ballad related to *The Merchant of Venice* and prose relations of *Midsummer Night's Dream* and *Hamlet*, she further observes that '[c]ross-textual characters also informed Pavier's investments in non-dramatic works'.[64] Like 'Eurialus and Lucretia', the prose *Hystorie of Hamblett* (1608) which Lyons mentions – along with an example Lyons does not note: 'Agincourt' or 'The history of HENRY the FIFT' – was similarly bundled with Shakespeare's plays in the Stationers' Register entries from 1626 onwards, presumably because they were potentially of interest as cross-textual, non-dramatic analogues to *Hamlet* and *Henry V* respectively.[65]

'Eurialus and Lucretia' may have been misguidedly included on the supposition that it was a spin-off of Shakespeare's poem, the Sienese heroine mistaken for her more famous Roman namesake.[66] As the romance's modern editor has observed, '[t]hat it is Lucretia's story is always

---

[63] Lyons, 'Serials, Spinoffs, and Histories', 189.

[64] Lyons, 'Serials, Spinoffs, and Histories', 195. Her argument that '[t]he stationer could market these nondramatic offshoots by exploiting audiences' theatrical knowledge of corresponding characters from the stage, perhaps even arranging to distribute the early play quartos alongside their offshoots' (195) seems eminently sensible. The *Merchant of Venice* analogue is the ballad, *Calebbe Shillocke, his Prophesie: or, the Jewes Prediction. To the tune of Bragandarie*. At London printed for T[homas]. P[avier] [1607]. STC (2nd ed.), 22434. The *Midsummer Night's Dream* analogue is *The historie of Titana, and Theseus. Verie pleasant for age to auoyd drowsie thoughts: profitable for youth to eschew wanton pastimes: so that to both, it brings the mindes content. Written by W.B.* London: Printed by T[homas]. C[reede]. for Thomas Pauier, and are to be solde at his shop in Cornhill, neare the Exchange, 1608. STC (2nd ed), 1980.

[65] *The hystorie of Hamlet.* London: Imprinted by Richard Bradocke, for Thomas Pauier, and are to be sold at his shop in Corne-hill, neere to the Royall Exchange, 1608. STC (2nd ed), 12734.5; it features on the list despite the absence of Shakespeare's *Hamlet*. I have not been able to trace the 'historye of Henry the fift', alternatively referred to as 'Agincourt', and cannot find how Pavier acquired his rights in it; Wiggins (1183) thinks it is an alternative name for Shakespeare's *Henry V*, which Pavier acquired on 14 August 1600 (Arber (ed.), *Stationers' Register*, 3.169), but the full entry of 4 August 1626 contradicts this, explicitly referring to two related but distinct texts: 'The historye of Henry the fift and the play of the same' (*Register of entries of copies: Liber D, 10 Jul 1620–1 Dec 1645*, p. 126 via *Literary Print Culture*, cf. Arber (ed.), *Stationers' Register*, 4.164).

[66] Although this is the likeliest possibility, it should also be noted that the romance 'in all probability owes something to the tale of Troilus and Cressida' (C. Mish (ed.), *Short Fiction of the Seventeenth Century* (New York: New York University Press, 1963), 287), which may have been an alternative point of connection to Shakespeare, and that Shakespeare himself is thought to have been familiar with the story. Bullough, noting Shakespeare's indebtedness to Montemayor in *The Two Gentlemen of Verona*, compares a maid letting a letter fall to Shakespeare's 'a charming stroke' of having Julia tear up the letter then attempt to decipher it. In fact, as Alan Stewart has shown, Shakespeare appears to have drawn on the Eurialus and Lucretia story for this incident: see G. Bullough, *Narrative and Dramatic Sources of Shakespeare* (London: Routledge and Kegan Paul, 1961), 1.206; and A. Stewart, *Shakespeare's Letters* (Oxford: Oxford University Press, 2008), 61–62. Shakespeare's use of 'Eurialus and Lucretia' as a source was first proposed by John A. Guinn: see J. A. Guinn, 'The

made abundantly clear'; an observation supported by the fact that an early owner of the Huntington copy of Aleyn's translation inscribed the name 'Luc$_{rec}$ia' on the verso of the final leaf.[67] That Shakespeare was well known for his *Rape of Lucrece* is evident from the poem's print history and from Francis Meres' celebration of the 'mellifluous & hony-tongued' Shakespeare's '*Venus* and *Adonis*, his *Lucrece*, [and] his sugred Sonnets'; moreover, it is worth noting that the 1655 edition of *Lucrece* offers evidence of precisely this compilation phenomenon, advertising on its titlepage '*The rape of Lucrece ... [w]hereunto is annexed, The banishment of Tarquin: or, the reward of lust. By J. Quarles*' – a text on related subject matter but explicitly announced as being by another author.[68]

The cross-textual 'offshoots of Shakespeare's plays' were never part of the planned series as such but would have been available for individual purchase from Pavier; customers could of course choose to buy (for example) Pavier's *Midsummer Night's Dream* (1600, i.e. 1619) and his prose *The historie of Titana, and Theseus* (1608) at the same time, and perhaps were encouraged to do so.[69] It is not clear when Pavier acquired his rights to the Aleyn translation, and therefore whether he may have envisaged a similar marketing strategy for this romance.[70] If, as Lyons has argued, 'Shakespeare' emerged as an available category for book organisation and acquisition by virtue of Pavier's seriality and historicity-driven 1619 collection, then it is more likely that 'Eurialus and Lucretia' only began to be associated in earnest with Shakespeare by publishers and

---

Letter Device in the First Act of The Two Gentlemen of *Verona*', *University of Texas Studies in English*, 20 (1940) 72–81, esp. 77.

[67] Aeneas Sylvius (Pius II), *Eurialus and Lucretia (1639)* in Mish (ed.), *Short Fiction of the Seventeenth Century*, 285–337; the Huntington copy of Aleyn's 1639 translation (shelfmark 59759) is available through EEBO (STC 2nd ed., 1973). It bears the signature of an 'Elisabeth Norden' on its final page (105), but the hand does not match the 'Lucrecia' inscription.

[68] Meres, *Palladis tamia*, fol.281^v; *The rape of Lucrece, committed by Tarquin the sixt; and the remarkable judgments that befel him for it. By the incomparable master of our English poetry, Will: Shakespeare gent. Whereunto is annexed, The banishment of Tarquin: or, the reward of lust. By J. Quarles.*, London: Printed by J.G. for John Stafford in George-yard neer Fleet-bridge, and Will: Gilbertson at the Bible in Giltspur-street, 1655. Wing (2nd ed)/S2943. See I. Donaldson, *The Rapes of Lucretia: A Myth and Its Transformations* (Oxford: Clarendon Press, 1982), 179 on the Quarles poem.

[69] Lyons, 'Serials, Spinoffs, and Histories', 195.

[70] See Greg, *BEPD*, Θ36. Aleyn flourished in the 1630s but is unknown prior to that period; the 1626 transfer by Pavier's widow suggests that Aleyn's translation can be antedated by at least thirteen years, but not earlier than that. An ESTC search yields four hits for Aleyn as translator: *The battailes of Crescey, and Poictiers* (London: Printed by Tho: Purfoot for T. K[night], 1631 and London: Printed by Thomas Harper, for Thomas Knight 1633), *The historie of that vvise and fortunate prince, Henrie of that name the seventh, King of England* (London: Printed by Tho. Cotes for William Cooke, 1638), and of course *The historie of Eurialus and Lucretia* (1639).

readers at a later stage. Throughout this discussion, my interest has been in the continued presence, but not necessarily the precise order of placement of 'Eurialus and Lucretia' in the Stationers' Register lists – when rights were transferred, the texts in question would not need to be re-inspected; the clerk would probably check the original entry or perhaps some kind of receipt listing the entered titles, hence the order of titles in the list need only have been arranged *once* and subsequently repeated.[71] That 'once' occurred in 1630, with the list associated with Richard Cotes's acquisition of titles; all subsequent entries repeat the order of Cotes's list. Whilst we do not quite have evidence of Cotes planning a bundle or series, Stationers' Register entries *can* sometimes correlate to such bundling; Pavier, for example, acquired first *Henry V* then *The First Part of the Contention* and *The True Tragedy of Richard, Duke of York* presumably because (as Lyons has suggested) 'these three plays were deemed more valuable together than apart', and reissued all three plays in 1619, the latter two together in a single quarto.[72] The admixing of Shakespeare's plays with prose analogues (or pseudo-analogues) in the list is, at the very least, suggestive, and Cotes may have been the first to envisage such an 'offshoot' role for 'Eurialus and Lucretia'.[73] He evidently changed his mind, probably by 1632 (when the publication of F2 was conspicuously *not* accompanied by the release of 'Eurialus and Lucretia' – or *The Rape of Lucrece*, for that matter – as a complement or supplement) and certainly by 1639, when Cotes' brother Thomas printed the Aleyn translation.[74] The subsequent repetition of 'Eurialus and Lucretia' in stationers' lists is likely the product of transferrals at Stationers' Hall rather than the plans of the subsequent rights-holders. By itself this pseudo-Shakespearean 'ghost' lost play may be of limited value, but it forms part of a broader pattern or context for Shakespeare's posthumous reputation. The ascription in the 1683 entry that makes the romance look like a Shakespeare play is a simple enough error; of greater interest is the continued presence of Aleyn's prose romance 'Eurialus and

---

[71] Ian Gadd offered this conjecture in personal correspondence (email 5 January 2015).

[72] Lyons, 'Serials, Spinoffs, and Histories', 186; see Arber (ed.), 3.169, 3.204. As Lyons reminds me (personal correspondence, 18 Feb 2015), when Blount and Jaggard registered their copies of sixteen plays for inclusion in the First Folio, on 8 November 1623 (Arber (ed.), *Stationers' Register*, 4.107), the order of the texts registered corresponds almost precisely to the order in which they ultimately appeared (albeit with some additional titles interspersed between them) in F1.

[73] As Lyons further suggests, '[b]y highlighting and prescribing organizational frameworks for readers, booksellers could hawk their books in a variety of pairs, sets, and sequences' ('Serials, Spinoffs, and Histories', 186).

[74] On texts that were apparently issued as supplementary volumes to F2 and the Beaumont and Fletcher F1 (1647), see E. Rasmussen and G. R. Proudfoot (eds.), *The Two Noble Kinsmen* (Malone Society Reprints) (Oxford: Oxford University Press, 2005), vii.

Lucretia' in Shakespearean stock owned by multiple stationers sixty years after the publication of the First Folio.

§

As Kirwan reminds us, writing in the context of the Third Folio's inclusion of seven plays now deemed spurious, '[t]he claims of most of the additional plays are now weak, according to modern priorities of individual author- ship, but in bibliographic terms, most of the additions had solid claims, better documented than those of several 1623 folio plays'.[75] I have shown that although the dubiousness of ascribing to Shakespeare the lost Apocryphal plays examined in this chapter might now seem clearer, the association of each title with Shakespeare followed a certain logic at the time of ascription. 'Iphis and Ianthe' is an atypical example in the forego- ing discussion as the only comedy. The attribution to Shakespeare suggests a general awareness of Shakespeare's fondness for Ovid, but only a weak grasp of the way Shakespearean comedy actually works. Moseley owned three pseudo-Shakespearean play manuscripts in 1660; the historical record of the Stationers' Register cannot offer evidence of an intention to publish a 'new works' volume in the vein of Moseley's recent publishing history, but it does implicitly permit such a possibility – in which case the Ovidian origin of 'Iphis and Ianthe' may have been sufficient to bundle it with other 'Shakespearean' Apocrypha.

The remaining titles are more of a piece with each other. The 'Duke Humphrey' example suggests the potential for Shakespeare's characters in serial history plays to emerge from their original contexts and become the subject of their own plays; a hypothesis which finds a non-dramatic parallel in the case of 'Eurialus and Lucretia' and the apparent market for prose analogues of historical characters' stories (here it is interesting that Shakespeare's narrative poetry was apparently at least as worthy of remem- brance as his drama). Seriality or clustering seems also to have generated the Shakespearean ascriptions of 'Henry II' and 'King Stephen', whose claims to Shakespearean authorship seem to depend on prior knowledge of the existence of 'Henry I' – a play which can only be confidently associated with Davenport, would thus have the appearance of an older play by 1653, and which may have entered Shakespeare's orbit purely on the basis of a perceived need for such a title in the repertory of Shakespeare's company at

[75] P. Kirwan, 'The Shakespeare Apocrypha and Canonical Expansion in the Marketplace', *Philological Quarterly*, 91(2) (2012), 247–275, 250.

a time when the competition were engaging with events from the reign of Henry I.

Unlike the extant Apocryphal plays, then, these lost plays do not paint a picture of instability or indeterminacy so much as consolidate a picture of Shakespeare's reception in the mid-late seventeenth century. (Picture Rubin's Vase with an enlarged, engorged vase, swelling out of proportion.) Inasmuch as they amplify, perhaps clumsily, the central tenets of the Shakespeare canon rather than pose a threat to unity, they are Apocryphal only in the sense that they were nominally associated with Shakespeare's name. Their exclusion from the Shakespeare canon rests on the weakness of attribution rather than any threat to homogeneity or purity; they are less clearly exceptions that prove the rule in the way that *The Merry Devil of Edmonton* (for example) is safely un-Shakespearean by virtue of both its genre and style.[76] These lost Apocryphal plays were known to at least some early moderns: stationers such as Moseley, if not playgoers necessarily (though for all we know, the plays *had* been performed). They affected the early modern perception of Shakespeare's posthumous reputation: the fact that stationers could ascribe these titles to Shakespeare is symptomatic of aspects of Shakespeare's reputation throughout the seventeenth century. By considering these lost plays alongside Shakespeare's surviving plays, we catch a glimpse of what Shakespeare's canon sometimes looked like to an early modern reader and in particular, which parts of his work were deemed worthy of amplification through the attribution of these supplementary examples.

---

[76] See Kirwan, *Shakespeare and the Idea of Apocrypha*, 5: 'Yet despite the range of genres and styles represented by the group and usually considered un-Shakespearean – from bourgeois magician comedy (*The Merry Devil of Edmonton*, anonymous but possibly by Thomas Dekker) to martyr play (*Thomas, Lord Cromwell*), domestic tragedy (*A Yorkshire Tragedy*) to comical romance (the anonymous *Mucedorus*) – the constitution of the group has remained surprisingly consistent'.

Conclusion

The visually experienced figure known as 'Rubin's Vase' contains two elements – a vase and faces – that give form to each other by virtue of their interconnected presence and shared contour. My contention throughout this book is notably simple: when we look at the Rubin's Vase-image of early modern drama, we see only the vase, but early modern playgoers saw the vase *and* the two silhouetted faces confronting each other. Moreover, our ability to perceive even the vase alone is somewhat limited; we have a general sense of its contours, but many of the details that were once apparent to an early modern playgoer blur into a more generalised outline from the vantage point of the twenty-first century. I propose that lost plays should be treated as a kind of 'negative space' that actively shapes our perception of the surviving early modern drama. I further argue that a shift in perspective is required before we can see what has always already been present but not prioritised. The surviving drama comes into sharper relief when its relationship to the lost drama is better understood.

After dispelling the unwarranted myths about the loss of plays being somehow correlated with quality, I offered quantifiable data to illustrate precisely how well lost plays performed at the box office. I then followed Rubin's lead and proceeded to take lost plays seriously as a vital context for understanding Shakespeare's work and his company's development between 1594 and 1613, and for adjusting our perception of how Shakespeare was received posthumously. Contemplating loss in this way led me to reappraise the crucial string of performances by the Admiral's and Chamberlain's Men at Newington Butts in 1594 in terms of the synergy between the companies' repertories and staging demands. It also prompted me to think about what gets lost when a company such as the Chamberlain's Men moves from one theatrical venue to an appreciably larger venue. Attending to lost plays also helps me see watershed moments in a dramatist's or company's career differently, such as when

Shakespeare's great 'Globe' plays, *Hamlet* and *Henry V*, are viewed in the context of the accrued symbolism of stage Denmark or of romantic comedy respectively. My pulling at loose threads opens up a space in which to ponder the possibility that entire genres of plays, such as the improbable biopics of 'felmelanco', 'pethageros' or 'the play*e* of tasso', have been lost, or to explore the ways in which companies flirted with danger by dramatising particularly sensitive material about still living persons ('Gowrie', 'The Silver Mine'; possibly 'The Spanish Maze'). Studying lost plays can also force us to acknowledge the limitations of what we know about early modern English theatre: we do not know, really, what effect (if any) the acquisition of the Blackfriars lease had on the King's Men's repertory, nor do we know precisely how plays were selected for performance at court during the revels seasons. Adding the evidence of lost plays to the mix complicates the picture, makes it a little less clean, a little less clear, but infinitely richer. It demands fresh eyes.

Indeed, fundamental to my metaphor throughout this book is the eye of the beholder and the prejudice associated with viewing the corpus of early modern drama by prioritising extant plays. Rubin was at pains to recognise that neither figure nor ground is clearer to perceive than the other: the 'most conspicuous feature' of the figure-ground 'is that the same area, seen as figure or as ground, appears completely different'; a single objective stimulus can be experienced differently under the right circumstances.[1] Rubin's work also seems to acknowledge the shaping power of the ground, to be more acting than acted upon. As Jörgen Pind summarises it in his study of Rubin:

> [t]he fact that a common contour separating two areas need not give shape or form to both of them, and that the contour has a stronger tendency to shape the figure, is of fundamental importance to the way the visual world appears to us.[2]

Lost plays thus form an indispensable role in shaping or forming the extant canon; extant plays are to a large extent 'produced' through their relationship not only to each other, but to their lost counterparts.

Analysing lost and extant plays together in this manner can be tremendously productive but it is vital to note that the conclusions are necessarily contingent upon the assumptions and inferences made. Transparency of argumentation and interpretation of evidence is key to the methodology, as is the need to be candid about alternative possibilities and the potential

---

[1] Pind, *Edgar Rubin*, 102.   [2] Pind, *Edgar Rubin*, 102.

flaws in a proposed hypothesis. Remaining vigilant about questioning assumptions and showing our working is vital if we are to avoid reproducing received narratives without interrogation and allowing theories to ossify into 'facts'.

Index

'Abraham and Lot', 41

'Adam and Eve', 54–55

Admiral's Men, 27–29, 32–38, 58–59, 72–75, 82, 87, 89, 91–94, 96, 99–116, 124, 189, 196, 205
   at Newington Butts, 59–61
   at the Fortune, 89
   biblical plays, 114–115
   size of repertory, 41–55

'Agamemnon', 51, 74

Agrippa, Cornelius, 111

Alahum, 5

Alamo, Antonio, 153

'albere galles', 18, 105, 108, 169

Alchemist, 142, 161, 163–164, 167, 175, 181–182

Alexander, Catherine, 92

'Alexander and Lodowick', 38

Aleyn, Charles (trans.)
   Historie of Eurialus and Lucretia, 198, 201–202

'Alice Pierce', 109

'All Fools but the Fool', 74

All is True (*Henry VIII*), 6–7

All's Lost by Lust, 24

All's Well That Ends Well, 7, 32

Allde, John, 12

Allen, Giles, 70

Alleyn, Edward, 48, 63, 73, 89, 101, 114–115, 163

Allot, Robert
   England's Parnassus, 11, 14, 52

'Amboyna', 5

Anne of Denmark, 177

'anti-Scots play', 33

Antonio and Mellida, 79

Antonio's Revenge, 79

'Antony and Cleopatra', 19

Antony and Cleopatra, 24, 171

Apology for Actors, 176

Appius and Virginia, 12

Arbuckle, W. F., 121–123

Arden of Faversham, 31, 75, 125, 185

Ariosto, Ludovico
   Orlando furioso, 100

Arrell, Douglas, 43

As You Like It, 7, 31, 78, 90

Astington, John H., 45, 84, 114, 144, 147–148

Atheist's Tragedy, 162

'Bad Beginning Makes a Good Ending', 161, 167, 175, 177–179

'Bad May Amend'. *See* 'Worse Afeared Than Hurt'

Baldwin, T. W., 12–13

Bancroft, Richard, 163

Barbé, Louis A., 123

Baret, John
   An Alvearie, 98

Barnes, Barnabe
   Devil's Charter, 144, 162, 176

Bartholomew Fair, 5

Bate, Jonathan, 196

Battle of Alcazar, 42–43

'Bear a Brain', 74

Beaumont, Francis, 63
   Captain, 175
   Comedies and Tragedies, 191
   Coxcomb, 162, 175
   Cupid's Revenge, 162
   King and No King, 156, 161
   Knight of the Burning Pestle, 175, 181, 184
   Maid's Tragedy, 160–161, 175
   Philaster, 142, 149, 160–161
   Wedding Masque of Olympian Knights, 178

Beckerman, Bernard, 2, 11, 17, 23, 29

'Belin Dun', 60, 66–70, 189

Bellamy, Henry
   Iphis, 196

Belleforest, François de, 99

'Bendo (or Byndo) and Richardo', 109

Bennett, Paul E., 154

Bentley, G. E., 108–109, 143–144, 147, 149, 166, 185, 187–188, 190–191, 196
Berry, Herbert C., 34
'Better Late Than Never'. *See* 'Bear a Brain'
Bevington, David, 179
Bird (Borne), William, 48, 113
  'Judas', 51, 55, 114
Bird, Robert, 193, 197
'Black Bateman of the North, parts 1 & 2', 92
'Black Dog of Newgate, part 1', 92
'Black Dog of Newgate, part 2', 79, 92
Blackfriars, 120, 137–149, 206
  Globe and, 143–147
'Black Joan', 43, 46
Blayney, Peter W. M., 8
Blind Beggar of Alexandria, 36, 38
Blind Beggar of Bethnal Green, part 1, 49, 53, 79–80, 156
'Blind Beggar of Bethnal Green with Tom Strowd, part 2', 49, 53, 79–80
Boar's Head, 34, 72–73, 89
Bodley, Sir Thomas, 7
Bower, Richard
  Appius and Virginia, 12
Bowes, Sir William, 123
Boyle, William
  Jugurtha, 49
'brandymer', 100–101, 104
Brayne, John, 71
Brazen Age, 43
Brewer, Thomas
  A Knot of Fools, 164–166
Brewster, Edward, 197
Brome, Richard
  Five New Plays, 191
  Late Lancashire Witches, 125
Brooke, C. F. Tucker, 185–187
Brooke, George, 133
Browne, Robert, 63–64
Brudenell, Charlotte, 198
Brulart, Pierre (Marquis de Sillery), 137
Bruster, Douglas, 37
'Brute Greenshield', 51
Bryan, George, 96
Buc, Sir George, 178, 194
  History of Richard III, 194
'Buckingham', 41, 193
Bullough, Geoffrey, 200
Burbage, Cuthbert, 70–71
Burbage, James, 71, 137
Burbage, Richard, 37, 70–71, 136–137, 141, 177
Burby, Cuthbert, 81, 85
Bye Plot, 131–135

'Caesar's Fall', 52
Calvin, John, 110
Camerarius, Joachim, 111–112
Campion, Thomas
  Wedding Masque of Stars and Statues Made Human, 178
Capell, Edward, 186
Captain, 161, 167, 175, 180–182, 184
Captain Thomas Stukeley, 36, 38
'Capture of Stuhlweissenburg', 105
'Cardenio', 1, 6, 151–153, 161, 184, 187
  at court, 175–183
  evidence for, 166–168, 173–174
  in repertory, 174–183
  subject matter of, 166–175
  Theobald and, 152–153, 168–170, 183
Cardenio und Celinde, 171
Carey Court, Blackfriars, 35
Carey, Henry, 59
Carleton, Dudley, 3, 35, 76, 132–134
Carson, Neil, 36, 45–46, 48, 50, 52, 56
Cartwright, William
  Comedies, Tragicomedies, 191
Case is Altered, 5
'Catiline's Conspiracy', 74
Cecil, Robert (Lord Salisbury), 137
Cecil, William (Lord Burghley), 33, 123, 131
Cervantes, Miguel de
  Don Quixote, 152, 167, 169–175, 183
Chamber Account warrants, 160–161, 166–168, 175
Chamberlain, John, 3, 121, 127–128, 131–132, 167
Chamberlain's Men, 2, 9, 11, 17, 28–38, 41, 55–57, 93, 95–96, 104, 113, 118, 165, 196, 203, 205
  at Newington Butts, 59–70
  at the Curtain, 70–87
  at the Globe, 89–91
  biblical plays, 114–115
  extant plays, 29–32
  formative moments, 59
  list of lost plays, 32–36
Chambers, E. K., 4, 11, 35, 42, 106, 140
Changeling, 24
Chapman, George
  'All Fools but the Fool', 74
  Blind Beggar of Alexandria, 36, 38
  'Chapman's three acts', 45, 47
  Chapman's (tragic?) playbook, 53
  Conspiracy of Charles, Duke of Byron, 119, 128, 137–138
  Eastward Ho, 78, 141
  'Fountain of New Fashions', 74
  Humorous Day's Mirth, 49

Chapman, George (cont.)
  'Ill of a Woman', 52
  'Old Joiner of Aldgate', 4, 15
  'Pastoral Tragedy', 47
  Sir Giles Goosecap, 105
  Tragedy of Charles, Duke of Byron, 119, 128, 137–138
  'Tragedy on Jonson's Plot', 45, 47
  untitled playbook, 47
  Wedding Masque of the Princes of Virginia, 178
  Widow's Tears, 162
'Chapman's three acts', 45, 47
Chapman's (tragic?) playbook, 53
Chapman's playbook, 47
Chettle, Henry, 85
  'Agamemnon', 51, 74
  'Black Bateman of the North, parts 1 & 2', 92
  Blind Beggar of Bethnal Green, part 1, 53, 79–80, 156
  'Catiline's Conspiracy', 74
  'Conquest of Brute', 51, 74
  'Danish Tragedy', 96
  'Earl Godwin and His Three Sons, parts 1 & 2', 92, 96, 102–103
  'Famous Wars of Henry I and the Prince of Wales', 190
  'felmelanco', 104–116, 206
  'Funeral of Richard Coeur de Lion', 34
  'Hot Anger Soon Cold', 5, 74–75
  John of Bordeaux, 39, 50
  'Life of Cardinal Wolsey', 113
  'Orestes' Furies', 51
  'Orphans Tragedy', 49
  'Pierce of Exton', 42, 47
  'Play for court', 47
  play in Chettle's pawn, 47
  'Rising of Cardinal Wolsey', 113
  'Robert II, King of Scots', 124
  Sir Thomas More, 10, 31, 113
  'Spencers', 74
  ''Tis No Deceit to Deceive the Deceiver', 74
  'Tobias', 114
  'Troilus and Cressida', 42, 74
  untitled play by Chettle and Day, 47
  'Woman's Tragedy', 47
Children of Paul's, 4
Children of the Chapel Royal, 31
Children of the Queen's Revels, 37, 119, 145, 162, 180
  at the Blackfriars, 137–141
'Chinon of England', 160
'Civil Wars of France, parts 1, 2 & 3', 74–75, 92
Clark, William, 132
'Cloth Breeches and Velvet Hose', 9, 35, 77–78, 88

Clubb, Louise George, 154, 160
Cobbes, James
  'Romanus', 16
Cobham, Eleanor, 194
Cobham, Lord, 133
Cockpit playhouse, 3
Coleridge, Samuel Taylor, 15
Collier, John Payne, 154
'Comedy of Cosmo', 40
Comedy of Errors, 7, 11, 29–30
'Comedy of Humours'. *See Humorous Day's Mirth*
Comical history of Don Quixote, 170
'Conan, Prince of Cornwall', 74
Conover, James H., 6
'Conquest of Brute', 51, 74
'Conquest of the West Indies', 169
Conspiracy of Charles, Duke of Byron, 119, 128, 137–138
Cook, Ann Jennalie, 144
Cooper, Helen, 159
Copley, Anthony, 131–134
Copley, John, 135
Copley, Sir Thomas, 131, 134
Coriolanus, 7
Cotes, Elinor, 197
Cotes, Richard, 193, 197–198, 202
Cotes, Thomas, 198
Cotgrave, Randle
  Dictionary of the French and English Tongues, 98
Cotton, William, 33
court performances, 29, 50, 129, 160–167, 175–183
Coxcomb, 162, 175
Craig, Heidi C., 189, 191
Craik, T. W., 94
Cranstoun, Thomas, 121
Cruel Brother, 162
Cupid's Revenge, 162
Curtain, 11, 14, 34, 57, 59, 70–88, 120, 142
'Cutlack', 60–61, 96
Cymbeline, 142, 149, 151–159, 172

D'Urfey, Thomas
  Comical history of Don Quixote, 170
Daemonologie, 119
'Danish Tragedy', 96
Danter, John, 85
Davenant, William
  Cruel Brother, 162
Davenport, Robert
  'Henry I', 24, 187–191, 203
  'Henry II', 187–191, 203

Dawkins, Richard, 25
Day, John, 140
 Blind Beggar of Bethnal Green, part 1, 53,
  79–80, 156
 'Black Dog of Newgate, part 1', 92
 'Black Dog of Newgate, part 2', 79, 92
 'Blind Beggar of Bethnal Green with Tom
  Strowd, part 2', 49, 53, 79–80
 'Conquest of Brute', 51, 74
 'Conquest of the West Indies', 169
 'History play including the death of Percy',
  54–55
 Lust's Dominion, 49
 'Maiden's Holiday', 189
 'Six Yeomen of the West', 54
 'Tom Dough, part 2', 54
 'Tom Strowd, part 3', 53, 79–80
 'Tragedy of Thomas Merry (Beech's
  Tragedy)', 49
 Travels of the Three English Brothers, 87
 untitled play by Chettle and Day, 47
de Voiture, Monsieur, 170
Deene Park, 198
Dekker, Thomas, 63
 'Agamemnon', 51, 74
 'Bear a Brain', 48, 74
 'Better Late Than Never'. *See* 'Bear a
  Brain'
 'Black Bateman of the North, parts 1 & 2', 92
 'Civil Wars of France, parts 1, 2 & 3', 74–75,
  92
 'Conan, Prince of Cornwall', 74
 'Earl Godwin and His Three Sons, parts 1 &
  2', 92, 96, 102–103
 'Fair Constance of Rome, parts 1 & 2',
  92
 'Famous Wars of Henry I and the Prince of
  Wales', 190
 'First Introduction of the Civil Wars of
  France', 47, 74–75, 92
 If This Be Not a Good Play, The Devil Is In It,
  163
 'Jephtha', 114
 'Keep the Widow Waking', 15–16
 Lust's Dominion, 49
 Noble Spanish Soldier, 44
 Northward Ho, 78
 Old Fortunatus, 53, 146
 'Orestes' Furies', 51
 'Page of Plymouth', 5
 'Phaeton', 109
 'Pierce of Exton', 42, 47
 'Pierce of Winchester', 74
 'Pontius Pilate', 51, 55, 114
 'Robert II, King of Scots', 124

Satiromastix, 31
Shoemaker's Holiday, 42, 77, 97
Sir Thomas More, 10, 31, 113
'Tasso's Melancholy', 113
'Troilus and Cressida', 42, 74
'Truth's Supplication to Candlelight', 44
'Two Shapes', 51–52
Welsh Ambassador, 10
Westward Ho, 78
Whore of Babylon, 44
Witch of Edmonton, 195
Wonder of a Kingdom, 43
'Worse Afeared Than Hurt', 52
'Dead Man's Fortune', 15
Deloney, Thomas
 Thomas of Reading, 54
Denmark on stage, 95–104
Dent, R. W., 179
Depledge, Emma, 189
Devereux, Robert (2nd Earl of Essex), 4–5, 126
Devil is an Ass, 5
Devil's Charter, 144, 162, 176
Dialogues and Dramas, 43
Digges, Leonard, 171
'Disguises', 49
Doctor Faustus, 36, 91, 99, 113, 115, 163–164,
 170
Dollerup, Cay, 95, 97
Don Quixote, 167, 169–175
Donaldson, Ian, 4–5
Doran, Gregory, 153
Double Falsehood, 152–153
Double PP, 135
Dowden, Edward, 151
Downton, Thomas, 105
Drayton, Michael
 'Black Bateman of the North, parts 1 & 2', 92
 'Caesar's Fall', 51–52
 'Civil Wars of France, parts 1, 2 & 3', 74–75,
  92
 'Conan, Prince of Cornwall', 74
 'Earl Godwin and His Three Sons, parts 1 &
  2', 92, 96, 102–103
 Englands Heroicall Epistles, 93, 193–194
 'Fair Constance of Rome, parts 1 & 2', 92
 'Famous Wars of Henry I and the Prince of
  Wales', 190
 'Funeral of Richard Coeur de Lion', 34
 'Owen Tudor', 91–95, 104, 116
 'Pierce of Exton', 42, 47
 'Pierce of Winchester', 74
 Poly-Olbion, 100
 Sir John Oldcastle, part 1, 12, 197
 'Sir William Longsword', 34
 'Two Shapes', 51

Drayton, Michael (cont.)
'William Longsword', 75
'Worse Afeared Than Hurt', 52
Dream of Judas' Mother Fulfilled, 51
Drummond, William, 5
Duchess of Malfi, 162
'Duke Humphrey', 187, 191–195, 203
Duke of York's Men, 163
Duncan-Jones, Katherine, 93
Dustagheer, Sarah, 3, 144–146
Dutch Courtesan, 163
Dutton, Richard, 90, 141, 176–178

'Earl Godwin and His Three Sons, parts 1 & 2',
92, 96, 102–103
'Earl of Hertford', 48
Early English Books Online, 18, 97–98, 108–109,
169–170
East, Thomas, 108
Eastward Ho, 78, 141
Edmund Ironside, 97, 102
Edward I, 49
Edward II, 14, 99
Edward III, 31, 185
Edward IV, parts 1 & 2, 12
Elizabeth I, 4, 110, 118, 127, 131, 138
Elizabeth Stuart (Princess Elizabeth), 160, 176
Englands Heroicall Epistles, 93, 193–194
English Traveller, 11
Enough is as Good as a Feast, 12
Erasmus, 110, 113
Erskine, Sir Thomas, 122
Esther und Haman, 16, 62–69
Eupolemia, 107
'Eurialus and Lucretia', 187, 197–203
Evans, Henry, 137
Every Man In His Humour, 31, 71, 76, 78,
80–81, 85, 87, 143, 164
Every Man Out of His Humour, 31, 76, 78, 127,
143

'Fair Constance of Rome, parts 1 & 2', 92
Fair Em, 103, 185, 189
'Fair Maid of Italy', 41
'Fair Maid of London', 34, 76, 88
Fair Maid of the West, part 2, 79
Faithful Shepherdess, 175, 181
Famous historie of Chinon of England, 159
'Famous Wars of Henry I and the Prince of
Wales', 190
Farmer, Alan B., 8–11
'felmelanco', 20, 91, 104–116, 206
Ferrar, Nicholas, 8
Ferrers, George
Mirror for Magistrates, 193

'First Introduction of the Civil Wars of France',
47, 74–75, 92
First Part of the Contention (2 Henry VI), 30, 82,
192–193, 195, 202
'Five Plays in One', 43
Flasket, John, 4
Fleay, Frederick Gard, 2, 20, 48–49, 52, 54,
96–97, 105–106, 190
Fletcher, John, 63
All is True (Henry VIII), 6–7
Captain, 161, 167, 175, 180–182, 184
'Cardenio', 1, 6, 151–153, 161, 166–184, 187
Comedies and Tragedies, 191
Coxcomb, 162, 175
Cupid's Revenge, 162
Faithful Shepherdess, 175, 181
Henry VIII (All is True), 158, 166
King and No King, 156, 161
Maid's Tragedy, 160–161, 175
Philaster, 142, 149, 160–161
Two Noble Kinsmen, 6, 151
Woman's Prize, 142
Foakes, R. A., 38
Ford, John
'Ill Beginning Hath a Good End', 179
'Keep the Widow Waking', 15–16
Witch of Edmonton, 195
Forman, Simon, 142, 146, 153, 156, 177
'Fortunatus, part 1', 53
'Fortunatus, part 2', 53, 55
Fortune playhouse, 3, 55, 72–74, 89, 115
'Fortune's Tennis, part 2', 15, 43
'Fountain of New Fashions', 74
'Four Plays in One', 39
Four Prentices of London, 43
Foxe, John, 102–103
Frazier, Harriet C., 168
'Frederick and Basilea', 15
Frederick V, Elector Palatine, 160, 176, 179
Frederyke of Jennen, 153
Freehafer, John D., 192
Freeman, Arthur, 154
Freeman, Janet Ing, 154
'Freeman's Honour', 35
'French Comedy, A', 52
'French Comedy, The', 52
Friar Bacon and Friar Bungay, 12, 50, 87
'Friar Francis', 41
Fulwel, Ulpian
Like Will to Like, 12
'Funeral of Richard Coeur de Lion', 34

Gabaleone, Sir Giovanni Battista, 167
Gadd, Ian, 98, 202
Game at Chess, 127, 138

Garnet, Henry, 132
Gayton, Edmund
   Pleasant Notes Upon Don Quixot, 54, 170
George-a-Greene, 41
Gerschow, Frederic, 105
Gesta Romanarum, 107
giants on stage, 100–101
Gib, John, 133
Globe, 32, 57, 59, 70, 72–73, 77–78, 85, 89–91,
   116, 119–120, 127, 142, 153, 156, 178,
   193–194, 206
   Blackfriars and, 143–147
Godly Queen Hester, 62
'God Speed the Plough', 41, 78
'Godfrey of Bulloigne, part 2', 43
'Gowrie', 118–128, 130–131, 134–135, 141,
   147, 206
Gowrie Conspiracy, 120–128, 134, 136
Granville-Barker, Harley, 143
Green, John, 63
Greenblatt, Stephen, 91, 127–128, 152
Greene, Robert
   Friar Bacon and Friar Bungay, 12, 50, 87
   John of Bordeaux, 39, 50
   Looking-Glass for London and England, 38
   Orlando Furioso, 39, 159
   Quip for an Upstart Courtier, 78
   Selimus, 46
Greg, W. W., 7, 9, 43–45, 47–48, 50, 52, 55,
   64, 83, 97, 106, 154, 188, 198
Greville, Fulke, 5
   Alaham, 5
   'Antony and Cleopatra', 5, 19
   Mustapha, 5
Grey, Lord, 133
Gryphius, Andreas
   Cardenio und Celinde, 171
Guilpin, Everard, 71, 73
'Guise'. *See Massacre at Paris*
Gunby, David, 162
Gunpowder Plot, 119, 135–136, 147
Gurr, Andrew, 2, 11, 23, 44–45, 47–51, 62,
   67–68, 71, 90, 114–115, 126, 129, 135
Guy of Warwick, 100
Guy of Warwick legend, 100–101

Hamlet, 1, 31, 90–91, 103–117, 124, 136, 142,
   172, 200, 206
   Denmark and, 95–104, 116–117
   'felmelanco' and, 104–117
   Wittenberg and, 111
Hampton Court, 146
Harbage, Alfred, 25, 188–190, 198
'Hardicanute', 102
'harey the vj' (*1 Henry VI*), 30, 39, 82

Harrington, Sir John, 14
Harrison, G. B., 29
'Harry the Fifth', 43
Hathway, Richard
   'Black Dog of Newgate, part 1', 92
   'Black Dog of Newgate, part 2', 79, 92
   'Fair Constance of Rome, parts 1 & 2', 92
   'Owen Tudor', 91–95, 104, 116
   Sir John Oldcastle, part 1, 12, 197
   untitled comedy, 45, 55
Haughton, William
   book by 'young' Haughton, 47
   'Blind Beggar of Bethnal Green with Tom
     Strowd, part 2', 49, 53, 79–80
   'Conquest of the West Indies', 169
   'Judas', 51, 55, 114
   Lust's Dominion, 49
   'Six Yeomen of the West', 54
   'Tom Dough, part 2', 54
   'Tom Strowd, part 3', 53, 79–80
   'Tragedy of Thomas Merry (Beech's
     Tragedy)', 49
   'William Cartwright', 48
Hazlitt, W. Carew, 105, 107
Hector of Germany, 35
Heminges, John, 160–161, 167
Henderson, Andrew, 122–123
'Hengist'. *See* 'Vortigern'
Henry Frederick, Prince of Wales, 175, 177–178
Henry I, 204
'Henry I', 24, 187–191, 203
'Henry II', 187–190, 203
Henry IV, 192
Henry IV, part 1, 31, 35, 50, 71, 87, 92, 161,
   167, 175, 177–181
Henry IV, part 2, 31, 80, 92, 94, 192
'Henry Richmond, part 1', 53
'Henry Richmond, part 2', 46, 53, 93
*Henry the Second, King of England; With The
   Death of Rosamond*, 190
'Henry the Una. . .', 24
Henry V, 13, 31, 35, 77, 82, 87, 90–95, 104,
   116, 158, 178, 192, 197, 200, 202, 206
Henry VI, 192, 194
Henry VI, part 1, 7, 192
Henry VI, part 2, 192–193
Henry VIII, 176
Henry VIII (All is True), 158, 166
Henslowe, Philip, 16, 28–29, 34, 36–55, 58–61,
   73–75, 96–97, 100, 105–106, 108–109,
   112–114, 143, 159–160
Herbert, Sir Henry, 7, 34, 76, 187–188, 190
'Hercules, parts 1 & 2', 43
'Herpetulus the Blue Knight and Perobia', 159
Herringman, Henry, 193, 198

Herz, E., 64
'Hester and Ahasuerus', 16, 33, 58, 60, 62–68,
     88
Heywood, John
   Two hundred epigrammes, 179
Heywood, Thomas, 11, 63
   'albere galles', 18, 105, 108, 169
   Apology for Actors, 176
   Brazen Age, 43
   Dialogues and Dramas, 43
   Edward IV, parts 1 & 2, 12
   English Traveller, 11
   Fair Maid of the West, part 2, 79
   Four Prentices of London, 43
   Iron Age, 43
   Late Lancashire Witches, 125
   Silver Age, 43
   Sir Thomas More, 10, 31, 113
   Tom a Lincoln (attrib.), 159
   untitled comedy, 45, 55
   Woman Killed With Kindness, 13
Hill, Abraham, 195
Hill, Alexandra, 10
Historie of Eurialus and Lucretia, 198, 201–202
Historie of Titana, and Theseus, 201
History of Richard III, 194
'History of Richard Whittington', 190
'History of the Solitary Knight', 159
'History play including the death of Percy',
     54–55
Holinshed, Raphael, 100, 153, 155
Hope, 72
'Hot Anger Soon Cold', 5, 74–75
Houlahan, Mark, 93
How, Agnes, 4
Hubbard, William, 136
Humorous Day's Mirth, 49
Humphrey of Lancaster, Duke of Gloucester,
     192–195
Hunsdon's Men, 85
Hunt, Christopher, 6, 12–13, 33
Hunter, G. K., 12–13
Huntington Library, 201
'Huon of Bordeaux', 41
Hutchings, Mark, 100
Hystorie of Hamblett, 99, 197, 200

Ieronimo, part 1, 31, 39
If This Be Not a Good Play, The Devil Is In It, 163
'Ill Beginning Hath a Good End', 179
'Ill of a Woman', 52
Illustrious Shepherdess, 170
Ingram, William, 61, 71
Iphis, 196
'Iphis and Ianthe', 187, 191, 195–196, 203

Iron Age, 43
'Isle of Dogs', 4, 6, 48, 75, 89

Jack Juggler, 12
Jacqueline of Hainault, 194
Jaggard, Isaac, 199
James I, 114, 118–119, 147, 167–168, 175, 183
   Bye Plot and, 131–135
   Daemonologie, 119, 176
   Gowrie Conspiracy and, 120–128, 134, 136
   Gunpowder Plot and, 119, 135–136
   Ruthven Raid and, 123
   satirised on stage, 138–141
James, Thomas, 7
Jastrow, Joseph, 24
'Jealous Comedy', 40
Jeffes, Humphrey, 105
Jenkins, Harold, 106–107, 110
'Jephtha', 114
'Jerusalem', 39
Jew of Malta, 36, 39–41, 60, 62, 65, 68, 70
John a Kent and John a Cumber, 49
John of Bordeaux, 39, 50
John of Brabant, 194
Johnson, Laurie, 61–62
Johnson, Robert, 173–174
Jones, Richard, 81
Jonson, Ben, 11, 143, 185–186
   Alchemist, 142, 161, 163–164, 167, 175,
        181–182
   Bartholomew Fair, 5
   Case is Altered, 5
   Devil is an Ass, 5
   Eastward Ho, 78, 141
   Every Man In His Humour, 31, 71, 76, 78,
        80–81, 85, 87, 143, 164
   Every Man Out of His Humour, 31, 76, 78,
        127, 143
   'Hot Anger Soon Cold', 5, 74–75
   'Isle of Dogs', 4, 6, 48, 75, 89
   Jonson's plot, 47
   'Joronymo', 37–38
   'Mortimer, His Fall', 19
   'Page of Plymouth', 5
   'Robert II, King of Scots', 124
   play publication and, 6
   Sejanus His Fall, 32
   'Tragedy on Jonson's Plot', 45, 47
Jonson's plot, 47
'Joronymo', 36–38, 55
'Joshua', 114
Jourdemayne, Margery, 194
Jowett, John, 31, 113
Juby, Edward
   'Samson', 114

'Judas', 51, 55, 114
'Jugurth', 49
Jugurtha, 49
Julius Caesar, 7, 31, 77, 161

Kahan, Jeffrey, 168
Karim-Cooper, Farah, 146
Karlstadt, Andreas, 111
Kastan, David Scott, 191
Kathman, David, 33, 35, 81
Kay, Dennis, 127
'Keep the Widow Waking', 15–16
Kempe, Will, 96
Ketterer, Elizabeth, 146
Kiefer, Frederick, 49
King and No King, 156, 161
King John, 7, 30, 142
King Lear, 32, 126, 176
'King Lud', 41
'King of England's Son and the King of
    Scotland's Daughter', 16, 34
'King Stephen', 187, 191, 196–197, 203
King, Ros, 94
King's Men, 2, 7, 16–17, 29, 32, 35, 50,
    118–121, 124–137, 147–150, 166–171,
    173–183, 188, 190, 193, 196, 199, 206
  at court, 29, 50, 129, 160–167, 175–183
  at Somerset House, 129
  at the Blackfriars, 141–147
  controversy and, 120–128
  their patron's interests, 120–137
Kirk, Maria, 14
Kirwan, Peter, 187, 203–204
Knack to Know a Knave, 39
Knack to Know an Honest Man, 36, 38
Knave of Clubs, 115, 163
Knave of Harts, 164
'Knaves, parts 1 & 2', 163–165
Knight of the Burning Pestle, 175, 181, 184
Knight, Heather, 71–72
Knight, Jeffrey Todd, 13
Knolles, Richard, 81
'Knot of Fools', 160, 164–166
Knutson, Roslyn L., 17, 24, 26, 32, 35, 59, 62,
    65, 71, 77, 79, 81, 89, 97, 115, 130, 142,
    144, 153, 179, 181, 193
Kozikowski, Stanley, 136
Kyd, Thomas
    Spanish Tragedy, 30–31, 36–39, 55

La Boderie, Antoine Lefèvre de, 137–140
Lady Elizabeth's Men, 163
Lake, Sir Thomas, 137, 139–140
Laneman, Henry, 71
Lardinois, André, 19

Larum for London, 31, 75, 77, 87, 124
Late Lancashire Witches, 125
Les Folies de Cardenio, 170
Lesser, Zachary, 8–11
Levenson, Jill L., 85–86
'Life and Death of Henry I', 189
'Life of Cardinal Wolsey', 113
Like Will to Like, 12
Literary Print Culture, 168, 188, 197, 200
Lloyd, Lodowick, 110
Locrine, 185
Lodge, Thomas, 33
    Looking-Glass for London and England, 38
'Long Meg of Westminster', 101
'Longshanks', 38, 49, 101
Look About You, 42–43, 49, 75–76
Looking-Glass for London and England, 38
Lope de Vega, 171
'Lord and his Three Sons', 18
lost plays
    'Abraham and Lot', 41
    actors' parts and, 16
    'Adam and Eve', 54–55
    'Agamemnon', 51, 74
    'albere galles', 18, 105, 108, 169
    'Alexander and Lodowick', 38
    'Alice Pierce', 109
    'All Fools but the Fool', 74
    'Amboyna', 5
    'anti-Scots play', 33
    'Antony and Cleopatra', 5, 19
    backstage plots and, 15
    'Bad Beginning Makes a Good Ending', 161,
        167, 175, 177–179
    'Bear a Brain', 48, 74
    'Belin Dun', 60, 66–70, 189
    'Bendo (or Byndo) and Richardo', 109
    'Better Late Than Never'. *See* 'Bear a Brain'
    biblical plays, 114–115
    'Black Bateman of the North, parts 1 & 2', 92
    'Black Dog of Newgate, part 1', 92
    'Black Dog of Newgate, part 2', 79, 92
    'Black Joan', 43, 46
    'Blind Beggar of Bethnal Green with Tom
        Strowd, part 2', 49, 53, 79–80
    book by 'young' Haughton, 47
    'brandymer', 100–101, 104
    'Brute Greenshield', 51
    'Buckingham', 41, 193
    'Caesar's Fall', 52
    'Capture of Stuhlweissenburg', 105
    'Cardenio', 1, 6, 151, 161, 166–175, 184, 187
    'Catiline's Conspiracy', 74
    censorship and, 4, 120
    Chapman's playbook, 47

lost plays (cont.)
  'Chapman's three acts', 45, 47
  Chapman's (tragic?) playbook, 53
  'Chinon of England', 160
  'Civil Wars of France, parts 1, 2 & 3', 74–75, 92
  'Cloth Breeches and Velvet Hose', 9, 35, 77–78, 88
  'Comedy of Cosmo', 40
  'Conan, Prince of Cornwall', 74
  'Conquest of Brute', 51, 74
  'Conquest of the West Indies', 169
  'Cutlack', 60–61, 96
  'Danish Tragedy', 96
  'Dead Man's Fortune', 15
  destroyed by accident, 3
  destroyed by fire, 3
  destroyed by rioters, 3
  'Disguises', 49
  'Duke Humphrey', 187, 191–195, 203
  'Earl Godwin and His Three Sons, parts 1 & 2', 92, 96, 102–103
  'Earl of Hertford', 48
  'Eurialus and Lucretia', 187, 197–203
  'Fair Constance of Rome, parts 1 & 2', 92
  'Fair Maid of Italy', 41
  'Fair Maid of London', 34, 76, 88
  'Famous Wars of Henry I and the Prince of Wales', 190
  'felmelanco', 20, 91, 104–116, 206
  'First Introduction of the Civil Wars of France', 47, 74–75, 92
  'Five Plays in One', 43
  'Fortunatus, part 1', 53
  'Fortunatus, part 2', 53, 55
  'Fortune's Tennis, part 2', 15, 43
  'Fountain of New Fashions', 74
  'Four Plays in One', 39
  'Frederick and Basilea', 15
  'Freeman's Honour', 35
  'French Comedy, A', 52
  'French Comedy, The', 52
  'Friar Francis', 41
  'Funeral of Richard Coeur de Lion', 34
  German redactions of, 16, 34, 62–69, 171
  giants in, 100–101
  'God Speed the Plough', 41, 78
  'Godfrey of Bulloigne, part 2', 43
  'Gowrie', 118–128, 130–131, 134–135, 141, 147, 206
  'Hardicanute', 102
  'Harry the Fifth', 43
  'Henry I', 24, 187–191, 203
  'Henry II', 187–191, 203
  'Henry Richmond, part 1', 53
  'Henry Richmond, part 2', 46, 53, 93

'Henry the Una. . .', 24
'Hercules, parts 1 & 2', 43
'Herpetulus the Blue Knight and Perobia', 159
'Hester and Ahasuerus', 16, 33, 58, 60, 62–68, 88
'History of Richard Whittington', 190
'History of the Solitary Knight', 159
'History play including the death of Percy', 54
'Hot Anger Soon Cold', 5, 74–75
'Huon of Bordeaux', 41
'Ill Beginning Hath a Good End', 179
'Ill of a Woman', 52
improbable biographical drama, 112
'Iphis and Ianthe', 187, 191, 195–196, 203
'Isle of Dogs', 4, 6, 48, 75, 89
'Jealous Comedy', 40
'Jephtha', 114
'Jerusalem', 39
Jonson's plot, 47
'Joronymo', 36–38, 55
'Joshua', 114
'Judas', 51, 55, 114
'Jugurth', 49
'Keep the Widow Waking', 15–16
'King Lud', 41
'King of England's Son and the King of Scotland's Daughter', 16, 34
'King Stephen', 187, 191, 196–197, 203
'Knaves, parts 1 & 2', 163–165
'Knot of Fools', 160, 164–166
legal notoriety and, 5
'Life and Death of Henry I', 189
'Life of Cardinal Wolsey', 113
'Long Meg of Westminster', 101
'Longshanks', 38, 49, 101
'Lord and his Three Sons', 18
'Love Prevented', 44
'Love's Labour's Won', 1, 6, 33, 78–80, 187, 196
lumping vs. splitting, 12, 35, 41–55, 96, 190
'Mack', 43
'Maiden's Holiday', 189
'Mark Antony (?)', 52
'Mortimer, His Fall', 19
'Mortimer', 48
'Mulmutius Dunwallow', 74, 82
'Muly Molocco', 39–40
Munday's court comedy, 47
'Nebuchadnezzar', 38
'Nobleman', 161–162, 166
'Old Joiner of Aldgate', 4, 15
'Olympio and Eugenio', 52
'Orestes' Furies', 51
'Orphans Tragedy', 49
'Owen Tudor', 91–95, 104, 116

'Page of Plymouth', 5
'Paradox', 38
'Pastoral Tragedy', 47
performance-based research and, 16
'Phaeton', 109
play in Chettle's pawn, 47
'Pierce of Exton', 42, 47
'Pierce of Winchester', 74
'Play for court', 47
'Play of Oswald', 149, 153–159
'Play of Poore', 16
'Play with a serenade scene', 141
playbook by 'mr Maxton', 47
playbook publication and, 8–11
plot-scenarios and, 16
'Pontius Pilate', 51, 55, 114
'Processus Satanae', 16
'Pythagoras', 38, 109, 112, 206
'Raymond, Duke of Lyons', 163, 166
reasons for loss, 2–11
repertory studies and, 17–20, 113–116, 120,
    124–128, 150, 193
'Richard the 2', 177, 193–194
'Richard the Confessor', 18, 41
'Rising of Cardinal Wolsey', 113
'Robert II, King of Scots', 124
'Robin Goodfellow', 35
'Romanus', 16
'Samson', 114
'Seleo and Olympo', 52
'Seven Deadly Sins (Tarlton's)', 33
'Seven Deadly Sins, part 1', 33
'Seven Deadly Sins, part 2', 33, 78, 81–83,
    87–88, 165
scholarship about, 15, 19, 41–56, 104–105,
    120, 125–130
self-censorship and, 5
'Silver Mine', 119, 128, 138–141, 206
'Sir John Mandeville', 113
'Sir John Oldcastle' (Chamberlain's), 35
'Sir William Longsword', 34
'Six Yeomen of the West', 54
'Spanish Comedy of Don Horatio', 39
'Spanish Fig', 44
'Spanish Maze', 118, 128–137, 147, 206
'Strange News Out of Poland', 110
'Sturgflatery', 43
'Tamar Cham, part 1', 38, 53
'Tamar Cham, part 2', 38–39, 53
'taner of denmarke', 20, 39–40, 74, 96–100,
    104
'Tapster fragment', 180
'Tartarian Cripple, Emperor of
    Constantinople', 34, 80–82, 85–86, 88, 116
'Tasso's Melancholy', 113, 206

theatregrams and, 153–160, 166, 172, 174,
    180, 183
'Tinker of Totnes', 38, 74
''Tis No Deceit to Deceive the Deceiver', 74
'Titus and Vespasian', 39
'Tom Dough, part 2', 54
'Tom Strowd, part 3', 53, 79–80
'Tragedy of Thomas Merry (Beech's
    Tragedy)', 49
'Tragedy on Jonson's Plot', 45, 47
'Troilus and Cressida', 42, 74
'Troy', 38, 43, 169
'Truth's Supplication to Candlelight', 44
'Turkish Mahomet and Hiren the Fair Greek',
    100
'Twins' Tragedy', 161–162, 166
'Two Angry Women of Abingdon, part 2', 74,
    76, 79
'Two Merry Women of Abingdon', 47, 74,
    76, 79
'Two Shapes', 51–52
untitled comedy by Hathway, 45, 55
untitled comedy by Heywood, 45, 55
untitled play by Chettle and Day, 47
untitled play(s) by Nashe, 33
'Ur-Hamlet', 1, 33, 58, 60–61, 90, 96, 99,
    104
value of, 36–42
'Vortigern', 38, 50
'White Witch of Westminster, or Love in a
    Lunacy', 195
'William Cartwright', 48
'William Longsword', 75
'William the Conqueror', 41, 103, 189
'Wise Man of Westchester', 48
'Woman's Tragedy', 47
'Worse Afeared Than Hurt', 52
Lost Plays Database, 1, 3, 5, 16, 20, 34–35, 50,
    56, 66, 74, 81, 93, 100, 140, 154, 157, 159,
    162, 169, 173, 178–180, 195
Lotti, Ottaviano, 139–141
'Love Prevented', 44
Love's Labour's Lost, 11–13, 29–30, 71, 78, 177
'Love's Labour's Won', 1, 6, 11–14, 33, 78–80,
    187, 196
Lust's Dominion, 49
Luther, Martin, 110
Lyly, John
    Sappho and Phao, 130
Lyons, Tara L., 199–202

Mabbe, James, 171
Macbeth, 7, 119, 125, 135–136, 146–147, 195
'Mack', 43
MacLean, Sally-Beth, 18, 29, 32–33, 97–98, 197

Maid's Tragedy, 160–161, 175
'Maiden's Holiday', 189
Malone, Edmond, 186, 190
Manley, Lawrence, 18, 32, 38–39, 97–98, 113, 197
Margeson, John, 138
'Mark Antony (?)', 52
Markham, Gervaise, 63
Markham, Sir Griffith, 133
Marlowe, Christopher, 63, 186
    Doctor Faustus, 36, 91, 99, 113–115, 163–164, 170
    Edward II, 14, 99
    Jew of Malta, 36, 39–41, 60, 62, 65, 68, 70
    'Maiden's Holiday' (attrib.), 189
    Massacre at Paris, 40, 114–115, 124
    Tamburlaine, part 1, 80–81
    Tamburlaine, part 2, 79–80
Marston, John, 139
    Antonio and Mellida, 79
    Antonio's Revenge, 79
    Dutch Courtesan, 163
    Eastward Ho, 78, 141
    playbook by 'mr Maxton', 47
Martin, John, 193, 197
Martin, Sarah, 198
Massacre at Paris, 40, 114–115, 124
Massai, Sonia, 199
Massinger, Philip, 63
    Three New Plays, 191
Masten, Jeffrey, 14
Master of the Revels, 7, 76, 126, 134, 137–138, 176–178, 183, 187–188, 190, 194
Mathew, Tobie, 76
May, Thomas
    Two Tragedies, 191
Maze, Southwark, 131, 134–135
McInnis, David, 16, 18, 24, 26, 53, 69, 90, 154
McMillin, Scott, 18, 26, 33
McQueen-Thomson, Douglas, 103
Measure for Measure, 6
Mee, Charles, 152
Melanchthon, Philip, 109–113
Menius, Friedrich, 63
Merchant of Venice, 11, 29, 31, 107, 129, 134, 200
Meres, Francis, 12, 14, 33, 45, 52, 196, 201
Merry Devil of Edmonton, 31, 143–144, 161, 165, 182, 204
Merry Wives of Windsor, 31, 76, 80, 161, 164, 193
Middleton, Christopher
    Famous historie of Chinon of England, 159
Middleton, Thomas
    'Caesar's Fall', 51–52

Changeling, 24
Game at Chess, 127, 138
Second Maiden's Tragedy, 10, 175
'Two Shapes', 51–52
Witch, 195
Midsummer Night's Dream, 11, 30, 77, 171, 200–201
Milward, John, 4
Mirror for Magistrates, 193
Miseries of Enforced Marriage, 142
Mish, Charles C., 201
Moncrieff, John (Laird of Pittencrieff), 121
Moore, Helen, 100
Moore, Mary, 130
More Knaues yet: The Knaues of Spades and Diamonds, 164
More, Sir Thomas, 113
'Mortimer, His Fall', 19
'Mortimer', 48
Moseley, Charles, 152
Moseley, Humphrey, 9, 168–170, 188–190, 192–196, 203–204
Mountfort, William, 190
Mucedorus, 30, 142–143, 185
Much Ado About Nothing, 31, 50, 76, 81, 86, 160–161, 164, 167, 172, 175, 179–182, 184
Muir, Kenneth, 171
Mullaney, Steven, 96
'Mulmutius Dunwallow', 74, 82
Mulready, Cyrus, 151, 159
'Muly Molocco', 39–40
Munday, Anthony
    'Caesar's Fall', 51–52
    'Fair Constance of Rome, parts 1 & 2', 92
    'Funeral of Richard Coeur de Lion', 34
    'Jephtha', 114
    John a Kent and John a Cumber, 49
    'Owen Tudor', 91–95, 104, 116
    Sir John Oldcastle, part 1, 12, 197
    Sir Thomas More, 10, 31, 113
    'Two Shapes', 51–52
    untitled comedy for court, 47
Munday's court comedy, 47
Munro, Lucy, 16, 139
Murray, John Tucker, 126
Museum of London Archaeology, 71–72
Mustapha, 5

Nashe, Thomas, 33
    'Isle of Dogs', 4, 6, 48, 75, 89
    Unfortunate Traveller, 110, 112
    untitled play(s) by, 33
'Nebuchadnezzar', 38
Newington Butts, 29, 33, 57–70, 72, 87, 90, 96, 205

Niccolls
  'Twins' Tragedy', 161–162, 166
Nice Wanton, 12
Nicolson, George, 33
'Nobleman', 161–162, 166
Noble Spanish Soldier, 44
North, Sir Thomas, 94
Northward Ho, 78
Nosworthy, J. M., 154

Old Fortunatus, 53, 146
'Old Joiner of Aldgate', 4, 15
Old Wives Tale, 77
Orlando Furioso, 39, 159
'Olympio and Eugenio', 52
'Orestes' Furies', 51
Ormerod, Oliver, 136
'Orphans Tragedy', 49
Othello, 32, 142, 161
Ovid, 203
  Metamorphoses, 195–196
'Owen Tudor', 91–95, 104, 116
Oxford's Men, 89
'Page of Plymouth', 5
Palmer, Barbara D., 84
Palsgrave's Men, 3
'Paradox', 38
Parr, Catherine, 176
'Pastoral Tragedy', 47
Pavier, Mary (Marie Percivall), 197
Pavier, Thomas, 13, 193, 197, 199–202
Peele, George
  Battle of Alcazar, 42–43
  Edward I, 49
  Old Wives Tale, 77
  Titus Andronicus, 24, 30, 41, 60, 68–69, 75, 83, 85–86, 142, 196–197
  'Turkish Mahomet and Hiren the Fair Greek', 100
Pembroke's Men, 48, 56, 89, 102
Percy, Algernon (10th Earl of Northumberland), 14
Pérez Díez, José A., 171
performance-based research, 144–146
Pericles, 6, 142, 151
Pett, Peter (?)
  'Strange News Out of Poland', 110
'Phaeton', 109
Philaster, 142, 149, 160–161
Philip II of Spain, 131
Phillips, Edward
  Illustrious Shepherdess, 170
'Pierce of Exton', 42, 47
'Pierce of Winchester', 74
Pind, Jörgen L., 28, 69, 91, 150–151, 206

plague, 118
Platt, Peter G., 133–134
Platter, Thomas, 77
play in Chettle's pawn, 47
'Play for court', 47
'Play of Oswald', 149, 153–159
'Play with a serenade scene', 141
playbook by 'm^r Maxton', 47
playhouses
  Blackfriars, 120, 137–149, 206
  Boar's Head, 34, 72–73, 89
  Carey Court, Blackfriars, 35
  Cockpit, 3
  Curtain, 11, 14, 34, 57, 59, 70–88, 120, 142
  Fortune, 3, 55, 72–74, 89, 115
  Globe, 32, 57, 59, 70, 72–73, 77–78, 85, 89–91, 116, 119–120, 127, 142–147, 153, 156, 178, 193–194, 206
  Hope, 72
  Newington Butts, 29, 33, 57–70, 72, 87, 90, 96, 205
  Red Bull, 73
  Rose, 60, 72–76, 89, 103, 160
  Swan, 34, 48, 72, 89
  Theatre, 11, 33, 57, 59, 70–72, 77–78, 82, 84–85, 88, 90, 120, 142
playing companies
  Admiral's Men, 27–29, 32–38, 58–61, 72–75, 82, 87, 89, 91–94, 96, 99–116, 124, 189, 196, 205
  Chamberlain's Men, 2, 9, 11, 17, 28–38, 41, 59, 70–87, 89–92, 95–96, 104, 113, 118, 165, 196, 203, 205
  Children of Paul's, 4
  Children of the Chapel Royal, 31
  Children of the Queen's Revels, 37, 119, 145, 162, 180
  Duke of York's Men, 163
  Hunsdon's Men, 85
  King's Men, 2, 7, 16–17, 29, 32, 35, 50, 118–121, 124–137, 147–150, 160–171, 173–183, 188, 190, 193, 196, 199, 206
  Lady Elizabeth's Men, 163
  Oxford's Men, 89
  Palsgrave's Men, 3
  Pembroke's Men, 48, 56, 89, 102
  Prince's Men, 163–165, 190
  Queen Anne's Men, 3, 86
  Queen's Men, 17, 59, 92, 142, 158
  Strange's Men, 18, 27, 32–33, 36–40, 81, 96–101, 109, 113, 189
  Sussex's Men, 27, 38, 41, 59, 78, 103, 189, 193
  Thomas Sackville's players, 63
  Worcester's Men, 27, 63, 89, 92

Pleasant Notes Upon Don Quixot, 54, 170
Poly-Olbion, 100
'Pontius Pilate', 51, 55, 114
Pope, Thomas, 97
Porter, Henry
    'Hot Anger Soon Cold', 5, 74–75
    'Spencers', 74
    Two Angry Women of Abingdon, part 1, 43–44,
        74, 76, 79
    'Two Angry Women of Abingdon, part 2', 74,
        76, 79
    'Two Merry Women of Abingdon', 47, 74,
        76, 79
Potter, Lois, 129
Pratt, Aaron T., 8
Pratt, Samuel M., 193
Prince's Men, 163–165, 190
Privy Council, 4–5
'Processus Satanae', 16
'Pythagoras', 38, 109, 112, 206

Quarles, John, 201
Queen Anne's Men, 3, 86
Queen's Men, 17, 59, 92, 142, 158

Ramsay, John, 121–122
Ramus, Peter, 114
Rankins, William
    'Mulmutius Dunwallow', 74, 82
Rape of Lucrece, 201–202
'Raymond, Duke of Lyons', 163, 166
Red Bull, 73
Revenger's Tragedy, 162
Rich, Sir Robert, 167
Richard II, 30, 71
Richard III, 30, 71, 193
'Richard the 2', 177, 193–194
'Richard the Confessor', 18, 41
Richards, Bernard, 153
'Rising of Cardinal Wolsey', 113
'Robert II, King of Scots', 124
Roberts, James, 77
'Robin Goodfellow', 35
Robinson, Richard
    Eupolemia, 107
    Gesta Romanarum, 107
Robinson, Richard (?)
    'felmelanco', 104–116, 206
'Romanus', 16
Romeo and Juliet, 30, 71, 75, 85–86, 142, 171
Roome, for a messe of knaues, 163
Rose, 60, 72–76, 103, 160
Rowlands, Samuel, 163–164
    Knave of Clubs, 115, 163
    Knave of Harts, 164

*More Knaues yet: The Knaues of Spades and
    Diamonds*, 164
Roome, for a messe of knaues, 163
Rowley, Samuel, 113
    'Joshua', 114
    'Judas', 51, 55, 114
    'Samson', 114
Rowley, William
    All's Lost by Lust, 24
    Changeling, 24
    'Keep the Widow Waking', 15–16
    Travels of the Three English Brothers, 87
    Witch of Edmonton, 195
Rubin, Edgar, 147–149
    Rubin's Vase, 20–25, 28–29, 57, 70, 88,
        90–91, 95, 119, 150–151, 168, 187,
        204–206
Ruthven, Alexander, 121–122
Ruthven, John (3rd Earl of Gowrie), 120–128
Rutter, Tom, 17

Sackville, Thomas, 63
'Samson', 114
Samson, Alexander, 171
Sappho, 19
Sappho and Phao, 130
Satiromastix, 31
Schoenbaum, S., 25, 198
Schofield, John, 110
Schoone-Jongen, Terence, 104, 135
Schuler, Robert M., 16
Scott, Robert, 198
Second Maiden's Tragedy, 10, 175
Sejanus His Fall, 32
'Seleo and Olympo', 52
Selimus, 46
Seven Champions of Christendom, 101
'Seven Deadly Sins (Tarlton's)', 33
'Seven Deadly Sins, part 1', 33
'Seven Deadly Sins, part 2', 33, 78, 81–83,
    87–88, 165
Shakespeare Documented, 70, 129, 156, 171, 177
Shakespeare, William, 17–18, 27, 129, 143–144,
    149–151, 161, 183–184
    All is True (Henry VIII), 6–7
    All's Well That Ends Well, 7, 32
    Antony and Cleopatra, 24, 171
    Arden of Faversham, 31, 75, 125, 185
    As You Like It, 7, 31, 78, 90
    at Newington Butts, 59–70
    at the Curtain, 70–87
    at the Globe, 89–91
    'Cardenio', 1, 6, 151–153, 161, 166–184, 187
    Comedy of Errors, 7, 11, 29–30
    Coriolanus, 7

Cymbeline, 142, 149, 151–159, 172
'Duke Humphrey' (attrib.), 187, 191–195, 203
Edward III, 31, 185
'Eurialus and Lucretia' (attrib.), 187, 197–203
First Folio, 7, 11, 32, 95, 203
First Part of the Contention (2 Henry VI), 30, 82, 192–193, 195, 202
forged allusion to, 154
Hamlet, 1, 31, 90–91, 95–117, 124, 136, 142, 172, 200, 206
'harey the vj' (*1 Henry VI*), 30, 38–39, 82
'Henry I' (attrib.), 24, 187–191, 203
'Henry II' (attrib.), 187–191, 203
Henry IV, part 1, 31, 35, 50, 71, 87, 92, 161, 167, 175, 177–181
Henry IV, part 2, 31, 80, 92, 94, 192
Henry V, 13, 31, 35, 77, 82, 87, 90–95, 104, 116, 158, 178, 192, 197, 200, 202, 206
Henry VI, part 1, 7, 192
Henry VI, part 2, 192–193
Henry VIII (All is True), 158, 166
'Iphis and Ianthe' (attrib.), 187, 191, 195–196, 203
Julius Caesar, 7, 31, 77, 161
King John, 7, 30, 142
King Lear, 32, 126, 176
'King Stephen' (attrib.), 187, 191, 196–197, 203
lost Apocrypha, 185–204
Love's Labour's Lost, 12–13, 29–30, 71, 78, 177
'Love's Labour's Won', 1, 6, 11–14, 33, 78–80, 187, 196
Macbeth, 7, 119, 125, 135–136, 146–147, 195
Measure for Measure, 6
Merchant of Venice, 11, 29, 31, 107, 129, 134, 200
Merry Wives of Windsor, 31, 76, 80, 161, 164, 193
Midsummer Night's Dream, 11, 30, 77, 171, 200–201
Much Ado About Nothing, 31, 50, 76, 81, 86, 160–161, 164, 167, 172, 175, 179–182, 184
Othello, 32, 142, 161
Pericles, 6, 142, 151
play publication and, 7
posthumous reputation, 185–187, 189, 191–192, 200–205
Rape of Lucrece, 201–202
Richard II, 30, 71
Richard III, 30, 71, 193
romance, 153–160

Romeo and Juliet, 30, 71, 75, 85–86, 142, 171
Second Folio, 198, 202
Sir Thomas More, 10, 31, 113
Spanish Tragedy, 37
Taming of the Shrew, 7, 16, 30, 60, 77
Tempest, 7, 151–152, 158–162, 172, 180–182, 184
Third Folio, 198, 203
Timon of Athens, 7
Titus Andronicus, 24, 30, 41, 60, 68–69, 75, 83, 85–86, 142, 196–197
Troilus and Cressida, 31, 142, 171
True Tragedy of Richard, Duke of York (3 Henry VI), 30, 82, 193, 202
Twelfth Night, 31, 195–196
Two Gentlemen of Verona, 6, 11, 30
Two Noble Kinsmen, 6, 151
Winter's Tale, 7, 151, 156, 158, 161, 172, 180, 184
Shakespearean bias, 56, 90–91, 116, 129, 147, 150–153
Shapiro, James, 96, 130
Sharpe, Robert B., 62, 114–115
Sharpe, Will, 156
Shelton, Thomas, 171–175, 182
Shirley, James
  Six New Plays, 191
Shoemaker's Holiday, 42, 77, 97
Sibley, Gertrude Manley, 198
Sidney, Sir Robert, 35
Silver Age, 43
'Silver Mine', 119, 128, 138–141, 206
Sir Giles Goosecap, 105
'Sir John Mandeville', 113
'Sir John Oldcastle' (Chamberlain's), 35
Sir John Oldcastle, part 1, 12, 197
Sir Thomas More, 10, 31, 113
'Sir William Longsword', 34
Sisson, C. J., 15
'Six Yeomen of the West', 54
Smith, W.
  'The Freeman's Honour', 35
  Hector of Germany, 35
Smith, Wentworth
  'albere galles', 18, 105, 108, 169
  'Black Dog of Newgate, part 1', 92
  'Black Dog of Newgate, part 2', 79, 92
  'Conquest of the West Indies', 169
'Spanish Comedy of Don Horatio', 39
'Spanish Fig', 44
'Spanish Maze', 118, 128–137, 147, 206
'Spanish Moor's Tragedy'. *See Lust's Dominion*
Spanish Tragedy, 30–31, 36–39, 55
'Spencers', 74
Star Chamber, 4

Stationers' Register, 9–12, 34–36, 67, 77, 80, 94, 100, 113, 115, 162, 168–170, 178, 185, 188–190, 192–193, 195–200, 202–203
Steevens, George, 186
Steggle, Matthew, 6, 17–18, 24, 44, 62, 67, 69, 96, 98, 108, 112, 157, 195
Stein, Suzanne H., 111
Stern, Tiffany, 168–169
Stewart, Alan, 200
Stewart, Ludovic (Duke of Lennox), 121–122
Stow, John, 100
'Strange News Out of Poland', 110
Strange's Men, 18, 27, 32–33, 36–40, 81, 96–101, 109, 113, 189
Street, Peter, 73
Stuart, Elizabeth (Princess Elizabeth), 179, 182
'Sturgflatery', 43
Suckling, John
    Fragmenta Aurea, 191
Sussex's Men, 27, 38, 41, 59, 78, 103, 189, 193
Swan, 34, 48, 72
Swinnerton, Sir John, 35, 167
Sylvius, Aeneas
    Historie of Eurialus and Lucretia, 198, 201–202
Syme, Holger, 32, 36–38, 55–56, 60, 65, 72–73

'Tamar Cham, part 1', 38, 53
'Tamar Cham, part 2', 38–39, 53
Tamburlaine, part 1, 80–81
Tamburlaine, part 2, 79–80
Taming of a Shrew, 30, 60, 65–66, 69, 77
Taming of the Shrew, 7, 16, 30, 60, 77
'taner of denmarke', 20, 39–40, 74, 96–100, 104
'Tapster fragment', 180
Tarlton, Richard, 164
    'Seven Deadly Sins', 33
'Tartarian Cripple, Emperor of Constantinople', 34, 80–82, 85–86, 88, 116
'Tasso's Melancholy', 113, 206
Taylor, Gary, 95, 152, 168, 177–178, 188
Tempest, 7, 151–152, 158–162, 172, 180–182, 184
Teramura, Misha, 4, 51, 140
Theatre, 11, 33, 57, 59, 70–72, 77–78, 82, 84–85, 88, 90, 120, 142
theatergrams, 153–160, 166, 171, 174, 180, 183
Theobald, Lewis, 170
    Double Falsehood, 152–153, 168–169, 183
Thomas Lord Cromwell, 12, 31, 113
Thomas of Woodstock, 193
Thomas Sackville's players, 63
Thomson, Leslie, 83–84, 147
Tilney, Edmund, 34, 76, 126, 137, 176–177
Timon of Athens, 7

'Tinker of Totnes', 38, 74
''Tis No Deceit to Deceive the Deceiver', 74
Tittman, Julius, 64
Titus Andronicus, 24, 30, 41, 60, 68–69, 75, 83, 85–86, 142, 196–197
'Titus and Vespasian', 39
'Tobias', 114
Tom a Lincoln, 159
'Tom Dough, part 2', 54
'Tom Strowd, part 3', 53, 79–80
Topcliffe, Richard, 4
Tourneur, Cyril
    Atheist's Tragedy, 162
    'Nobleman', 161–162, 166
    Revenger's Tragedy (attrib.), 162
Tragedy of Charles, Duke of Byron, 119, 128, 137–138
'Tragedy of Thomas Merry (Beech's Tragedy)', 49
'Tragedy on Jonson's Plot', 45, 47
Travels of the Three English Brothers, 87
'Troilus and Cressida', 42, 74
Troilus and Cressida, 31, 142, 171
Troublesome Reign of King John, 142
'Troy', 38, 43, 169
True Tragedy of Richard, Duke of York (3 Henry VI), 30, 82, 193, 202
'Truth's Supplication to Candlelight', 44
'Turkish Mahomet and Hiren the Fair Greek', 100
Turner, Gustavo, 125–126
Twelfth Night, 31, 195–196
'Twins' Tragedy', 161–162, 166
Two Angry Women of Abingdon, part 1, 43–44, 74, 76, 79
'Two Angry Women of Abingdon, part 2', 74, 76, 79
Two Gentlemen of Verona, 6, 11, 30
Two hundred epigrammes, 179
Two Lamentable Tragedies, 49
'Two Merry Women of Abingdon', 47, 74, 76, 79
Two Noble Kinsmen, 6
'Two Shapes', 51–52

Udall, William, 4
Unfortunate Traveller, 112
unnamed play by Chettle and Day, 47
untitled comedy by Hathway, 45, 55
untitled comedy by Heywood, 45, 55
'Ur-Hamlet', 1, 33, 58, 60–61, 90, 96, 99, 104

Verreyken, Ludovic, 35
Villa, Francesco, 167
Vogt, George McGill, 106
'Vortigern', 38, 50

Wager, William
  Enough is as Good as a Feast, 12
Warburton, John, 3, 178, 188–190, 192
Warner, William
  Albion's England, 113
Warning for Fair Women, 31, 75, 87, 124–125
Watson, William, 132
Webster, John
  'Caesar's Fall', 51–52
  Duchess of Malfi, 162
  'Keep the Widow Waking', 15–16
  Northward Ho, 78
  'Two Shapes', 51–52
  Westward Ho, 78
Wedding Masque of Olympian Knights, 178
Wedding Masque of Stars and Statues Made Human, 178
Wedding Masque of the Princes of Virginia, 178
Welsh Ambassador, 10
Wengert, Timothy J., 111–112
Werstine, Paul, 7
West, Richard
  Wits A.B.C., 78
Westward Ho, 78
Whipday, Emma, 16
White, Paul Whitfield, 51
Whitehall palace, 160–161, 167
'White Witch of Westminster, or Love in a Lunacy', 195
Whitgift, John, 163
Whore of Babylon, 44
Whyte, Rowland, 35
Wickham, Glynne, 4
Widow's Tears, 163
Wiggins, Martin, 1, 11, 26, 29, 32–35, 42, 47, 49–55, 63–65, 75–77, 79–81, 86–87, 100, 106, 113, 129, 135–136, 139–140, 142, 154, 162–164, 192–193, 199–200

Wilkins, George
  Miseries of Enforced Marriage, 142
  Pericles, 6, 142, 151
  Travels of the Three English Brothers, 87
'William Cartwright', 48
'William Longsword', 75
'William the Conqueror', 41, 103, 189
Wilson, Richard, 169, 179, 182
Wilson, Robert
  'Black Bateman of the North, parts 1 & 2', 92
  'Catiline's Conspiracy', 74
  'Earl Godwin and His Three Sons, parts 1 & 2', 92, 96, 102–103
  'Fair Constance of Rome, parts 1 & 2', 92
  'Funeral of Richard Coeur de Lion', 34
  'Henry Richmond, part 2', 46, 53, 93
  'Owen Tudor', 91–95, 104, 116
  'Pierce of Exton', 42, 47
  'Pierce of Winchester', 74
  Sir John Oldcastle, part 1, 12, 197
Winter's Tale, 7, 151, 156, 158, 161, 172, 180, 184
Winwood, Ralph, 121, 129, 131
'Wise Man of Westchester', 48
Witch, 195
Witch of Edmonton, 195
Woman Killed With Kindness, 13
Woman's Prize, 142
'Woman's Tragedy', 47
Wonder of a Kingdom, 43
Wood, Michael, 173–174
Woodson, William C., 136
Worcester's Men, 27, 63, 89, 92
'Worse Afeared Than Hurt', 52
Wotton, Sir Henry, 167
Woudhuysen, H. R., 79

Yarrington, Robert
  Two Lamentable Tragedies, 49
Yorkshire Tragedy, 197